Media Clusters

NEW HORIZONS IN REGIONAL SCIENCE

Series Editor: Philip McCann, *Professor of Economic Geography, University of Groningen, The Netherlands and Professor of Economics, University of Waikato, New Zealand*

Regional science analyses important issues surrounding the growth and development of urban and regional systems and is emerging as a major social science discipline. This series provides an invaluable forum for the publication of high quality scholarly work on urban and regional studies, industrial location economics, transport systems, economic geography and networks.

New Horizons in Regional Science aims to publish the best work by economists, geographers, urban and regional planners and other researchers from throughout the world. It is intended to serve a wide readership including academics, students and policymakers.

Titles in the series include:

Technological Change and Mature Industrial Regions
Firms, Knowledge and Policy
Edited by Mahtab A. Farshchi, Odile E.M. Janne and Philip McCann

Migration and Human Capital
Edited by Jacques Poot, Brigitte Waldorf and Leo van Wissen

Universities, Knowledge Transfer and Regional Development
Geography, Entrepreneurship and Policy
Edited by Attila Varga

International Knowledge and Innovation Networks
Knowledge Creation and Innovation in Medium Technology Clusters
Riccardo Cappellin and Rüdiger Wink

Leadership and Institutions in Regional Endogenous Development
Robert Stimson and Roger R. Stough with Maria Salazar

Entrepreneurship and Regional Development
Local Processes and Global Patterns
Edited by Charlie Karlsson, Börje Johansson and Roger R. Stough

Endogenous Regional Development
Perspectives, Measurement and Empirical Investigation
Edited by Robert Stimson, Roger R. Stough and Peter Nijkamp

Media Clusters
Spatial Agglomeration and Content Capabilities
Edited by Charlie Karlsson and Robert G. Picard

Spatial Scenarios in a Global Perspective
Europe and the Latin Arc Countries
Edited by Roberto Camagni and Roberta Capello

Creative Knowledge Cities
Myths, Visions and Realities
Edited by Marina van Geenhuizen and Peter Nijkamp

Societies in Motion
Innovation, Migration and Regional Transformation
Edited by Amnon Frenkel, Peter Nijkamp and Philip McCann

Media Clusters

Spatial Agglomeration and Content Capabilities

Edited by

Charlie Karlsson

Professor of the Economics of Technological Change, Jönköping International Business School, Jönköping University, Jönköping, Professor of Industrial Economics and Organization, Blekinge Institute of Technology, Karlskrona, Sweden and President of the European Regional Science Association (ERSA)

Robert G. Picard

Director of Research, Reuters Institute, University of Oxford, UK and Hamrin Professor of Media Economics, Jönköping International Business School, Jönköping University, Jönköping, Sweden

NEW HORIZONS IN REGIONAL SCIENCE

Edward Elgar

Cheltenham, UK • Northampton, MA, USA

Published by
Edward Elgar Publishing Limited
The Lypiatts
15 Lansdown Road
Cheltenham
Glos GL50 2JA
UK

Edward Elgar Publishing, Inc.
William Pratt House
9 Dewey Court
Northampton
Massachusetts 01060
USA

A catalogue record for this book
is available from the British Library

Library of Congress Control Number: 2011927322

FSC
www.fsc.org
MIX
Paper from responsible sources
FSC® C018575

ISBN 978 0 85793 268 6

Typeset by Servis Filmsetting Ltd, Stockport, Cheshire
Printed and bound by MPG Books Group, UK

Contents

Contributors

Leona Achtenhagen is a professor of business administration, with special focus on entrepreneurship and business development, at Jönköping International Business School in Sweden. She is the Assistant Director of the Media Management and Transformation Centre (MMTC) and Head of the department 'Entrepreneurship, Strategy, Organization and Leadership' (ESOL) at the same school. Her main research interests concern entrepreneurial and strategic activities of media companies and her work has been published in *Entrepreneurship: Theory & Practice*, *Entrepreneurship & Regional Development*, *International Journal of Media Management* and *Journal of Media Business Studies* and other journals. She received her PhD from the University of St. Gallen in Switzerland.

Leon Barkho is manager of Media Content Practices and Effects Project at Sweden's Jönköping University. He holds a master's degree in applied linguistics and a doctorate in media and communication science. Previously, he held positions at Reuters News Agency as bureau chief and the Associated Press as staff writer. A specialist in journalism and discourse, he is the author of *News from the BBC, CNN, and Al-Jazeera: How The Three Broadcasters Cover The Middle East* and *Where Swedes Get it Wrong When Writing English* and his research has been published in *International Journal of Business Studies*, *Journalism Studies*, *Journal of Pragmatics*, *Studies in Language and Capitalism*, *Journal of Arab and Muslim Media Research*, and *American Communication Journal.*

Trevor Barnes is a professor of Geography and Distinguished University Scholar at the University of British Columbia, Canada. His research is on Vancouver's new urban economy, British Columbia's old forestry economy, and the history of economic geography. He has authored or edited nine books, and has published nearly 150 papers in journals and edited volumes. He is on the editorial boards of six journals, and an editor of *Environment and Planning A*.

Harald Bathelt holds the Canada Research Chair in Innovation and Governance at the Department of Political Science, University of Toronto. He is also cross-appointed in the Department of Geography and Program in Planning and Zijiang Visiting Professor at East China

Normal University, Shanghai. His research interests include clusters, innovation systems and knowledge-creation, political economy, industrial restructuring, globalization, and regional policy and governance. Publications encompass books on the relational economy (OUP, 2011), relational economic geography (UTB, 2002 and 2011), industrial restructuring in the German chemical industry (edition sigma, 1997) and regional growth in US and Canadian high-technology regions (Springer 1991). He has published conceptual and empirical articles in leading journals, such as *Economic Geography*, *Environment and Planning*, *European Planning Studies*, *Journal of Economic Geography*, *Progress in Human Geography* and *Regional Studies*.

Neil M. Coe is a reader in economic geography at the University of Manchester. His research interests are in the areas of global production networks and local economic development; the geographies of local and transnational labour markets; the geographies of innovation; and institutional and network approaches to economic development. These concerns have been explored through empirical research into computer services and temporary staffing in the UK, Europe and Asia Pacific, the film and television industry in the UK and Canada, and retailing in the UK, East Asia and Eastern Europe. He has published over 60 articles and book chapters on these topics, and is a co-author of *Spaces of Work: Global Capitalism and the Geographies of Labour* (Sage, London, 2003) and *Economic Geography: A Contemporary Introduction* (Blackwell, Oxford, 2007), and co-editor of *The Globalization of Retailing* (2 vols, Edward Elgar, Cheltenham, 2009) and *The Economic Geography of the UK* (Sage, London, 2010).

Gary Cook is senior lecturer in applied economics and Head of Economics at the University of Liverpool Management School. He holds an MSc. in Economics from the University of Warwick and PhD from the University of Manchester. He is co-editor of the book series on New Technology-Based firms in the New Millenium. He publishes in the areas of broadcasting, industrial clusters and small firm insolvency and turnaround in journals including *Environment and Planning A*, *Small Business Economics*, *International Small Business Journal* and *International Journal of the Economics of Business*.

Charles H. Davis holds the Edwards S. Rogers Sr Research Chair in Media Management and Entrepreneurship at Ryerson University in Toronto, Canada. He is a professor in the School of Radio and Television Arts (Faculty of Communication and Design) and is cross-appointed in the Entrepreneurship and Strategy Department in the Ted Rogers School of Management. Charles teaches courses in media management, media innovation, and political economy, and his current research has to do with innovation in experience goods, especially new product development, new firm formation and growth, and consumer behaviour in the media and experience industries. He earned his M.A. from the University of Notre Dame (Indiana), and his Ph.D. from the Université de Montréal. Before joining Ryerson University in 2004, Charles held the NSERC-SSHRC-NB Power-Xerox Research Chair in the Management of Technological Change at the University of New Brunswick in Saint John.

Harry Dugmore is MTN Chair of Media and Mobile Communication at the School of Journalism and Media Studies at Rhodes University, in Grahamstown, South Africa. He is also the Interim Director of the Discovery Centre for Health Journalism at Rhodes and project manager of the Knight Foundation funded 'Iindaba Ziyafika' Citizen Journalism project. Harry has a PhD in history from the University of the Witwatersrand.

Sören Eriksson is a professor of Economic Geography at Jönköping International Business School, Sweden. His research activities focus on technology diffusion and innovation, globalization processes and regional economic development. He is an authority on East and Southeast Asian geography. His research has been published in *International Journal of Technology Transfer and Commercialisation*, *International Journal of Logistics Economics and Globalization*, *Technovation* and *Asian Geographer*.

Ben Goldsmith is a senior research fellow in the ARC Centre of Excellence for Creative Industries and Innovation and the Institute for Social Research at Swinburne University of Technology, Australia. He is the co-author of *The Film Studio: Film Production in a Global Economy* and *Local Hollywood: Global Film Production and the Gold Coast*.

Erik Hitters is Associate Professor at the Erasmus School of History, Culture and Communication of Erasmus University Rotterdam. He has founded and is director of ERMeCC, the Erasmus Research Centre for Media, Communication and Culture. He holds a PhD in Social Sciences from Utrecht University. Erik's research interests lie in the broad field of transformations in the media and cultural industries. His research and publications have a focus on three issues. His first strand of research deals with the changing logics of institutional and field dynamics in the media and cultural industries, including the film and music industries. His second interest is in local and regional cultural industries. His third is in media clustering and creative cities.

Jennifer Johns is a Lecturer in Management and International Business at University of Liverpool Management School, University of Liverpool UK. She previously lectured at the Department of Geography, University of Liverpool and the School of Geography, University of Manchester. Jennifer is an economic geographer working on research issues of inter-disciplinary interest including globalisation, the agglomeration of economic activities and global trade and production networks. She is currently co-authoring a text titled *Fieldwork in Human Geography* for Sage and has published in journals including *Journal of Economic Geography*, *Environment and Planning A* and *Urban Studies*.

Charlie Karlsson is Professor of the Economics of Technological Change at Jönköping International Business School (JIBS), Jönköping, Sweden; Professor of Industrial Economics and Organization at Blekinge Technical University, Karlskrona, Sweden and Associate Professor ('docent') in Regional Planning at the Royal Institute of Technology, Stockholm, Sweden. At JIBS he is director of INA (the Institute of Industrial Research). Charlie Karlsson is the president of the European Regional Science Association (ERSA) since 1 January 2009. In his research, Charlie Karlsson has focused on infrastructure economics, urban economics, the economics of innovation and technological change, regional economics, spatial industrial dynamics, entrepreneurship and small business economics, international trade and the economics of R&D and higher education. He has published articles in the *Papers in Regional Science*, *Entrepreneurship and Regional Development*, *Regional Studies*, *Environment and Planning A*, *Growth and Change*, *The Annals of Regional Science*, *Industry and Innovation*, *Research Policy* and *Small Business Economics*, and served as editor for more than 20 books published by Springer-Verlag, Edward Elgar, Routledge and Cambridge University Press, and for a number of special issues of international scientific journals.

Johanna Mavhungu is a media researcher and lecturer at the Sol Plaatje Institute for Media Leadership (SPI) at Rhodes University. Her research looks at trends in Media Management, using and producing data and knowledge that helps in developing the training curriculum of Media Management courses. Johanna attended the University of the Witwatersrand where she achieved a first-class honours certificate and then graduated with Honours in Dramatic Arts. She started work as a tutor in film, visual and performing arts at Wits University. Johanna has worked with South African media organizations as a researcher for broadcast television programmes on community development, which increased her involvement with research and development communication. At the SPI she has worked and collaborated on research projects with the International Research and Exchanges Board (IREX), the Open Society Foundation for South Africa (OSF-SA), the Media Development and Diversity Agency (MDDA) and the Department of Communications, whose funding made participation in this project possible.

Tom O'Regan is professor of Cultural and Media Studies in the School of English, Media Studies and Art History at the University of Queensland, Australia. He is the co-author with Susan Ward and Ben Goldsmith of *Local Hollywood: Global Film Production and the Gold Coast* (2010) and with Ben Goldsmith of *The Film Studio: Film Production in the Global Economy* (2005) and *Cinema Cities, Media Cities: The Contemporary International Studio Complex* (2003). He is also the author of *Australian National Cinema* (1996) and *Australian Television Culture* (1992). With Susan Ward and Ben Goldsmith he has been researching the changing environments of Australian film and television production.

Robert G. Picard is Director of Research at the Reuters Institute in the Department of Politics and International Relations at the University of Oxford, UK, and Hamrin Professor of Media Economics at Jönköping International Business School, Sweden. A specialist in media economics and policy, he is the author and editor of 25 books, including *Value Creation and the Future of News Organizations*, *The Economics and Financing of Media Companies*, *The Internet and the Mass Media*, and *Media Firms: Structure, Operations, and Performance.* He is editor of the *Journal of Media Business Studies* and was previously editor of *The Journal of Media Economics*. Picard received his PhD from the University of Missouri, Columbia, and has been a fellow at the Shorenstein Center at the John F. Kennedy School of Government at Harvard University and the Reuters Institute at University of Oxford. He has consulted and carried out assignments for governments in North America, Europe, Africa, and Asia and for international organizations including the European Commission, UNESCO, and the World Intellectual Property Organization. He has been a consultant for leading media companies in North America, Europe, Asia, Africa, and Latin America.

Andy C. Pratt is a professor of Culture, Media and Economy at King's College London.He specializes in the social organization of economic development, cities and economic spaces. He is the author of *The Secret Life of Cities* and *Creativity and Innovation in the Cultural Economy*. His research has been published in *Environment and Planning A*, *Land Use Policy*, *City*, *Culture and Society*, and *Journal of Rural Studies*. He is a fellow of the Institute of British Geographers / Royal Geographical

Society (IBG/RGS), and the Royal Society of Arts, Manufacture and Commerce (RSA).

Susan Ward is a researcher with the School of Arts and Social Sciences, Southern Cross University, Lismore, Australia. She is co-author of *Local Hollywood: Global Film Production and the Gold Coast*, and specializes in studying production cultures and the spatial dynamics of film and television production.

Preface

This book results from discussion among media and regional science researchers about the growth in the number of media clusters worldwide and the enthusiasm of policymakers toward organizing and funding their activities as part of efforts supporting information and communication industry developments and the cultural economy. In those discussions, it became apparent that there was limited evidence about the efficacy of media clusters in economic and regional development terms or about their impact on creativity and output of media products.

Interest in those questions ultimately led the Media Management and Transformation Centre at Jönköping International Business School in Sweden to organize a research project on the effectiveness of clustering strategies and public support. The three-year project, supported by funds from the Carl-Olof and Jenz Hamrin Foundation, assembled an extraordinary group of researchers from around the world to develop knowledge and understanding of media clusters. It sponsored two conferences related to the topic (Stockholm 2009 and London 2010) and a themed programme at the Uddevalla Symposium in Bari, Italy, in 2009.

To comprehensively cover the topic, it incorporated perspectives from economic geography and economics, public development and industrial policy, organizational studies, entrepreneurship, and media studies in the project. The project took a coordinated three-prong approach focusing on conceptual issues, comparative understanding, and specific case studies of clusters.

This book, the first to focus on the phenomenon of media clusters, is the ultimate result of that work. It provides a context for understanding media clusters, their rationales and purposes, how they compare to clusters in other industries, and the significant differences in purposes, characteristics, development processes, and drivers among media clusters worldwide.

It is hoped that this book will help inform policy makers, media practitioners, and scholars about the underlying challenges of media firm agglomerations, their potential, and their effects. Its case studies from Asia, Africa, Europe, the Middle East, and North America provide critical insight into clustering from a wide variety of initiatives, showing the globalized and highly networked nature of media industries, and reasons why the media activities are not the same as producing raw materials and manufactured products that are usually the focus of cluster activities.

Charlie Karlsson
Robert G. Picard

PART I

Clusters and agglomeration

1. Media clusters: what makes them unique?

Charlie Karlsson and Robert G. Picard

The global media industry is characterized from a geographical point of view by a heavy concentration[1] to a limited number of large cities, where large media clusters have emerged (Krätke & Taylor, 2004). 'Media industries are highly clustered, and the clusters are practically always in major urban areas' (Davis, Creutzberg and Arthurs, 2009, p. 203). These large media cities are today connected by worldwide networks operated by a limited number of large global media firms working on a global scale and controlling a global network of branch offices and subsidiaries, i.e. they are local and national nodes in global media networks. Global media firms today pursue strategies focusing on opening up new markets and increasing market shares, which necessitates a presence in the cities that are large global media centres. A presence in these large cities allows the large media firms access to the latest trends and developments in the general culture industry as well as to the latest technological developments affecting the media industry. Around the large media firms that function as anchors in the large media cities, there have emerged clusters of small, often very small, specialized media firms engaged as subcontractors and in project-oriented production forms by the large media firms. These clusters function as creative urban milieus characterized by intensive and flexible forms of inter-firm networking and they allow the global media firms to tap the globally distributed creative potential of entertainment and content production.

Where clustering of media industries takes place is, of course, a critical question. Krugman (1991) stresses that history matters, which implies that path-dependent processes generating industrial clustering might emerge at unexpected locations due to the individual decisions and actions by key economic agents, as well as to random factors. Media firms are generally looking for locations that can support their special types of business activities, i.e. (1) the production and distribution of entertainment and content (Beck, 2002) and (2) the acquisition, preparation, compilation and distribution of information (Beck, 2002) and the sales of advertisements to advertisers (Ferrando, Gabszewicz, Laussel and Sonnac, 2008). For this reason, the clustering of media firms occurs, in particular, in those locations that can accommodate a large number of planned as well as chance and random encounters with both similar and different producers and customers, i.e. locations that can support the mediation, iteration and heuristic action that is integral to the production in media industries. Such locations are mostly large cities.

Media clusters promote and improve production of entertainment and content by connecting producers through private and public partnerships, networks and projects, i.e. making media production more efficient. In the past decades, media companies spontaneously created clusters to gain individual and mutual benefit, but today national and regional development authorities and entrepreneurs are increasingly promoting and investing in the creation of media clusters to improve productive capabilities, spur economic development and create financial gain.

Media clusters also stimulate media innovation. However, innovation in media industries is special since it is driven by innovation at three different connected and interacting levels of the media sector: (1) the physical infrastructure level, (2) the software level and (3) the content level (Benkler, 2006). It is here important to observe that, while infrastructure and software innovations are driven by R&D, the spending on content innovations is normally not classified as R&D. Neither are content innovations connected to formal R&D institutions with the possible exception of the more technical needs in digital media. Content innovation generates experience goods (Nelson, 1970),[2] which create economic value not through improved production efficiency but by offering consumers experience, affect and meaning. What has stimulated the growth of the media sector in recent decades is the growing ability of media firms to generate content that is tradable and consumable and thus create economic value. It seems reasonable to assume that clustering of media firms increases their efficiency in creating content, i.e. to generate content innovations.

Clusters exist when there is a large enough concentration of media (and related) firms in a city or a metropolitan area. Several firms are normally gathered in a specific, often central location in the city, but the cluster may include other firms in the surrounding area. An important element of clusters is that the cluster firms share resources, such as labour, contract services information and knowledge, and interact directly or indirectly for mutual advantage and benefit – although the degree of interaction among individual members may vary widely and may even be unintentional. It should also be noted that some cluster firms may also have significant interactions with players outside the cluster or in other locations.

Media clusters are a specialized form of cluster designed to produce mediated *content*, such as motion pictures, television programmes/videos, broadcasts, audio recordings, books, newspapers, magazines, games, photography and designs, websites and mobile content for customers that often are based elsewhere. These clusters may have significant relations with other industries and clusters such as cultural industries (music and theatrical performance, museums and heritage sites, festivals), sports and entertainment activities (professional sports teams and venues, amusement parks), information and communication technologies (computers, software, telecommunications) and hardware manufactures (television and radio receivers, set-top boxes, game consoles, DVD players, etc).

Against this background rise questions of what media sector clustering looks like today in different parts of the world and what issues are common in such clusters. These are the basic motivation for this book, which brings together leading scholars on the subject from different countries. The result is a state-of-the-art overview of clustering in the media sector as well as of the trends in the field. This book raises the question whether they are special cases. Several of the authors in this book argue that there are many elements supporting exceptionalism compared to clusters in other economic sectors.

At the fundamental level, they differ because media clusters involve a complex interplay among cultural, economic and political objectives. This creates a milieu in which far more complex objectives than merely promoting job creation and economic growth are present. In media cluster development, issues of national and regional identity, language and culture play significant roles, as well as desires to promote domestic content production to counter foreign content.

Media clusters also typically do not represent pioneering involvement of government in media industries. Typically, there is significant government involvement in media prior to the emergence or creation of clusters, particularly in the areas of broadcasting, film and performance industries. Structural and behavioural regulation of broadcasting is universal, and state support for cinema, public broadcasting and the arts is common. In most cases governments play a significant role in development and promotion of audiovisual media because they rely on public spaces – airwaves and regulated distribution systems (cable, satellite, broadband).

Most cluster literature conceptualizes the internal configuration of clusters as providing the incentives for colocation and its benefits. These benefits are to varying degrees derived from flexibility, informal networks based on frequent face-to-face interaction, trust-based interconnections among some large and many small firms and their subcontractors, specialized local infrastructures and institutions, a common skilled labour pool and the rapid diffusion of knowledge and ideas (cf. May, Mason and Pinch, 2001). Many authors stress that the perhaps most important benefit a cluster brings is a particular information and knowledge advantage due to the potential for frequent face-to-face interaction that colocation generates. The information and knowledge is communicated through what Marshall (1927) calls 'industrial atmosphere', Grabher (2002) calls 'noise' and Bathelt, Malmberg and Maskell (2004) and Storper and Venables (2004) call 'buzz'. The face-to-face interaction brings distinct information including persistent updates, planned and unplanned learning and the development of similar interpretation schemes,[3] shared understanding of new knowledge and new technologies, local institutions and similar cultural traditions and habits in the long run. However, these benefits do not come for free. Economic agents have to establish and invest and reinvest in links to other economic actors to build the necessary trust, which demands both time and economic resources (Karlsson, Johansson and Stough, 2005).[4]

However, colocation benefits seem not to be the only driving force in media clusters, where external forces and processes – not least in the form of large global media firms – are highly significant and promote reconfiguration of internal activities. Thus, the traditional view of why clusters work and what makes them successful may not apply fully to media industries. In media clusters, the external linkages of firms may not always be restricted to the local economic milieu. Because of competition becoming more global and the need to serve demand elsewhere to be able to take advantage of economies of scale, some media firms extend the geographical scale and scope of their external linkages (Nachum and Keeble, 2003).

The location of media clusters within cities reflects different purposes and perceptions of company needs and cluster benefits. In some cases, clusters are located within industrial zones when they involve physical production and distribution; in other cases they are located in science parks – especially when media technology is involved; some are located in incubator facilities and these are especially attractive to startup digital media firms; others are located within free trade zones to take advantage of tax and export advantages. In less organized clustering, companies may be spread out across cities or provinces or locate within neighbourhoods that provide specific amenities.

MEDIA CLUSTERING IN 'THE WEIGHTLESS ECONOMY'

Technological development and fast structural adjustments have characterized industrial economies for more than a hundred years, and still they feature pronounced structures. One structural characteristic of industrial economies is that economic activities tend to colocate, i.e. cluster in space. This phenomenon has interested researchers during the whole 20th century (see e.g. Marshall, 1920; Hotelling, 1929; Christaller, 1933; Schumpeter, 1934; Lösch, 1943; Dahmén, 1950; Perroux, 1955), but it was first with the contributions by Krugman (1991, 1998) and Porter (1985, 2000) that research on clusters really took off. While Porter (1985) mainly focuses on clusters from a nation-state perspective[5] and how they generate competitive advantages, Krugman (1991) discusses clusters as something developing at the regional level due to specific centripetal forces inducing firms in individual industries to colocate.

According to Krugman (1991), the geographic concentration of production is evidence for the pervasive influence of some kind of increasing returns. When many firms in one sector cluster together, there exists an industrial or sectoral cluster. Clusters are, generally speaking, non-random (Ellison and Glaeser, 1997) geographical agglomerations of firms with similar or highly complementary capabilities (Richardson, 1972). Inside such clusters, one can identify several forms of direct and/or indirect interactions. Increasing returns are obtained when such interactions generate positive economic externalities for firms belonging to the cluster.

Economic geographers have to a high extent accepted the economic analysis of clustering processes but have at the same time stressed that social, cultural and institutional factors also play an important role for clusters to develop, grow and possibly decline and disappear (Martin and Sunley, 1996). Scott (1998b) claims, for example, that clusters can only create new knowledge and new products and continue to grow if they have linkages with external markets and utilize a mix of local and non-local transactions. Thus, the effects of local interaction and learning are much stronger if they are continuously supported by impulses from other regions and clusters (Bathelt, 2005). According to economic geographers (cf. Bathelt, 2005), clusters should be analysed along five dimensions: (1) the vertical dimension, (2) the horizontal dimension, (3) the power dimension, (4) the institutional dimension and (5) the external dimension.

There is currently a strong belief in many countries and regions that clusters can be the major vehicle for economic development and growth. In particular, clusters can influence economic growth in three ways: (1) by increasing the productivity of the firms located in the cluster through internal and external economies of scale, (2) by increasing the pace of innovation through rapid knowledge exchange and (3) by stimulating the formation of new firms, i.e. entrepreneurship (Huggins, 2008).

One sector known for a strong tendency to cluster is the media sector.[6] There is today a growing literature dealing with media clusters and in particular with large media clusters (van den Berg, Braun and van Winden,

2001), sometimes characterized as 'global media cities' (Krätke, 2003). There are several obvious reasons why media firms tend to cluster. One reason is that many products from the media sector, like films, are produced in the form of projects, which run for limited periods of time. Each such project needs to engage a large number of different specialists on a temporary basis. Only a relatively large cluster will offer a diverse enough supply of specialists to make such projects economically feasible.[7] Another reason why media sector firms cluster is that many media industries are creative industries within or closely related to the cultural sector. The tendency of creative cultural industries to cluster has been documented often in the literature in recent decades (Scott, 1997; Hitters and Richards, 2002; Mommaas, 2004).

A parallel process to the emergence of large media clusters in large cities has been the marked trend towards the globalization of a number of large media firms (Robins, 1995; Pratt, 2000). The growth of media firms, not least through mergers and acquisitions, has led to the formation of very large media groups, which not only occupy a prominent position in the cultural sector in individual countries, but are also creating increasingly global networks of branch offices and subsidiaries with presence in many large media clusters (Krätke, 2003). These large media groups tend to pursue a strategy that involves the integration and recombination of the media value chains at both the national and the global level. Another crucial strategy is the ambition to take advantage of diversification, i.e. the simultaneous or almost simultaneous distribution and exploitation of the same 'content' via different media, e.g. the print media, television programmes and internet services. Furthermore, the globalization of media firms is related to the increased importance of intellectual property rights and in particular copyrights. Copyrights provide the means for controlling information and entertainment products and ensuring that they can be exclusively exploited in a particular national market (Bettig, 1996).

In recent decades the media sector has been strongly affected by technological changes. We can today observe that the developments within information and communication technologies (ICT) are stimulating the birth of new media services including the creation, manipulation and distribution of digital content (Gillespie, Ricardson and Cornford, 2001). An interesting characteristic of these new services, which include software, databases, electronic libraries, new media, videos, broadcasting, etc, is that they do not just embody knowledge – they are knowledge and behave as such (cf. Arrow, 1962). These new services represent what Quah (1999) calls 'the weightless economy',[8] i.e. an economy whose products are nonexcludable, infinitely replicable and electronically transportable costlessly through space, like knowledge in Arrow (1962). This observation might lead to the conclusion that the location of the production of media products is a non-issue, since there are no raw materials that should be transported to the producer and no physical goods that should be distributed from the producer to the customers. Media firms could locate anywhere and the urban regions would no longer host any clusters of media firms. So why do media firms continue to cluster?

At the same time as 'the weightless economy' develops, we can also observe tendencies of technology-related industry convergence (Rosenberg, 1963; Sahal, 1985; Dosi, 1988) in the emerging digital economy but also a break-up of old value chains (Evans and Wurster, 1997) followed by a new structuring of value chains where takeovers and strategic alliances play a significant role (Hagel III and Singer, 1999).[9] There are today numerous claims that industries like telecommunications, computing and entertainment are converging and one day might evolve into one huge multimedia industry (Collis, Bane and Bradley, 1997; The Economist, 2000) – an industry that has received particular attention recently (Brail and Gertler, 1999; Egan and Saxenian, 1999). This convergence of the telecommunications, media and information technology sectors might even have been increasing in recent years with the emergence of the internet and with the increasing capability of existing networks to carry both telecommunications and broadcasting services (Knieps, 2003). Developments in digital technologies and software are creating a large innovative technological potential for the production, distribution and consumption of information services. Convergence, characterized as the ability of different network platforms to carry essentially similar kinds of services, may have very different faces: telecommunications operators may offer audiovisual programming over their networks, broadcasters may provide data services over their networks, cable operators may provide a range of telecommunication services, etc.

In the 1980s and early 1990s, some cyber prophets and technological optimists predicted that the emergence of the digital economy would kill distance and make clustering in urban regions superfluous (Cairncross 1997; Knoke 1996; Naisbitt 1995; Negroponte 1995; Toffler 1980), at the same time eliminating the scale disadvantages of smaller and more peripheral regions.[10] The basic idea was that the spread of the use of ICT has the potential to replace face-to-face activities that formerly occurred in central locations, which would strongly reduce or even eliminate agglomeration economies and hence make economic activities totally foot-loose. At the beginning of the 21st century, however, it has become clear that this picture is at least single-sided. New technologies are likely to remain grounded in existing urban regions, which implies that these regions will keep their locational attractiveness and that clusters will remain or even grow. Thus, the ICT has not rendered work and organization 'spaceless' (Neff, 2005).

There is also increasing evidence that the digital revolution actually reinforces the position of leading urban regions (Castells 1989, 1996; Hall 1998; Wheeler, Aoyama and Warf, 2000). So why do media firms cluster, when the technological opportunities have seemingly reduced the necessity of proximity in operations between inter-linked firms? Actually, it seems as if the clustering tendencies are even more dominant in media industries than in many traditional industries. Ogawa (2000) shows, for example, that ICT development may not necessarily encourage the dispersal of economic activities due to the network effects and the technology effects of ICT infrastructure supply. Cities are a means of reducing the fixed travel costs involved in face-to-face interactions. Even if in principle improvements in ICT could eliminate the demand for face-to-face interactions and make cities obsolete, empirical results point in the direction that telecommunications are mainly a complement to face-to-face interactions (Gaspar and Glaeser 1998).

A major effect of the rapid diffusion of ICT is a dramatic reduction in transport and communication costs, which will alter the incentives for clustering of media industries as well as other industries. It is too early to observe the final results of the diffusion of ICT but it is possible to identify some possible effects (Venables, 2001), since ICT reduces

- the search and matching costs in product markets, but closeness by customers may still be essential, in particular for products with rich and fluent characteristics;
- the direct shipping costs since many products can be delivered in digital form;
- the control and management costs for geographically and organizationally fragmented operations;
- the cost of time in transit, i.e. the shipping to and communication with distant locations;
- the costs of personal interactions, stimulating knowledge spillovers;
- the costs of commuting and of travelling in agglomerations;
- the costs of replicating products; and
- the costs of relocation.

These effects are not specific for the media sector. However, due to the character of the media sector's products, ICT might have stronger effects on the media sector than on other sectors. It is by no means clear how these factors will affect clustering in the media sector even if it is obvious that the ICT revolution makes it possible for media firms to go from a physical to a virtual value chain as well as to eliminate stages in the value chain (Benjamin and Wigand, 1995; Ghosh, 1998). This implies that it is an empirical issue to find out how the clustering in the media sector as a whole as well as its different industries is affected by the ICT revolution.

THE NATURE AND CONTENT OF MEDIA CLUSTERS

In order to understand the impetus towards clustering among media firms one must be cognizant of the fact that media are undergoing tremendous structural and organizational changes caused by technological, economic and social changes. These changes are provoking developments in media industries that are different from other sectors of the economy. Deregulation of broadcasting and telecommunications, the growth of advertising and marketing activities of all kinds and internationalization of media markets have made media industries grow faster than most other sectors of the economy.

However, media activities tend to be concentrated in certain locations and in certain sectors that can be unequally promoted and developed in different locations. Media clusters include many small, specialized firms as well as establishments of large media corporations with a potential to generate external economies of scale. They facilitate a fast spread of new ideas and of creative impulses between the media firms and establishments present in the cluster.

Media are an important category for policymakers for economic and cultural reasons, but many tend to see them as tightly knit with other industries, such as arts and performance. Media sectors differ widely from those other industries and among themselves, however, and the environments in which they operate and the processes in which staff work vary widely between the advertising, television, film, music, computer games and newspaper sectors. In some ways the concern about media may be more for occupations than companies because the part-time nature of employment and the heavy use of freelance employees leads to serial employment.

Although many media are represented in clusters, the music industry is not so strongly incorporated as other industries, but there is some colocation where video production and design services are available. Game production and animation has tended to cluster on its own or near software firms and clusters rather than with other media industries.

ARE MEDIA CLUSTERS DIFFERENT FROM OTHER CLUSTERS?

Today there exists a rich general literature on the cluster phenomena (see, e.g. Karlsson, Johansson and Stough, 2005; Karlsson, 2008a, 2008b). Three analytically distinct forms of spatial industrial clustering have been identified (Gordon and McCann, 2000):

- the classical model of pure agglomeration, referring to job matching and service and information economies of scale and scope;
- the industrial-complex model, referring to explicit links of sales and purchases between firms;
- the network or club model, also referred to as the social network model, which focuses on social ties and trust.

All these forms of industrial clustering have a common focus on the spatial concentration of similar firms, i.e. firms belonging to the same industry. Thus, clusters have a horizontal dimension, which through untraded interdependencies may generate a number of different static and dynamic external economic advantages (Harrison, Kelley and Gant, 1996), i.e. different kinds of increasing returns (Krugman, 1991). These external economies might concern superior accessibility to inputs, labour skills and infrastructure but also collective visibility and reputation. It is in this connection important to observe that even if there are very limited vertical relationships between firms (i.e. input-output relations) there are many other reasons why clustering is an advantage for firms in an industry.

There can be no doubt that these forms of spatial industrial clustering also prevail within the media sector. However, one interesting question concerns whether the media sector in certain aspects is different and thus exhibits special traits and possibly other clustering tendencies than industries in general. One such special trait is the specific characteristics of media products, such as their public goods character, the clear scale economics in media production and particular in media distribution, the high degree of product differentiation, the advertising content demand interdependence and the existence of network externalities (Rosse and Dertouzos, 1978a, 1978b; Owen and Wildman, 1992).

Media refers to economic activities directed towards entertaining and informing, normally seeking to reach and influence a large audience. According to a traditional definition it involves communication between a sender and typically large numbers of receivers (audience), where the relationship between them is one-directional and impersonal

(Vogel, 1990). However, the existence of letters to the press, web-based debates, phone-in-programmes, chat pages, blogs, etc shows that this definition is somewhat too strict. The output of the media activities has to be distributed to the widest possible audience, in order to maximize the returns on the investment costs incurred in the course of production, making the distribution function a critical determinant of economic success (Vogel, 1990).

An important and fundamental characteristic of many activities in the media sector is that they are creative activities. There is a constant need for creativity and innovation in product design and development. Each output is a one-off item that must be experienced by consumers as new or different, if only minimally. Thus, the creation of media output is heavily dependent upon talent, typically a single individual or a small group of people: the writer in books, the actor(s) in film, the musician(s) or conductor in music, the copywriters and designers in advertising, etc. It is well known that creative activities only develop in specific milieus characterized by diverse activities and competencies with synergetic potential, instability and uncertainty, great tolerance and critical mass (Andersson, 1985). Such milieus are normally found only in large cities.

Another important characteristic of media products is that they are rapidly evolving products, which implies that important external advantages and stimuli are derived from the incentives of the media firms involved to generate competing goods and services (Maskell, 2001; Malmberg and Maskell, 2002). Firms in media industries, which are creative industries, cannot reproduce their earlier products since their ability to compete depends upon their ability to generate new products that their customers find visually and functionally novel and superior to the earlier products. This implies that it is critical for firms in media industries to actively monitor the products of their competitors, and transform and improve their own products accordingly. Presence for a media firm in a cluster with other media firms nearby makes it easier to formally and informally monitor and study the products of these other firms. This kind of monitoring is an important part of the creative process, which stimulates innovation, imitation and competition[11] (Britton, 2007). Innovation in media industries is often incremental and requires new combinations or applications of existing tacit and/or codified knowledge building on past creative successes and an expanding skill base (Wolfe, Davis and Lucas, 2005).

Scott (1999, p. 811) remarks, based on studies of different cultural industries, that the spatial clustering of (media) producers facilitates 'unstable, finely grained, frequent and mediated face to face contact' and moreover that mediation, iteration and heuristic development involves 'not only concrete practices and technologies, but also the emotive content of products'. Thus, learning in media industries is the result of a trial, feedback and evaluation process, which occurs when firms and individuals exploit new technologies and meet new expectations of clients (Teece and Pisano, 1998). Such learning-by-doing activities create increasing returns within a cluster through knowledge spillovers.[12] It is against this background not difficult to understand the recent emphasis that localized innovation policies should focus not only on the R&D-based generation of innovations but also on the need in a broader sense to accelerate learning and the creation of new product varieties through systemic improvements and the reduction of information and transaction costs, furthering of trust-based cooperation, the supply of services and the improvement of the capacity for collective action (Laranja, Uyarra and Flanagan, 2008).

A third important characteristic of the activities in important parts of the media sector is that they are organized as intra- and inter-firm projects with a limited time span, which can be described as project-based temporary production networks.[13] This solution to the problem of organizing and coordinating production is in the literature known as 'flexible specialization' (Piore and Sabel, 1985) and is very common in the media sector (Starkey, Barnatt and Tempest, 2000; Sydow and Staber, 2002; Mossig, 2004; Ferriani, Corrado and Boschetti, 2005). The flexible specialization model makes it possible for the leading media firms to use the freelancers and the different small firms in the media cluster as a reserve labour pool and to reduce risks by relying to a high extent on short-term contracts (Christopherson, 2005, 2006). Project-based production is true for film production, music production, book production, software development, etc, and it has been proposed that such networks, so-called project based enterprises, is the archetypical form of the emerging new media industries, as well as of many industries in the cultural sector (Grabher, 2002; Pratt, 2002).[14] Thus, the single talented individual or small group of people is part of a larger production network using a varied supply of specialists. The development and continuous updating of software, for example, demand the employment of large in-house as well as outsourced teams of designers and managers, preferably with good opportunities for frequent face-to-face communication (Cusumano, 1991; Cusumano and Selby, 1996). Hansen, Vang-Lauridsen and Asheim (2005) stress that in the entertainment sector, which is part of the media sector, production systems often are based on the assembling of new teams of actors, writers and other specialized workers for each new project. Carefully selected staff from different firms,[15] which, for a limited period, dedicate some or all their time to the tasks specified for the project, constitute such inter-firm projects. These inter-firm projects are based on a rigorous division of labour within the production chain, i.e. vertical disintegration, and a specialization in small areas of production.

Overall, the media production system is characterized by many different specialized functions and dense inter-firm relationships, in which geographical proximity increases the efficiency of transactions, information exchange and inter-active learning between producers thus enhancing the core competencies of the localized firms (Scott, 1998a; Bathelt and Boggs, 2003; Picard, 2011). Many projects may over time create a strong social basis for the transfer of tacit knowledge via face-to-face contacts but will function only if the local skilled labour pool is large enough. Only large regions contain a large potential local demand and the variation in skills, competencies and services that are needed to host this kind of flexible production system and to generate the necessary learning effects (Arthur, 1990, 1994). Thus, we should expect strong tendencies for the media sector activities to cluster in large dense regions where geographical proximity makes it possible to reduce transaction costs through more efficient transactions and information exchange.[16] It is also well known that many major metropolitan centres, such as London, Los Angeles, New York, Paris and Tokyo possess media clusters.

A fourth important characteristic of the media industry is the existence of a group of large global media oligopolists (McChesney, 1999) and of strategic alliances between such oligopolists. One common picture of industrial clustering is the colocation of many small firms in the same locality. Recognizing the importance of large global actors in the industry makes it necessary to think differently about media clustering. Obviously, large anchor media firms may play a critical role for the clustering of small and medium-sized media firms. Today the large media firms play a strategic role in the production and delivery of media products, which implies that corporate structure, strategy, management and behaviour can have a significant influence on industrial clustering of media firms.

To discuss the role of global media oligopolists for the clustering of media firms it is necessary to discuss some important characteristics of these firms (Chan-Olmsted and Chang, 2003):

- They offer dual, complementary media products of content and distribution.
- They rely on dual revenue sources from consumers and advertisers.
- Most media content products are non-excludable and non-depletable public goods, whose consumption by one individual does not exclude another individual to consume it but instead adds to scale economies in production.

- Many media content products are marketed under a windowing process in which a specific content is delivered to consumers via multiple outlets sequentially in different time periods.
- Media products are highly subjective to the cultural preferences and existing communication infrastructure of each geographical market and are often subject to regulatory control in different countries.

There are several reasons including cost and risk reduction for these large media corporations not to produce all content in-house, but instead either outsource part of the content production to subcontractors or do it in the form of individual projects within project companies set up for each individual project. It is well established that costs may be reduced through outsourcing of production to subcontractors (Williamson, 1975, 1985). However, numerous empirical studies give evidence that strong control over subcontractors may require frequent face-to-face contacts and inspection of products, and hence the subcontractors need to cluster in the same location as the large corporation to get the needed geographical proximity (cf. Scott, 1988).

A fifth important characteristic is that the firms in media clusters reveal a number of common characteristics (Scott, 1996; Brail and Gertler, 1999; Egan and Saxenian, 1999; Bathelt, 2001). Most of the firms in these clusters are fairly young but often serve older, larger, established media firms. Often they have only existed for a few years. They are normally small in terms of employment. The local growth processes of many of the media clusters are driven by innovative regional startups. They have often been started by teams of entrepreneurs rather than by individual entrepreneurs and they have relied heavily on owner capital. These clusters emerge in inner cities rather than in suburban locations (Storper and Christopherson, 1987; Eberts and Norcliffe, 1998; Brail and Gertler, 1999).

MEDIA CLUSTERS AND POLICY

Policies concerning media industries are implemented at both the national and the regional level. At the national level policy goals, such as freedom of expression and diversity of expression, have made policymakers concerned about the effects of media structure and ownership (Hendriks, 1995). The political discussions have concerned not least mergers between newspapers and the diversification of newspaper companies into radio and TV broadcasting activities. The result has been a diverse set of policy measures including special tax regulation, subsidies, the acceptance of price cartels, and (cross-)ownership regulation that varies from country to country and over time. What is interesting with this experimentation with different policy measures is that policymakers have shown little interest in the underlying economic theory and contributions in media economics,[17] which explains the development of market structures in the media sector and the strategic behaviour of media firms. Another important issue in the national policy debate in recent years has been the so-called digital divide, i.e. the unequal access to information among different social and economic groups in society (Perrons, 2004). Media industries are also affected by the national infrastructure and innovation policies. However, content innovations are mainly unknown in innovation policy circles and they do not fit easily into traditional innovation policy frameworks (Davis et al., 2009). This is problematic in a time when media industries function as growth industries and when the creative abilities in media industries might play a strategic role in stimulating creativity and innovation in other industries not least in terms of their design capabilities (Vinodrai, Gertler and Lambert, 2007; Potts and Cunningham, 2008). The media policies at the regional level have had a different focus. Here the target has tended to be towards generating new employment and regional economic growth and to rejuvenate old industrial sites often in central city locations.

There is evidence that national media policy may drive regional agglomeration more than regional policy and economic benefits. National policies, particularly in regard to broadcasting, are particularly significant in terms of promoting centralization or regionalization of media services and production. Because media are used to promote economic and cultural goals, policy choices may in some cases conflict if agencies involved pursue separate objectives. Some policies may promote only economic or cultural goals, and these can create tensions where clusters are involved. Media clusters are not easily tweakable in policy terms to create high performing clusters.

It is important to recognize that the corporate, operational and production locations often differ for the same media firm. They may agglomerate functions in different locations to obtain different benefits. Corporate offices may be located near suppliers in the financial industry, whereas production may be located near other producers to access shared resources.

For the most part and as a result of a well-established legacy, media that tend to produce the greatest economic value and employment tend to be left outside of clusters and policymakers' interests in clusters. Newspaper, magazine and printing enterprises are rarely considered to be parts of clusters by policymakers. Newspaper houses, for example, tend not to be moved by redevelopment authorities to be parts of new clusters, but those authorities may move their production and distribution activities to other types of industrial parks to make way for other redevelopment efforts at their original location.

The ability to use media industries for policy purposes varies because of their differing market structures. Film has a more national than regional structure; television typically has a national or regional structure (and in some cases, local structure) based on the location of public and commercial broadcasters; and advertising typically has a local, regional and national structure.

The location of media agglomeration is not always about costs and benefits. Clearly, there are locations in which low real-estate costs, tax incentives, etc provide advantages, but location is often more about operational needs and labour. Thus, agglomeration will occur in high-cost locations when beneficial for face-to-face interaction in making deals, when labour markets require it or when other facilities are unavailable.

It must also be recognized that some functions and productions are more geographically mobile because they are less dependent on external resources and staff. Such activities are more likely to be relocated to low-cost agglomeration locations, and others require infrastructure-led planning for digital television, cable and broadband services.

The impetus for development of media clusters differs depending on location conditions. Its purpose may be to attract existing firms to a location to benefit from their activity, it may be to benefit by supporting the development of new media industries in the location, it may be to redevelop existing locations where media firms are already present and/or it may be to redevelop other quarters.

In general, there is recognition that some media industries are currently leading industries for economic growth and employment creation. Consequently policymakers have promoted agglomeration in both large and small cities and regions. Agglomeration in large cities follows different patterns in that subsectors and firms tend to have more opportunity to spread. In some cases micro-agglomerations of specific sectors – advertising or television production, for example – may appear, whereas in others these may be more colocated. The extent of the spread depends on geography and particular urban dynamics such as population density and transportation systems.

The reasons for the widespread pursuit of media clusters vary and it is often difficult to determine whether the fundamental dynamic is intended to be city transformation or media industry development. Media clusters can be created to help transform and extend inner city spaces – in which case they often involve residential redevelopment, shopping and entertainment development – or they may be created specifically to gain benefits from media developments.

Media clusters may have some linkages to educational institutions but this is not always the case. Unlike high-tech and emerging technology clusters where such linkages are crucial, many media do not rely on research activities in educational institutions. Consequently, educational institution involvement in clusters tends to be limited to cases where newer digital media are involved or where technical training is required.

THE PERFORMANCE OF MEDIA CLUSTERS

In order to consider the performance of media clusters, this book explores clusters worldwide, with in-depth study of clusters in Cape Town (South Africa), Dubai (United Arab Emirates), Hilversum (The Netherlands), London (United Kingdom), Manchester/Liverpool (United Kingdom), Munich (Germany), Singapore, Sydney (Australia), Toronto (Canada), Trollhättan (Sweden) and Vancouver (Canada).

The researchers have identified a variety of characteristics of clusters that are useful in determining the performance[18] of media clusters and the media firms they contain and have attempted to gather that information from each of the case clusters:

- The development processes for creation and improvement. This considers whether clusters are spontaneously created, self-generated clusters, planned clusters created by industry or governmental agencies or real-estate related clusters designed primarily by real-estate developers.
- Structural/operational characteristics of clusters, such as whether they are managed clusters led by professional staffs that promote and support collaborative activities, cooperative clusters operated without paid staff but relying on resources from within members to serve joint interests or unmanaged clusters that are mere agglomerations of firms without organized joint activities.
- The size of the cluster evidenced by the number of players and total turnover.
- The age and size of companies, number of employees, spin-offs, etc.
- Profitability of firms in the cluster.
- The connectedness of clusters indicated by the number and value of transactions among members of the cluster and the number and value of transactions with firms outside the cluster.
- The extent to which international linkages are forged by the cluster itself and its members.

- What spillover effects are found with cultural industries, ICT, telecommunication, sports and entertainment, etc.
- The prospects for cluster sustainability evidenced through renewal and adaptation.

THE CONTENT OF THIS BOOK

In subsequent chapters in Part I of this book, existing literature on clusters and agglomeration generally and media clusters are reviewed, as are policy implications of clusters. In Part II, the individual cases are reported, gathered together in sections that consider well-established clusters that are working to maintain or reinvigorate their media leadership positions, clusters that are expanding or improving their positions and startup and emerging clusters. Finally, conclusions and implications for policy are discussed in Part III.

In the next chapter Sören Eriksson provides a discussion of the various approaches to clustering from economics, economic geography, regional science and related fields, revealing the development of the idea, the main themes and issues in its research and definitions that underpin studies. Leona Achtenhagen and Robert G. Picard then look specifically at media clusters, their definitions, specific challenges they pose and how past researchers have attempted to deal with them. In the final introductory chapter, Charles Davis explores policy issues related to media clusters, showing how governmental approaches to media clusters differ because of the intersection of industrial, cultural and media-specific policies.

The case studies reveal a range of conditions and objectives and means of pursuing them through media clusters. Erik Hitters leads off a discussion of existing clusters that are seeking to reinvigorate themselves or maintain their positions with a view of the Hilversum cluster in the Netherlands. Andy Pratt explores the diffusion of media-related clusters across London and its implications, while Harald Bathelt explores how the Munich media cluster has changed to account for industry and national transformations.

The effects of the expansion and new roles for a combined cluster in Manchester and Liverpool are studied by Gary Cook and Jennifer Johns, and Tom O'Regan, Ben Goldsmith and Susan Ward explore how the Sydney cluster has altered and shifted into different zones of the city. Two Canadian studies reveal how Toronto and Vancouver have vied to play international and national in audio-visual and game production. Charles Davis shows how national cultural policies have promoted domestic television and film production in Toronto and have used international productions to improve the economic base of the cluster there. Neil Coe and Trevor Barnes reveal that Vancouver's audiovisual production and electronic games industries have developed more organically but have gained more public financial support as they have matured and become more important to the evolving local economy.

Startup clusters are explored in a number of locations. Robert G. Picard and Leon Barkho study the Dubai Media Cluster, showing how objectives other than media development have driven that agglomeration. Harry Dugmore and Johanna Mavhungu explore an emerging cluster in Cape Town, South Africa, and how the nation failed to pursue opportunities for a broader national cluster after the World Cup in 2010. Sören Eriksson reveals the strategic thinking and highly planned approach being used in creation of the Singapore Media Cluster and Leona Achtenhagen underscores the roles of individuals and strength of commitment in her study of the Trollhättan, Sweden, cluster.

The chapters in this book together provide a crucial insight into the multiple ways that clusters develop and are promoted and the prospects for such clusters. They reveal strengths and weaknesses of such clusters, emerging challenges and the extent to which they serve traditional and emerging objectives and purposes of clusters.

NOTES

1. Miller, Botham, Gibson, Martin and Moore (2001) estimate, for example, that 70–90 per cent of the total UK employment in different media industries is located in London.
2. Experience goods have special economic properties because of the high uncertainty of demand and thus an exceptionally vital role in the development of markets, of quality-signalling mechanisms, such as word-of-mouth in consumer networks, reviews of critics and different recommendation systems.
3. The development of similar interpretation schemes involves a substantial risk in the long term in the sense that the economic agents in a cluster might not correctly interpret the importance of, for example, new emerging technologies and too long continue to invest in the old established technologies.
4. It is certainly a misunderstanding, when Bathelt (2005, p. 109) claims that 'Participating in a cluster's buzz does not require particular investments'.
5. Porter (2000, p. 254) goes even further and defines a cluster as 'a geographically proximate group of interconnected companies and associated institutions in a particular field, linked by commonalities and complementarities. The geographic scope of a cluster can range from a single city or state to a country or even a group of neighboring countries'. One can for many reasons question this kind of all-embracing definition. The concept of proximity totally loses its meaning due to Porter's fuzziness regarding the spatial boundaries of clusters.
6. In the literature one finds the term 'new media' which is a concept mainly launched by the 'new media' sector to distinguish itself, as a group of leading-edge industries, from the traditional media sector (Backlund and Sandberg, 2002). Given the transformation in recent decades in all media industries, it does not seem meaningful to try to make a

distinction between 'new' and 'old'. The use of the term media sector here is intended to cover all media industries.

7. There are examples of attempts to run such projects outside clusters, such as Trollywood in Trollhättan, Sweden, but such attempts are feasible only because of public subsidies.
8. Quah (1999) remarks that the weightless economy also can be described as the knowledge economy, the intangible economy, the immaterial economy or simply the new economy. Kling & Lamb (2000) suggest the use of the term 'information economy' to include all informational products such as publishing, R&D, legal and insurance services, entertainment and teaching in all forms, and the term 'internet economy' to address only those products whose development, production, sale or distribution is critically dependent upon digital technologies. Piazolo (2001, p. 30) defines the digital economy as 'an economy where both final output and intermediate input increasingly consist of information and where the modern (digital) information and communication technologies provide world-wide access to almost any available information'.
9. One example of the break-up of value chains in the media sector is the increasing role of content intermediaries (Hess and von Walter, 2006).
10. Already McLuhan (1964) wrote that new technologies would lead to activities leaving the centre and going to the periphery, to create a uniform 'global village', and Bairoch (1988) suggested that one of the causes of the 'break up of cities', i.e. urban sprawl, was the development of television.
11. Competition in media markets is achieved by means of differentiated products (Rosse & Dertouzos, 1978a). To avoid the head-to-head competition in homogeneous markets, media firms engage in Hotelling-type competition to distinguish their content products (Hotelling, 1929). The maximum number of differentiated products in monopolistically competitive markets is determined by exogenous variables, such as market size, distribution of taste groups, size of entry barriers, operation costs, etc, which are difficult for the individual media firms to influence (Mankiw and Whinston, 1986; Waterman, 1989/1990).
12. However, this observation does not imply that media firms do not seek information and knowledge from other regions by other means including the internet.
13. There exists a rich literature about networks of firms and their relationships and the different scales over which such networks may operate and be facilitated by new technologies (Castells, 1996; Karlsson et al., 2005).
14. For the cultural industries Scott (2000) uses the concept 'multi-faceted industrial complexes'.
15. These firms are overwhelmingly made up by small businesses, micro-businesses and self-employed freelancers, which can be described as dependent entrepreneurs (Burton-Jones, 1999).
16. Media activities are typically concentrated in small districts of large cities.
17. Media economics centres around examinations of the interactions among media firms due to their strategic behaviour, the structural development of the media business environment and the public policy towards media markets with a focus on how this results in the performance of media markets and media firms.
18. It is important to observe that media performance measures often go beyond the traditional economic performance measures to include also political and social measures such as freedom of speech, public order, diversity, access, equality, participation and cohesion (cf. Fu, 2003).

REFERENCES

Andersson, Å.E. (1985), *Kreativitet – Storstadens Framtid: en Bok om Stockholm (Creativity – The Future of the Metropolis: A Book about Stockholm)*, Stockholm, SWE: Prisma.

Arrow, K.J. (1962), 'Economic Welfare and the Allocation of Resources for Invention', in Richard R. Nelson (ed), *The Rate and Direction of Inventive Activity*, Princeton, NJ, USA: Princeton University Press, pp. 609–26.
Arthur, W.B. (1990), 'Silicon Valley Locational Clusters: When do Increasing Returns Imply Monopoly?', *Mathematical Social Sciences*, **19**, 235–51.
Arthur, W.B. (1994), *Increasing Returns and Path Dependency in the Economy*, Ann Arbor, MI, USA: University of Michigan Press.
Backlund, A.-K. and Å. Sandberg (2002), 'New Media Industry Development: Regions, Networks and Hierarchies – Some Policy Implications', *Regional Studies*, **36**(1), 87–91.
Bairoch, P. (1988), *Cities and Economic Development: From the Dawn of History to the Present*, Chicago, IL, USA: Chicago University Press.
Bathelt, H. (2001), 'The Rise of a New Cultural Products Industry Cluster in Germany: The Case of the Leipzig Media Industry', *IWSG Working Papers 06-2001*, Frankfurt am Main, DEU: Johann Wolfgang Goethe-Universität.
Bathelt, H. (2005), 'Cluster Relations in the Media Industry: Exploring the "Distanced Neighbour" Paradox in Leipzig', *Regional Studies*, **39**(1), 105–27.
Bathelt, H. and J.S. Boggs (2003), 'Toward a Reconceptualization of Regional Development Paths: Is Leipzig's Media Cluster a Continuation or a Rupture with the Past?', *Economic Geography*, **79**(3), 265–93.
Bathelt, H., A. Malmberg and P. Maskell (2004), 'Clusters and Knowledge: Local Buzz, Global Pipelines and the Process of Knowledge Creation', *Progress in Human Geography*, **28**(1), 31–56.
Beck, H. (2002), *Medienökonomie: Print, Fernsehen und Multimedia*, Berlin, DEU and New York, NY, USA: Springer.
Benjamin, R. and R. Wigand (1995), 'Electronic Markets and Virtual Value Chains on the Information Superhighway', *Sloan Management Review*, **36**(2), 67–72.
Benkler, Y. (2006), *The Wealth of Networks: How Social Production Transforms Markets and Freedom*, New Haven, CT, USA: Yale University Press.
Bettig, R.V. (1996), *Copyrighting Culture: The Political Economy of Intellectual Property*, Bolder, CO, USA: Westview Press.
Brail, S.G. and M.S. Gertler (1999), 'The Digital Regional Economy: Emergence and Evolution of Toronto's Multimedia Cluster', in Hans-Joachim Braczyk, Gerhard Fuchs and Hans-Georg Wolf (eds), *Multimedia and Regional Economic Restructuring*, London, UK and New York, NY, USA: Routledge, pp. 76–103.
Britton, J.N.H. (2007), 'Path Dependence and Cluster Adaptation: A Case Study of Toronto's New Media Industry', *International Journal of Entrepreneurship and Innovation Management*, **7** (2/3/4/5), 272–97.
Burton-Jones, A. (1999), *Knowledge Capitalism: Business, Work and Learning in the New Economy,* Oxford, UK and New York, NY, USA: Oxford University Press.
Cairncross, F. (1997), *The Death of Distance: How the Communications Revolution Will Change Our Lives*, Boston, MA, USA: Harvard Business School Press.
Castells, M. (1989), *The Informational City: Information Technology, Economic Restructuing and the Urban-Regional Process*, Oxford, UK: Blackwell.
Castells, M. (1996), *The Rise of the Network Society. The Information Age: Economy, Society, and Culture, Vol. 1*, Oxford, UK: Blackwell.
Chan-Olmsted, S.M. and B.-H. Chang (2003), 'Diversification Strategy of Global Media Conglomerates: Examining Its Patterns and Determinants', *Journal of Media Economics*, **16**(4), 213–33.

Christaller, W. (1933), *Die zentralen Orte in Süddeutschland*, Jena, DEU: Gustav Fischer.

Christopherson, S. (2005), 'Divide and Conquer: Regional Competition in a Concentrated Media Industry', in Greg Elmer and Mike Gasher (eds), *Contracting Out Hollywood: Runaway Productions and Foreign Location Shooting*, Lanham, MD, USA and Oxford, UK: Rowman & Littlefield, pp. 21–40.

Christopherson, S. (2006), 'Behind the Scenes: How Transnational Firms are Constructing a New International Division of Labour in Media Work', *Geoforum*, **37**(5), 739–51.

Collis, D.J., P.W. Bane and S.P. Bradley (1997), 'Winners and Losers: Industry Structure in the Converging World of Telecommunications, Computing, and Entertainment', in David B. Joffe (ed), *Competing in the Age of Digital Convergence*, Boston, MA, USA: Harvard Business School Press, 159–99.

Cusumano, M.A. (1991), 'Factory Concepts and Practices in Software Development', *Annals of the History of Computing*, **13**(1), 3–32.

Cusumano, M.A. and R.W. Selby (1996), *Microsoft Secrets: How the World's Most Powerful Software Company Creates Technology, Shapes Markets, and Manages People*, London, UK: Macmillan.

Dahmén, E. (1950), *Entrepreneurial Activity and the Development of Swedish Industry 1919–1939*, Homewood, IL, USA: American Economic Association Translation Series (1970).

Davis, C.H., T. Creutzberg and D. Arthurs (2009), 'Applying an Innovation Cluster Framework to a Creative Industry: The Case of Screen-based Media in Ontario', *Innovation: Management, Policy & Practice*, **11**(2), 201–14.

Dosi, G. (1988), 'Sources, Procedures and Microeconomic Effects of Innovation', *Journal of Economic Literature*, **26**(3), 1120–71.

Eberts, D. and G.B. Norcliffe (1998), 'New Forms of Artisanal Production in Toronto's Computer Animation Industry', *Geographische Zeitschrift*, **86**, 120–33.

Economist, The (2000), 'The Great Convergence Gamble', *The Economist 357*, 7 December 2000, 67–8.

Egan, E.A. and A. Saxenian (1999), 'Becoming Digital: Sources of Localisation in the Bay Area Multimedia Cluster', in Hans-Joachim Braczyk, Gerhard Fuchs and Hans-Georg Wolf (eds), *Multimedia and Regional Economic Restructuring*, London, UK and New York, NY, USA: Routledge, pp. 9–23.

Ellison, G. and E.L. Glaeser (1997), 'Geographic Concentration in U.S. Manufacturing Industries: A Dartboard Approach', *Journal of Political Economy*, **105**(5), 889–927.

Evans, P.B. and T.S. Wurster (1997), 'Strategy and the New Economics of Information', *Harvard Business Review*, **75**(5), 70–82.

Ferrando, J., J.J. Gabszewicz, D. Laussel and N. Sonnac (2008), 'Intermarket Network Externalities and Competition: An Application to the Media Industry', *International Journal of Economic Theory*, **4**(3), 357–79.

Ferriani, S., R. Corrado and C. Boschetti (2005), 'Organizational Learning Under Organizational Impermanence: Collective Ties in Film Project Firms', *Journal of Management and Governance*, **9**(3), 257–85.

Fu, W. (2003), 'Applying the Structure-Conduct-Performance Framework in the Media Industry Analysis', *The International Journal on Media Management*, **5**(4), 275–84.

Gaspar, J. and E.L. Glaeser (1998), 'Information Technology and the Future of Cities', *Journal of Urban Economics*, **43**(1), 136–56.

Ghosh, S. (1998), 'Making Business Sense on the Internet', *Harvard Business Review*, **76** (2), 126–35.

Gillespie, A., R. Richardson and J. Cornford (2001), 'Regional Development and the New Economy', *European Investment Bank Papers*, **6**(1), 109–31.

Gordon, I.R. and P. McCann (2000), 'Industrial Clusters: Complexes, Agglomeration and/or Social Networks?', *Urban Studies*, **37**(3), 513–32.

Grabher, G. (2002), 'Cool Projects, Boring Institutions: Temporary Collaboration in Social Context', *Regional Studies*, **36**(3), 205–14.

Hagel III, J. and M. Singer (1999), 'Unbundling the Corporation', *Harvard Business Review*, **77**(2), 133–41.

Hall, P. (1998), *Cities in Civilization: Culture, Innovation and Urban Order*, London, UK: Weidenfeld & Nicolson

Hansen, H.K., J. Vang-Lauridsen and B.T. Asheim (2005), 'The Creative Class and Regional Growth: Towards a Knowledge Based Approach', paper presented at 'Regional Growth Agendas' conference, Regional Studies Association, Aalborg, DNK, 28–31March 2005

Harrison, B., M.R. Kelley and J. Gant (1996), 'Innovative Firm Behavior and Local Milieu: Exploring the Intersection of Agglomeration, Firm Effects, and Technological Change', *Economic Geography*, **72**(3), 233–58.

Hendriks, P. (1995), 'Communications Policy and Industrial Dynamics in Media Markets: Toward a Theoretical Framework for Analyzing Media Industry Organization', *Journal of Media Economics*, **8**(2), 61–76.

Hess, T. and B. von Walter (2006), 'Toward Content Intermediation: Shedding New Light on the Media Sector', *International Journal on Media Management*, **8**(1), 2–8.

Hitters, E. and G. Richards (2002), 'The Creation and Management of Cultural Clusters', *Creativity and Innovation Management*, **11**(4), 234–47.

Hotelling, H. (1929), 'Stability in Competition', *Economic Journal*, **39**(153), 41–57.

Huggins, R. (2008), 'The Evolution of Knowledge Clusters: Progress and Policy', *Economic Development Quarterly*, **22**(4), 277–89.

Karlsson, C. (ed) (2008a), *Handbook of Research on Cluster Theory*, Cheltenham, UK and Northampton, MA, USA: Edward Elgar.

Karlsson, C. (ed) (2008b), *Handbook of Research on Innovation and Clusters: Cases and Policies*, Cheltenham, UK and Northampton, MA, USA: Edward Elgar.

Karlsson, C., B. Johansson and R.R. Stough (eds) (2005), *Industrial Clusters and Inter-Firm Networks*, Cheltenham, UK and Northampton, MA, USA: Edward Elgar.

Karlsson, C., B. Johansson and R.R. Stough (2005), 'Industrial Clusters and Inter-Firm Networks', in Charlie Karlsson, Börje Johansson and Roger. R. Stough (eds), *Industrial Clusters and Inter-Firm Networks*, Cheltenham, UK and Northampton, MA, USA: Edward Elgar, pp. 1–25.

Kling, R. and R. Lamb (2000), 'IT and Organizational Change in Digital Economies: A Sociotechnical Approach', in Erik Brynjolfsson and Brian Kahin (eds), *Understanding the Digital Economy: Data, Tools, and Research*, Cambridge, MA, USA: The MIT Press, pp. 295–324.

Knieps, G. (2003), 'Competition in Telecommunications and Internet Services: A Dynamic Perspective', in Claude E. Barfield, Günter Heiduk and Paul J.J. Welfens (eds), *Internet, Economic Growth and Globalization: Perspectives on the*

New Economy in Europe, Japan and the US, Berlin, DEU and New York, NY, USA: Springer, pp. 217–27.

Knoke, W. (1996), *Bold New World: The Essential Road Map to the Twenty-First Century*, New York, NY, USA: Kodansha.

Krätke, S. (2003), 'Global Media Cities in a World-wide Urban Network', *European Planning Studies*, **11**(6), 605–28.

Krätke, S. and P.J. Taylor (2004), 'A World Geography of Global Media Cities', *European Planning Studies*, **12**(4), 459–77.

Krugman, P.E. (1991), *Geography and Trade*, Cambridge, MA, USA: The MIT Press.

Krugman, P.E. (1998), 'What's New About the New Economic Geography?', *Oxford Review of Economic Policy*, **14**(2), 7–17.

Laranja, M., E. Uyarra and K. Flanagan (2008), 'Policies for Science, Technology and Innovation: Translating Rationales into Regional Policies in a Multi-level Setting', *Research Policy*, **37**(5), 823–35.

Lösch, A. (1943), *Die Räumliche Ordnung der Wirtschaft*, Stuttgart, DEU: Gustav Fischer

Malmberg, A. and P. Maskell (2002), 'The Elusive Concept of Localization Economies: Towards a Knowledge-based Theory of Spatial Clustering', *Environment and Planning A*, **34**(3), 429–49.

Mankiw, N.G. and M.D. Whinston (1986), 'Free Entry and Social Inefficiency', *Rand Journal of Economics*, **17**(1), 48–58.

Marshall, A. (1920), *Principles of Economics*, 8th edn, London, UK: Macmillan

Marshall, A. (1927), *Industry and Trade: A Study of Industrial Technique and Business Organisation; and of Their Influences on the Conditions of Various Classes and Nations*, 3rd edn, London, UK: Macmillan.

Martin, R. and P. Sunley (1996), 'Paul Krugman's Geographical Economics and Its Implications for Regional Development Theory: A Critical Assessment', *Economic Geography*, **72**(3), 260–93.

Maskell, P. (2001), 'Towards a Knowledge-based Theory of the Geographical Cluster', *Industrial and Corporate Change*, **10**(4), 921–43.

May, W., C. Mason and S. Pinch (2001), 'Explaining Industrial Agglomeration: The Case of the British High-Fidelity Industry', *Geoforum 32*, 363–76

McChesney, R.W. (1999), 'The New Global Media: It's a Small World of Big Conglomerates', *The Nation*, 29 November 1999, 11–15.

McLuhan, M. (1964), *Understanding Media: The Extensions of Man*, Cambridge, MA, USA: The MIT Press.

Miller, P., R. Botham, H. Gibson, R. Martin and B. Moore (2001), *Business Clusters in the UK – A First Assessment*, report for the Department of Trade and Industry.

Mommaas, H. (2004), 'Cultural Clusters and the Post-industrial City: Towards the Remapping of Urban Cultural Policy', *Urban Studies*, **41**(3), 507–32.

Mossig, I. (2004), 'The Networks Producing Television Programmes in the Cologne Media Cluster: New Firm Foundation, Flexible Specialization and Efficient Decision-making Structures', *European Planning Studies*, **12**(2), 155–71.

Nachum, L. and D. Keeble (2003), 'Neo-Marshallian Clusters and Global Networks: The Linkages of Media Firms in Central London', *Long Range Planning*, **36**(5), 459–80.

Naisbitt, J. (1995), *The Global Paradox*, New York, NY, USA: Avon Books.

Neff, G. (2005), 'The Changing Place of Cultural Production: The Location of

Social Networks in a Digital Media Industry', *Annals of the American Academy of Political and Social Science*, **597**(1), 134–52.
Negroponte, N. (1995), *Being Digital*, New York, NY, USA: Vintage Books
Nelson, P. (1970), 'Information and Consumer Behavior', *Journal of Political Economy*, **78**(2), 311–29.
Ogawa, H. (2000), 'Spatial Impact of Information Technology Development', *The Annals of Regional Science*, **34**(3), 537–51.
Owen, B.M. and S.S. Wildman (1992), *Video Economics*, Cambridge, MA, USA and London, UK: Harvard University Press.
Perrons, D. (2004), 'Understanding Social and Spatial Divisions in the New Economy: New Media Clusters and the Digital Divide', *Economic Geography*, **80**(1), 45–61.
Perroux, F. (1955), 'Note sur la notion de « pôle de croissance »', *Economie Appliquée*, **8**(1)–(2), 307–20.
Piazolo, D. (2001), 'The Digital Divide', *CESifo Forum*, **3/2001**, 29–34.
Picard, R.G. (2011), *The Economics and Financing of Media Companies*, 2nd edn, New York, NY, USA: Fordham University Press.
Piore, M.J. and C.F. Sabel (1984), *The Second Industrial Divide: Possibilities for Prosperity*, New York, NY, USA: Basic Books.
Porter, M.E. (1985), *Competitive Advantage*, New York, NY, USA: Free Press.
Porter, M.E. (2000), 'Locations, Clusters, and Company Strategy', in Gordon L. Clark, Maryann P. Feldman and Meric S. Gertler (eds), *The Oxford Handbook of Economic Geography*, Oxford, UK and New York, NY, USA: Oxford University Press, pp. 253–74.
Potts, J. and S. Cunningham (2008), 'Four Models of the Creative Industries', *International Journal of Cultural Policy*, **14**(3), 233–47.
Pratt, A.C. (2000), 'New Media, the New Economy and New Spaces', *Geoforum*, **31**(4), 425–36.
Pratt, A.C. (2002), 'Hot Jobs in Cool Places. The Material Cultures of New Media Product Spaces: The Case of South of the Market, San Francisco', *Information Communication and Society*, **5**(1), 27–50.
Quah, D.T. (1999), 'The Weightless Economy', *Centrepiece*, **4**(2, Summer), 30–2.
Richardson, G.B. (1972), 'The Organisation of Industry', *Economic Journal*, **82**(327), 883–96.
Robins, K. (1995), 'The New Spaces of Global Media', in R.J. Johnston, Peter J. Taylor and Michael J. Watts (1995) (eds), *Geographies of Global Change: Remapping the World in the Late Twentieth Century*, Oxford, UK and Cambridge, MA, USA: Blackwell, pp. 248–62.
Rosenberg, N. (1963), 'Technological Change in the Machine Tool Industry, 1840–1910', *The Journal of Economic History*, **23**(4), 414–446.
Rosse, J.N. and J.N. Dertouzos (1978a), 'Economic Issues in Mass Communication Industries', in Federal Trade Commission (eds), *Proceedings of the Symposium on Media Concentration*, Volume 1, Washington, DC, USA: Government Printing Office, pp. 40–192.
Rosse, J.N. and J.N. Dertouzos (1978b), 'The Evolution of One Newspaper Cities', in Federal Trade Commission (eds), *Proceedings of the Symposium on Media Concentration*, Volume 2, Washington, DC, USA: Government Printing Office, pp. 429–71.
Sahal, D. (1985), 'Technological Guideposts and Innovation Avenues', *Research Policy*, **14**, 61–82

Schumpeter, J. (1934), *The Theory of Economic Development: An Inquiry into Profits, Capital, Credit, Interest, and the Business Cycle*, Oxford, UK: Oxford University Press.

Scott, A. J. (1988), *New Industrial Spaces*, London, UK: Pion.

Scott, A.J. (1996), 'The Craft, Fashion, and Cultural-Products Industries of Los Angeles: Competitive Dynamics and Policy Dilemmas in a Multisectoral Image-Producing Complex', *Annals of the Association of American Geographers*, **86**(2), 306–23.

Scott, A.J. (1997), 'The Cultural Economy of Cities', *International Journal of Urban and Regional Research*, **21**(2), 323–39.

Scott, A.J. (1998a), 'From Silicon Valley to Hollywood: Growth and Development of the Multimedia Industry in California', in Hans-Joachim Braczyk, Philip Cooke and Martin Heidenreich (eds), *Regional Innovation Systems: The Role of Governances in a Globalized World*, London, UK: UCL Press, pp. 136–62.

Scott, A.J. (1998b), *Regions and the World Economy: The Coming Shape of Global Production, Competition, and Political Order*, Oxford, UK and New York, NY, USA: Oxford University Press.

Scott, A.J. (1999), 'The Cultural Economy: Geography and the Creative Field', *Media, Culture and Society*, **21**(6), 807–17.

Scott, A.J. (2000), *The Cultural Economy of Cities*, London, UK and Thousand Oaks, CA, USA: Sage.

Starkey, K., C. Barnatt and S. Tempest (2000), 'Beyond Networks and Hierarchies: Latent Organizations in the U.K. Television Industry', *Organization Science*, **11**(3), 299–305.

Storper, M. and S. Christopherson (1987), 'Flexible Specialisation and Regional Industrial Agglomerations: The Case of the U.S. Motion Picture Industry', *Annals of the Association of American Geographers*, **77**(1), 104–17.

Storper, M. and A.J. Venables (2004), 'Buzz: Face-to-face Contact and the Urban Economy', *Journal of Economic Geography*, **4**(4), 351–70.

Sydow, J. and U. Staber (2002), 'The Institutional Embeddedness of Project Networks: the Case of Content Production in German Television', *Regional Studies*, **36**(3), 215–27.

Teece, D.J. and Pisano, G. (1998), 'The Dynamic Capabilities of Firms: An Introduction', in Giovanni Dosi, David J. Teece and Josef Chytry (eds), *Technology, Organization, and Competitiveness: Perspectives on Industrial and Corporate Change*, Oxford, UK and New York, NY, USA: Oxford University Press, pp. 193–212.

Toffler, A. (1980), *The Third Wave*, New York, NY, USA: Bantam Books.

van den Berg, L., E. Braun and W. van Winden (2001), 'Growth Clusters in European Cities: An Integral Approach', *Urban Studies*, **38**(1), 185–205.

Venables, A.J. (2001), 'Geography and International Inequalities: The Impact of New Technologies', paper presented for World Bank Annual Conference of Development Economics, Washington, DC, USA, May 2001.

Vinodrai, T., M.S. Gertler and R. Lambert (2007), 'Capturing Design: Lessons from the United States and Canada', in *Science, Technology and Innovation Indicators in a Changing World: Responding to Policy Needs*, Paris, FRA: OECD, pp. 65–85.

Vogel, H. (1990), *Entertainment Industry Economics*, 3rd edn, Cambridge, UK and New York, NY, USA: Cambridge University Press.

Waterman, D. (1989/1990), 'Diversity and Quality of Information Products in Monopolistically Competitive Markets', *Information Economics and Policy*, **4**(4), 291–303.
Wheeler, J.O., Y. Aoyama and B. Warf (eds) (2000), *Cities in the Telecommunications Age. The Fracturing of Geography*, London, UK and New York, NY, USA: Routledge.
Williamson, O. (1975), *Markets and Hierarchies: Analysis and Antitrust*, New York, NY, USA: The Free Press.
Williamson, O. (1985), *The Economic Institutions of Capitalism*, New York, NY, USA: The Free Press.
Wolfe, D.A., C. Davis and M. Lucas (2005), 'Global Networks and Local Linkages: An Introduction', in David A. Wolfe and Matthew Lucas (eds), *Global Networks and Local Linkages: The Paradox of Cluster Development in an Open Economy*, Kingston, CAN: McGill-Queen's University Press, pp. 1–25.

2. Promotion of company and local economic growth through clusters

Sören Eriksson

Media clusters are rooted in policy changes over the past century in which governments have taken a prominent role in promoting economic growth and the development of industries. To understand the nature and significance of media clusters, one must comprehend this broader context, the bases of governmental action and underlying economics of clusters as a whole.

Economic geography, along with several other economic and social sciences, is firmly linked to a theoretical approach with the aim of explaining local, regional and national economic growth in terms of clusters. This chapter is a general survey of the concept of clusters – a term underlying a multitude of ideas. The subject is indeed broad with extensive literature rendering research focus a necessity. The emphasis is laid on the historical development of research in localized growth and the main themes and concepts used. Internal versus external influences, weaknesses of research, definitions and new approaches of research in clusters are also discussed.

The renewed interest in agglomeration and localized economic growth research has come from a variety of disciplines, but ideas and thoughts about local thickening have a much older origin. Research in local agglomeration and embeddedness converges through expressions such as cluster, industrial districts, innovative milieu and networks. Not all spatial agglomerations of firms in the same or related sectors necessarily comprise a cluster.

The profound changes in the world economy in the last few decades accompanied by the displacements in parts of the old industrial cores and the duality between deterritorializing and territorializing forces have intensified interest in localized growth in the spatial economy. Alongside significant changes such as the increased importance of East and Southeast Asia, especially China, the old industrial core has seen the emergence of new industrial spaces (various high-tech clusters, etc). The revitalization of industrial areas such as Third Italy and Baden-Württemberg and the rise of 'world cities', around which intense interdisciplinary debate is taking place, are part of this process (Conti, 2005).

The topic of clustering is a fundamental issue when discussing the relationship between the local and the global. We live in what is now considered a globalized world, a term which is widely used by many to bundle together a number of processes facing contemporary societies. According to the sociologist Castells (1996), the forces of globalization are replacing the 'space of places' with a 'space of flows', thus more or less assuming that anything can be located anywhere and thus moved somewhere with ease. But Dicken (2007, p. 18) criticizes Castells's argument:

> Seductive as such ideas might seem, they are highly misleading. The world is both a 'space of places' and a 'place of flows'. Production networks don't just float freely in a spaceless/placeless world. Although transportation and communications technologies have, indeed, been revolutionized, both geographical distance and, especially, place are fundamental. Every component in a production network – every firm, every economic function – is, quite literally, 'grounded' in specific locations.

Economic activities are not only located somewhere, they also tend to be concentrated into various kinds of spatially localized agglomerations, where different groups and different mixes of activities tend to be clustered together in different places (Gordon and McCann, 2000).

The phenomenon was first observed by Alfred Marshall. He noted a tendency for specialized firms to cluster together in a way that produces geographic concentrations of expertise and economic activity. In his 1890 book, *Principles of Economics*, he observes 'how great are advantages which people following the same skilled trade get from near neighbouring to one another . . .'. This finding mostly resembles that of an industrial district (economists refer to them as Neo-Marshallian nodes). In subsequent editions of his work he mentions the industrial atmosphere ('were in the air') found in some industrial areas, with a supply of skilled people and cooperation between different businesses and firms.

Marshall's analysis largely overlooked the importance of the role of entrepreneurs. In the 1930s, Joseph Schumpeter acknowledged Marshall's original insight, but highlighted the role of the self-interested economic agent, who took risks in order to generate substantial profits. In *Business Cycles: A Theoretical, Historical and Statistical Analysis of the Capitalist Process* Schumpeter (1939) proposes the idea of 'cluster-of-innovation hypothesis', which is an early contribution to cluster thinking.

An early contribution to what has later been labelled clusters was made by Professor Erik Dahmén (1950). Although not so well known outside Scandinavia, his ideas of synergistic development blocks have, in a historical retrospect, had an influence on other researchers.

During the 1950s, the dominant trend in Europe and North America was one of spatial concentration. The 1950s, as well as the 1960s, observed a decline in the intensity of local industrial linkages in many European countries, which seems to have reflected new forms of industrial organization. Falling transport costs allowed firms to transfer semi-finished products and components between factories over considerable distances (Keeble, 1976).

The influential growth pole concept (Perroux, 1955) was based on input-output data that identified not only the upstream sectors on which other sectors relied for inputs, but also forward (downstream) linkages. A distinction was made between growth poles, set in an economic space of input-output relations, and growth centres, propulsive industries set in a regional context (Moseley 1974; Polenske 1988). Growth centres were tied to optimism concerning the process of 'trickle-down' or 'spread effects', based on Hirschman (1958) and Myrdal (1957a) and the formation of industrial complexes (Czamanski, 1971). From the early 1970s, the general emphasis switched to the observation and explanation of spatial dispersion (Keeble, 1976).

To understand the main themes from the 1980s and onwards we need to widen the approach and look at the development which took place in France during the 1970s. In a preparatory work, Lipietz (1974) begins with a spatial regime which he labels 'the Economic and Social Division of Space' based on the mechanisms when space reproduces itself under the private initiative of property developers. In 1970, Lipietz formulates the coexistence of different types of regions in the national space. Another fruitful approach has been the new spatial division of labour (Aydalot, 1976) as a consequence of the hierarchical dispersion of functions by large multi-plant industrial complexes.

Local milieus are regarded as nurseries, an approach implying that innovative behaviour is as much dependent on variables defined at the local and regional level as on national-scale influences. Access to technological know-how, the availability of local industrial linkages and inputs, the impact of close market proximity and the existence of a pool of qualified labour are important factors determining which are the successful areas and which are not (Aydalot and Keeble, 1988).

Another very important strand of interest arising from the early 1970s, also influencing the research agenda later on, was the emergence of new industrial regions based on high-technology activities.

MAIN RESEARCH THEMES

From the 1980s onwards an important stream of research originated in Italy, mainly influenced by Giacomo Becattini who revitalized and elaborated Marshall's old ideas of the advantages of geographical agglomeration of specialized firms in the so-called 'industrial districts'. He extended the analysis of purely economic effects of agglomeration to a broader perspective, including social, cultural and institutional foundations on local economic and industrial growth.

Usually regarded as the single most important contribution is Piore and Sabel's (1984) *The Second Industrial Divide*, in which the authors use the Italian districts as the main example in their macro-historical analysis. This new industrial divide has been attributed in effect on the one hand to the professionalism of the workforce and on the other hand to decentralized innovation and coordination.

One of the most valuable books about the Italian districts is Pyke, Becattini and Sengenberger's (1990) *Industrial Districts and Inter-firm Co-operation in Italy*. In the sociological literature, interest in spatial clustering has been underpinned by an interest in the relationship between an individual's environment and the development of 'embedded' social networks of communication and influence (Granovetter, 1985, 1992) which may transcend either firm or industry boundaries.

A variant of the approach of industrial districts is the term 'innovative milieu' (Aydalot, 1986; Camagni, 1991a; Hansen, 1992). A milieu is a coherent whole in which a territorial production system, a technical culture, and firms and institutions are linked (Maillat and Lecoq, 1992). In a milieu, trust and reciprocity are based on a system of implicit rules or cultural norms (or modes of social regulation) as well as on institutions that support innovation and flexibility.

The role of regional and local institutions is a key aspect of a milieu, an example of which is the introduction of courses in micro-technical engineering in the Swiss Jura region's five technical colleges (Maillat et al., 1995). The links in a territorial network of this kind are structural, but they are above all cultural and serve principally to reduce uncertainty (Camagni, 1991b). Irrespective of the use of 'industrial districts' or 'innovative milieu', the milieu can be seen as a community or collective entrepreneur, with not only firms, but inter-firm associations, worker organizations, financial institutions and governmental agencies playing important roles.

During the 1980s, Paul Romer (1990) developed a knowledge-centred theory of economic growth suggesting that technological progress is caused by the search for new ideas by researchers interested in profiting from their innovations. Although he does not explicitly equate entrepreneurship with innovation, his theory interprets growth as a process through which the research sector creates new products for the market. The model proves theories for high-tech clusters.

Within economics much interest in geographical dimensions draws primarily on applications of modern trade theory (Helpman and Krugman, 1985). In the 1990s the interest in geographical clustering was emphasized in the writings of some leading economists and management theorists, notably Paul Krugman (1991a, 1991b, 1995), Michael Porter (1990) and Kenichi Ohmae (1995). The best-known contribution is Porter's (1990) identification of regional clusters in several countries.

The Californian school of economic geography represented by Allen Scott and Michael Storper, impressed by the growth of their state and particularly Los Angeles, emphasizes the interest in so-called New Industrial Districts arising primarily from observations of the spatial organization of production in several key industries, such as electronics in California (Storper 1992; Scott 1993), and electronics and computer industries in California and Massachusetts (Saxenian, 1994). These forms of districts have led to a re-awakening of the possibilities for a renewed public policy role in local economic development issues (Castells and Hall, 1994).

A study by Markusen (1996) rejects the New Industrial District model in either its Marshallian or the Italianate form. Instead, she identifies three additional types. The findings suggest that the study of industrial districts requires a broader institutional approach. Markusen's paper urges a larger focus on external influences as well as the importance of advances in transportation and information.

During the 1980s a common explanation was that of reduced transaction costs occurring in local and regional systems due to social trust and social capital (Dei Ottati, 1994). Later on this explanation was accompanied by the strategic role of knowledge accessibility. This would be higher in clusters and districts and would strengthen and accelerate collective learning processes (Capello, 1999; Keeble and Wilkinson, 1999; Maskell, 2001). Physical and social proximity favours communication and knowledge access, which would explain why large multinationals locate subsidiaries in small clusters, like biomedical (Biggiero, 2002) and packaging (Belussi, 2003).

While most cluster literature maintains the importance of local knowledge and spillovers as key drivers of cluster competitiveness, some researchers question this view, emphasizing the need to focus more on external linkages (Bathelt et al., 2004; Breschi and Lissoni, 2001; Boschma and ter Wal, 2007). But the role of external linkages is not new. Sweeney (1987) states that the level of innovativeness in an area depends on the degree to which firms are linked to both local networks of suppliers and external global markets. Regions with a technical culture (Sweeney, 1991) are able to adjust to changing conditions, such as the dramatic shock which took place in the watch-making region of Jura when electronic technology replaced mechanical technology (Glasmeier, 1991). The Swiss district had to build both internal and external links in order to learn and incorporate the new technology and to add a fashion element on which it could capitalize in the Swatch (D'Aveni, 1994).

Bathelt et al. (2004) question the view that tacit knowledge transfer is confined to local milieus whereas codified knowledge may roam the globe almost frictionless. They highlight the conditions under which both tacit and codified knowledge can be exchanged locally and globally. This implies that particularly successful clusters are the ones that are able to build and maintain a variety of channels, labelled 'global pipelines', for exchange of knowledge between relevant hot-spots around the world (Bathelt, 2001).

The structure of some high-technology industries seems to conceal globalization and regionalization through a small number of connections: the local dimension is connected globally through some bridge firms. Due to their local and global connections, a few local firms are able to absorb non-local knowledge and transmit it into other firms or clusters (Eriksson, 2000; Owen-Smith and Powell, 2004; Trippl and Tödtling, 2007). Biotechnology and aerospace industries suggest this type of structure, although there is a need for additional empirical studies (Biggiero and Sammarra, 2010). Aerospace clusters are characterized by major geographical inertia due to heavy sunk costs in large plants with costly and complex sophisticated equipment that cannot be easily moved from one location to another (Niosi and Zhegu, 2005).

Studying the Austrian biotechnology sector, Trippl and Tödtling (2007) maintain that cluster relations go beyond the dichotomy of 'local buzz and global pipelines' (Bathelt et al., 2004) as they find evidence for 'global buzz' as well as 'local pipelines'. The importance of both strong local and global connections is highlighted in the development of a high-tech aerospace cluster in Taiwan (Eriksson, 2006), which is referred to as 'design, manufacturing and innovation networks'.

WHEN IS A 'CLUSTER' A CLUSTER?

As previously discussed, we have many names for things or phenomena that are very similar or closely related and are seldom sufficiently defined. Many studies of localized growth and embeddedness use different overlapping terms and expressions such as clusters, industrial districts, regional innovation systems, innovative milieu, learning regions, networks, etc. For instance, Becattini (1989) defines industrial districts as 'a particular type of agglomeration, characterized by a localized "thickening" of inter-industrial relationships which is reasonably stable over time'.

Not all spatial agglomeration of firms in the same or related sectors necessarily comprises a cluster. Of three textile regions examined in France, Italy and the UK, only the Italian case represents a reasonable number of specialized and connected firms (Cento Bull et al., 1991). Thus, a functioning local network in a local area is an essential prerequisite for cluster development.

According to Doeringer and Terkla (1995), industrial clusters are a variation on the theme of agglomeration economies and the identification of clusters starts with linkages and proximity; and becomes dynamic through face-to-face collaboration economies. Dynamic local economies are open to giving as well as taking information and, like innovative firms, they continually search for information and maintain good internal information flows (Sweeney, 1987). The combination of sophisticated needs of customers and technical expertise in suppliers leads to mutually supportive interaction (De Bresson, 1989).

How then to define a cluster? The definition used depends partly, but not completely, on the scientific background of the researcher and partly on the purpose of the study. According to Nooteboom and Woolthuis (2005), economists and management scholars emphasize the economic and technological features of a cluster; spatial economists and geographers emphasize spatial effects of localization. But scanning cluster-related literature, it is not hard to find definitions with different orientations.

According to Porter (1990), clusters are geographical concentrations of firms involved in similar and related activities; however, in a later book he defines them as a 'geographically proximate group of interconnected companies and associated institutions in a particular field, linked by communalities and complementaries' (Porter, 1998, p. 199).

To Cooke and Huggins (2003) a cluster represents 'geographically proximate firms in vertical and horizontal relationships involving a localized enterprise support infrastructure with shared developmental vision for business growth, based on competition and cooperation in a specific market field' (p. 52).

The latter definition differs from Porter's as it reveals a sense that there is an awareness of shared goals, that is planning and growth dimensions of a cluster.

A basic way to define clusters is to have them divided into two major types (Dicken, 2007):

> generalized clusters and specialized clusters. Both are based on the notion of externalities, the 'spillovers' created when activities in a particular place are connected with one another, either directly (by specific transactions) or indirectly. Both rely on the idea that the 'whole' (the cluster) is greater than the sum of the parts because of the benefits that spatial proximity provides.

Generalized clusters occur when human activities tend to agglomerate to form urban areas, which traditionally have been labelled urbanization economies. Such clustering of activities creates the basis for sharing the costs of a whole range of services. Larger aggregate demand in a large urban area encourages the emergence and growth of a variety of infrastructural, economic, social and cultural facilities.

Specialized clusters reflect the tendency of firms in the same or closely related industries to locate in the area to form what is often termed 'industrial districts' (spaces), which are often labelled localization economies. The bases of specialized clusters arise from the geographical proximity of firms performing different, and linked, functions in specialized production networks.

Clusters generate two types of interdependencies, traded interdependencies and untraded interdependencies. The first are direct transactions between firms in the cluster, such as specialized input of intermediate products and services. Untraded interdependencies are less tangible benefits, ranging from an appropriate pool of labour to particular kinds of institutions like universities, business associations, government institutions, etc. This also implies a broader socio-cultural context in which face-to-face contacts, social and cultural interaction as well as knowledge and innovation are embedded.

Once established, a cluster tends to grow through a process of cumulative, self-reinforcing development involving attraction of linked activities, stimulation of entrepreneurship, deepening and widening of local labour market, thickening of local institutions and intensifying of the social-cultural milieu (Dicken, 2007).

The history and origin of specific geographical clusters are highly contingent and often shrouded in the mist of history. Many years ago Myrdal (1957b, p. 26) wrote:

> Within broad limits the power of attraction today of a center has its origin mainly in the historical accident that something once started there, and not in a number of other places where it could equally well or better have started, and that the start met with success.

Without doubt most clusters are the outcome of the historical process of cumulative, path-dependent growth although a few are the deliberate creations of regional or national policies, such as the Hsinchu Science-Based Industry Park, Taiwan (Mathews, 1997; Mathews and Cho, 2000; Yeung et al., 2006).

Policy initiatives to develop clusters have been very common in many countries in the last few decades. Governments with widely different ideologies and philosophies have instituted cluster promotion policies, such as Canada and the USA, Australia, New Zeeland, Malaysia, Singapore, Taiwan (Asia-Pacific) and in particular the European Union.

With such different governments all adopting cluster-based strategies, it is easy to conjecture that we have either stumbled across universal truths or mass delusion, or used the same words to describe very different programs (Enright, 1998).

Proposals for policy initiatives to develop clusters need to include actual interaction rather than single-sector clusters or linked sectors on the basis of national-scale input-output linkages (De Bresson, 1989; Held, 1996; Rosenfeld, 1995).

The nature of innovation makes it difficult to plan industrial clusters (Feldman et al., 2005). The path of emerging industries is difficult to predict as new technology is extremely fluid, and planning efforts based on current assumptions will never be able to anticipate future scientific developments or the direction that technology may take (Lambooy and Boschma, 2001). The basis of localized knowledge clusters lies in several characteristics of the innovation process that are highly sensitive to geographical distance and proximity (Howells, 2000, pp. 58–9).

WEAKNESSES OF CLUSTER RESEARCH AND NEW APPROACHES

It is important to stress that a single unique interpretation or theory of localized economy does not exist. There are a number of different approaches often contradictory and sometimes not so well defined. In general there is a limited understanding of how innovative clusters take hold and transform regional economies (Feldman et al., 2005).

The conventional cluster model is often criticized because clusters tend to be treated as static instead of dynamic entities, which implies that development of clusters is taken for granted and a great deal of emphasis is placed on the virtues of a cluster as if it were, and will ever remain, in a perfect state. Another issue is the inherent tension in the cluster model between the general (as ideal type) and the particular, that is that each cluster tends to be considered as almost unique. Many cluster-model approaches have an inbuilt normative stance since the emphasis has been on positive rather than negative effects. Locked-in effects are taken for granted or ignored altogether. When adopting a dynamic perspective to clusters, both positive and negative aspects of formation can be taken into account (Boschma and Kloosterman, 2005, pp. 1–2).

Another tension in the cluster concept that is almost impossible to reduce is related to one inherent cluster characteristic, namely the spatial concept (a geographic concentration), in which spatial processes play an important role. On the one hand, such a definition implies that there is a need to determine at what spatial scale clusters operate. On the other hand, there is increasing awareness that drawing geographical boundaries is an almost impossible task, because of the many processes (inter-firm linkages, knowledge spillovers, social networks, etc) that take place at different spatial scales at the same time, and because the spatial range of these processes will change over time (Martin and Sunley, 2003).

Rutten and Boekema (2005) suggest that researchers should take the spatial dimension as an outcome rather than a starting point when analysing processes and activities related to clusters. It is important to know if policymakers and planners can initiate and stimulate the development of successful clusters and if so under what conditions. What determines the sustainability of clusters and can strong clusters delay the renewal of regional economies (Karlsson et al., 2005)?

Besides, there is a need to broaden the research agenda regarding clusters by looking into other dimensions, such as development of more dynamic cluster models, which includes changes over time and differences of profitability and sustainability between various clusters. Other important research questions concern internal and external connectedness of clusters, including economic and technological spillover/transfer and supply chains. There is a need to understand more of the market dimension, that is the demand side, as well as the role of various cluster engines.

It is within this context that this book explores media clusters, a specific type of industrial agglomeration that has gained strong interest from policymakers as developed economies shift to post-industrial societies in which information, creative and cultural industries play significant roles.

REFERENCES

Aydalot, P. (1976), *Dynamique spatiale et développement inégal*, Paris: Economica.

Aydalot, P. (1986), *Milieux innovateurs en Europe*, Paris: GREMI.

Aydalot, P. and D. Keeble (eds) (1988), *High-Technology Industry and Innovative Environments: The European Experience*, London, UK and New York, NY, USA: Routledge.

Bathelt, H. (2001), 'The Rise of a New Cultural Products Industry Cluster in Germany: the Case of the Leipzig Media Industry', Institut für Wirtschafts- und Sozialgeographie. Universität Frankfurt Main (IWSG) Working Papers 06-2001.

Bathelt, H., A. Malmberg and P. Maskell (2004), 'Clusters and Knowledge: Local Buzz, Global Pipelines and the Process of Knowledge Creation', *Progress in Human Geography*, **28**(1), 31–56.

Becattini, G. (1989), 'Sectors and/or Districts: Some Remarks on the Conceptual Foundations of Industrial Economics', in Edward Goodman and Julia Bamford

with Peter Saynor (eds), *Small Firms and Industrial Districts in Italy*, London, UK: Routledge, pp. 123–135.
Belussi, F. (2003), 'The Generation of Contextual Knowledge Through Communication Processes. The Case of the Packaging Machinery Industry in the Bologna District', in Fiorenza Belussi, Giorgio Gottardi and Enzo Rullani (eds), *The Technological Evolution of Industrial Districts*, Amsterdam, NL: Kluwer Academic Publishers, pp. 341–365.
Biggiero, L. (2002), 'The Location of Multinationals in Industrial Districts: Knowledge Transfer in Biomedicals', *Journal of Technology Transfer*, **27**(1), 111–122.
Biggiero, L. and A. Sammarra (2010), 'Does Geographical Proximity Enhance Knowledge Exchange? The Case of the Aerospace Industrial Cluster of Centre Italy', *International Journal of Technology Transfer and Commercialisation*, **9**(4), 283–305.
Boschma, R.A. and R.C. Kloosterman (2005), *Learning from Clusters: A Critical Assessment from an Economic-Geographical Perspective*, Dordrecht, NL: Springer.
Boschma, R.A. and A.L.J. ter Wal (2007), 'Knowledge Networks and Innovative Performance in an Industrial District: The Case of a Footwear District in the South of Italy', *Industry and Innovation*, **14**(2), 177–199.
Breschi, S. and F. Lissoni (2001), 'Knowledge Spillovers and Local Innovation Systems: A Critical Survey', *Industrial and Corporate Change*, **10**(4), 975–1005.
Camagni, R. (ed) (1991a), *Innovation Networks: Spatial Perspectives*, London, UK: Belhaven-Pinter.
Camagni, R. (1991b), 'Local "Milieu", Uncertainty and Innovation Networks: Toward a New Dynamic Theory of Economic Space', in Roberto Camagni (ed), *Innovation Networks: Spatial Perspectives*, London, UK: Belhaven-Pinter, pp. 121–144.
Capello, R. (1999), 'Spatial Transfer of Knowledge in High-technology Milieux: Learning Versus Collective Learning Processes', *Regional Studies*, **33**(4), 353–365.
Castells, M. (1996), *The Information Age: Economy, Society and Culture*, 3 vols, Oxford, UK: Blackwell.
Castells, M. and P. Hall (1994), *Technopoles of the World: The Making of 21st Century Industrial Complexes,* New York, NY, USA: Routledge.
Cento Bull, A., M. Pitt and J. Szarka (1991), 'Small Firms and Industrial Districts, Structural Explanations of Small Firm Viability in Three Countries', *Entrepreneurship & Regional Development*, **3**(1), 83–99.
Conti, S. (2005), 'A Systematic Perspective on Local Development', in Ron A. Boschma and Robert C. Kloosterman, *Learning from Clusters: A Critical Assessment from an Economic-Geographical Perspective*, Dordrecht, NL: Springer, pp. 19–50.
Cooke, P. and R. Huggins (2003), 'High-Technology Clustering in Cambridge (UK)', in Fabio Sforzi (ed), *The Institutions of Local Development*, IGU Series on Local Development, Aldershot, UK: Ashgate, pp. 51–72.
Czamanski, S. (1971), 'Some Empirical Evidence of the Strengths of Linkages Between Groups of Related Industries in Urban-Regional Complexes', *Papers of the Regional Science Associations*, **27**(1), 136–150.
Dahmén, E. (1950), *Svensk Industriell företagarverksamhet: Kausalanalys av den Industriella Utvecklingen 1919–1939, I-II*, Stockholm, SE: Industrins Utredningsinstitut.

D'Aveni, R.A. and R. Gunther (1994), *Hypercompetition: Managing the Dynamics of Strategic Maneuvering*, New York, NY, USA: Free Press.
De Bresson, C. (1989), 'Breeding Innovation Clusters: A Source of Dynamic Development', *World Development*, **17**(1), 1–16.
Dei Ottati, G. (1994), 'Trust, Interlinking Transactions and Credit in the Industrial District', *Cambridge Journal of Economics*, **18**(6), 529–546.
Dicken, P. (2007), *Global Shift: Mapping the Changing Contours of the World Economy* (5th edn), London, UK, Thousand Oaks, CA, USA, New Delhi, IN: Sage Publications.
Doeringer, P.B. and D.G. Terkla (1995), 'Business Strategy and Cross-Industry Clusters', *Economic Development Quarterly*, **9**(3), 225–237.
Enright, M.J. (1998), *The Globalization of Competition and the Localization of Competitive Advantage: Policies toward Regional Clustering*, Paper presented at the Workshop on the Globalization of Multinational Enterprise Activity and Economic Development, University of Strathclyde, Glasgow, UK.
Eriksson, S. (2000), 'Technology Spillover from the Aircraft Industry: The Case of Volvo Aero', *Technovation*, **20**(12), 653–664.
Eriksson, S. (2006), 'Cluster Creation and Innovation Within an Emerging Taiwanese High Tech Sector', *International Journal of Technology Transfer and Commercialisation*, **5**(3), 208–236.
Feldman, M.P., J. Francis and J. Bercovitz (2005), 'Creating a Cluster While Building a Firm: Entrepreneurs and the Formation of Industrial Clusters', *Regional Studies*, **39**(1), 129–141.
Glasmeier, A.K. (1991), *The High-Tech Potential: Economic Development in Rural America,* New Brunswick, NJ, USA: Center for Urban Policy Research.
Gordon, I.R. and P. McCann (2000), 'Industrial Clusters: Complexes, Agglomeration and/or Social Networks?', *Urban Studies*, **37**(3), 513–532.
Granovetter, M. (1985), 'Economic Action and Social Structure: The Problem of Embeddedness', *American Journal of Sociology*, **91**(3), 481–510.
Granovetter, M. (1992), 'Problems of Explanations in Economic Sociology', in Nitin Nohria and Robert G. Eccles (eds), *Networks and Organizations: Structure, Form and Action*, Cambridge, MA, USA: Harvard Business School Press, pp. 25–56.
Hansen, N. (1992), 'Competition, Trust, and Reciprocity in the Development of Innovative Regional Milieux', *Papers in Regional Science*, **71**(2), 95–105.
Held, J.R. (1996), 'Clusters as an Economic Development Tool: Beyond the Pitfalls', *Economic Development Quarterly*, **10**(3) 249–261.
Helpman, E. and P. Krugman (1985), *Market Structure and Foreign Trade: Increasing Returns, Imperfect Competition, and the International Economy*, Cambridge, MA, USA: MIT Press.
Hirschman, A.O. (1958), *The Strategy of Economic Development*, New Haven, CT, USA: Yale University Press.
Howells, J. (2000), 'Knowledge, Innovation and Location', in John R. Bryson, Peter W. Daniels, Nick Henry and Jane Pollard (eds), *Knowledge, Space, Economy*, London, UK: Routledge, pp. 50–62.
Karlsson, C., B. Johansson and R.R. Stough (eds) (2005), *Industrial Clusters and Inter-Firm Networks*, Cheltenham, UK, Northampton, MA, USA: Edward Elgar.
Keeble, D. (1976), *Industrial Location and Planning in the United Kingdom*, London, UK: Methuen.

Keeble, D. and F. Wilkinson (1999), 'Collective Learning and Knowledge Development in the Evolution of Regional Clusters of High Technology SMEs in Europe', *Regional Studies*, **33**(4), 295–303.

Krugman, P. (1991a), 'Increasing Returns and Economic Geography', *Journal of Political Economy*, **99**(3), 483–499.

Krugman, P. (1991b), *Geography and Trade*, Cambridge, MA, USA: MIT Press.

Krugman, P. (1995), *Development, Geography and Economic Theory*, Cambridge, MA, USA: MIT Press.

Lambooy, J.G. and R.A. Boschma (2001), 'Evolutionary Economics and Regional Policy', *Annals of Regional Science*, **35**(1), 113–131.

Lipietz, A. (1974), *Le tribut foncier urbain*, Paris, FR: Maspero.

Maillat, D. and B. Lecoq (1992), 'New Technologies and Transformation of Regional Structures in Europe: The Role of the Milieu', *Entrepreneurship & Regional Development*, **4**(1), 1–20.

Maillat, D., B. Lecoq, F. Nemeti and M. Pfister (1995), 'Technology District and Innovation: The Case of the Swiss Jura Arc', *Regional Studies*, **29**(3), 251–63.

Markusen, A. (1996), 'Sticky Places in Slippery Space: A Typology of Industrial Districts', *Economic Geography*, **72**(3), 293–313.

Marshall, A. (1895), *Principles of Economics*, 3rd edn, London, UK: Macmillan.

Martin, R. and P. Sunley (2003), 'Deconstructing Clusters: Chaotic Concept or Policy Panacea?', *Journal of Economic Geography*, **3**(1), 5–35.

Maskell, P. (2001), 'Towards a Knowledge-based Theory of the Geographical Cluster', *Industrial and Corporate Change*, **10**(4), 921–943.

Mathews, J.A. (1997), 'A Silicon Valley of the East: Creating Taiwan's Semiconductor Industry', *California Management Review*, **39**(4), 26–54.

Mathews, J.A. and D-S. Cho (2000), *Tiger Technology: The Creation of a Semiconductor Industry in East Asia*, Cambridge, UK: Cambridge University Press.

Moseley, M.J. (1974), *Growth Centres in Spatial Planning*, Oxford, UK: Pergamon Press.

Myrdal, G. (1957a), *Economic Theory and Underdeveloped Regions*, London, UK: G. Duckworth.

Myrdal, G. (1957b), *Rich Lands and Poor: The Road to World Prosperity*, New York, NY, USA: Harper and Brothers.

Niosi, J. and M. Zhegu (2005), 'Aerospace Clusters: Local or Global Knowledge Spillovers?', *Industry and Innovation*, **12**(1), 5–29.

Nooteboom, B. and R.K. Woolthuis (2005), 'Cluster Dynamics', in Ron A. Boschma and Robert C. Kloosterman (eds), *Learning from Clusters: A Critical Assessment from an Economic-Geographical Perspective*, Dordrecht, NL: Springer, pp. 51–67.

Ohmae, K. (ed) (1995), *The Evolving Global Economy: Making Sense of the New World Order*, Boston, MA, USA: Harvard Business Review Press.

Owen-Smith, J. and W.W. Powell (2004), 'Knowledge Networks as Channels and Conduits: The Effects of Spillovers in the Boston Biotechnology Community', *Organization Science*, **15**(1), 5–21.

Perroux, F. (1955), 'Note sur la Notion de Pole Croissance', *Economie Appliquée*, **8**(1)–(2) 307–320, translation in Ian Livingston (ed) (1971), *Economic Policy for Development: Selected Readings*, Harmondsworth, UK: Penguin, pp. 279–289.

Piore, M.J. and C.F. Sabel (1984), *The Second Industrial Divide: Possibilities for Prosperity*, New York, NY, USA: Basic Books.

Polenske, K.R. (1988), 'Growth Pole Theory and Strategy Reconsidered: Domination, Linkages, and Distribution', in Benjamin Higgins and Donald J. Savoie (eds), *Regional Economic Development: Essays in Honour of Francois Perroux*, Boston, MA, USA: Unwin Hyman, pp. 91–111.

Porter, M.E. (1990), *The Competitive Advantage of Nations*, New York, NY, USA: Free Press.

Porter, M.E (1998), *On Competition*, Boston, MA, USA: Harvard Business School Publishing.

Pyke, F., G. Becattini and W. Sengenberger (eds) (1990), *Industrial Districts and Inter-firm Co-operation in Italy*, Geneva, CH: International Institute for Labour Studies (ILO).

Romer, P.M. (1990), 'Endogenous Technological Change', *Journal of Political Economy*, **98**(5), Part 2, S71–S102.

Rosenfeld, S.A. (1995), *Industrial Strength Strategies: Regional Business Clusters and Public Policy*, Washington, DC, USA: Aspen Institute.

Rutten, R. and F. Boekema (2005), 'Competitiveness in Regional Clusters: The Case of Océ's "Knowledge Industry Clustering" project', in Ron A. Boschma and Robert C. Kloosterman (eds), *Learning from Clusters: A Critical Assessment from an Economic-Geographical Perspective*, Dordrecht, NL: Springer, pp. 225–245.

Saxenian, A. (1994), *Regional Advantage: Culture and Competition in Silicon Valley and Route 128*, Cambridge, MA, USA: Harvard University Press.

Schumpeter, J. (1939), *Business Cycles: A Theoretical, Historical, and Statistical Analysis of the Capitalist Process*, New York, NY, USA, Toronto, CA, London, UK: McGraw-Hill.

Scott, A.J. (1993), *Technopolis: High-Technology Industry and Regional Development in Southern California*, Berkeley and Los Angeles, CA, USA: University of California Press.

Storper, M. (1992), 'The Limits to Globalization: Technology Districts and International Trade', *Economic Geography*, **68**(1), 60–93.

Sweeney, G.P. (1987), *Innovation, Entrepreneurs, and Regional Development*, New York, NY, USA: St Martin's Press.

Sweeney, G.P. (1991), 'Technical Culture and the Local Dimension of Entrepreneurial Vitality', *Entrepreneurship & Regional Development*, **3**(4), 363–378.

Trippl, M. and F. Tödtling (2007), 'Developing Biotechnology Clusters in Non-high Technology Regions: The Case of Austria', *Industry & Innovation*, **14**(1), 47–67.

Yeung, H.W., W. Liu and P. Dicken (2006), 'Transnational Corporations and Network Effects of a Local Manufacturing Cluster in Mobile Telecommunications Equipment in China', *World Development*, **34**(3), 520–540.

3. Media clusters: development paths and core issues

Leona Achtenhagen and Robert G. Picard

In recent years, the academic interest in media clusters has increased in correspondence with the enhanced focus of cultural and media policy-making on attempting to support the agglomeration of media companies. Such policies typically aim at supporting existing clusters or at stimulating the emergence of new clusters, leading to different development paths of media clusters. The current policy focus on supporting media clusters is driven by the observation that media industries can be a key engine of contemporary urban economic growth as well as the explosive growth of the creative sectors in terms of production output, employment and export trade (Howkins, 2001).

In this chapter we will review existing academic publications on media clustering to outline different typical paths of development as well as important issues arising from those studies and the interpretation of them.

THE PHENOMENON OF MEDIA CLUSTERS

Policymakers and academic scholars have long recognized geographically defined regional clusters of specialized firms as socio-economic engines for the competitiveness and growth of regions as well as countries (Krugman, 1991; Porter, 1990, 1998). Since the 1970s, but drawing on Marshall's (1890) definition of the concept of industrial districts, the regional agglomeration of (technology-based) companies has received substantial academic attention from different disciplines. The seminal study by Piore and Sabel (1984) triggered much research activity to search for explanations of the phenomenon of regional clustering of primarily small and medium-sized companies, often around one or several incumbent companies (cf. Keeble and Wilkinson, 2000, p. 1). Industrial districts have been characterized by three specific factors, and these same factors appear to be common to media clusters as well. First, they are a regional agglomeration of small companies, which typically are specialized in certain product types, components or process stages. Secondly, they are held together by a network of personal contacts and a shared socio-culture of employees, entrepreneurs and politicians in a region. And thirdly, they are characterized by an industrial atmosphere in which information is exchanged, professional training offered and the diffusion of innovation supported (Bianchi, 1998).

Silicon Valley has developed into a role model of regional clusters and has inspired many regions to attempt creating technology-based clusters. Its success has been largely attributed to the cooperation between its many small high-tech companies. Thereby, local knowledge bases and relationships could be exploited to generate new markets, products and applications (Saxenian, 1994a, p. 44). These specialized companies were competing with each other while at the same time learning from each other regarding market and technology changes. Interestingly, many entrepreneurs in Silicon Valley were not locals but had moved to the region, which contradicts a common assumption in entrepreneurship research that entrepreneurs tend to found their companies close to home. Nonetheless, the aspect that these entrepreneurs were often alone and in a new environment has been ascribed to their propensity to take risks and to experiment (Saxenian, 1994a, p. 45). The example of Silicon Valley suggests that the success of regional networks might be based on the relationships between companies and actors, rather than a mere agglomeration of (old and/or new) companies in a region (Saxenian, 1994b, p. 51). This is similar to media clusters, where relationships tend to play a key role for deal-making and project delivery.

Media clusters, like other regional agglomerations of companies, display substantial heterogeneity regarding firm size, performance, structure and strategies (cf. Lazerson and Lorenzoni, 1999). Nonetheless, the common assumption about (media) clusters is that locating inside a regional agglomeration of related actors brings certain advantages for firms ('agglomeration economics') and that the interrelations and interactions between the actors matter for the shape and efficiency of the agglomerations (Fuchs and Koch, 2005, p. 234). This assumption makes media clusters especially interesting to study, as they primarily create non-physical goods and services (Picard, 2008). A key difference is that even though physical goods – such as film rolls, DVDs or books – might be the outcome of a media production process, these products are not where value is created, they are simply the means of distributing the content, which can usually be stored in digital, non-physical format. Thus, they might not benefit from a number of the advantages that have previously been ascribed to the cluster phenomenon. Instead, media clusters typically combine local agglomerations of facilities and resources with a global (and mobile) network of specialized skills and creative inputs. Thereby, media clusters move beyond the common academic conceptualization of clusters as functional regions. However, other scholars have argued against such 'death of distance' arguments (e.g. Pratt, 2002), by claiming that many media products have in fact a physical form, which for example in the case of broadcasting can be highly significant, when products must meet exacting technical as well as creative standards (Cook & Pandit, 2008, p. 282).

In any case, various similarities to clusters in other industries can be identified. Media clusters appear to be mainly comprised of specialized, small to medium-sized companies that are interdependent in their work and heavily rely on personal network ties. This interdependence is the result of the very nature of many media production processes, which are typically project-based. In film production many specialized companies exist which focus on different steps in the value chain between pre-production and content production (such as screenplay writing, project management, casting/artist agencies, costume designers, film financing and insurances, multimedia design), production (such as rental studios, camera equipment, film, material, cutter equipment, lighting technicians, make-up artists, special effects, stunts), post production (such as optical post production including electronic imaging, computer animation, optical effects, film cutting, sound tracks/recording studios, synchronization) and distribution (such as promotion agencies, media agencies, publicity agencies, cinema advertising, retail trade of video, DVD and multimedia) (cf. Krätke, 2002). As film production is typically organized as project-based work, different specialized companies in different constellations deliver their services for the making of different films. As the workload for each company fluctuates, companies often prefer to keep hired staff to a minimum and instead rely on contract workers who are hired in for the duration of a specific film project only. Similar processes can be found in television and game production. One-shot production is almost the norm and many firms are established specifically for a single production.

By relying on personal networks, companies need to be less regionally bound. Instead, film directors and performers as well as specialized companies (e.g. special effects companies) can move internationally between film sets, creating what Picard (2008, p. 5) names virtual media clusters, thereby putting into question the long-term advantages and sustainability of regionally agglomerated media clusters. Personal networking facilitates increased geographic mobility, contradicting traditionally asserted clustering benefits. This can especially be expected to be the case where local and regional governments and agencies promote and finance the building of clusters by demanding local effects to be created in return by the companies recruited to the cluster. Such local effects could refer to a certain percentage of premises hired for the production process, percentage of the budget spent locally or percentage of the film to be shot in the region.

Media clusters differ from each other. Four different broad orientations of media clusters have been identified, print media clusters, audiovisual clusters, new media clusters and creative industry clusters (Picard, 2008, p. 10). As different media sectors have different value chains and business models, cluster characteristics also differ between agglomerations. The groups of companies making up a media cluster might also be more or less homogeneous with each other. If clusters are made up of rather homogeneous firms – for example, firms specializing in print media or firms focused on new media – they tend to reduce spillover effects to other related sectors. However, if clusters are made up of more heterogeneous firms – such as television firms, performing arts firms and graphic designers – spillover effects might be stronger, but at the same time conflicts can develop because of the firms' disparate business models, cultures and types of staff. But clusters representing the same media sector might also differ from each other, for example due to their different development paths. Such different development paths will be outlined in the next section.

DEVELOPMENT PATHS OF MEDIA CLUSTERS

Historically, a number of media clusters have developed spontaneously, i.e. without explicit policy support. Examples of such clusters are most prominently Hollywood, but also New York, London, Berlin, Tokyo and Bollywood. The trend towards policy-driven cluster development is rather recent and aims at obtaining benefits for regional economic development. In the following we will describe different typical ways of promoting media cluster formation.

Creating 'Greenfield' Clusters

Due to the assumed benefits of the clustering of media (and other creative) firms, policymakers sometimes attempt to develop clusters even where no or little previous activities in that sector have taken place. Bayless (2007) reports on an attempt to build a creative industry cluster in Dublin, the Digital Hub. This project was intended to become a digital district boasting an industry with assumed future potential and employing thousands of media, technology and creative people and was planned to comprise an entire district of flats, shops and leisure activities. In the Digital Hub, digital media enterprise and entrepreneurship were thought to link with R&D and educational sectors to develop external knowledge links claimed to be important for cluster development. However, as Bayless (2007) assesses, six years after inception, only two out of the total nine acres of the site have been in any way developed and the project faces collapse following the closure of its key tenant, Media Lab Europe. Bayless identifies several weaknesses in this attempt of cluster development. Firstly, there was a failure to establish links between research/education and enterprise. Secondly, the aims of the project were overambitious – at the same time, developing property was prioritized above developing talent, and yet the property development took too long. Thirdly, the project was initiated exactly as the dot-com bubble burst, and ICT entrepreneurs received a negative image. Policy measures appear especially relevant in relation to creative industry cluster development. Gwee (2009) presents a detailed case study of Singapore's embarking on the development of a creative industries cluster in order to shift the city-state's economic focus from manufacturing to innovation. The aspect of innovation in creative industry clusters is in focus also in Davis, Creutzberg and Arthurs' (2009) study of the screen-based media sector in Ontario, defined as the film, TV and interactive media sectors. The authors outline different challenges of approaching a creative industry cluster in terms of innovation – which in the policy discourse often plays an important role. They also elaborate on how the Ontario cluster differs from other technology-based clusters. The companies in the Ontario media cluster are primarily oriented towards local and regional customers, the cluster is much larger in terms of number of member firms than most technology-based clusters, it has a strong identity and has rather weak linkages with proximate or distant R&D institutions, except for the digital media companies (which also report higher growth prospects). The media cluster firms do not report deep involvement in community organizations that provide services to members and support collective action. Thus, the attempt to create a greenfield media cluster in locations where production had not previously been strong leads to the question of the sustainability of the established activities. O'Regan and Ward (2008), for example, are critical of such ventures as they often lack creative infrastructure and staff and merely offer media-friendly locations at (temporary) low costs. The authors also provide a detailed account of the challenges and struggles to put the film production activities at the greenfield location Gold Coast in Queensland, Australia, on firm feet (Goldsmith, Ward and O'Regan, 2010). Other greenfield film production clusters that have been developed through policy measures are Wilmington and Vancouver. Similarly, Clancy and Twomey (1997) argued that the lack of an established music industry in Ireland, hosting neither strong domestic recording companies nor support services such as legal services, management, marketing and production firms, would undermine policy efforts to create an Irish music industry cluster, despite domestic and international appreciation of the artists.

Reviving of Old Media Clusters through New Initiatives

Bathelt (2002) analyses how the former print cluster in Leipzig was revived as an audiovisual media cluster in Leipzig. He discusses the origins of Leipzig as an industrial district before World War II, when it played a leading role in the German book trade, printing and publishing industry, with more than 800 publishers and booksellers with over 3000 employees. Bathelt and Boggs (2003) conclude for the earlier print media cluster in Leipzig that regional development paths consisted of bundles of various technological trajectories. Its book publishing industry dominated the German book trade from the eighteenth to the mid-twentieth century. After World War II, Leipzig lost this role, ‘as it was integrated into the cold war international socialist division of labor’ (Bathelt and Boggs, 2003, p. 267). After reunification in 1990, Leipzig was ill prepared to compete against West German publishers. But, as the authors argue, the region recovered from the crisis as its actors continually rebundled local assets until they found a combination that generated growth, namely Leipzig’s unrelated growth of its broadcasting, film and digital media industry. In result, the industry is not embedded into traditional industrial structures and institutional settings (Bathelt, 2002). Rather, it can be related to local start-up processes and the establishment of branch facilities. Companies are interconnected with each other as well as with the region’s two most important actors in the industry, the MDR (Mitteldeutscher Rundfunk, the mid-German TV and broadcasting service) and the Leipzig convention centre. The media companies have benefited from the formation of localized capabilities, such as the development of particular institutional structures, a regional customer basis, local labour market relations as well as a distinct local identity (Bathelt, 2002, p. 590). Thus, the growth of the cluster has occurred quite spontaneously and is not the result of policy measures. However, a local initiative aiming to support Leipzig’s development as a media cluster, Förderverein Medienstadt Leipzig, had been founded by local planners, politicians and members of institutions already in 1990, coordinating public activities to promote the vision of Leipzig as a media cluster. In a later paper (Bathelt, 2005), the same author finds that clusters can only create new knowledge and continue to grow if the cluster firms have linkages with external markets and employ a mix of local and non-local transactions. The combination of local and global, or translocal, creates a dynamic process of knowledge creation. Bathelt concludes for the further development of the Leipzig cluster that companies neither network enough locally nor have overly strong contacts with firms outside of the cluster, leading to a lack of learning.

Developing a Cluster around Existing Incumbents

A number of different studies have pointed out that the agglomeration of media companies often happens around existing incumbents, and indeed combining new and old economy firms in complementary ways and cooperating with other clusters has been claimed to be one road to success (Bresnahan and Gambardella, 2004). Such clustering grants access to skilled staff. Yet, such incumbents are not necessarily industry incumbents, as commonly suggested in academic literature. Rather, Vang (2007) shows that the agglomeration of newspapers in the largest metropolitan areas is not due to the knowledge externality factors typically emphasized in the cluster literature. He argues that instead the spatial organization reflects a need for physical proximity to 'central powers' and major events taking place in these areas. In addition, Oakey, Kipling and Wildgust (2001) propose that local spin-offs from incumbent companies may explain the physical intensity of clusters, both in terms of a reluctance to move far away when relocating and a preference for locating near to the firm from which new entrepreneurs have spun off. The authors conclude that a rich supply of relevant local labour skills can stimulate the growth of a cluster, but that this form of clustering does not necessarily imply functional linkages.

Fuchs and Koch (2005, p. 245) find that multimedia activities in Germany are concentrated mainly in the urban agglomerations with dense population, low unemployment rates and a high number of employees in the service sector. Inside those agglomerations, they find that multimedia firms seem to prefer representative locations (such as inner-city neighbourhoods) with interesting architecture (such as old industrial buildings or old army buildings). They point out the importance of traditional media for the multimedia sector: multimedia companies in Hamburg benefit from the presence of publishing houses there, in Cologne they are mainly dependent on the public and private TV industry located there, and in Munich multimedia companies benefit from a publishing and movie industry concentration as well as the closeness to the electronics company Siemens.

A large literature exists on film production clustering in Hollywood (e.g. Christopherson and Storper, 1986; Miller and Shamsie, 1996; De Fillippi and Arthur, 1998; Goldsmith and O'Regan, 2003) and the changes this cluster has undergone since inception. For example, Christopherson and Storper (1986) find that the 'new' Hollywood was based on two main structural changes. Firstly, Hollywood underwent vertical disintegration and spatial dislocation, leading to the emergence of a 'transactions-intensive' entertainment cluster in Los Angeles and the emergence of satellite production clusters in other countries (such as the film industry in Vancouver, see Coe, 2001). Secondly, film marketing and distribution underwent a process of vertical integration and globalization as studios were integrated into larger international conglomerates. As a result, studios functioned increasingly as gatekeepers (rather than film factories) controlling access to the sources of finance for producing, marketing and distributing films (and related products) in major markets around the world; the six major studios now account for over 90 per cent of revenues in the US film industry (Currah, 2006, p. 440).

While most of these authors discuss Hollywood as a flexibly specialized district, Cook and Pandit (2008) point out that Aksoy and Robins' (1992) findings would characterize it more as a hub-and-spoke district, 'with major studios calling the tune and independent production companies being highly dependent' (p. 275). On the basis of analysing Hollywood both from flexible specialization and systems-house forms of production, Scott (2002) argues that Hollywood is deeply bifurcated into two systems, namely the majors and their cohorts of allied firms on the one hand and the mass of independent production companies on the other hand. He finds that Hollywood continues to be an attractive agglomeration for motion picture production, but that the major firms extend their global reach by more aggressive marketing and distribution divisions. While clusters have been claimed to contribute to enhanced innovation, Currah (2006) finds that executives of Hollywood studios openly recognize the projected benefits of legal file sharing but have limited incentives to pursue emerging markets at an early stage of their development. Instead, he argues that executives have powerful incentives to protect the existing spatial and temporal structure of 'release windows', which is currently dominated by DVDs as a physical commodity format (Currah, 2006, p. 442).

Cook and Pandit (2008) studied the UK broadcasting industry and found that around 70 per cent of employment in film and TV is concentrated in London. They find that in this industry, 'there is a very strong concentration on an area of approximately one square mile in Soho. Programme production is dominated by the main incumbent BBC, which is responsible for another 36 per cent of programme production. The independent television broadcasters account for around another 25 per cent. Another 25–30 per cent of the market is accounted for by the about 50 medium-sized, mainly London-based independent production companies (many of which are owned by larger media concerns) and the remaining 10 per cent is accounted for by around 500 very small companies' (Cook and

Pandit, 2008, p. 279). The authors find that broadcasting in the UK does not really fit any of the existing typologies of clusters and instead stress the importance of the 'microclimate' within the cluster (ibid, p. 288).

Thus, as the review of different cluster development paths above has shown, clusters typically emerge out of existing activities in traditional media or are built on spin-offs and new ventures around existing incumbents. But they can also be initiated as greenfield endeavours. A number of core issues appear as relevant in relation to media clusters and these are discussed below.

CORE ISSUES RELATED TO MEDIA CLUSTERS

Media Clusters as Engines for Regional Economic Development

Media clusters are often proclaimed to be engines for regional economic development. Especially new media companies are often considered an engine for growth as well as for job and wealth creation and have therefore become an important part of regional economic policy in many countries (see Kinder and Molina, 1999). Some authors claim that the difference between new media and 'traditional' media is that new media activities would be generically similar to other new economy sectors such as IT or biotechnology (Cooke, 2006, p. 284), where such positive economic development effects have been noted. Yet, critical voices point out that it is not certain that new media activities are preferable to other forms of economic activity, which might be more sustainable or better suited to address the specific development problems in an area (Backlund and Sandberg, 2002). New media industries are based on digital technology, which often changes in a discontinuous fashion with relatively short product life cycles, making companies relatively vulnerable. Therefore, innovation and learning are a crucial part of firm survival and growth strategies (Pratt, 1999). As Picard (2009) notes, conceptually the idea of clusters contradicts the underlying purposes of and transformations created by contemporary information technologies, particularly the idea that it reduces the importance of place (Cairncross, 1994). The internet and related information and communication technologies render communication and commerce easy and reduce the costs and time required for communication, and they also reduce the advantages of colocation. This is especially true for media clusters whose players often were early adopters of digital technologies and who can therefore be expected to employ them in a broader way than other industries. Thus, the centripetal forces of agglomeration are counteracted by centrifugal forces of ICT (cf. Giovanetti, Neuhoff and Spagnolo, 2007).

Advantages and Disadvantages of Locating in a Media Cluster

One commonly assumed advantage of clusters is the level of networking and resource flows among companies belonging to the agglomeration. Oakey et al. (2001) studied the non-broadcast visual communication industry in the South East, including digital media activities (video, internet, multimedia, etc). Surprisingly, they found that the majority of SMEs had low proportions of purchases and sales occurring within their local area. Only very small companies, with two to four employees, were found to rely on customers in the local market to a significant degree. The authors suspect that a partial explanation of the tendency for newer high technology activities to be less susceptible to clustering might be one of sheer complexity: new media do not have the well-defined but disintegrated production functions upon which local concentration could be built.

Yet, this does not imply that agglomeration cannot be of advantage for media companies. Cooke and Hughes (1999) studied a new media cluster in Cardiff and found that one third of the companies interviewed considered colocation to be important. But the authors also identified a range of possible disadvantages of being part of a cluster, such as too much competition and price discounting. Smaller firms felt insecure about networking and sharing information with larger firms. Fuchs and Koch (2005, p. 246) argue that it is not the cooperative networks between firms but rather the links to customers that are responsible for the differences in organization of production, the qualification of the employees and the product-specific expertise. Among other things, they find that the specialization of traditional media industries has direct effects on the organization of the new multimedia sector, which also becomes more specialized.

Based on the case of an emerging British new media cluster in Brighton and Hove, Perrons (2004) attempts to understand social and spatial divisions. In her interpretation, the cluster then emerges less as a new technology cluster and more as a reflection of increasing social division in the new economy. She points out the importance of a social network for sharing knowledge and ideas as well as informing about job opportunities but finds that some groups, such as female respondents and 'techie' programmers, feel excluded from this networking, which often takes place in the wine bars. Also, in order to avoid offering permanent contracts to staff, much use is made of freelancers, whose wages remain rather low due to the large pool of experienced freelancers available. The author warns that future growth of the cluster might be hampered as the rationale for expansion might come into conflict with the values and objectives of people who work in the industry (Perrons, 1994, p. 56). For example, as large multinational firms took over some of the most dynamic firms, it was feared that the working atmosphere would change considerably. A larger company size tends to make jobs more rigid and correspondingly less attractive. As the new media cluster has attracted high-skilled labour with above-average salaries, prices for houses have increased dramatically in the area, making them unaffordable for many people outside the cluster. Thus, the benefits of the cluster for the region as a whole might be questionable.

In a study of a British new media cluster, Blackburn and Conway (2008) find that several of the factors typically ascribed to clusters do not apply to their case, especially in relation to local supply side, customer base and competitiveness factors. As success factors they identify the contextual benefits of environmental attractiveness (namely the sea and countryside location) together with the benefits of a readily available supply of appropriately skilled labour (access to qualified graduate staff and experienced freelancers at a relatively lower cost compared to London salaries), which all were important aspects. At the same time they saw the need for the businesses to go beyond the immediate locality in order to find clients. The niche market strategy practised by the companies in their sample tended to take them beyond the immediate locality for clients, thereby reducing any general benefits a cluster may have to offer.

Based on a study of the Soho cluster in London, Cook and Pandit (2008) conclude that cluster benefits such as informal knowledge flows and personal interaction vary significantly by precise location and line of activity. More critically, Gornostaeva (2008, p. 47) finds that 89 per cent of companies in film and television production have less than five employees, and that they typically run one project at a time, with significant gaps in between. Financing of the projects is often fragmented and small-scale, rendering the companies unable to cover overheads or inner-city rents. Therefore, it has become common for companies to move away from the Soho cluster and be run from home. Gornostaeva presents data that point at decreasing cluster activity and employment. She argues that while some, affluent, producers, who can draw on an established network and track record, successfully integrate the business into their lifestyle, the majority of producers have completely different economic imperatives (2008, p. 49). The same Soho cluster of activities associated with film and TV production has been studied by Nachum and Keeble (2003b), as in Soho the entire chain of film and TV production (film production and post production, film distribution and sales agents, design, photography, music and advertising) is available in a very small area.

Globalization of Local Agglomerations

Nachum and Keeble (2003a) argue that Soho is not only a centre of British media firms, but also a global media centre and a monitoring post for world media trends, hosting Hollywood film producers, advertising multinational companies and music groups. In a comparison between foreign and indigenous companies in the cluster, they find that foreign film producers more often rely on the other MNCs for provision of capital. Likewise, the distribution of film and music is often handled internally within the MNC. However, the links between MNCs are used mainly for such inputs, while for more specialized inputs the companies are similar to the indigenous firms in making use of the cluster, especially when drawing on networks of personal relationships. Due to the project-based organizing of film production, the Soho cluster is in constant flux in terms of movement of different types of inputs (such as labour and service providers) with network organizations being constantly created and recreated. Therefore, Nachum and Keeble argue (2003a, p. 181) that the companies need to develop competencies in the coordination and integration of different inputs for collaboration on each project (see also DeFillippi and Arthur, 1998; Miller and Shamsie, 1996). Such competencies are based on deep local knowledge and require high levels of integration in the local cluster. MNC subsidiaries have to develop these competencies locally and acquire the necessary knowledge independently of the parent company, similar to the indigenous firms in the cluster. Moreover, Nachum and Keeble (2003a, p. 183) find that the proximity to customers does not play a major role; rather, the location has an important signalling function regarding creativity and credibility rather that in facilitating accessibility. They conclude their study by proposing that MNCs balance between internal and external sources of learning depending on the type of knowledge concerned – while codified knowledge can be developed internally in the MNC as a substitute for cluster linkages, the MNCs are similar to indigenous firms dependent on local linkages for tacit knowledge. In another paper, the same authors (Nachum and Keeble, 2003b) stress that within the cluster of Soho a critical network of inter-firm transactions exists which holds the complex together as a spatial agglomeration, and further develop the argument of balancing local and global aspects.

Also Turok (2003) takes a rather critical stance when he concludes that the film and TV industries in Scotland have a more modest economic impact than commonly assumed, and he suggests that national and transnational organizations as well as government regulations are more important than localized networks in influencing their scale and durability.

CONCLUSIONS

The first conclusions that can be drawn from this literature review on media clusters are of a method-related nature (see Table 3.1). While many previous studies on media clusters provide fascinating stories of single case studies, very little work of a comparative nature has so far been conducted. This partly explains why knowledge on media clusters has remained rather fragmented to date. In addition, there appears to be a need of more reliable primary data on clusters, providing sufficient details on what is happening inside the clusters (Blackburn and Conway, 2008). Such studies, based on in-depth, qualitative work, are important to help explain how clusters function and what challenges they meet. Yet there appears to be a trend emerging to put individuals and small companies as well as the challenges they meet into the forefront of media cluster research. Thus, more social and societal issues are put into focus than in many cluster studies of other industries that take a more distant approach of analysing network externalities, policy measures and such.

Despite many policy efforts to promote cluster building, it remains questionable whether such efforts would be an effective use of resources. Martin and Sunley (2003), for example, argue that all firms, whether clustered or not, could benefit from support and that diversity rather than specialization could be more important to cluster development and regional adaptability. Therefore, further research into the phenomenon of media clusters is called for to assess the performance of such clustering approaches as well as the possible benefits to the companies as well as the regions as a whole. One challenge of policy-planned media or creative industry clusters is that the rationale for such policies might not be formed out of concern for those industries, but rather as a mechanism to solve other public challenges. Mommaas (2004), for example, has shown how Dutch cluster development efforts have been more about urban regeneration than about media.

An important aspect of media cluster development is that the cluster needs effective organization to help it achieve stated goals (Britton, 2007; Knell and Oakley, 2007; Kaiser and Liecke, 2007). Media companies cannot just be agglomerated into the same region, hoping for positive cluster effects to happen automatically. Instead, policymakers need to see to it that coordination and interaction between companies is facilitated, as well as access to production financing and production distribution mechanisms (Picard, 2009, p. 881). Yet, in media clusters, such organization might be difficult to achieve as artistic temperaments and sensibilities might not respond well to being directed and organized (cf. Bresnahan and Gambardella, 2004, p. 355).

Table 3.1 Major literature on media clusters and their contributions

Author(s) (year)	Media cluster (type) studied	Focus of study	Empirical basis	Main results
Bathelt (2002)	Leipzig	Analyse and evaluate the development of Leipzig's media industry cluster	Survey of 68 firms, in which over 100 interviews were conducted based on a structured questionnaire, plus 20 expert interviews	The Leipzig media industry cluster shows similar tendencies and characteristics as those displayed by multimedia and cultural products industries in Los Angeles, San Francisco and Toronto, albeit on a much smaller scale. The growth process of the media industry has been driven by spontaneous start-up activities and is not the consequence of a political master plan.
Bathelt (2005)	Leipzig	Processes of knowledge creating as decisive for explaining how clusters are established, why they grow and how they reproduce themselves	More than 100 interviews with media firms as well as 25 expert interviews	Clusters can only create new knowledge and continue to grow if the cluster firms have linkages with external markets and employ a mix of local and non-local transactions. The combination of local and global or translocal creates a dynamic process of knowledge creation. Firms in the Leipzig cluster were found to neither network locally nor have strong contacts with firms outside of the cluster, leading to a lack of learning.

Table 3.1 (continued)

Author(s) (year)	Media cluster (type) studied	Focus of study	Empirical basis	Main results
Bathelt and Boggs (2003)	Leipzig (from print to TV/film and interactive digital media)	Reconceptualize regional development to incorporate the effect of sectoral, technological and political crises and interactive learning	N/A (but presumably same as in Bathelt, 2002)	Regional development paths consist of bundles of various technological trajectories. Regions recover from crises as their actors continually rebundle local assets until they find a combination that generates growth, here demonstrated by the demise of Leipzig's book publishing industry and the unrelated growth of its broadcasting, film and digital media industry.
Bathelt and Gräf (2008)	Film and TV industry in Munich	Show that deficits in social relations can impact a cluster's growth potential	Participatory observations, semi-structured interviews with 65 firms in Munich as well as with planners and media experts	After WWII, Munich grew into a national centre of media industries in Germany, but the recent advertising crisis and the dissolution of the Kirch Group have reinforced existing dilemmas. The authors suggest that the growth prospects of the industry are limited due to a lack of reflexive, interconnected communication and interaction patterns.
Bayless (2007)	Creative industry cluster: Dublin's Digital Hub	Derive lessons to be learned from this attempt to plan and develop a creative digital cluster	N/A	Weaknesses: - (1) failure to establish links between research/education and enterprise, (2) overambitious aims of the project – at the same time, developing property was prioritized above talent, and yet the property development took too long, (3) the project was initiated exactly as the dot-com bubble burst, and ICT entrepreneurs received a negative image.

Blackburn and Conway (2008)	New media cluster on the south coast of England (Brighton-Hove)	Relevance of cluster concept to small firms in the media industry	Interviews with 17 managing directors	New media clusters meet few of the conditions and benefits widely assumed from colocation; customers and competitors not colocated; limited networking behaviours between companies, but evidence of knowledge spillovers in terms of the labour market and use of freelancers.
Britton (2007)	Toronto's new media cluster	Path dependence and cluster adaptation	Employment database for data on 600 new media firms in Toronto as well as over 50 company interviews	Many new media products and the skills used in their design reflect the developmental trajectory of antecedent activities, especially those related to services for the entertainment sector and the local business market. The paper concludes that to understand learning processes the dynamic analysis of clusters is a necessary research strategy.
Cook and Pandit (2008)	TV broadcasting, UK	Causes and effects of agglomeration of broadcasting in particular cities	Econometric study on financial data of 1213 broadcasting firms in the UK; 72 interviews conducted with firms in London, Bristol and Glasgow; questionnaire survey of 204 firms in London	Importance of the microclimate within the cluster; UK broadcasting does not fall into any typology; centripetal forces are very strong, as are knowledge transfer and information sharing, as well as formation of social capital in London.

Table 3.1 (continued)

Author(s) (year)	Media cluster (type) studied	Focus of study	Empirical basis	Main results
Currah (2006)	Hollywood	Collision between the Hollywood studios and the internet (as a decentralized electronic architecture that has enabled peer-to-peer file sharing between networked computers)	150 interviews with 'elites' in the studios and other related firms in the Hollywood region	Studios behave oligopolistically in response to emergence of file sharing, trying to preserve the oligopolistic structure of the industry by promoting a business model oriented around centralized client-server architectures, which provide tight control over digital commodities.
Davis et al. (2009)	Screen-based media in Ontario	Application of an innovation cluster framework to a media cluster	N/A	Five challenges in approaching a media industry as innovation cluster: accurately understanding the innovation process in media; facilitating the linkages, spillovers and externalities that are believed to be most significant; factoring the cluster's translocal external linkages; implementing innovation policy measures for labour, entrepreneurs and small firms; identifying cluster-specific implications of actual or potential policy measures.

Fuchs and Koch (2005)	Multimedia	Comparison between biotechnology and multimedia clusters to better understand how and why agglomerations emerge and what are the advantages for firms inside them	Econometric study of the locations of multimedia companies in Germany; two surveys of multimedia companies in one German state; expert interviews and case studies	Point out spatial disequilibrium in the location pattern of firms in the two sectors and argue against the popular belief that clustering firms in the same neighbourhood will in itself trigger innovation; point out importance of traditional media sector location for multimedia company location.
Goldsmith et al. (2010)	Film production at the Australian Gold Coast	Development of Gold Coast into an outpost of Hollywood productions	Interviews	Global Hollywood operations need to include the many location interests, financial contributors and other actors in the globally dispersed production; outline how the Gold Coast could participate in international film production. The international film producer and financier Dino De Laurentiis played a major role in developing the activities at the Gold Coast.
Gwee (2009)	Singapore	Emergence of creative industry clustering in Singapore	N/A	Creative cluster of a small nation such as Singapore can enable developing a national innovation system, but it took two decades for this cluster to gain visibility and credibility as an enabler for innovation.
Kaiser and Liecke (2007)	Munich feature film cluster	Assess the role that a secondary feature film cluster can play in an industry dominated by Hollywood studios	N/A	Major corporate actors that established a core group within the cluster have turned the industry towards specialized niche products and have become significantly supported by public policy measures.

Table 3.1 (continued)

Author(s) (year)	Media cluster (type) studied	Focus of study	Empirical basis	Main results
Krätke (2002)	Potsdam/ Babelsberg	Point out the need for quality cluster analysis, based on the ability to identify its specific strengths or weak points and inadequacies of cluster formation	Network analysis	Cluster analysis should focus on three aspects: (1) concentration, number and structural features of the companies in the cluster, (2) extent of the functional differentiation in the regional area of the cluster, (3) establishment of the density, cohesion and degree of centralization of corporate relations in the cluster and supra-regional links.
Mossig (2004)	Cologne Media Cluster	How localized production networks arise and how they function; the role of the founding of new firms for the cluster; decision structures; how parts of particular production chains are linked together to guarantee smooth production	Analysis of three volumes of Cologne Media Handbook; 19 semi-structured expert interviews	Point out importance of one local financing partner which accepted immaterial goods such TV rights and licences as securities for agreed credits; interaction on the political level between local and state governments; role of personal networks and informal networking; decision-making structures based on implicit rules of the game which people follow without questioning.

Nachum and Keeble (2003a)	Media cluster of Central London (Soho)	Examine operations of MNCs in clusters to understand the impact of cluster participation on the organization of international activities and the generation of competitive advantages	Interviews with companies and industry experts; comparison of 23 international with 26 indigenous firms	The major factor affecting the advantages accruing to MNCs from cluster participation is the effect with which internal linkages within MNCs substitute for local cluster linkages.
Nachum and Keeble (2003b)	Media cluster of Central London (Soho)	Paint a picture of the nature of external linkages of firms in the media industries in Soho and the dynamics of the global and the local in shaping their competitive advantages	Interviews with companies and industry experts; comparison of 23 international with 26 indigenous firms	Linkages between locally clustered media firms are vital for their competitiveness, but are insufficient by themselves to gain access to expertise and knowledge which is increasingly shaped on a global basis.
Oakey et al. (2001)	Non-broadcasting visual communications cluster in South East England	Evidence of physical concentration of firms at a regional level and linkages between these	Questionnaire survey with 455 responses	Local spin-offs may explain the physical intensity of clusters, both in terms of a reluctance to move far away when relocating and a preference for locating near to the firm from which new entrepreneurs have spun off. Rich supply of relevant local labour skills can stimulate the growth of a cluster, but does not necessarily imply functional linkages.
Perrons (2004)	New media cluster on the south coast of England (Brighton-Hove)	Focus on social and spatial divisions in developing holistic framework for economic geography	In-depth interviews in 55 companies	New media cluster emerges less as a new technology cluster and more as a reflection of increasing social divisions in the new economy.

Table 3.1 (continued)

Author(s) (year)	Media cluster (type) studied	Focus of study	Empirical basis	Main results
Scott (2002)	Hollywood	Reinterpretation of the economic geography of the so-called new Hollywood	N/A	On the basis of analysing Hollywood both from flexible specialization and systems-house forms of production, it is argued that Hollywood is deeply bifurcated into two systems, namely the majors and their cohorts of allied firms on the one hand and the mass of independent production companies on the other hand. Hollywood continues to be an attractive agglomeration for motion-picture production, but majors extend global reach by more aggressive marketing and distribution divisions.
Smith et al. (2004)	New media cluster Vancouver	Is this cluster really a cluster or a temporary, economic phenomenon?	70 interviews (51 with companies and individuals, 19 with industry and government representatives)	The Vancouver cluster consists of four sub-clusters: e-learning, gaming, animation, web services.

Sydow and Staber (2002)	Cologne/Düsseldorf and Berlin/Babelsberg	Explore the significance of institutional thickness for the performance of project networks in TV content production in the two clusters	Semi-structured interviews with producers and managing directors of 16 production firms and CEOs of four broadcasting stations; expert interviews, in total more than 70 interviews	Media region of Cologne/Düsseldorf was found to be institutionally thicker than Berlin/Babelsberg, as reflected by higher degrees of mutual awareness, levels of contacts and intensity of information exchange. Institutional thickness cannot be created entirely at will. The organizational and financial endowments of the key actors are important. Collective structures of signification and legitimation that support coordination of project activities are not spatially tied to a particular institutional context.
Turok (2003)	Glasgow film and TV activities	Analyse the forces affecting the performance of the film and television industries in Scotland	Background information, 25 interviews with key informants	Film and TV industries in Scotland are found to have a more modest economic impact than commonly assumed and national and transnational organizations and government regulations are more important than localized networks in influencing their scale and durability.

Table 3.1 (continued)

Author(s) (year)	Media cluster (type) studied	Focus of study	Empirical basis	Main results
Vang (2007)	Danish newspapers	Question the role of knowledge externalities for clustering of creative industries	Interviews with around 25 experts; quantitative data are also incorporated from a different study by the same author	Location of newspapers in largest metropolitan areas is not due to the knowledge externality factors emphasized in the cluster literature; instead the spatial organization reflects a need for physical proximity to 'central powers' and major events.
Wilson and Stokes (2004)	Music industry in the UK	How cultural entrepreneurs in the music industry market to networks that control the resources necessary to support entrepreneurial ventures	18 industry expert interviews, telephone survey of 310 music businesses, postal survey of 410 banks; seven case studies of music companies	Dividends from creative clusters appear to result in part from the related increased cognitive and pragmatic legitimation the geographic closeness brings.

Further research needs to seek answers to questions regarding the extent to which media clusters contribute financially, whether they actually improve local employment when they are constructed by development agencies, the extent of internal and external financial flows, the effects of clusters on images of communications and whether the duration of various benefits is short or long. While in many cases this is difficult to achieve, Clower and Weinstein (2008) provide an example of assessing the economic and fiscal impacts of a concentration of companies located within the same business incubator. Research also needs to consider where the boundaries of clusters are actually located in light of network effects and the roles of key actors in media cluster development and operation.

However, perhaps even more importantly, more research is needed that moves away from the aggregate level of considering the media cluster as a whole and that looks more closely at managerial issues of the cluster firms involved – for example, what strategic, organizational and entrepreneurial issues these companies face as a result of being part of a cluster. While much research attention to date has focused on why clusters emerge and whether they make sense as an overall economic phenomenon, little is known about the performance and managerial implications of being part of a cluster for the individual firm. Such research should also pay attention to potential negative effects of cluster membership, such as being locked into certain standard ways of behaviour or doing business, or institutionalized ways of receiving contracts. Basically, such research would answer the question for media companies whether it would make sense for them to agglomerate or not.

The studies in this book represent an effort to further develop the understanding of how clusters actually work and what internal and external challenges they face, thus providing clearer understanding of their contributions and their desirability to firms and policymakers.

REFERENCES

Aksoy, A. and K. Robins (1992), 'Hollywood for the 21st Century: Global Competition for Critical Mass in Image Markets', *Cambridge Journal of Economics*, **16**(1) 1–22.

Assmo, P. (2005), 'Creative Clusters – Ideas and Realities for Cluster Growth: The Example of Film in Väst in the Region of Västra Götaland, Sweden', in Charlie Karlsson, Börje Johansson and Roger R. Stough (eds), *Industrial Clusters and Inter-Firm Networks*, Cheltenham, UK and Northampton, MA, USA: Edward Elgar, pp. 453–474.

Backlund, A.-K. and Å. Sandberg (2002), 'New Media Industry Development:

Regions, Networks and Hierarchies – Some Policy Implications', *Regional Studies*, **36**(1), 87–91.

Bathelt, H. (2002), 'The Re-emergence of a Media Industry Cluster in Leipzig', *European Planning Studies*, **10**(5), 583–611.

Bathelt, H. (2005), 'Cluster Relations in the Media Industry: Exploring the "Distanced Neighbour" Paradox in Leipzig', *Regional Studies*, **39**(1), 105–127.

Bathelt, H. and J.S. Boggs (2003), 'Toward a Reconceptualization of Regional Development Paths: Is Leipzig's Media Cluster a Continuation of or a Rupture with the Past?', *Economic Geography*, **79**(3), 265–293.

Bathelt, H. and A. Gräf, (2008), 'Internal and External Dynamics of the Munich Film and TV Industry Cluster, and Limitations to Future Growth', *Environment and Planning A*, **40**(8), 1944–1965.

Bayless, D. (2007), 'Dublin's Digital Hubris: Lessons from an Attempt to Develop a Creative Industrial Cluster', *European Planning Studies*, **15**(9), 1261–1271.

Bianchi, G. (1998), 'Requiem for the Third Italy? Rise and Fall of a Too Successful Concept', *Entrepreneurship & Regional Development*, **10**(2), 93–116.

Blackburn, R. and C. Conway (2008), 'Clusters in the New Media Industry: Relevant Model or Artifact?', in Urs Fueglistaller, Thierry Volery and Walter Weber (eds), *Innovation, Competitiveness, Growth and Tradition in SMEs*, St. Gallen: KMU Verlag HSG.

Bresnahan, T. and A. Gambardella (eds) (2004), *Building High-Tech Clusters: Silicon Valley and Beyond*, Cambridge, UK and New York, NY, USA: Cambridge University Press.

Britton, J.N.H. (2007), 'Path Dependence and Cluster Adaptation: A Case Study of Toronto's New Media Industry', *International Journal of Entrepreneurship and Innovation Management*, **7**(2)–(5), 272–297.

Cairncross, F. (1994), *The Death of Distance*, London, UK: Orion Business Books.

Christopherson, S. and M. Storper (1986), 'The City as Studio; The World as Back Lot: The Impact of Vertical Disintegration on the Location of the Motion Picture Industry', *Environment and Planning D: Society and Space*, **4**(3), 305–320.

Clancy, P. and M. Twomey (1997), *Clusters in Ireland: The Irish Popular Music Industry: An Application of Porter's Cluster Analysis*, Dublin: National Economic and Social Council.

Clower, T.L. and B.L. Weinstein (2008), 'Should Local Governments Invest in Technology Incubators? A Case Study of Richardson, Texas, USA', in Iréne Bernhard (ed), *Uddevalla Symposium 2008: Spatial dispersed production and network governance: papers presented at the 11th Uddevalla Symposium, 15–17 May, 2008, Kyoto, Japan*, Research Reports 2008:03, University West, Trollhättan, Sweden, pp. 213–219.

Coe, N.M. (2001), 'A Hybrid Agglomeration? The Development of a Satellite-Marshallian Industrial District in Vancouver's Film Industry', *Urban Studies*, **38**(10), 1753–1775.

Cole, A. (2008), 'Distant Neighbours: The New Geography of Animated Film Production in Europe', *Regional Studies*, **42**(6), 891–904.

Conford, J. and K. Robins (1992), 'Development Strategies in the Audiovisual Industries: The Case of North East England', *Regional Studies*, **26**(5), 421–435.

Cook, G.A.S. and N.R. Pandit (2008), 'Clustering in the Broadcasting Industry', in Charlie Karlsson (ed), *Handbook of Research on Cluster Theory*, Cheltenham, UK and Northampton, MA, USA: Edward Elgar, pp. 274–291.

Cooke, P. (2001), 'Regional Innovation Systems, Clusters, and the Knowledge Economy', *Industrial and Corporate Change*, **10**(4), 945–974.

Cooke, P. (2006), 'New Media and New Economy Cluster Dynamics', in Leah A. Lievrouw and Sonia Livingstone (eds), *The Handbook of New Media: Updated Student Edition*, London, UK and Thousand Oaks, CA, USA: Sage, pp. 266–286.

Cooke, P. and G. Hughes (1999), 'Creating a Multimedia Cluster in Cardiff Bay', in Hans-Joachim Braczyk, Gerhard Fuchs and Hans-Georg Wolf (eds), *Multimedia and Regional Economic Restructuring*, London, UK and New York, NY, USA: Routledge, pp. 197–209.

Currah, A. (2006), 'Hollywood Versus the Internet: The Media and Entertainment Industries in a Digital and Networked Economy', *Journal of Economic Geography*, **6**(4), 439–468.

Davis, C.H., T. Creutzberg and D. Arthurs (2009), 'Applying an Innovation Cluster Framework to a Creative Industry: The Case of Screen-based Media in Ontario', *Innovation: Management, Policy & Practice*, **11**(2), 201–214.

DeFillippi, R.J. and M.B. Arthur (1998), 'Paradox in Project-Based Enterprise: The Case of Film Making', *California Management Review*, **40**(2), 125–139.

Fuchs, G. and A. Koch (2005), 'Biotechnology and Multimedia: Cluster Development in New Industries', in Charlie Karlsson, Börje Johansson and Roger R. Stough (eds), *Industrial Clusters and Inter-Firm Networks*, Cheltenham, UK and Northampton, MA, USA: Edward Elgar, pp. 231–259.

Giovanetti, E., K. Neuhoff and G. Spagnolo (2007), 'Trust and Virtual Districts: Evidence from the Milan Internet Exchange', *Metroeconomica*, **58**(3), 436–456.

Goldsmith, B. and T. O'Regan (2003), *Cinema Cities, Media Cities: The Contemporary International Studio Complex*, Brisbane: Australian Film Commission, Screen Industry, Culture and Policy Research Series.

Goldsmith, B., S. Ward and T. O'Regan (2010), *Local Hollywood: Global Film Production and the Gold Coast*, St.Lucia: University of Queensland Press.

Gornostaeva, G. (2008), 'The Film and Television Industry in London's Suburbs: Lifestyle of the Rich or Losers' Retreat?', *Creative Industries Journal*, **1**(1), 47–71.

Gwee, J. (2009), 'Innovation and the Creative Industries Cluster: A Case Study of Singapore's Creative Industries', *Innovation: Management, Policy & Practice*, **11**(2), 240–252.

Howkins, J. (2001), *The Creative Economy: How People Make Money from Ideas*, London, UK: Penguin.

Kaiser, R. and M. Liecke (2007), 'The Munich Feature Film Cluster: The Degree of Global Integration and Explanations for its Relative Success', *Industry and Innovation*, **14**(4), 385–399.

Keeble, D. and F. Wilkinson (2000), 'High-Technology SMEs, Regional Clustering and Collective Learning: An Overview', in David Keeble and Frank Wilkinson (eds), *High-Technology Clusters, Networking and Collective Learning in Europe*, Aldershot, UK: Ashgate, pp. 1–20.

Kinder, T. and A. Molina (1999), 'From Purposiveness to Sustainability in the Formation of Multimedia Clusters: Governance and Constituency Building in Scotland', in Hans-Joachim Braczyk, Gerhard Fuchs and Hans-Georg Wolf (eds), *Multimedia and Regional Economic Restructuring*, London, UK and New York, NY, USA: Routledge, pp. 210–232.

Krätke, S. (2002), 'Network Analysis of Production Clusters: The Potsdam/

Babelsberg Film Industry as an Example', *European Planning Studies*, **10**(1), 27–54.

Krugman, P.R. (1991), *Geography and Trade*, Cambridge, MA, USA: MIT Press.

Lazerson, M.H. and G. Lorenzoni (1999), 'The Firms that Feed Industrial Districts: A Return to the Italian Source', *Industrial and Corporate Change*, **8**(2), 235–266.

Marshall, A. (1890), *Principles of Economics*, London, UK: Macmillan, reprint Amherst, NY, USA: Prometheus Books, 1997.

Martin, R. and P. Sunley (2003), 'Deconstructing Clusters: Chaotic Concept or Policy Panacea?', *Journal of Economic Geography*, **3**(1), 5–35.

Miller, D. and J. Shamsie (1996), 'The Resource-based View of the Firm in Two Environments: The Hollywood Film Studios from 1936 to 1965', *Academy of Management Journal*, **39**(3), 519–543.

Mommaas, H. (2004), 'Cultural Clusters and the Post-Industrial City: Towards the Remapping of Urban Cultural Policy', *Urban Studies*, **41**(3), 507–532.

Mossig, I. (2004), 'The Networks Producing Television Programmes in the Cologne Media Cluster: New Firm Foundation, Flexible Specialization and Efficient Decision-making Structures', *European Planning Studies*, **12**(2), 155–171.

Nachum, L. and D. Keeble (2003a), 'MNE Linkages and Localised Clusters: Foreign and Indigenous Firms in the Media Cluster of Central London', *Journal of International Management*, **9**(2), 171–192.

Nachum, L. and D. Keeble (2003b), 'Neo-Marshallian Clusters and Global Networks: The Linkages of Media Firms in Central London', *Long Range Planning*, **36**(5), 459–480.

Oakey, R., M. Kipling, and S. Wildgust (2001), 'Clustering Among Firms in the Non-Broadcast Visual Communications (NBVC) Sector', *Regional Studies*, **35**(5), 401–414.

O'Regan, T. and S. Ward (2008), 'Managing Uncertainty: Defining the Location Interests of a Greenfield Location'. In the Table of Contents, the title of the chapter is '"Managing Uncertainty" on the Gold Coast and the Production Services Industry', in Janet Wasko and Mary Erickson (eds), *Cross-border Cultural Production: Economic Runaway or Globalization*, Youngstown, NY, USA: Cambria Press.

Perrons, D. (2004), 'Understanding Social and Spatial Divisions in the New Economy: New Media Clusters and the Digital Divide', *Economic Geography*, **80**(1), 45–61.

Picard, R.G. (2008), *Media Clusters: Local Agglomeration in an Industry Developing Networked Virtual Clusters*, Jönköping: Jönköping International Business School Working Paper Series No. 2008-3, 16pp.

Picard, R.G. (2009), 'Media Clusters and Regional Development: Reflections on the Significance of Location in Media Production', in Iréne Bernhard (ed), *The Geography of Innovation and Entrepreneurship*, Research Reports 2009:02, Trollhättan: University West, pp. 877–885.

Piore, M.J. and C. Sabel (1984), *The Second Industrial Divide*, New York, NY, USA: Basic Books.

Porter, M.E. (1990), *The Competitive Advantage of Nations*, New York, NY, USA: Free Press.

Porter, M.E. (1998), 'Clusters and the New Economics of Competition', *Harvard Business Review*, November – December 1998, 77–90.

Porter, M.E. (2000), 'Location, Competition and Economic Development: Local Clusters in a Global Economy', *Economic Development Quarterly*, **14**(1), 15–34.
Pratt, A.C. (2002), 'Hot Jobs in Cool Places: The Material Cultures of the New Media Product Spaces: The Case of South of the Market, San Francisco', *Information, Communication & Society*, **5**(1), 27–50.
Saxenian, A. (1990), 'Regional Networks and the Resurgence of Silicon Valley', *California Management Review*, Fall 1990, **33**(1), 89–112.
Saxenian, A. (1994a), 'Lessons from Silicon Valley', *Technology Review*, July 1994, **97**(5), 42–51.
Saxenian, A. (1994b), *Regional Advantage: Culture and Competition in Silicon Valley and Route 128*, Cambridge, MA, USA: Harvard University Press.
Scott, A.J. (2002), 'A New Map of Hollywood: The Production and Distribution of American Motion Pictures', *Regional Studies*, **36**(9), 957–975.
Smith, R., J. McCarthy and M. Petrusevich (2004), 'Cluster or Whirlwind? The New Media Industry in Vancouver', in David A. Wolfe and Matthew Lucas (eds), *Clusters in a Cold Climate: Innovation Dynamics in a Diverse Economy*, Montreal and Kingston: McGill-Queen's University Press, 195–221.
Sydow, J. and U. Staber (2002), 'The Institutional Embeddedness of Project Networks: The Case of Content Production in German Television', *Regional Studies*, **36**(3), 215–227.
Turok, I. (2003), 'Cities, Clusters and Creative Industries: The Case of Film and Television in Scotland', *European Planning Studies*, **11**(5), 549–565.
Vang, J. (2007), 'The Spatial Organization of the News Industry: Questioning Assumptions About Knowledge Externalities for Clustering of Creative Industries', *Innovation: Management, Policy & Practice*, **9**(1), 14–27.

4. Media industry clusters and public policy

Charles H. Davis

Over the past two decades, public policies and programmes in support of industry clusters have become widespread in policy domains devoted to regional, metropolitan or sectoral development. Although cluster policies and programmes are found in many different industries, cluster approaches to media industries are relatively unfamiliar, and the scholarly literature on public policy for media clusters is very thin. It is the task of the present chapter to draw out and explore the policy implications of cluster approaches to media industries.[1]

An industry cluster is a geographically bounded production system encompassing related industries and consisting of colocated and functionally interlinked firms and their customers and suppliers, as well as supporting institutions, service producers, labour, associative bodies, public agencies and governance institutions. Clusters can be characterized according to seven key parameters that must be taken into account in the design and implementation of cluster policy: geographical concentration, industrial specialization, variety of actors, mixture of competitive and cooperative behaviour, critical mass and stage in evolutionary life cycle (Andersson, Schwaag Serger, Sörvik and Wise Hansson, 2004, pp. 13 and 19). Clustering is a natural occurrence in most industries in the absence of countervailing forces (Krugman, 1994). Media industries are no exception. The effects of competition, technological change and economies of scale make clustering likely to be a strong tendency in media industries into the foreseeable future (Noam, 2009).

Although the Hollywood film industry has attracted much attention since the mid-1980s as a leading example of post-Fordist flexible specialization, it has had nowhere near the influence on cluster theory or practice as Silicon Valley, a much-imitated paradigm of industry clustering.[2] The earliest explicit cluster policies for media industries made their appearance in the 1990s in connection with digital media and e-commerce initiatives. Cluster approaches to media industries have since gained traction under the impulsion of digital convergence, globalization, the rise of metropolitan regions as economic motors and media industry deregulation and transnationalization. Older media industries (print, film and broadcasting) are being brought into cluster policy frameworks, often through inclusion in cluster-like metropolitan or regional policy initiatives aimed at broader groups of cultural or creative industries, creative cities or digitally converged media sectors (Birch, 2008; Conference Board of Canada, 2008; Creative Metropoles, 2010; HAL, 2009; PWC, 2009; UNCTAD, 2008).[3]

More than a hundred media agglomerations around the world have been identified and described (Achtenhagen and Picard, 2009; Picard, 2008). The public policies that affect them, enabling them to thrive or survive, reflect a wide variety of sectoral and jurisdictional arrangements and conceptual frameworks. All levels of government are involved in cluster policies. Subnational governments, which are closest to local economic constituencies, often originate and implement cluster initiatives in federal states. For national governments, cluster policies offer a way of customizing and regionalizing national policies. International or supranational institutions, notably the OECD, UNIDO and the European Union, have played a key role in diffusing cluster approaches and associated cluster policy practices among national and subnational governments.

Public policy for media clusters differs from prevailing media policy in two important respects. First, although industry cluster policy practically always requires involvement of national policymakers and national programmes at multiple points, it speaks first and foremost to local economic development concerns. Media cluster policy is no exception, with the added twist that 'local' usually refers to the major metropolitan regions where media agglomerations are found, not small towns or rural regions. Media policy proper, in contrast, practically always falls under the jurisdiction and operational responsibility of the national government, although subnational governments often play a role in media policy through industry support and incentive programmes, and in a few countries policy responsibilities in key media sectors such as broadcasting are delegated to subnational authorities. Further, the involvement of private actors in the design and implementation of cluster policy, as well as cluster governance, is usually expected and encouraged, while media policy proper is nominally under the sole control of the state, which may seek policy guidance through elaborate public consultations.

Secondly, media cluster policy, like other cluster policies, has an overarching economic development orientation, seeking to increase the economic fortunes of the host jurisdiction through improvement of the performance of the firms in the cluster. National media policy, on the other hand, has a very different agenda, which historically is concerned with balancing the demands on the national media system, especially the broadcasting sector, in order to ensure market competition, diversity of voices, variety of opinion and national cultural expression, all in the name of national cultural sovereignty and democratic political process. These regulatory principles were developed in the period of mass communication and competition for broadcasting frequencies and now must urgently be overhauled for interactive broadband-based media environments with their proliferating channels, communicative abundance and strong likelihood of being provided by vertically integrated conglomerates.

This chapter unpacks and assesses public policy for media clusters. I first briefly review several characteristics of media industries that differentiate them from other industries, giving them a unique policy environment, which makes a cluster approach to media industries a more complex undertaking than in other industries. I then consider contemporary industry cluster policy thought and practice, examining the issues and challenges involved in extending cluster policy approaches to media industries for economic development purposes. In a concluding section I consider how media cluster policy in an age of communicative abundance could provide a way to fulfil national media policy's longstanding normative commitments regarding pluralism, diversity, localism and civic engagement.

MEDIA POLICY AND THE DISTINGUISHING CHARACTERISTICS OF MEDIA INDUSTRIES

Media are 'one of the most lucrative and important growth areas of global capitalism', and media industries 'do not hesitate to undertake the political activity necessary to promote their interests' (Raboy, 2005). Media policymaking is highly political, and the media industry is dominated by powerful interests that can shape the policymaking process, as Freedman (2008) shows in his study of the politics of media policymaking in the USA and the UK. The overall trend in media policies is towards regulatory relaxation and market liberalization regarding ownership and content origin (van Cuilenberg and McQuail, 2003). This trend, however, does not represent the withdrawal of the state from media policymaking generally, but instead represents a changing state role. Concurrent trends towards expansion of the role of the state include greater stringency in extension and enforcement of intellectual property rights, a vigorous increase in surveillance activities, involvement in negotiating and enforcing international trade agreements and increased participation of subnational governments in economic development initiatives involving media industries, including media cluster initiatives.

Three characteristics distinguish media industries from other industries and complicate placing media in an industry cluster policy framework designed primarily to produce local economic development, which is the principal orientation of most cluster policies.

First, media in liberal democracies are expected to serve 'public interest, convenience and necessity' (in the words of the US Communications Act of 1934). Mass media are a public good with significant positive externalities (Blosser, Scott, Kenney, Kimmelman and Manishin, 2006). The advent of apparently limitless media channels does not change the fact that media are central to the production of social meaning and are critical to democratic processes (Curran, 2002; Freedman, 2008; Silverstone, 2007 and 1999). This is the case to such an extent that 'media policy to a significant degree is citizenship policy' (Hutchison, 1999, p. 69). Historically the media industry has been considered by policymakers as not just one more economic sector but rather as a critical enabler of social cohesion and political expression. Dual economic and civic-cultural functions of media are widely acknowledged in media scholarship and in national and international law (Just, 2009; Napoli, 2001). As political authorities have known for centuries, media are powerful. The growing ubiquity of networked communication increases the potency of the media (Castells, 2009). Media industries provide essential domestic services in the form of connectivity, communication and content that support cultural citizenship, civic engagement, social inclusion and democratic political practices. Historically, few countries have left the provision of media-based goods and services entirely to the market, and in liberal democracies telecommunications, broadcasting and to a lesser extent the press are subject to regulatory oversight to ensure competition, adequate geographic coverage, diversity of voices, privacy and freedom of speech. The broadcast industry in particular is closely regulated to ensure competition and diversity of voices – ideals that speak to concerns about concentration of ownership or political control of the media industry. Furthermore, many countries actively protect and promote indigenous mediated cultural expression through dedicated programmes and policy instruments. Contemporary media cluster policies, on the other hand, almost by definition aim to increase economic performance of particular subnational jurisdictions, rarely addressing media's non-economic values or involving stakeholders other than the business and economic development communities in policy processes. To the extent that media cluster policy seeks to promote economic competitiveness and wealth generation, it represents a very selective application of national policy (more closely akin to industrial policy than mainstream media policy) at the local level.

Secondly, media industries are assuming a strategic economic role. Along with information and communication technologies, media industries are key players in the rapidly emerging cognitive-cultural capitalist economy as drivers of innovation and economic growth (Scott, 2008). Most of the principal media industry clusters are located in major metropolitan areas, which in many cases are also national or regional political capitals (Krätke, 2003; Krätke and Taylor, 2004). Positional improvement in the world hierarchy of media cities is likely to yield considerable economic and political value. The creative-city and creative-class movements have inspired many cities to race to assemble the necessary conditions and infrastructure to attract and grow cognitive-cultural industries, among which the media industries are particularly appealing because of their high potential for multiple positive externalities. Media industries produce and amplify symbols, images and meanings that circulate widely, potentially yielding many indirect economic benefits to media cluster host jurisdictions. In addition to directly generating revenue and employment, successful media clusters yield domestic and international 'soft power' by magnifying political and commercial communication and by augmenting metropolitan visibility, which can be leveraged to create economic opportunities. Media industries help to brand the host city, spotlighting urban amenities and spurring consumption of downtown leisure and entertainment services. A screen industry cluster brings celebrities and their halos, while a vigorous and visible interactive media cluster suggests that the host city is at the leading edge of cognitive-cultural production and consumption. These features of media clusters appeal not only to the creative class of transient professionals and corporate executives, but also to diverse stakeholders in the urban cultural economy: local politicians, policymakers, geeks, bohemians, culture makers, downtown universities and retailers, sophisticated consumers, real estate developers and investors, and gentrifiers – the metro condo crowd – creating relatively diverse support for 'growth coalitions' around media industries.

Thirdly, media industries are currently in a state of extreme flux driven by massive networked digital convergence. Rapid improvements in software, computing and telecommunications technologies have resulted in dramatically lowered cost of content reproduction and distribution and spectacular expansion of user-generated content. Consumption of digital media content, which is increasingly delivered via portable, personal devices connected to interactive broadband networks, is pushing older media to the sidelines and inflicting economic damage on them by undermining their business models. All three layers of the media industry (transport, software and content) are affected by convergence, blurring the boundaries among the multiple historically distinct older media subsectors such as printing, magazine or book publishing, broadcasting, advertising and motion pictures, spurring the emergence of newer media subsectors such as electronic games, mobile video and social media, and generally disrupting the value chain of suppliers, infrastructure providers, advertisers, distributors and customers. Businesspersons and policymakers face considerable uncertainty regarding media business models, industry trajectories and endpoint scenarios. Rapid change and the indeterminate state of the industry imply that multiple evolutionary pathways are possible, requiring flexibility, bet-hedging and very adept policy and programme management capabilities. From a cluster perspective this requires concurrently addressing early-stage path creation issues as well as technology and business model migration issues affecting the major mature subsectors of the industry. Media innovation also blurs geographical boundaries and creates new sets of opportunities and tradeoffs between the local and the external which media cluster policy must address. Thus domestic adoption and consumption of media innovations is, or should be, as much a concern of media cluster policy as export or competitiveness, which are invariably the goals of cluster policy initiatives.

CLUSTER POLICIES AND POLICY INSTRUMENTS

The overarching goal of industry cluster policy is to enhance the economic welfare of the jurisdiction in question by improving the performance of an industry agglomeration. It does this by facilitating the exploitation of positive externalities in clusters:

> The fundamental rationale for policy intervention in clusters is to facilitate the exploitation by firms and workers of potential local external economic benefits from input-output linkages and knowledge spillovers and hence increase productivity and generate growth (Potter, 2009).

Industry clustering is regarded as a means to an economic development goal, not as an end in itself: 'Clusters are today recognised as an important *instrument* for promoting industrial development, innovation, competitiveness and growth' (Andersson et al., 2004, p. 1, emphasis added). What can policymakers hope to achieve through cluster policies? Industry clusters compete with each other nationally and internationally, so established clusters must be improved and new clusters incubated in an ongoing economic development effort. In the case of media cluster policy, the main emphasis is often on digital media, which are in an early enough stage of their life cycle to permit the hope that policy intervention will trigger a clustering process leading to the development of a superior competitive position. Media cluster policies that encompass older media industries also invoke the challenge of convergence and digital transformation as a major area of focus.

Policymakers usually define 'cluster' very broadly. Many initiatives use the term 'cluster' as a loose label for a local collection of firms and other players without addressing questions of cluster structure, evolution or performance. Several commentators from a range of countries have observed that, in practice, clusters are defined so loosely as to permit a wide variety of policies and policy interventions (Burfitt, MacNeill and Gibney, 2007; Duranton, 2009; Martin and Sunley, 2003; Navarro Arancegui, 2003; Taylor, 2010; Torre, 2008, 2006; Wrobel, 2009). This is probably one reason why clusters remain such a popular and heterogeneous area of public policy. Consequently, 'there is no single "generic" cluster policy but rather a myriad of interventions that prove difficult to classify' (Peck and Lloyd, 2008, p. 396). This is because cluster policies are customized local bundles or mixes of national policies. Cluster policy plays the particular role of customizing national policy (usually innovation, industrial, or regional development policy) to suit the needs and circumstances of particular localities (Nauwaelers, 2003). According to the OECD, cluster policy is often implemented with the intention of joining up existing policies. In these cases, the choice of instruments is limited by established governmental practice. This means that what actually takes place under the rubric of 'cluster policy' is tightly conditioned by a wide range of government systems from the technology, economic, utilities and scientific policy areas.

Explains the European Commission in a recent overview of European cluster policies:

> *Typically, policies in support of cluster development are not explicitly called 'cluster policies'* but are part of broader strategies aiming at regional and business development. These are in [sic] often those having the strongest impact. Similarly, different methods may be used, ranging from hands-on methods, like providing information, contacts, assistance, advice or direct funding to hands-off methods, like lobbying, marketing, monitoring and reporting. This makes it inadvisable to define 'cluster policies' in a strict and uniform way, although they could in general be described as policy mixes to support the development of such regional systems (EU, 2008, emphasis in original).

It is to be noted that most cluster policy instruments are not specific to clusters. Other than cluster-specific governance and promotion organizations, cluster policy is a domain of public policy without unique or dedicated instruments. Most cluster policy instruments are sourced from existing programs in other policy domains:

> [C]luster policies do not exist as a new policy area but rather as an innovative combination of existing policy instruments from traditional policy fields . . . Cluster policy becomes a mean to use these instruments in a more focused way, taking better into account the specific environments in which firms operate (Nauwaelers, 2003: 24).

The key challenge for public policymakers and their cluster partners is to operationalize cluster policy in such a way as to improve the economic performance of the cluster. Cluster policy is operationalized through an array of incentives and disincentives administered via various policy instruments. Eight broad classes of cluster policy instruments are employed (EU, 2008): information and contact brokerage, practical assistance and advice, direct financing and facilities, events and training, networking and events, lobbying, marketing, and monitoring and reporting (see also OECD, 2007).

Cluster policy must necessarily assume that appropriate interventions can improve the aggregate performance of firms in the cluster:

> [W]ith the right local networks, and the appropriate local levels of trust, learning, competencies, social capital, and institutional support, a place can generate local social capital and can become innovative, productive and internationally competitive within a global mosaic of economic activities (Taylor 2010: 278).

By providing strategic vision and policy integration at the metropolitan or subregional level, cluster policies provide a way of combining 'different aspects of regional development into a holistic policy framework: e.g. technology innovation, regional productivity advantages, and growing versus declining sector balancing' (OECD, 2006: 109).

In practice, cluster promotion usually means promoting innovation, with its anticipated performance-enhancing effects (Arthurs, Cassidy, Davis and Wolfe, 2009). Inventories of cluster policy instruments show that most policy instruments used for cluster development have to do with innovation or regional economic development and are usually under the auspices of ministries of science-technology-research-innovation, regional development, industry or finance-economy (Oxford Research, 2008). Nauwelaers' 2003 examination of the main instruments of cluster policy in Europe found projects relating to infrastructure, consulting, inward investment, competence centres, specialized R&D centres, brokers and intermediaries, SME networks, collaborative R&D, inter-firm partnerships, cluster animation, regulatory measures, education and training, risk capital, technology transfer and commercialization, policy consultation, strategic planning and foresight, assistance for technology adoption and upgrading, and regional branding, all assembled into various configurations in different national and regional cluster policy initiatives (see also Andersson et al., 2004, p. 95). An analogous inventory of policy instruments at work in a media cluster would include many of these same instruments, as well as some instruments that are specific to media policy but are not necessarily implemented in a cluster framework: ownership regulations, content production subsidies, tax incentives to attract foreign productions, national origin requirements, etc. Also, since media clusters are usually located in central urban cores, large media physical infrastructure projects such as sound stages and exhibition centres usually involve expensive real estate and bring public and private real estate interests into play in schemes to redevelop and brand specific metropolitan neighborhoods or districts (Goldsmith and O'Regan, 2005).

Cluster initiatives often aim to induce collaboration among firms and other cluster players. Cluster champions report that physical proximity does not necessarily or automatically induce relational proximity (cooperative behaviour) among firms in a cluster – instead it needs to be developed through leadership and consensus-building (Tremblay and Cecilli, 2009). The same could be said of competition among specialized service providers in a cluster, such as institutions of higher education. The value of a cluster approach in the eyes of senior governments is that, if cluster players can be induced to present partnership projects, the political liability of selecting one particular firm or higher-education institution over another for investment purposes is removed.

Contrary to policymaking based on ignorance, dogma, hope or special interests, 'fact-based' and 'evidence-based' policymaking require reliable empirical inputs and clear understanding of causes and effects, but cluster policymaking raises significant epistemological issues regarding policy elaboration, execution and performance measurement. Policy is supposed to be based on an accurate understanding of the system whose behaviour is to be affected by policy interventions, but maps and models of cluster systems are always very approximate at best. Performance measurement requires that explicit assumptions be made about key linkages, dynamics, outcomes, cluster boundaries, ways to attribute impacts and ways to measure performance (Schmiedeberg, 2010). This is especially challenging in the case of media clusters, where spillovers, convergence, rapid product innovation and hybrid combinations of economic and non-economic policy goals are common (Davis, Creutzberg and Arthurs, 2009). Most cluster initiatives include provisions for performance benchmarking and include a set of indicators for intermediate and final performance outcomes (Arthurs et al., 2009; Davis et al., 2009; Meier zu Köcker and Rosted, 2010; Wise, Langkilde and Bertelsen, 2008). National statistical agencies generally do not produce data that are regionalized in such a way as to be useful as indicators to cluster policymakers or managers, and standard industrial accounting categories such as NAICS do not provide the resolution necessary to track innovation in emerging areas such as digital media. Therefore, customized empirical observations to monitor cluster behaviour must be produced on a regular basis, and this can be an expensive and time-consuming proposition for policymakers and industry stakeholders alike. Furthermore, many kinds of impacts or policy outcomes, such as improvement in cluster brand, leadership, educational infrastructure, collaborations, or technology and human resource flows can only be ascertained via customized surveys, raising the question what is the proper 'dependent variable' of cluster policy interventions (Arthurs et al., 2009; see also Gagné, Townsend, Bourgeois and Hart, 2010).

CAPABILITIES OF MEDIA CLUSTERS

Cluster policymaking is now in its fourth or fifth generation, and thousands of scholarly papers and policy reports on clusters have been published. One reliable take-away from this body of research and policy experience is that no single superior structure for an industry cluster exists. Just as differences in firm performance among superficially identical firms are determined by firm-level capabilities, not by structural differences or similarities with other firms, the same is true of industry clusters, local production systems, or economic regions, as proposed by Lawson (1999). Capabilities can be distributed among cluster players in different ways, so a variety of configurations is possible in any given cluster as well as in any given group of clusters in the same industry. The policy lesson is that structural mimetism is a misplaced objective: policy interventions are just shooting in the dark when their goal is to produce a particular configuration of cluster actors believed to cause superior performance in some other cluster. Instead, a capabilities-oriented policy framework is the key to strategic cluster policy, and policy intervention should aim to improve specific cluster capabilities, not necessarily to produce specific configurations of structures, linkages, knowledge flows or processes.

To explore a cluster policy framework that focuses on capabilities we need a workable and accurate typology of principal cluster capabilities. However, only a small body of research brings a capabilities perspective (drawn from the resource-based view of the firm and its variants) to cluster theory.[4] Röttmer and Katzy (2005) use six constructs to characterize cluster capabilities: rule setting and enforcement, strategic decision making, reconfiguration of assets, opportunity recognition, networking and learning. Hervás-Oliver and Albors-Garrigós (2007) use seven constructs: skilled labour, social interactions, business sophistication, supplier linkages, network, R&D support and training. The following discussion reviews eight key cluster capabilities that were identified in the course of development of a performance measurement framework for a technology-based cluster in Canada (Arthurs et al., 2009; Davis et al., 2009) and discusses how they might be operationalized or adapted in the case of the software and content layers of media industry clusters.

Novelty-Creation Capability

Cluster theory is premised on the idea that enhanced industrial performance requires innovation, which is assumed to be technological innovation. Thus cluster policy always seeks to deepen the cluster's capability to produce or source scientific and technical knowledge and deliver it to local firms, and to influence the supply, quality and effectiveness of R&D, technology transfer and commercialization, technical support services and scientific and technical education and training. The problem with this approach, from the perspective of media industries, is that it captures innovation processes in the technology-intensive transport and software layers but not in the content layer, where formal R&D is rarely undertaken yet where very high rates of innovation take place.[5] Media clusters tend to support R&D initiatives for exploring various new combinations of digital technologies rather than R&D for storytelling, narration, entertainment, documentaries or journalism. Prevailing creative-class and creative-city doctrines and practices try to solve the content innovation problem by developing urban places, events or associations that intermediate between the creative practitioner communities and the organizations that finance and commercialize cultural products and services (Cohendet, Grandadam and Simon, 2010). Media cluster policy that seeks to improve the rate and quality of novelty creation in the content layer needs to develop stronger and more effective incentives and support mechanisms for 'soft' or aesthetic innovation (Stoneman, 2010), for example by modifying the innovation support regime to make firm-level investment in content R&D eligible for tax incentives in ways analogous to scientific, technical and engineering R&D and by creating incentives for firms in non-media sectors to use media products and services as intermediate inputs (cf. Bakhshi and McVettie, 2009).

Product and Service Innovation Capability

This capability refers to the effectiveness of firm-level processes to source knowledge and other inputs, transform them into new offerings and deliver them to paying customers. As proxy measures of this capability, innovation surveys use the per cent of sales generated from new products or services, the fraction of revenues generated through exports and the degree of novelty of the innovation (firm-first, region-first, world-first, etc). Effectiveness of innovation is an important question in cluster policy in light of evidence that firms in clusters have lower rates of product and service innovation but higher rates of commercially successful innovation than out-of-cluster firms, underlining that knowledge flows and spillovers in clusters are about market learning as well as about technological learning (Breschi and Lissoni, 2001; Cornish, 1997). In the case of media firms, the challenges of effective new product development are great. The pervasiveness of the 'nobody knows' principle in media product innovation culture (Caves, 2000) is understandable since many media products are pure experience goods, but at the same time the relative neglect of audience and consumer research in support of product innovation in the media industries works against reduction of uncertainty concerning product acceptance. Media clusters can improve the product and service innovation capabilities of firms through policy instruments that accelerate market learning by providing incentives and opportunities to adopt improved new product development routines and by encouraging development of local competences in media product innovation and in media-related consumer behaviour research, and by stimulating demand of indigenous media products.

Entrepreneurship, New Firm Formation and Early Stage Investment Capability

These entrepreneurial capabilities refer to the ability of the cluster to renew itself and grow the population of viable firms in the cluster. This capability can be measured by the rate and quality of new firm formation and by assessment of the investment situation in the cluster. Policy measures designed to improve entrepreneurship, new firm formation and early stage investment encompass training, education, incubation, business acceleration, establishment of angel networks and investment incentives. Such measures are very common in industry cluster policy portfolios, and they are practically always found in digital media cluster policies. Media cluster policies need to consider capabilities for entrepreneurship, new firm formation and investment very carefully. Media clusters exhibit high rates of new firm formation but low average rates of firm growth. The population of media firms is dominated by micro-enterprises, which are usually constituted by freelance workers (Davis, 2010). Most are not intended to grow or resourced with growth in mind. Media clusters need to consider ways to improve the generally precarious working conditions of media labour. Since full-time permanent salaried employment is no longer the norm in media industries, a stronger emphasis in media cluster policy on support measures for entrepreneurs and new firms is very much warranted. Management capabilities are notoriously weak among small media content and software firms (Davis, Vladica and Berkowitz, 2008) and media cluster policy needs to address this challenge. This might be accomplished through executive workshops and seminars with invited speakers, preparation of case studies and assistance in recruiting seasoned executives from high-performing firms in other clusters.

Export Capability

Export capability refers to the ability of firms to identify and reach distant markets that are large enough and dynamic enough to support growth. Secondary media clusters must often be satisfied with import substitution efforts and low levels of exports. A challenge to media firms in countries with relatively small national markets is the 'cultural discount' – a product's loss of economic value when crossing cultural borders (Davis and Nadler, 2009; Fu and Sim, 2010; Hoskins and Mirus, 1988). This discount affects the exportability of media products and therefore their profitability. Media cluster policies can improve the cluster's export capability by supporting the development of market intelligence, trade missions, participation in expositions and festivals and international co-production arrangements.

Business Development Capability

This capability is a corporate entrepreneurial practice to extend the firm's value creation activities into areas that are relatively new to the firm (Davis and Sun, 2006). It includes competences for opportunity recognition, idea generation and qualification, new product development, commercialization, licensing or acquisitions. Business development capability is notably required by firms that participate in the production and delivery of integrated solutions, either as members of a business consortium or as integrators, as may be the case in the digital media sector. Media cluster policy can support the improvement of business development capability through specialized training and mentoring programmes and through the establishment of business development networks and missions.

Branding

Branding refers to the capability to communicate the cluster's value proposition with strength and clarity. Its effectiveness is measured by brand recognition – familiarity with the cluster and with its offerings. A cluster's branding capability can be improved by identifying and communicating the cluster's areas of business, creative and technological strength and its unique value proposition (which can include such factors as urban amenities, weather, travel time, quality of secondary schools, ranking among competitors on various scales, cost of housing and so forth).

Leadership and Operational Capability

This capability refers to the ability to get things done at the cluster level on behalf of the cluster and its members. It includes communication, advocacy, organization of events, networking, strategic planning, foresight and strategic intelligence, project development and execution, cluster monitoring and assessment, consensus building, policy engagement and overall cluster governance. Although industry clusters often have informal governance processes based on central firms or public institutions, a cluster's operational capabilities are usually based in formal dedicated cluster organizations that can offer services to their members and also represent the cluster to outsiders. Agile and effective governance of media industry clusters is hindered when industry subsectors are organized into multiple distinct trade associations, labour unions and craft guilds, public programmes and policy frameworks such that it is a challenge to engineer collective action on behalf of the cluster as a whole.

Public Policy Capability

Public policy capability refers to the ability of cluster players, especially subnational public organizations and private groups with a cluster mandate, to coordinate policy interventions and implement policy solutions. By virtue of their bundling of policies and programmes from across horizontal and vertical jurisdictions, which can lead to 'congestion' of the state (Burfitt and MacNeill, 2008), cluster interventions pose significant management and governance challenges. The media policy environment 'grows more complex with each passing year and each new technological innovation' (Napoli, 2001, p. 1). Although there is wide variation among national media regimes, in no case does a single unified policy framework apply to telephones, broadcast, cable, internet, advertising, motion pictures and print. Media clusters therefore must operate in a complex multi-jurisdictional policy framework requiring multi-level governance (Shaver and Shaver, 2006). As noted earlier, practically all of the key policy domains affecting media clusters fall under the jurisdiction of senior governments. These key domains include: the intellectual property regime;

regulation of the telecommunications and broadcasting system in matters concerning foreign investment, ownership, licensing of services, and business practices such as internet traffic shaping; regulation of capital markets; establishment of labour standards; public service broadcasting; and delivery of educational services, R&D support programs, provision of specialized public sector technical standards and R&D-performing institutions.

It is a challenge for any government to develop coherent and consistent policy across all media industries and technologies. Media policymakers currently face four main sets of issues:[6] how to ensure successful transition to a digitally converged media system; how to understand and respond to the cultural ramifications of vastly expanded transnational circulation of media products; what standards should apply to national media content, ownership of the media and concentration of media ownership; and the appropriate civic, cultural and public service roles of media and how they can be secured. The way these issues are addressed and resolved at the national level will necessarily have implications for media clusters and media cluster policies. For their part, media cluster activities mainly involve delivery of some services to cluster members, animation and coordination of activities within the cluster, facilitation of the cluster's external commercial linkages and management of the cluster's policy linkages.

CONCLUSION: MEDIA CLUSTERS AND THE FOUNDATION PRINCIPLES OF MEDIA POLICY

Approached as engines of wealth creation, media clusters raise management and policy issues that are analogous to those of other industry clusters. While it is not entirely straightforward to apply cluster principles to an industry that specializes in the production and distribution of experience goods, prevailing cluster policy models are sufficiently flexible to accommodate media industries, and much can be learned by media cluster policymakers from cluster development experiences in other industries.

Media industries have massive social and cultural spillovers that make them so substantively different from other industries, however, most governments see fit to regulate them in the public interest. Modern democracies historically have regulated mass media, especially broadcasting, to protect and promote civic, cultural and public values that ensure democratic deliberation and support national cultural sovereignty. The foundation principles of communication policy, as identified by Napoli (2001), are the public interest, marketplace of ideas, diversity, competition, universal service, localism and freedom of speech; the purpose of promoting these values is to protect liberty, check government power, enhance the democratic process, provide community cohesion and ensure that the truth is told.

The normative framework and the regulatory measures that many governments have put in place for mass media are being relaxed. The rise of internetworked broadband communication has enabled a massive increase in communication channels, radically reducing entry barriers to content production and distribution. The contemporary media environment contains a superabundance of choices for consumers, an apparently full spectrum of political opinion for citizens to consider and a multitude of opportunities to interact and contribute. Thus, some argue, the policy objectives concerning diversity, pluralism and democracy that were pursued in the period of mass media using various regulatory measures are being achieved through technological change and market liberalization in the contemporary period of broadband-based internetworked interactive media, allowing media industries to fulfil their dual economic and civic-cultural functions without need for further policy intervention. As Freedman observes, the foundation principles of contemporary media policymaking 'are based on an increasingly narrow and instrumental commitment to market forces as the central dynamic of contemporary communications' (2008, p. 78). Regulators have relaxed their oversight of media concentration and cross-media ownership, apparently motivated by concerns to lessen the present economic hardships of indigenous mass media firms or allow national firms to grow so that they can compete globally (Doyle, 2007; Napoli, 2010). For example, in Canada many public media support programmes aim specifically at development of multi-platform media content for *broadcasters*, a move that endorses cross-media ownership among domestic media conglomerates and does not address the specific growth and competitiveness concerns of small indigenous digital media firms.

Recent commentary on media policy in a digital environment urges the reinterpretation of traditional media policy principles to support the development of 'a broader conception of media pluralism that is not concerned only with consumer choice or specific issues like media ownership but more broadly with a more democratic distribution of communicative power in the public sphere' (Karppinen, 2009, p. 167). Cluster policy provides a way to apply national policies to specific local needs and circumstances, and media cluster policy has a largely unrealized opportunity to bring national media policy's longstanding foundation principles into the ambit of cluster policy alongside economic development objectives and apply them in local circumstances. This requires addressing the normative propositions about media value creation drawn from, and inspired by, national media policy.

Media clusters, especially ones encompassing broadcasting, the press and motion pictures, are found mainly in larger metropolitan areas, regions with great social and cultural diversity, highly heterogeneous economies and a variety of media organizations encompassing the private for-profit media sector as well as the professional sector, the social market sector, the civic sector and the public service sector (Curran, 2002). These latter sectors are typically ignored by media cluster policies, and they create economic and social value in ways that are usually unrecognized by innovation policy or cluster theory. Bringing normative media policy principles into cluster policy requires rethinking the usual 'dependent variable' or expected outcome of cluster policy intervention, economic performance, and adding measures of diversity, pluralism, democratic engagement or other public-good outcomes as proxy indicators of innovation in the public interest.

I am suggesting, in sum, to broaden the media cluster policy framework to address the normative dimensions of media policy regarding communication rights, citizenship, diversity and localism. That few media cluster policies currently consider these dimensions of national media policy is an indication of how thoroughly media cluster policy has been subsumed under economic development-oriented innovation and industrial policy. Broadening the cluster policy approach from exclusive concern with economic development to encompass civic and non-commercial cultural functions of media would bring the full spectrum of media impacts, effects, spillovers, innovation and normative propositions regarding media value creation into media policymaking at the cluster level, concurrently enhancing economic welfare and civic-cultural well-being in the cluster's jurisdiction.

NOTES

1. The analysis in this chapter pertains mainly to media systems in contemporary democracies with comparatively advanced, open economies, whose major cities are culturally diverse and where freedom of speech is exercised. In such countries the media system enjoys relative political autonomy, consumers' choices are relatively unconstrained, the telecommunications system is relatively up to date, niche media exist alongside mainstream media, the system encompasses a mix of public, private and not-for-profit media outlets, and the state remains more or less committed to democratic processes, pluralism, free speech, a free press and national cultural expression through various combinations of regulatory intervention, publicly owned media and encouragement of indigenous content production. Also, the state tolerates critical political discourse and does not encourage or tolerate intimidation of journalists. The range of media systems I have in mind corresponds roughly to those encompassed by Hallin and Mancini's (2004) three models of media systems: liberal, democratic corporatist and polarized pluralist, which vary in terms of the degree of development of the mass press, professionalization

of journalism, media partisanship (political parallelism) and state intervention. I leave it to others to investigate and theorize agglomerative media industry behaviour and related policy issues in media regimes that are highly centralized, intolerant, violent or lawless.
2. See for example Miller and Côté (1987).
3. Film, television and animation constitute the group of industries most frequently found in creative-city policies (Evans, 2009).
4. For a recent assessment of the resource-based view see Lockett, Thompson and Morgenstern (2009).
5. For a fuller discussion of these points see Davis et al., (2009).
6. See, among others, Benkler (2006), Freedman (2008), Hutchison (1999) and Napoli (2001).

REFERENCES

Achtenhagen, L. and R.G. Picard (2009), 'Challenges and Success Factors in Media Cluster Development', paper presented at the *12th Uddevalla Symposium: The Geography of Innovation and Entrepreneurship*, Bari, Italy, 11–13 June 2009.

Andersson, T., S. Schwaag Serger, J. Sörvik and E. Wise Hansson (2004), *The Cluster Policies Whitebook*, Malmö: IKED – International Organisation for Knowledge Economy and Enterprise Development.

Arthurs, D., E. Cassidy, C.H. Davis and D. Wolfe (2009), 'Indicators to Support Innovation Cluster Policy', *International Journal of Technology Management*, **46**(3/4), 263–279.

Bakhshi, H. and E. McVittie (2009), 'Creative Supply-chain Linkages and Innovation: Do the Creative Industries Stimulate Business Innovation in the Wider Economy?', *Innovation: Management, Policy & Practice*, **11**(2), 169–189.

Benkler, Y. (2006), *The Wealth of Networks: How Social Production Transforms Markets and Freedom*, New Haven, CT, USA and London, UK: Yale University Press.

Birch, S. (2008), *The Political Promotion of the Experience Economy and Creative Industries – Cases from UK, New Zealand, Singapore, Norway, Sweden and Denmark*, Frederiksberg, Denmark: Imagine.

Blosser, L.A., B. Scott, J. Kenney, G. Kimmelman and G.B. Manishin (2006), 'Introduction', in Mark N. Cooper (ed), *The Case Against Media Consolidation: Evidence on Concentration, Localism and Diversity*, New York: Fordham University, pp. 1–19.

Breschi, S. and F. Lissoni (2001), 'Knowledge Spillovers and Local Innovation Systems: A Critical Survey', *Industrial and Corporate Change*, **10**(4), 975–1005.

Burfitt, A. and S. MacNeill (2008), 'The Challenges of Pursuing Cluster Policy in the Congested State', *International Journal of Urban and Regional Research*, **32**(2), 492–505.

Burfitt, A., S. MacNeill and J. Gibney (2007), 'The Dilemmas of Operationalizing Cluster Policy: The Medical Technology Cluster in the West Midlands', *European Planning Studies*, **15**(9), 1273–1290.

Carlsson, B. (2006),'The Role of Public Policy in Emerging Clusters', in Pontus Braunerhjelm and Maryann Feldman (eds), *Cluster Genesis: Technology-Based Industrial Development*, Oxford, UK and New York, NY, USA: Oxford University Press, pp. 264–278.

Carpentier, N. (2008), 'The Belly of the City: Alternative Communicative City Networks', *International Communication Gazette*, **70**(3)–(4), 237–255.
Castells, M. (2009), *Communication Power*, Oxford, UK and New York, NY. USA: Oxford University Press.
Caves, R.E. (2000), *Creative Industries: Contracts between Art and Commerce*, Cambridge, MA, USA: Harvard Business School.
Cohendet, P., D. Grandadam and L. Simon (2010), 'The Anatomy of the Creative City', *Industry & Innovation*, **17**(1), 91–111.
Conference Board of Canada (2008), *Valuing Culture: Measuring and Understanding Canada's Creative Economy*, Ottawa: Conference Board of Canada.
Cornish, S.L. (1997), 'Product Innovation and the Spatial Dynamics of Market Intelligence: Does Proximity to Markets Matter?', *Economic Geography*, **73**(2), 143–165.
Creative Metropoles (2010), *Creative Metropoles: Situation Analysis of 11 Cities. Final Report*, available at http://www.creativemetropoles.eu/uploads/files/report_cm_final_formatted_02.2010.pdf.
Curran, J. (2002), *Media and Power*, London, UK and New York, NY, USA: Routledge.
Davis, C.H. (2010), 'New Firms in the Screen-based Media Industry: Startups, Self-Employment, and Standing Reserve', in Mark Deuze (ed), *Managing Media Work*, Thousand Oaks, CA, USA and London, UK: Sage, pp. 165–178.
Davis, C.H. and J. Kaye (2010) 'International Production Outsourcing and the Development of Indigenous Film and Television Capabilities: The Case of Canada', in Greg Elmer, Charles H. Davis, Janine Marchessault and John McCullough (eds), *Locating Migrating Media*, Lanham, MD, USA: Rowman and Littlefield /Lexington Books, pp. 57–78.
Davis, C.H. and J. Nadler (2009), 'International Television Co-productions and the Cultural Discount: the Case of *Family Biz*, a Comedy', in Iréne Bernhard (ed), *Uddevalla Symposium: The Geography of Innovation and Entrepreneurship*, Trollhattan, Sweden: University West, Research Reports, pp. 359–378.
Davis, C.H. and E. Sun (2006), 'Business Development Capabilities in Information Technology SMEs in a Regional Economy: An Exploratory Study', *Journal of Technology Transfer*, **31**(1), 145–161.
Davis, C.H., T. Creutzberg and D. Arthurs (2009), 'Applying an Innovation Cluster Framework to a Creative Industry: The Case of Screen-based Media in Ontario', *Innovation: Management, Policy & Practice*, **11**(2), 201–214.
Doyle, G. (2007), 'Undermining Media Diversity: Inaction on Media Concentrations and Pluralism in the EU', in Katharine Sarikakis (ed), *Media and Cultural Policy in the European Union*, Amsterdam: Rodopi, pp. 135–156.
Duranton, G. (2009), '"California Dreamin": The Feeble Case for Cluster Policies', Toronto: University of Toronto, unpublished paper, *Review of Economic Analysis*, forthcoming.
EU (2007). *Innovation Clusters in Europe: A Statistical Analysis and Overview of Current Policy Support*, Brussels: European Commission, Enterprise and Industry Directorate-General.
Evans, G. (2009), 'Creative Cities, Creative Spaces and Urban Policy', *Urban Studies*, **46**(5), (6), 1003–1040.
Freedman, D. (2008), *The Politics of Media Policy*, Cambridge, UK and Malden, MA, USA: Polity Press.

Fu, W.W. and C. Sim (2010), 'Examining International Country-to-Country Flow of Theatrical Films', *Journal of Communication*, **60**(1), 120–143.
Gagné, M., S.H. Townsend, I. Bourgeois and R.E. Hart (2010), 'Technology Cluster Evaluation and Growth Factors: Literature Review', *Research Evaluation*, **19**(2), 82–90.
Goldsmith, B. and T. O'Regan (2005), *The Film Studio: Film Production in the Global Economy*, Lanham, MD, USA: Rowman & Littlefield.
HAL (2009), *Ontario's Creative Cluster Study*, Report prepared for the Ontario Ministry of Culture. Ottawa: Hicklings Arthurs Lowe.
Hallin, D.C. and P. Mancini (2004), *Comparing Media Systems: Three Models of Media and Politics*, Cambridge, UK and New York, NY, USA: Cambridge University Press.
Hervás-Oliver, J.L. and J. Albors-Garrigós, 'Do Clusters Capabilities Matter? An Empirical Application of the Resource-based View in Clusters', *Entrepreneurship and Regional Development*, **19**(2), 113–136.
Hoskins, C. and R. Mirus (1988), 'Reasons for the US Dominance of the International Trade in Television Programs', *Media, Culture & Society*, **10**(4), 499–504.
Hutchison, D. (1999), *Media Policy: An Introduction*, Oxford, UK and Malden, MA, USA: Blackwell.
Just, N. (2009), 'Measuring Media Concentration and Diversity: New Approaches and Instruments in Europe and the US', *Media, Culture & Society*, **31**(1), 97–117.
Karppinen, Kari (2009), 'Rethinking Media Pluralism and Communicative Abundance', *Observatorio*, **3**(4), 151–169.
Krätke, S. (2003), 'Global Media Cities in a World-wide Urban Network', *European Planning Studies*, **11**(6), 605–628.
Krätke, S. and P.J. Taylor (2004), 'A World Geography of Global Media Cities', *European Planning Studies*, **12**(4), 459–477.
Krugman, P. (1994), 'Location and Competition: Notes on Economic Geography', in Richard P. Rumelt, Dan E. Schendel and David J. Teece (eds), *Fundamental Issues in Strategy*, Boston, MA, USA: Harvard Business School Press, pp. 463–494.
Lawson, Clive (1999), 'Towards a Competence Theory of the Region', *Cambridge Journal of Economics* **23,** 151–166.
Lockett, A., S. Thompson and U. Morgenstern (2009), 'The Development of the Resource-based View of the Firm: A Critical Appraisal', *International Journal of Management Reviews*, **11**(1), 9–28.
Markusen, A. (2010), 'Organizational Complexity in the Regional Cultural Economy', *Regional Studies*, **44**(7), 813–828.
Martin, R. and P. Sunley (2003), 'Deconstructing Clusters: Chaotic Concept or Policy Panacea?', *Journal of Economic Geography*, **3**(1), 5–35.
Meier zu Köcker, G. and J. Rosted (eds) (2010), *Promoting Cluster Excellence: Measuring and Benchmarking the Quality of Cluster Organisations and Performance of Clusters*, Berlin and Copenhagen: VDI/VDE Innovation + Technik GmbH, FORA.
Miller, R. and M. Côté (1987), *Growing the Next Silicon Valley: A Guide for Successful Regional Planning*, Lexington, MA, USA: Lexington Books.
Napoli, P.M. (2001), *Foundations of Communications Policy: Principles and Process in the Regulation of Electronic Media*, Cresskill, NJ, USA: Hampton Press.

Napoli, P.M. (2010), 'Persistent and Emergent Diversity Policy Concerns in an Evolving Media Environment: Toward a Reflective Research Agenda', paper presented at the Bits Without Borders Conference, Michigan State University College of Law, East Lansing, MI, USA, 24–25 September 2010.
Nauwelaers, C. (2003), *Innovative Hot Spots in Europe: Policies to Promote Trans-Border Clusters of Creative Activity*, Background Paper on Methods for Cluster Policies, European Trend Chart on Innovation, Trend Chart Policy Workshop, 5–6 May 2003, Brussels: European Commission.
Navarro Arancegui, M. (2003), 'Análisis y políticas de clusters: teoría y realidad', *Ekonomiaz,* **53**(2), 14–49.
Noam, E.M. (2009), *Media Ownership and Concentration in America*, Oxford, UK and New York, NY, USA: Oxford University Press.
OECD (2007), *Competitive Regional Clusters: National Policy Approaches*, Paris: Organisation for Economic Co-operation and Development.
OECD (2006), *Competitive Cities in the Global Economy*, Paris: Organisation for Economic Co-operation and Development.
OECD (2001), *Innovative Clusters: Drivers of National Innovation Systems*, Paris: Organisation for Economic Co-operation and Development.
Oxford Research (2008), *Cluster Policy in Europe. A Brief Summary of Cluster Policies in 31 European Countries*, Kristiansand, Norway: Oxford Research.
Peck, F. and C.E. Lloyd (2008), 'Cluster Policies and Cluster Strategies', in Charlie Karlsson (ed), *Handbook of Research on Innovation and Clusters: Cases and Policies*, Cheltenham, UK and Northampton, MA, USA: Edward Elgar, pp. 393–410.
Picard, R.G. (2009), 'Media Clusters and Regional Development: Reflections on the Significance of Location in Media Production', in Iréne Bernhard (ed), *The Geography of Innovation and Entrepreneurship*, Research Reports 2009:02, Trollhättan, Sweden: University West, pp. 877–885.
Picard, R.G. (2008), *Media Clusters: Local Agglomeration in an Industry Developing Networked Virtual Clusters*, Jönköping: Jönköping International Business School Working Paper Series No. 2008-3, 16pp.
Potter, J. (2009), 'Policy Issues in Clusters, Innovation and Entrepreneurship', in Jonathan Potter and Gabriela Miranda (eds), *Clusters, Innovation and Entrepreneurship*, Paris: Organisation for Economic Co-operation and Development, pp 21–41.
PWC (2009), *Global Entertainment & Media Outlook 2009–2013*, New York, NY, USA: PriceWaterhouseCoopers.
Raboy, M. (2005), 'Making Media: Creating the Conditions for Communication in the Public Good', Vancouver: 2005 Spry Memorial Lecture, available at http://www.com.umontreal.ca/spry/spry-mr-lec.html.
Raboy, M. and D. Taras (2004), 'Transparency and Accountability in Canadian Media Policy', *Communications*, **29**, 59–76.
Röttmer, N. and B. Katzy (2005), *Regional Innovation Capabilities*, Munich: University of Munich, Center for Technology and Innovation Management Working Paper No. 3505.
Schmiedeberg, C. (2010), 'Evaluation of Cluster Policy: A Methodological Overview', *Evaluation*, **16**(4), 389–412.
Scott, A.J. (2008), *Social Economy of the Metropolis: Cognitive-Cultural Capitalism and the Global Resurgence of Cities*, Oxford, UK and New York, NY, USA: Oxford University Press.

Shaver, D. and M.A. Shaver (2006), 'Directions for Media Management Research in the 21st Century', in Alan B. Albarran, Sylvia M. Chan-Olmsted and Michael O. Wirth (eds), *Handbook of Media Management and Economics*, Mahwah, NJ, USA: Lawrence Erlbaum, pp. 639–654.

Silverstone, R. (2007), *Media and Morality: On the Rise of the Mediapolis*, Cambridge, UK and Malden, MA, USA: Polity Press.

Silverstone, R. (1999), *Why Study the Media?* London, UK and Thousand Oaks, CA, USA: Sage.

Spencer, G.M., T. Vinodrai, M.S. Gertler and D.A. Wolfe (2010), 'Do Clusters Make a Difference? Defining and Assessing their Economic Performance', *Regional Studies*, **44**(6), 697–715.

Stoneman, P. (2010), *Soft Innovation: Economics, Product Aesthetics, and the Creative Industries*, Oxford, UK and New York, NY, USA: Oxford University Press.

Taylor, M. (2010), 'Clusters: A Mesmerising Mantra', *Tijdschrift voor Economische en Sociale Geografie*, **101**(3), 276–286.

Torre, A. (2008), 'First Steps Towards a Critical Appraisal of Clusters', in Uwe Blien and Gunther Maier (eds), *The Economics of Regional Clusters: Networks, Technology and Policy*, Cheltenham, UK and Northampton, MA, USA: Edward Elgar, pp. 29–40.

Torre, A. (2006), 'Clusters et Systèmes Locaux d'Innovation – un Retour Critique sur les Hypothèses Naturalistes de la Transmission des Connaissances à l'Aide des Catégories de l'Économie de la Proximité', *Région et Développement*, **24**, 15–44.

Tremblay, D.-G. and E. Cecilli (2009), 'The Film and Audiovisual Production in Montreal: Challenges of Relational Proximity for the Development of a Creative Cluster', *Journal of Arts Management, Law and Society*, **39**(3), 157–186.

UNCTAD (2008), *Creative Economy Report 2008: The Challenge of Assessing the Creative Economy Towards Informed Policy-making*, Geneva: United Nations Conference on Trade and Development.

van Cuilenburg, J. and D. McQuail (2003), 'Media Policy Paradigm Shifts: Towards a New Communications Policy Paradigm', *European Journal of Communication*, **18**(2), 181–207.

Wise, E., L. Langkilde and M. Degn Bertelsen (2008), *The Use of Data and Analysis as a Tool for Cluster Policy: an Overview of Good Practices and Perspectives Prepared for the European Commission*, Brussels: European Commission, DG Enterprise and Industry.

Wrobel, M. (2009), 'Das Konzept regionaler Cluster: zwischen Schein und Sein? Eine kritische Analyse gängiger Annahmen der aktuellen Clusterdiskussion', *Jahrbuch für Regionalwissenschaft*, **29**(1), 85–103.

PART II

Media cluster studies

Section A Clusters maintaining or reinvigorating media leadership

5. Back to Hilversum: consolidation of the Dutch broadcast cluster

Erik Hitters

In most countries broadcasting and the associated television industry is clustered in the capital, or at least in one of the country's major cities. However, the Dutch television industry is not located in Amsterdam, but in a 'leafy suburban hamlet' 20 km southeast of the capital (Ourrossof, 2007). Hilversum is a medium-sized town of 84,000 inhabitants, but it is home to most of the television and broadcast-related companies and institutions in the Netherlands. About a third of all jobs in this city are related to the media. The focal point of the broadcasting cluster is the Media Park, a relatively clearly defined area, almost exclusively for media businesses, that houses some 200 companies. Throughout the city a number of organizations and businesses in the broadcasting industry are located, scattered in the green suburban area. Although broadcasting is the main focus of the Hilversum media cluster, it is also a city that has a strong presence in adjacent fields of multimedia, ICT and creative industries.

The broadcasting industry is clearly dominant in the Hilversum economy, but it is also the major cluster of that industry in the Netherlands. Furthermore, the closely related music and film industry is also clustered here. The cluster is, however, losing ground to its main competitor in this industry, Amsterdam. 'Media are swapping Hillywood for Amsterdam' was the headline in an article in a major newspaper in June 2010 (Ali, 2010). Until the beginning of the 21st century, the broadcasting industry has grown steadily in Hilversum, but in the last decade this growth has slowed down, and employment has been falling since 2008 (Immovator, 2010). The advent of digitalization and internet distribution certainly plays a role in the hard times that have hit upon the traditional broadcasting industry. Nonetheless, the town of Hilversum is increasingly less appealing for new media companies and start-ups to locate in. But also the traditional broadcasters are reconsidering their location in the cluster. Recently, a number of large broadcasters have left the Hilversum area and have relocated to Amsterdam.

In this chapter I will closely follow the characteristics laid out in this book's introduction. I will draw on several data sources such as statistical and economic data offered by LISA (the Laboratory for Interdisciplinary Statistical Analysis). I will also use secondary analyses of a number of reports on Dutch media, such as the Cross Media Monitors (Immovator, 2006, 2008 and 2010).

DEVELOPMENT PROCESS

The Hilversum media cluster has developed slowly but gradually, along with the advent of radio and television in the daily lives of the Dutch. The location of the associated industry in the city of Hilversum can only be understood if we take a closer look at its history, more specifically the history of public service broadcasting. What emerges is a highly path-dependent development process with many contingent factors that are related to the unique composition of the Dutch broadcasting policy.

Let me then, first, briefly outline the basic principles of that policy, before explaining the development of the broadcasting cluster in Hilversum. As in many other western countries, media policy is rooted in freedom of expression and is guided mainly by principles of independence, diversity and access (Ministry of Education, Culture and Science, 2006). Dutch public service broadcasting has a unique organizational structure rooted in 'pillarization' of Dutch society as a whole. Consequently, the public broadcasting system is not operated directly by a government agency, but 'outsourced' to private associations. Broadcasting time on the public radio and television channels is shared by a large number of broadcasting associations and several other non-profit organizations. All of these are granted broadcasting licences either because they are deemed representative of a particular section of the population or on the basis of a specific programme remit. Until 2000 these organizations operated under a self-appointed general management (ibid., p. 94). Various broadcasting associations representing different schools of thought and groups within the Dutch society are still at the heart of the Dutch public broadcasting system. In 2006, eight broadcasting associations shared responsibility for the bulk of public radio and television: KRO (Catholic), NCRV (Protestant), EO (Protestant), AVRO (neutral), TROS (family viewing), BNN (the young), VARA (progressive) and VPRO (progressive) (ibid., p. 95).

The path-dependent development of Hilversum as a broadcast cluster is intertwined with the history of radio and television broadcasting in the Netherlands and the Dutch government intervention therein. In 1923 a radio manufacturing company (NSF) located in Hilversum started radio transmissions, renting out airtime. In the following years broadcast associations were established for Catholics, Protestants, labourers and the general public, which all located in Hilversum, close to the NSF transmission tower. Quite clearly, these years can be identified as the path creation of the Hilversum development. In the 1950s television broadcasting started, initiated by Philips, the owner of the NSF. Facilitated by the Hilversum city council, the emerging television industry located naturally close to the already existing radio activities, as the television airwaves were operated in a similar way by the broadcast associations. In 1954 the Broadcast Quarter was developed in the north of Hilversum, featuring a large transmission tower, ample space for studios and offices as well as housing for the television staff. In the following years all television and radio activities became clustered in that area, which was later renamed Media Park. Path reproduction became established in the 1950s in Hilversum with the advent of television, thereby speeding up clustering in the municipality at a pace that could never be matched by any competing location, if there had been any. Hilversum became the household name to refer to television in the Netherlands. 'Back to Hilversum' are still the closing words of any journalist or presenter reporting on location.

A major recent development is the privatization of the facilities monopoly at the end of the 1990s. The Media Park properties were owned by that same large state-owned facilities company (NOB), which was completely privatized and split up in the 2000s. In 2003 the real estate was sold to property developer TCN. It has developed the Media Park into a 'thematic business park where a clustering of media-related companies generates a unique synergy' (http://www.mediapark.nl). The Media Park covers 36 hectares with 300,000 m^2 of buildings. The park is operated by TCN Media Park, which is in charge of developing the park further, as well as overseeing the daily management. TCN is working closely on the further development of the Media Park with broadcasting organization and co-owner NOS, the municipality of Hilversum and the province of Noord-Holland (http://www.tcn.nl).

SIZE OF THE CLUSTER

The size of the media and entertainment cluster is large in Hilversum. In number of jobs provided, only Amsterdam has more in that category. The employment structure in Hilversum is dominated by this sector. One in five jobs is directly within this sector, and about a third of total employment is both indirectly and directly dependent on it (see Table 5.1).

Table 5.1 Hilversum: persons employed, total, creative industries and media and entertainment 2005–2008

Persons employed	**2005**	**2006**	**2007**	**2008**
Hilversum	**46,740**	**47,600**	**48,500**	**49,560**
Creative Industries	12,425	12,912	13,143	13,324
% Creative Industries in total	27	27	27	27
Media and Entertainment	9,064	9,532	9,576	9,658
% Media and Entertainment in total	19	20	20	19

Source: LISA.

Table 5.2 Hilversum: structure of Media and Entertainment 2008

Business activity	**Number of firms**	**Persons employed**	**Avg. firm size**
Publishing	68	1,011	14.9
Photography	55	140	2.5
Film	247	1,288	5.2
Broadcasting Org.*	28	5,643	201.5
Production and support Radio / TV*	87	1,502	17.3
Other entertainment	8	28	3.5
Press & Journalism	26	46	1.8
Total 2008	519	9,658	18.6
* Core Broadcasting Structure	110	7,145	65

Source: LISA.

There are 519 companies in the media and entertainment sector in Hilversum, employing almost 10,000 people. Most of that employment, however, is highly concentrated in certain specific parts of that sector, namely the reproductive and distributive parts (see Table 5.2). Within the sector in Hilversum, the broadcast associations account for up to 60 per cent of all employment (see Figure 5.1). Furthermore, a large amount of employment is concentrated in broadcast facilities companies, which are usually quite large firms such as Dutchview, United Broadcast Facilities, Team Facilities and Technicolor. Given the dominance of large organizations and companies in Hilversum, the average firm size is 18.6 employees, which is exceptionally high for the media and entertainment industries, which are usually characterized by the presence of many very small firms (SMSEs) (cf. Bathelt, 2001). In the broadcast sector the average firm size

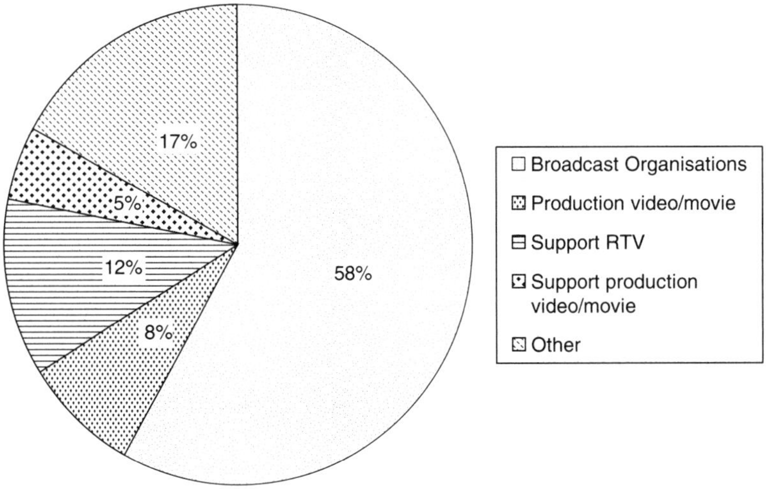

Source: LISA

Figure 5.1 Employment Media and Entertainment Hilversum 2008 in %

is as high as 62, while in the other sub-sectors of the media and entertainment sector the average firm size is much smaller.

Within the boundaries of the Media Park over 200 firms are clustered. The Media Park is the main focus of the Hilversum broadcasting activities. It is home to large television and radio broadcasters, associations such as VPRO, VARA and NPS that operate on the PSBS, as well as commercial broadcasters such as RTL. The area has numerous studios and studio facilities companies. There are also offices for music major Sony and production companies such as Endemol, Studio 100 and Fremantle. Furthermore, the Media Park also has educational facilities, the Media Academy and Veronica Radio School. One of its architectural eye catchers is the National Institute for Sound and Vision, the national broadcasting archives including a museum and an interactive media experience.

CONNECTEDNESS

The Hilversum media cluster has a strongly embedded structure that is rooted in its traditional audiovisual broadcasting functions. A limited number of firms are at the core of this structure, consisting of the broadcasting organizations, production companies and facilities companies. These are 115 firms that make up 75 per cent of all employment in the

Hilversum media cluster (see Table 5.2). This core consists of both commercial and public broadcasters, facilities companies and production companies. It functions according to a traditional broadcasting business model, producing and distributing programming that can be supplied to specified audiences. Around this core a periphery of smaller audiovisual or multimedia firms has emerged, most of which are dependent on commissions from the core. The peripheral firms are usually small, flexible and specialized; they are entrepreneurial and innovative (Gemeente Hilversum, 2010).

Following Leyshon's (2001) analysis of the music industry, we can differentiate between three interrelated networks that make up the structure of the media industry. First is the creative network, which consists of core creative staff (artists) and specialized institutions (for education and presentation) as well as specialized technical facilitators; this network is usually highly spatially concentrated in urban areas. Second is the reproductive network around cultural producers such as the audiovisual production companies and their ancillary industry. Here, the creative work of the first network can be capitalized into profitable products. These reproductive networks are very capital- and technology-intensive and subject to economies of scale. They are usually located close to the creative network but also close to the market. Third is the distributive network, which packages 'commodified creativity' to be distributed to the end users. Here, economies of scale and standardized production methods are dominant. Distribution, then, does not profit from agglomeration economics, but will mainly seek for cost effectiveness (Leyshon, 2001).

The Hilversum media cluster, then, can be characterized as a reproductive network for the broadcasting industry. It is highly vertically integrated around a number of broadcasters. As is commonly found in the television industry, production is fairly standardized and routinized, with a tendency towards outsourcing of creative and productive functions. However, in the Hilversum cluster, such functions have also been integrated and consolidated into the large dominant firms. This typical structure of the Hilversum cluster sets it apart, functionally as well as spatially and organizationally, from that other Dutch cluster for audiovisual industries, Amsterdam. Van der Groep (2004) explicitly makes this point, explaining how both clusters operate with a specific division of labour, with Hilversum focusing on broadcasting and Amsterdam on filmmaking, advertising and new media. He concludes that 'the Hilversum cluster exist [sic] of large-scale mass-like production conglomerates that produce mostly in-house. The executive work is done by technicians, camera staff and others that are on the pay list. [. . .] A periphery of small firms function as a back up reservoir yet as well as a repository in which small-scale technological innovations can thrive' (van der Groep, p. 13). Consequently, Hilversum is strong in the distributive and reproductive networks but has limited connectedness to creative networks. Parts of the creative and reproductive force in broadcasting production in Hilversum are integrated into large consolidated and internalized conglomerates, thereby routinizing and standardizing their symbolic production.

Although the Hilversum Media Cluster has a significant economic importance for the overall Hilversum economy, the connection to other economic sectors is generally deemed limited (Gemeente Hilversum, 2010). The Hilversum City Council rightly observes this in its economic vision document 2007–2020. The media cluster is under threat from technological revolutions and national and international competition and fails to innovate and spill over into the adjacent economic sector. The city attributes itself with the tasks to stimulate effective networking, expand the knowledge infrastructure, strengthen cluster connections and facilitate the large flagship firms and organizations in order to keep them in the city (ibid.). What appears is a picture of a cluster that is over-embedded (cf. Uzzi, 1997), with production, facilities and distribution firms tightly interrelated, causing lock-in effects that allow for effective routinized production but lack in innovation and competitiveness (cf. Bathelt, 2001).

PROFITABILITY

Claims on the profitability of the Hilversum media cluster cannot be made based on hard data such as figures on turnover or profits of the firms that make up the media cluster. Although such data might be available for a number of firms, there are no aggregate data available that allow for conclusions on financial performance of the media sector as such. The Cross Media Monitor 2008 (Immovator, 2008, p. 46) gives some data on turnover of the larger sector of ICT and creative industries. From these figures it becomes clear that more than 25 per cent of the turnover of the Hilversum economy comes from these sectors. In comparison to the national average of 6.4 per cent, obviously ICT and creative industries are very central to the Hilversum economy. The annual growth of turnover in these sectors is 4 per cent, only fractionally more than average (ibid., p. 40). Nonetheless, some indicators exist that can suggest a somewhat closer analysis of profitability developments concerning the cluster.

A first indicator is the employment growth in the cluster. Here we can distinguish between the overall Hilversum economy and the creative industries. Widening up the scope to the creative industries allows us to get a view of the media industries together with the closely related sectors

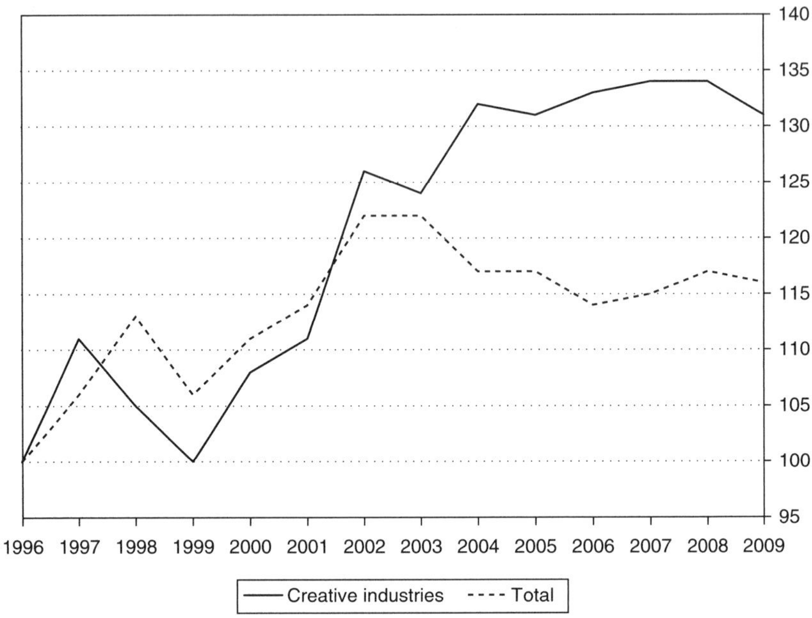

Source: LISA.

Figure 5.2 Employment growth in Hilversum for total economy and creative industry (1996–2009)

of entertainment, arts and creative services such as advertising. As Figure 5.2 shows, the creative industries have grown at a rapid pace since 1999. Even when the growth of the overall economy slowed down after 2002, the creative industries kept creating more jobs in Hilversum. Most of those jobs were in the broadcasting industry, especially since the rapidly growing commercial broadcasting firms and their adjacent production and facilities companies also located in Hilversum. Since 2008, the radio and television industry is losing jobs. This loss is not being compensated by growth in related media industries (Immovator, 2010).

A second indicator modifies this image somewhat. Due to a number of factors, the television industry in Hilversum was faced with severe cutback and cost-efficiency measures. The factors causing this lie in the saturation of the television market, with many newly entered networks and only limited numbers of viewers as well as a limited market for advertisers. Another factor was the advent of the internet and the increasing competition in screen-based entertainment. An additional reason was the cost-cutting measures that were imposed on public broadcasters since 2004. All

Table 5.3 Hilversum: Employment and Location Coefficient (LQ) in Media and Entertainment by subsector

Hilversum	Jobs 2007	Annual employment growth 1996–2007	LQ 2007	LQ tendency
Media and entertainment	**9744**	**2.3 %**	**2148**	–
Publishing	1008	4.0 %	496	–/+
Photography	126	3.4 %	278	–/+
Film	1194	0.1 %	1676	–
Broadcasting Org.	5599	0.6 %	12033	–
Production and support Radio / TV	1478	26.3 %	3613	–
Other entertainment	29	15.4 %	199	n.a.
Press & Journalism	43	-0.2 %	220	–
Advertising	499	5.8 %	156	–
			NL = 100	

Source: LISA

of these led to a general economizing of programming for all broadcasters, resulting in consolidation tendencies but also in the loss of employment in the periphery of firms operating around the core of the Hilversum cluster structure. Also, a major commercial network, Talpa (Tien), located on the Media Park, went bankrupt in 2007 and was taken over by RTL which continued broadcasting but cut down most locally produced programmes.

Table 5.3 shows how media and entertainment is a sector that has shown stunning growth figures over the last ten years. Furthermore, the dominance of the broadcasting industry in Hilversum is overwhelming, with location coefficients skyrocketing for broadcasting organizations and production and support for television. However, that relative dominance appears to be waning, as concluded by analyses carried out by the Immovator Cross Media Network in 2008 and 2010 (Immovator, 2008, 2010). They show the tendency for the location coefficients decreasing for broadcast organizations, radio and television production and support, journalism and film. Specifically the film sector is concentrating in Amsterdam, whereas the location of two networks (SBS and MTV) in Amsterdam could also induce other producing and supporting firms to (re)locate in the capital (Immovator, 2008, p. 69). Radio network Q-Music has left Hilversum for Amsterdam, and two newly entered public broadcasting associations (PowNed and WNL) have chosen to locate in Amsterdam (Ali, 2010). Recently, a number of major production companies such as Endemol and Eyeworks have also decided to locate in Amsterdam or close or downsize their Hilversum offices.

STRUCTURE AND OPERATIONAL CHARACTERISTICS

If we look at the operational characteristics of the Hilversum media cluster, we have to make a distinction between the cluster as a whole and the more tightly geographically confined Media Park. The latter is managed very transparently, whereas the former involves several governance structures, but on a less obvious level.

The media cluster in Hilversum is very clearly a planned cluster, that is to say, a cluster that originated in a concentration of broadcasting facilities, around which, by government intervention, a cluster of broadcasting organizations and production and facilities companies gathered. As became clear earlier in this chapter, cluster development was closely planned both from the municipal level and from the state level.

In the current situation, it is mainly the municipal level, i.e. the Hilversum city council, that seizes the opportunity to actively develop a 'cluster policy' in order to safeguard the leading position as media city in the Netherlands. The Hilversum Media City policy will be more closely discussed in the next section. However, it is interesting at this point to elaborate on a number of policy initiatives that deal directly with the managerial and operational characteristics of the cluster.

Only since around 2000 has the city of Hilversum actively started to intervene in the media sector. Before that time public broadcasting was fairly non-commercial as it was closely linked to the pillarization model (as discussed above). With the entry of commercial broadcasting in the 1990s the sector became more economically embedded, and its connection to the town of Hilversum became reinforced with the installation of the first Hilversum alderman for Media Affairs. Thus, only by the end of the 1990s did the city become aware of the enormous growth of the sector and its importance, if not centrality, to the city's economy and to the city's reputation. In 2000 the alderman initiated a network organization (Stichting Multi Media Hilversum) together with the province, the chamber of commerce and representatives of the AV, IT and telecom industry, in order to maintain and strengthen the multimedia sector in the Hilversum region. There have been a number of subsequent initiatives, for instance a very typical and practical planning intervention in order to improve the traffic flow in the city and the accessibility of media firms as well as the subsidizing of networking events and educational activities. The city is also actively involved in a project to realize a fibre optic infrastructure for both households and businesses in order to facilitate high-speed and high-density data traffic. On the administrative level the city participates in a number of regional economic development boards aimed at regional cooperation and strengthening regional economic growth. One of these is the so-called Creative Axis, a cooperation of creative towns and cities in the Amsterdam area; another is the Amsterdam Metropolitan Regional Platform (Gemeente Hilversum, 2007, 2010). The actual achievements of such cooperation structures, however, remain rather vague.

A very central organization in the interaction between the media business and policy actors is Immovator Cross Media Network. This organization has a cooperative structure; it is a very active non-profit organization mainly managing knowledge transfer opportunities. It originated from a policy initiative but became an autonomous non-profit association for the media industry. Although it is located in Hilversum, it has a broader scope, aiming at stimulating national cooperation and trade of Dutch media companies. Nonetheless, geographically, its focus is on the north wing of the Randstad, the area roughly from Utrecht to the Amsterdam metropolitan region. Its main function is that of a network, with a strong focus on innovation. It serves that function by actively connecting policy, education and business with a range of activities. It is supported by European subsidies, city, province and state subsidies, educational institutions and semi-public media companies. There is also some sponsoring by for-profit companies.

Management at a much more concrete level can be found in the operations of the Media Park. Since its privatization in 2003 the Media Park is managed by TCN Media Park, the management company of the owner of the park, property developer TCN. TCN Media Park is responsible for developing the park further, as well as overseeing the daily management. TCN Media Park and the users together aim at creating a good working environment, something that for a long time has been lacking in this area. Spearheads of management are the image of the park, public safety and accurate support services, such as childcare and fitness (http://www.mediapark.nl). The former broadcast quarter that later became the Media Park always had the charm of any other industrial estate. However glamorous things were inside the studios, outside hardly any of that appeal persisted. The Media Park, then, was an utterly boring place, with nothing but a few canteens and company restaurants for lunch or a quick dinner, but no other attractions for staff and visitors. Broadcasting staff would usually come in in the morning, or whenever their shift began, and go home as soon as they were done. That home typically would be in Amsterdam for the creative staff and in the suburban region for the facilities staff. TCN, as manager and developer of the park, has set itself a goal to turn this boring image of the Media Park around and change it into a pleasant place to work as well as a place to visit. For media staff, the park has already become more attractive by the removal of the physical barriers such as gates and fences that used to close the park off, for security reasons, from its environment. A number of other improvements include public transport, parking, mail services and a coffee bar. For potential visitors, the park is becoming increasingly attractive with the new Institute for Sound and Vision, as mentioned before, and a stronger focus on organizing events and fairs around the theme of broadcasting specifically for visitors. This will be further explored in the next section.

CLUSTER ENGINES

The main engines in the Hilversum cluster have always been the large broadcasting organizations and facilities companies. As explained above, these companies make up the reproductive core of the cluster, with a large number of specialized small firms catering to specific needs of the core. The current position of Hilversum is, however, threatened as a result of several market trends. The necessity for media firms to be located in Hilversum has diminished considerably. There is competition from neighbouring regions that are also seeking the growth potential of the media industries. Furthermore, there are limits to the locational appeal of Hilversum, both in the concrete locational factors (accessibility, rents, space) as well as in atmosphere and character. As an innovative milieu, Hilversum no longer appeals to new media start-ups. The departure of media companies not only implies a direct loss in employment, but also an indirect loss of income and jobs in adjacent business activities (Freriks and Menkveld, 2009). Subsequently, I will focus in this section on the efforts of the municipality as well as the Media Park property developer and their strategies to maintain a strong media cluster in Hilversum.

The policy of the municipal government aims at sustaining the core companies in broadcasting while at the same time enhancing growth in the periphery. The first focus area is innovation. Hilversum wants to develop milieux of innovation for the media and broadcasting sector, but also with a wider appeal in order to generate spillover into the creative industries, health care and tourism. The above-mentioned Cross Media Network Immovator has an important role in this matter, but it is also central in the second focus area, that of networking. The city wishes to actively promote networking among policy makers, educators and media compa-

Source: http://www.mediapark.nl

Figure 5.3 Hilversum Master Plan Media Park 2020

nies. Knowledge transfer, both formal and tacit, is considered essential. The third focus area is the enhancement of the city's profile as a media city. Here the city clearly ties in to the concept of reputation economies. Knowledge and value in the cultural industries are crucially related to reputation and the dynamics of taste. Reputational economies affect the value of products and are very often related to and supported by the reputation of the place where they are brokered and sold. Thus the value of a city's reputation and status for brokering high quality and innovative culture and entertainment is important to the products brokered there but also to the city's ability to sustain a global market hub. It is also argued that reputational economies accrued within the cultural industries can spill over to other sectors of the economy. However, such a policy can be effective, but only if the reputation of the city is very good. For the Hilversum case, this remains to be seen. It definitely has the image of the broadcast city, but that does not necessarily transform easily into an innovative media city.

The development of the Media Park follows two tracks that have been laid down in a Master Plan (see Figure 5.3). On the one hand, it will remain a media business park, enhancing its appeal to media firms.

The business park will accommodate new media-related companies by developing the available space in the park from 300,000 m^2 to 447,000 m^2, an addition of some 50 per cent. A planned business support centre will furthermore provide residents with new services such as a fitness centre, a health centre or day care facilities. The second track in the Master Plan is the development of a theme park with an expected huge public appeal. In December 2006, Media Experience of the Netherlands Institute for Sound and Vision opened its doors at the Media Park. Media Experience consists of a high-profile interactive presentation and a unique museum collection covering more than 80 years of broadcasting history. New functions like a Grand Café, a multiplex cinema and hotel facilities will further enhance the attraction of Media Experience. In terms of planning, the Media Park will be made accessible by two new entrances, in order to separate the expected 200,000 visitors annually from the media staff working in the park. The southern entrance at the Institute of Sound and Vision gives access to the television studios that are located on the so-called Walk of Fame. The northern side of the park will be for staff only. A new traverse over the main road will connect the Media Park to the train station (http://www.mediapark.nl).

SPILLOVER

Spillover effects are generally considered to be an important aspect of media clustering. The Immovator Cross Media Monitor is especially designed to monitor such effects for the Northwing Region. Their starting point is not the media industry as such, but the assumption that both ICT and creative industries are important buttresses for the regional economy, and that these sectors are inextricably tied together by content production. Content-producing companies, specifically in the media and entertainment industry, can be classified as part of the ICT sector as well as the creative industries (Immovator, 2008, p. 1). Where the ICT sector deals with the creation, production, publishing, distributing and facilitating of (electronic/digital) information and communication, the creative industries do the same with symbolic products; hence the term cross media. However, the ICT sector produces not only content but also hardware and technical services. Hilversum is specifically strong in the content part of the ICT sector. Here the overlap with the media is quite clear. Growth rates for both parts are fairly equal (some 2 per cent annually) although below average compared to the rest of the region. Spillover effects are thus fairly clear with respect to the relation between the media cluster and the ICT-content cluster. Many of the firms in the latter cluster will be part of the periphery of the Hilversum cluster. Van der Groep (2004) uses the example of young specialized firms in niche activities, where new innovations are invented and tested in a network of young ambitious entrepreneurs, amateurs and hobbyists, while the broadcasters keep a close watch on them. Thus, at the end of the 1990s the multimedia industry evolved alongside the broadcasters. 'When the broadcasters finally understood their relevance, they were consolidated in order to organize television shows accompanied by Internet sites' (Immovator, 2008, p. 12).

Other spillovers are taking place in the events and tourism market, but many of these markets are yet to be developed. For instance, RTL started the so-called 'Hillywood Tours' in 2009, modelled after the Hollywood star tours, where visitors are taken in a small train across the Media Park visiting sites of interest such as studios and the Walk of Fame, but also the site where politician Pim Fortuyn was shot in 2002. The Media Experience in the new National Institute for Sound and Vision is also generating a large number of visitors to Hilversum, particularly to the Media Park, but up to this moment there have not been many clear spillovers visible from this. Future tourism development is, nevertheless, incorporated in the TCN Master Plan for the area.

OWNERSHIP

Van der Groep (2004) explains the consolidation and internalization tendencies in the Hilversum media cluster from specific historical developmental paths of the broadcasting industry, as well as strategic conduct driven by economies of scale and an oligopolistic structure in a saturated and competitive television market. Over ten channels are operated by three clusters of broadcasting agencies, one of which is the consortium of public broadcasters. This oligopoly compels independent producers to use price-competitive strategies, while at the same time smaller facility suppliers are driven out of the market and efficient and large all-purpose suppliers are the ones that survive. Facilities companies have started using 'package deals', renting out complete sets ranging from light installations, sound-recording equipment and cameras to staff and assistants. The system offers efficiency benefits, as it saves producers' coordination time and results in lower production and administrative costs (ibid., pp. 11–12). Van der Groep concludes that in Hilversum 'the regime of broadcasters and government forces the facility suppliers and producers to realise economies of scale. Networks of small firms have not replaced the large conglomerates in the audiovisual industry, even in the production phase.

It turned out that both modes of production existed and continue to exist even in a phase of economic transition' (ibid., pp. 16–17).

Most firms in the cluster are domestic, or at least domestic in origin, which is understandable given the development of broadcasting in the Netherlands. The monopoly of public service broadcasting existed until 1990, resulting in many firms having spun off from the non-profit broadcasters and the state-owned facilities companies. The core of public broadcasting is the broadcasting associations that operate three TV and six radio channels, overseen by a board of the Netherlands Public Broadcasting system, which is publicly accountable. The entry of commercial broadcasters into the system resulted in many foreign capital ties entering the, up until then, fairly closed television cluster. Commercial broadcasting is obviously all private and foreign-owned (e.g. Bertelsmann for RTL). The commercial broadcasters have also used internalization and consolidation strategies in order to remain competitive. Consolidation here mainly existed in the taking over of originally Dutch television broadcasters or production companies to get a foothold in the market. The first decade of RTL in the Netherlands was dominated by one production company, Endemol, which could be considered its in-house production company. Later RTL stared its own production company, Blue Circle, which was brought under the international RTL Group umbrella and now operates as part of Fremantle Media. RTL in 2009 also took over the bankrupt Talpa network, which was initiated by John de Mol, general director and founder of Endemol.

The entry of commercial television also dramatically changed the landscape for facilities suppliers, resulting in a similar consolidation tendency. The state-owned facility monopolist was gradually dismantled. When it became semi-privatized, it lost its monopoly position. But as van der Groep explains (van der Groep, 2004, p. 12) the new semi-privatized facility supplier (NOB) used governmental funding to widen its tasks from registration assistance towards pre- and post-production facilities. Other facility suppliers that newly entered the market were forced to do the same to remain competitive. Consequently, all facilities companies present themselves nowadays as all-purpose facility suppliers. Cutbacks and efficiency measures furthermore reinforce the tendency towards consolidation.

SUSTAINABILITY

The central position of Hilversum as a cluster for broadcasting and media is still undisputed. The small city has some 10,000 jobs in media and entertainment and an additional 4000 in the adjacent sectors of ICT and creative industries. One in three jobs in the city is in that field, while one in five is in media. Only Amsterdam, which is ten times bigger, has more jobs in media and entertainment (12,000), with an emphasis on publishing and film (Immovator, 2008, p. 51). Media and broadcasting are hugely over-represented in Hilversum, owing to a strong path-dependent development of the broadcasting industry in this city.

However, there are many trends that can start to challenge this position. On the macro level these trends are mainly technological. Agglomeration in the broadcasting industry has long since become obsolete from a technological point of view. The advent of cable made the proximity to the transmission tower no longer necessary, and now that the whole process from creation to transmission is done digitally, the transactions and communications between the different links in the production and distribution chain can be taken care of over large distances. Still, the cluster in Hilversum can be characterized by strong ties (cf. Granovetter, 1973), and the cluster is institutionally thick (Hitters, 2009) with many traded and untraded transactions taking place among cluster firms.

On the level of the cluster itself, there are significant threats to its sustainability in the long term. The above-mentioned technological possibilities are causing less location of new start-up firms in Hilversum. The city is trying to break this trend by offering incubator buildings with advanced technological infrastructure to businesses willing to locate in the city. Nonetheless, the competition from Amsterdam is significant, as new entrants are much more likely to locate in Amsterdam. The location coefficients for the core media firms are falling, indicating a loss of firms to other areas. Large firms such as production firms Endemol and Eyeworks and broadcasters MTV and SBS have very consciously decided not to locate in Hilversum. For media staff, Amsterdam is also a much more attractive place to live and work, with its extensive creative network branching out to arts and new media. The Hilversum networks are mainly reproductive and distributive, along with the presence of many large media organizations and companies, giving it a somewhat boring image. The reputational economy of Hilversum, then, is under severe threat. Its image is closely linked to the traditional broadcasters and has failed to adapt sufficiently to new media developments and innovation. A quite obvious lock-in can be observed here, caused by the dominance of strong ties between large broadcasters and technical facilities (cf. Bathelt, 2001). The Hilversum City Council as well as the property owner of the Media Park are actively intervening in order to reverse the trend. Both are keen on stimulating innovation and networking within the Hilversum cluster. Both are also attempting to turn around Hilversum's traditional broadcasting image into a more innovative and lively new media image. Likewise, the development of the Media Park as a tourist destination fits into this reputation policy.

CONCLUSIONS

The Hilversum cluster can be characterized as a dinosaur. Clearly the overwhelming presence of the media in this relatively small city makes it a very interesting case to study. Its position as the centre of the broadcasting industry in the Netherlands is unchallenged, and employment has grown steadily since the mid-1990s. Hilversum can be characterized as mono-disciplinary, having a very dominant specialization in traditional broadcasting. Recently, employment has been decreasing in that sector, which is not being compensated by growth in related media sectors, creative industries and ICT.

The cluster has a very typical structure with a core of a limited number of firms, consisting mainly of large commercial and public broadcasters, facilities companies and production companies. It functions according to a traditional broadcasting business model, producing and distributing programming that can be supplied to specified audiences. Around this core a periphery of smaller audiovisual or multimedia firms has emerged, most of which are dependent on commissions from the core. The peripheral firms are usually small, flexible and specialized; they are entrepreneurial and innovative. The Hilversum media cluster, then, can be characterized as a reproductive network for the broadcasting industry. It is highly vertically integrated around a number of broadcasters. As is commonly found in the television industry, production is fairly standardized and routinized, with a tendency towards outsourcing of creative and productive functions. However, in the Hilversum cluster, such functions have also been integrated and consolidated into the large dominant firms. This typical structure of the Hilversum cluster sets it apart, functionally as well as spatially and organizationally, from that other Dutch cluster for audiovisual industries, Amsterdam.

Most theory suggests that cultural industries clusters consist of many small, socially embedded firms that work closely together in relationships that are based on mutual trust and knowledge exchange. The Hilversum cluster, however, shows a very different picture, due to its specific mode of organization rooted in historical and institutional developmental paths. What appears is a picture of a cluster that is over-embedded, with production, facilities and distribution firms tightly interrelated, causing lock-in effects that allow for effective routinized production but lack in innovation and competitiveness. Consequently, the relative dominance of Hilversum in the media and entertainment business is diminishing; location coefficients are decreasing for broadcast organizations, radio and television production and support, journalism and film. In these fields, Hilversum is clearly losing ground to Amsterdam, which is growing at a rapid pace in the fields of film production, advertising and supporting audiovisual industry. Recently, even broadcasting networks are concentrating in Amsterdam followed by a number of production firms.

With the market for television viewers as well as the market for television advertising being saturated, large incumbents can still profit from economies of scale using strategies of consolidation and integration. The overall image, however, is that the golden days are over and large cutbacks and efficiency operations have put a pressure on content producers to deliver similar goods for lower prices. This in turn, might force them out of the tightly-knit reproductive network of Hilversum, trying their luck in the much more open and creative network of Amsterdam.

Between 2005 and 2009 we have witnessed a move of creative production away from Hilversum to Amsterdam. This shift of more production activities into the capital is not being made up for by the use of better transportation or uses of ICT and the internet. The city is effectively losing production to Amsterdam. Furthermore, the internet-supported networks that used to strengthen – or at least facilitate – the clustering in Hilversum are also moving their focus to Amsterdam, thereby converging with the already existing strong creative and artistic network in the capital. Van Oort et al. (2010) have argued that specialization can certainly lead to positive economic results, but that also holds for sectoral diversity. Diversity can, for instance, be seen as an important source of creativity, innovation and economic revitalization. After all, innovation often follows knowledge spillovers and new associations between existing economic sectors. Urban economic variety then, could well offer a firmer basis for additional economic growth than a strengthening of clustered specialization. So-called related diversification, with different industry branches and sectors that can benefit from each other's presence and proximity, can stimulate economic growth. This then, would call for the establishment of new linkages between the diverse specializations and clusters within the Randstad region (van Oort et al., 2010).

As Hilversum seems to suffer from lock-in and is lacking in self-reinforced innovative capacity, its added value as a cluster in its own right appears to be waning. An active public policy would be needed in order to turn around the exodus of creative productivity to Amsterdam. However, a small town such as Hilversum does not have many means to do so. The current alderman for media affairs explains why there is not much room for growth: 'Amsterdam has a lot of means for attracting young talent, money to develop incubators for example. Our financial means are very limited compared to that' (Ali, 2010). The city's policy is twofold. On the one hand it aims to diversify the media industry in other adjacent sectors. The current policy of the city is more aimed at facilitating, stimulating and developing multi- and cross-media applications, for instance in health care and tourism. The other strategic choice is to collaborate with Amsterdam in the Northwing Region in order to compete internationally with other media clusters such as London and Paris. The latter could be an effective policy away from the view of Hilversum as a stand-alone media cluster towards integration of the broadcasting industry into a much broader cross-media cluster in the Amsterdam region.

The horror scenario for Hilversum would be the departure of content producers and the innovative periphery of firms, leaving only the support and facilities industry and distribution functions. With an active city council trying to turn the tide, and a property developer hoping to sell the Tinseltown glamour, the question remains whether the dinosaur can survive and adapt. New value and economic growth could be generated by the combination and collaboration between industry branches and across economic sectors. Innovative concepts are examples such as serious gaming in health care, which Hilversum has successfully developed. Especially in the context of media, convergence and digitalization can add to the heterogeneity of clusters (Immovator, 2010). But industry branches also need to be tied in to educational and knowledge institutions. Here, public policy plays an important role. Local and regional policymakers could therefore utilize the opportunities that are offered by related diversification. The reinvigoration of Hilversum can only be successful if the mono-disciplinary broadcast cluster can be effectively integrated into the diversified creative, innovative and competitive network of the entire Amsterdam region.

REFERENCES

Ali, H. (2010), 'Media verruilen Hillywood voor Amsterdam', *De Volkskrant*, 1 June 2010, 50.

Bathelt, H. (2001), *The Rise of a New Cultural Products Industry Cluster in Germany: The Case of the Leipzig Media Industry*, Frankfurt, DEU: IWSG Working Papers 06-2001.

Freriks, G. and J.W. Menkveld (2009), *Versterking positie Hilversum Mediastad*, Hilversum, NLD: Two Minds.

Gemeente Hilversum (2007), *Multimedia Land(t)* [Policy document] Hilversum, NLD: Gemeente Hilversum.

Gemeente Hilversum (2010), *Economische Visie Hilversum 2007–2020; Uitvoeringsplan versterking positie Hilversum Mediastad*, Hilversum, NLD: Gemeente Hilversum.

Granovetter, M. (1973), 'The Strength of Weak Ties', *American Journal of Sociology*, **78**(6), 1360–1380.

Groep, R. van der (2004), 'Spatial Clustering and Culture Barriers: An Exploration in the Geography of Audiovisual Firms', paper presented at the City Futures International Conference, 8–10 July 2004.

Hitters, E. (2009), 'Exploring the Creation of Urban Media Clusters in the Creative City', in Alan Albarran, Paulo Faustino and Rogério Santos (eds), *The Media as a Driver of the Information Society. Economics, Management, Policies and Technologies*, Lisbon, PRT: MediaXXI/Formalpress.

Immovator Cross Media Network (2006), *Cross Media Monitor 2006*, Hilversum, NLD: Immovator.

Immovator Cross Media Network (2008), *Cross Media Monitor 2008*, Hilversum, NLD: Immovator.

Immovator Cross Media Network (2010), *Cross Media Monitor 2010*, Hilversum, NLD: Immovator.

Leyshon, A. (2001), 'Time-space (and Digital) Compression: Software Formats, Musical Networks, and the Reorganisation of the Music Industry', *Environment and Planning A*, **33**(1), 49–77.

LISA (database), see http://www.lisa.nl.

Ministry of Education, Culture and Science (2006), *Cultural Policy in the Netherlands*, Amsterdam, NLD: Boekmanstudies.

Oort, F. van, I. van Aalst, M. Burger, B. Lambregts and E. Meijers (2010), *Clusters en netwerkeconomie in de Noordvleugel van de Randstad*, Utrecht, NLD: Universiteit Utrecht.

Ourroussof, N. (2007), 'Heaven, Hell and Purgatory, Encased in Glass', *The New York Times*, 26 May 2007.

Uzzi, B. (1997), 'Social Structure and Competition in Interfirm Networks: The Paradox of Embeddedness', *Administrative Science Quarterly*, **42**(1), 35–67.

Internet Sources

http://www.mediapark.nl/, accessed 7 March 2010.

http://www.tcn.nl/, (address recently changed to www.tcnpp.com), original was accessed 7 March 2010.

6. Microclustering of the media industries in London

Andy C. Pratt

Along with a select number of cities in the world, London is commonly regarded as a centre for media. Like most capital cities it has the headquarters of major media organizations, and it has proximity to national politics and economic power, often the content of news and other media stories. In addition, many of the media organizations are international in scope and networked. However, we have to ask if this means that London has media power. This is a dimension of research that has been overlooked. Generally the symbolic or representational aspect of the media is given priority (even in geography texts, see for example Adams, 2009), where attention paid to the material and economic aspects is shorn of a focus on space and place (see Herman and McChesney, 1997). However, in this chapter the focus is on the socio-economics of organization and operation of media industries, that is corporate or economic power of media organization and activity and on the question whether it makes London a 'media cluster'. This chapter addresses the second of these issues, but additionally suggests that this answer might help to engage with the former question. In particular, in its efforts to describe and understand the concentration of media activity in London, this chapter examines the utility of the cluster model to account for it.

A critical function of any analytical exercise is to reflect upon the key terms and definitions. In this case the chapter is critical of the coherence and utility of the very notion of media industry. The chapter highlights that there are multiple industries with varied structures and organization, as well as markets and technologies, that could sit under the umbrella term 'media'. In addition, they might include relevant and related activities that would not normally be included under technical aspects of production or distribution.[1] I argue that these differences – within media industries and between other media industries and non-media industries – are critical in explaining the locational forms and organization as well as consequences of clustering. Secondly, and related, the chapter is critical of the notion of business clusters in their normal presentation, colocation (Porter, 1996):

we stress the interaction (social and economic) and social action across firms and projects that constitute what we might better term actually existing clusters.

In the discussion I am keen to examine the scale at which clusters might be said to exist. As I outline, the constitutive industries may have an organizational footprint that crosses the globe. Which precise activities are clustered, and at which scale, which are not, which are located in the city and which are not is important. Finally, the chapter stresses the need for subtle and detailed work on the qualitative organization of work and project networks of media organizations and their governance, as well as the tensions and overlaps between them and their workers. We begin the chapter with a discussion of definitions followed by a brief context setting of London and then a more detailed exploration of the spatial scale of clusters in London.

DEFINITIONAL ISSUES

A problem that besets all research, especially in fast-changing areas of technology or economic practice, is definition. The field of the media is a case in point, one that has become more complicated with the technological and organizational convergence that has occurred as the impacts of digitization have unfolded. Clearly, the once separate industries of analogue media (radio, film, television, books, press) have both begun to intersect and transform and to proliferate new industries (so-called new media, computer games, social networks, internet applications and intermediation of any other activity). To complicate matters further, some of these industries already were under intersecting ownership, a process that has been suddenly accelerated by digitization and the scramble for new product markets and audiences.

As a result of both trends the location pattern of media is a problematic question. In such a maelstrom there are further complex questions about the causes and trajectory of media growth. Many have pointed to the articulation with a vastly expanded and rapidly growing cultural and creative economy: this is not simply a case of spillover but real integration that is creating new products; moreover, the direction of causality (that is with the cultural industries or the rest of the economy) and the definition of what the spillover is (economic, social or cultural value; know-how or know-what) remains an important issue. There is strong evidence that the cultural economy is a fully-fledged driver of urban economic fortunes, not simply candy floss. A recent report for the European Commission provides authoritative data on the contribution of the media and creative industries to the economy, jobs and economic growth (KEA European Affairs, 2006). More specifically, in London, data underline the fact that the creative economy has become the third most important economic sector, media industries playing a significant part in this contribution (GLA Economics, 2002).

There are also questions about what clustering might mean in media industries. Traditionally, economic geographers have taken the head office as the locus of power: is this relevant to the media? In a new media environment where project networks are the dominant organizational form, does such a term have the same meaning? Others might point to the notion of the death of distance that might afflict media in cities. On this latter point the research is clear, if anything new media are more rooted in place (Pratt, 2000); moreover, the social relations and social networks that they are embedded in are also critical.

These questions lead us into a tricky empirical field. First, on the issue of definition I would argue that the notion of media industry must be emphatically plural – the media industries, which are necessarily diverse. In that sense, we must attend to the particular industries. Accordingly, this chapter focuses on the film, radio and television industries and the advertising industries; new media and newspapers are also discussed. There are three arguments for the particular subset of industries that are focused on here (although they are different). First, that they do have an interlocking labour market (not overlapping); and secondly, they work in intersecting markets (advertising is used in both film, radio and TV; film, radio and TV are the media of much advertising). Thirdly, as these are older industries they have existing census data taxonomies that allow their identification (albeit partially), something we cannot find for, say, computer games or new media.

Returning to the theoretical sphere, questions can be raised as to the applicability of business cluster theory or simply traditional economics or even economic geography to these industries. As noted above, the organizational form, especially project-based firms, creates quite different business imperatives: markets and users as well as producers have quite different relationships with one another and also space and place. At its simplest the minimization of transaction costs or costs of moving materials is less relevant; arguably, the social and organizational aspects of those items that are normally in the residuals category of economic modelling are centre stage in these industries. This is a further reason why clustering in the media industries does not fit the normal expectations of business cluster theory.

A final question can be asked with regard to global cities and media cities (see Kratke, 2003, 2006; Kratke and Taylor, 2004). The global cities literature implies that advertising, for example, is an advanced producer service that intermediates with finance to enable global city functions. However, first, as has already been noted, the term media is misleading; but, taking advertising as an example, there the problem is that the organizational forms are such that enumerating headquarters does not signify that which it does in other industries (see discussion below). Moreover, there are additional issues about the precise relation of media industries to the financial sector: critically, are they dependent or independent? The traditional view is that they are dependent, and culture is either a consumption lure for finance or manufacturing or a means to market financial products. Evidence is emerging that the media industries, in common with many cultural industries, may be propulsive, not dependent, industries (Pratt, 2008a).

So, there are lots of questions that need to be carefully navigated in any investigation of media industries and the city. Definitions and conceptualizations of what the industry is, and the nature of its relations with other industries, with workers and the wider social, cultural and political fields all matter. For this reason this chapter is rather circumspect and careful in its analysis about the choice of industry and indicators of its activity. The substantive analysis is preceded by some contextualization of media industries in London.

LONDON: THE FIRST MEDIA INDUSTRIES AND THE END OF A CLUSTER

London is a global city, a multi-functional economic hub and site of political and cultural power, constituting a node of many international networks. In this sense one would expect it to be a media centre, if one takes as a definition a concentration of head or strategic offices. The question is: is this necessary or indeed sufficient for a media cluster? The analytic questions would have to resolve on activities. In that sense it would be important to consider which activities are concentrated in London (if not all?): Is it production or consumption or employment and turnover, or is it content sourcing and generation?

Once these questions are posed it becomes clear that any analysis of clustering, or concentration, requires a more fine-grained analysis, moreover, one that is sensitive to the historical dynamics of particular industries. Furthermore, there are questions about which scale we take to measure concentration: the city, the quarter, the ward, the block or street? Is there one cluster or many: are clusters on one or more media industries related to, and constitutive of, the media cluster'? A good introduction to these problems is a survey of the first media industries in London, printing and publishing, in particular newspapers.

It was to London that William Caxton brought his printing press in the late 15th century, his apprentice Wynkyn de Worde setting up the first printing press in Fleet Street in 1500 and later establishing a bookstall in nearby St Paul's churchyard, which became an early locus of the UK book trade. In 1702 the *Daily Courant* established its offices in Fleet Street. Close by, in the mid-18th century, Dr Johnson lived and compiled his first English dictionary. By the mid-20th century Fleet Street was a by-word for the British newspaper industry. It appeared to be an excellent example of an industrial cluster, albeit dominated by a number of large companies (and media barons such as the Lords Beaverbrook, Northcliffe and Rothermere). Clearly, proximity to the City of London and Parliament (more or less equidistant), as well as places to wine and dine sources and to find instant legal advice, proved very accommodating. Perhaps surprisingly, it can be noted that by the 1990s every newspaper had departed from Fleet Street (Wintour, 1989); the death-knell finally sounded in 2005 when the news agency Reuters also departed for Canary Wharf (East London) in London's docklands.

This shift was precipitated by a complex and interlocking set of events. In no small part were the attempts to break union control and to restructure the industry (to save costs) and to move to digital production, all of this in the context of a political agenda by the Thatcher government to destroy the unions.[2] The battering ram to break the unions was News International (the *Times*, *Sun*), which established an integrated production plant at Wapping (inner East London) in 1986. Other newspapers gradually separated printing from newsrooms for the first time: news offices relocating to the discounted rents of Canary Wharf, and printing plants to the regions and outer London (Burns Owens Partnership, 2004). However, a decade later, as the Canary Wharf rent reviews came in and market values were reasserted, news offices (shedding permanent staff and multitasking those that remained) once again moved: in recent years we have seen moves to Victoria (the *Telegraph*), Kensington (the *Mail* and the *Independent* share a site) and King's Cross (the *Guardian*). At the time of writing only the *Mirror* and the news agency Reuters remain in Canary Wharf; in 2003 the Press Association moved to Howden, a small town near to Leeds, Yorkshire.

So, the lesson is that what appear to be the most robust clusters can break up and move at the drop of a hat. In this case, much of the dispersal has been from one street to other parts of inner London for content production and to the regions and outer London for printing and distribution. However, it is a significant shift. One could point to digital production, to rent levels, to the emergence of web services, to convergence, continuous news and to multitasking. All have a part to play; the whole is a more complex story than there is space to cover here. However, it is fair to point to the fact that unlike most media industries, newspapers tend to lose money, hence their business models are particularly unusual, but then again, compared to the standard manufacturing industry, each media industry is peculiar in its own way. In the rest of this chapter we take a restrictive focus on film, radio, TV and advertising and discuss the notion of clustering in their particular cases.

THE BIG PICTURE

The aim of this section of the chapter is to provide a broader empirical insight into a specific group of clusters of the media industries in London. The analysis begins with a general overview of employment mapping in the film, TV, radio and advertising industries; this is followed by an analysis of the location of firms, which focuses particularly on the micro scale. As will be noted, scale and organization are the motifs of this chapter: we stress the overflowing of particular scales, and the extreme micro-geographies; also, that organizational forms configure location practices and the particular activities undertaken in one cluster or another.

We begin by using employment data from the Annual Business Inquiry, the most comprehensive business census available. However, the analysis is significantly constrained by the fact that the ABI relies on the taxonomy of the standard industrial classification (SIC), which significantly under-represents and presents a partial view of the media industries; in addition its coverage of micro-enterprises is extremely limited.[3] This data source is the default one for the identification of business clusters (see DTI, 2001). The discussion below illustrates how partial the grasp of clustering can be captured in this way.

Bearing the methodological caveats in mind, one can at least grasp the broad pattern of employment concentration in a select group of industries that are covered by the SIC taxonomy. Table 6.1 shows first and foremost that these industries (the closest we can get to the media) are concentrated in London and the South East and East region, but fully half of all those employed are to be found in London, compared to just 15 per cent for other industries. The geography of these industries in the UK beyond the concentration in London is more widely that they have an urban focus, mainly concentrated in the cities of Manchester, Bristol and Glasgow (for TV and radio). Advertising is spread more widely across secondary cities. Film is predominantly a London activity.

Moving down the scales we can see that 41 per cent of total employment in the media industries in the UK is located in Inner London and 11 per

Table 6.1 AFTV industry by sub-sector, % of Great Britain

Area	7440: Advertising	9211: Motion picture and video production	9212: Motion picture and video distribution	9220: Radio and television activities	All AFTV	All Industries
	% employed					
W1 postcode area	9.43	25.87	19.38	7.43	10.88	0.98
Inner London	34.38	51.41	73.08	44.05	41.18	9.15
Outer London	7.80	9.20	7.35	13.37	10.10	6.29
London	42.17	60.62	80.43	57.41	51.28	15.44
London, South East and East	61.27	76.95	88.63	60.90	63.74	38.36
Great Britain	**100.00**	**100.00**	**100.00**	**100.00**	**100.00**	**100.00**

Source: ABI, 2007

cent in just one postcode district (W1[4]). If we were to present a cursory analysis of a media industry cluster via concentration of employment, we surely have it here. However, as I will discuss, such analyses should be considered as a starting point: the material geography of media industries is more complex and fine-grained. The key point that the SIC taxonomy fails to pick up is the specific organization of media industries' production chains; in short, using this data set it is not clear which activities are clustered. Secondly, the SIC categories tend to lump together quite different industries and segments of industries that have different markets and modes of production. Thirdly, as hinted at already, this level of analytical resolution does not provide insight into the very local patterns of these industries. It is to this that I turn next.

THE CLOSE-UP: MICRO CLUSTERS IN INNER LONDON

In order to take the analysis to a different scale, it is necessary to shift both sources and our analytic lens. Instead of employment, it is necessary to focus on the location of enterprises, sourced from industry directories.[5] As with the census, such sources are prone to inaccuracies due to the extraordinarily high turnover of companies in this sector, especially project-based enterprises that may routinely survive less than a year: the length of a project. To minimize this effect, industry trade directories used by practitioners were used as a primary source where there was an incentive to be accurate and timely.

It is not possible to weight these location data by employment, but separately from census data it is known that the average firm size tends to be five or less, or that of an exceptional few of several hundred, added to which are a huge number of freelance workers who do not show up in ABI returns. This section is organized around particular industries: new media (for which there is no SIC classification), radio and television, and film; we begin with advertising.

Advertising

The advertising industry is in many ways central to the media industries cluster in London. Physically it is located in Soho, with an epicentre in Golden Square, but extending north of Oxford Street and east to Tottenham Court Road and Clerkenwell. The majority of companies are within a square of a couple of hundred metres. In terms of their markets, TV and film are critical; media buying is a fundamental aspect of advertising. Moreover, advertising specializes in cutting-edge practice from film and television making. In this sense there is an overlapping labour market (though not precisely the same one, as each discipline has its own skills).

However, the critical issue about the advertising industry is its organizational structure. As is pointed out elsewhere, the advertising industry, although international by name, is in fact embedded in national markets of regulation and media buying, and of audience taste. Moreover, the international groups that dominate the advertising world are very complex amalgams of usually three companies or more that effectively compete against one another.[6] Additionally, there is a degree of vertical disintegration where services are contracted from other companies (media buying, creative services) within the same group (see Grabher, 2001, 2002a, b, c; Pratt, 2006).

At the local scale this means that the industry comprises a large number of small but internationally successful boutique creative companies who have a relatively short life. The (especially creative and executive) staff moves between companies and the larger holding companies as their careers develop. Physical proximity enables this flux, with staff able to effectively work in the same place. Moreover, a critical part of the modality of advertising is reputation. The cut-throat competition that signifies advertising is sustained via close mutual surveillance of all participants.

Thus keen attention is paid to who is doing what, for whom, at all times. Informal information exchange in an industry where everyone works with everyone else takes place in the workplace and in the numerous bars and restaurants where clients are entertained. The most cutting-edge advertising companies have sought to locate away from Golden Square and Soho, and closer to Shoreditch. This represents a convergence of sorts between new media and advertising.

New Media

Non-advertising related new-media activity has continued to increase market share and employment. Although there are no definitive figures for employment (in fact there are no figures, as according to census taxonomies new media, like the computer games industry, do not exist), survey work has highlighted that new media employment is dominated by London, although like advertising it is scattered in a minor way across all major cities. The surprising and significant outlier is the new media cluster in Brighton (Perrons, 2003; Pratt, Gill and Spelthann, 2007). In London the new media industry was itself embedded in, and grew out of, another cluster of fine artists (who constituted the Young British Artists and were themselves critically obsessed with the advertising image). As the new media industry has developed, the art-related activities have remained in the *genius loci* Shoreditch and Spitalfields; the advertising-related activities migrated west to Clerkenwell (see Hutton, 2006; Pratt, 2009; Oakley and Pratt, 2010).

Although starting from quite different roots, London's new media cluster is in part converging with advertising as online advertising has come to such prominence. This is manifest by the incorporation and takeover of a number of new media companies and the specialist development of new media advertising. These companies have tended to not co-locate precisely with old advertising, preferring the Tottenham Court Road area and Clerkenwell, the latter being an area between the City and Soho, and Shoreditch (Hoxton).

Within London, new media is drawn to those whom it works with. This is not as proponents of advanced producer services would imagine, the finance industry. It is in fact old media, and its synergies of work process and expertise that matter most (Pratt et al., 2007). So, the production of film and TV special effects, animation and 'idents'[7] are something that overlaps with the practices of new media businesses and has been a significant part of the changing visual landscape of the media in recent years. Finally, perhaps the most significant grouping of new media expertise in the world, this time under one roof, is to be found in Bush House at

Aldwych (to the south-east of Soho and next to Fleet Street), the home of the BBC World Service, but also the offices of the most read news website in the world: BBC online.

Television and Radio

The clustering of radio and television activities in London is a story of organizational change first and technology second (see Pratt and Gornostaeva, 2009). Inevitably, the location of radio and television has been influenced by the legacy of the public broadcasting service. The BBC, like other national broadcasters, was a fully integrated commissioner, maker and broadcaster of programmes. The location of its radio headquarters was established north of Oxford Circus and its TV centre in west London, Shepherds Bush. The BBC had its own studio space, smaller London theatres commonly being used for live broadcasts that required an audience present. Independent TV had a smaller presence in London, based next to the South Bank arts complex.

Fundamental changes occurred in the wake of regulatory reconfiguration led by the establishment of Channel 4 in 1982; an innovation in TV, in an organizational parallel to the book industry, the channel acted as a publisher only. Channel 4's offices were initially just north of Soho, although latterly have relocated to Victoria. Critically, this regulatory change generated a market for independently produced TV programmes (Darlow, 2004); independent production companies clustered around the commissioning body.

In subsequent years both the BBC and independent TV have followed the C4 model; the BBC has a quota of at least 25 per cent contracted-out programme making. The location of Soho, and a sub-cluster in West London, is attractive to companies to be close to the commissioners. Moreover, in the years since 1998 both independent broadcasters and the BBC have committed to shifting as much as 50 per cent of production spending outside of London. Despite the relic regional structure of broadcasting of the BBC,[8] the shift announced in 2004 for the BBC to relocate programme making in at least two key areas (Sport and Children's TV) to a new Media City in Manchester is dramatic. The implications for both London and Manchester will take many years to become clear.

Regulatory changes at the BBC – the contracting out of programme making – further added to the growth of independent production companies and the clustering around Soho, further facilitated by the concentration of post-production expertise (again, outsourced). In the midst of this the BBC has developed a new TV centre at White City, ironically, the soon-to-be-disused old centre being proposed as a cultural cluster. The other significant shift in the TV landscape is the multichannel environment of digital TV; independent production has further been boosted by this market expansion, as has the establishment of new channels. TV from smaller providers has not all been located in Soho and West London; a significant outlier is Camden in North London, home to, amongst others, MTV.

Film

The story of film in London, as elsewhere, is one of governance and organization change mediating technological shifts. With regard to film, the complex organization of production and changes in ownership and investment patterns complicate the picture. By contrast with TV, film is dominated by international, specifically US, investment and ownership. The reason for US majors locating headquarters in London is rooted in numerous regulatory changes: to dodge quotas and taxation and to benefit from dollar/pound currency fluctuation (Pratt and Gornostaeva, 2009).

Historically, the footprint of film has been bifurcated: one foot in Soho, Wardour Street to be precise, and the other in outer North and West London Studios (for example, Pinewood and Shepperton).[9] The Soho focus has been on distribution and finance. There the story might have ended with the decline of British filmmaking in the 1960s and London a refuge for runaway production (Nachum and Keeble, 2003). However, the US investment happened to be in a series of films requiring special effects. This laid the foundations for a booming digital effects economy in the late 1990s that has projected London to the forefront of digital effects production in the world (Culkin, Morawetz and Randle, 2005); this group of companies is mainly located in Marlborough Street, just south of Oxford Street in Soho.

London companies, both in TV and film, invested in a novel digital infrastructure (Sohonet) that allowed massive capacity transfer of data not only between the burgeoning post-production companies clustered in Soho, but also direct to Hollywood. Moreover, Sohonet, established in 1995, was a private initiative: a classic case of ultra-competitive companies collaborating to enable global competitiveness. This foundation and the continuous reinvestment in skill and technology is perhaps London's greatest asset in the media industries cluster. Whilst the industry is growing (the demand driven by the fact that as much as 80 per cent of the frames in a non-animated film may have some form of digital manipulation added), the workflow is precarious. Recently, a major digital effects studio announced the withdrawal from film to concentrate on advertising as the industry was more stable (Kemp, 2007).

For filmmaking as a whole impermanence is the norm; it has been so especially since the 1990s when project-based firms became a dominant force in the industry. As in TV, film production companies are formed for single projects (in part as a tax-avoidance vehicle), finance and distribution deals are arranged and making begins. The deregulation of labour, as we have already noted in newspapers, has long been a characteristic of film and is now endemic (Blair, 2001; Blair, Grey and Randle, 2001). For freelancers, the need to sustain regular employment leads to a necessity of colocation so that it is possible to move from job to job without massive relocation costs, or for firms, to avoid significant startup costs and long lead times.

DISCUSSION

This chapter has sought to critically examine the notion of media clusters through the empirical example of London's media industries clusters. It has established a number of points. First, that the notion of media industry is problematic. Potentially, such a notion can disguise the significant diversity that exists within the media industries and between them and other industries. In this sense we echo the call of Miège (1987), who argued a similar point for the cultural industries (as opposed to the term coined by Adorno (1991): the culture industry). Within this plural concept I have illustrated considerable variance of experience, organization and form of clustering. Accordingly, in this chapter I chose to highlight particular industries: advertising, film, television and radio, as well as newspapers and publishing and new media.

Thus, in London at least, I argued that analytically there are multiple and overlapping media industries clusters. Moreover, and this is important, the nature of overlap, or interaction, produces a second level of interaction that needs to be analysed. In a very simplistic sense this is the spillover. However, the use of this term in normative literature does not touch upon the complexities of social, cultural, political and economic hybridizations that take place and are constitutive (not simply contextual) of the media industries clusters.

Secondly, this chapter pointed to another critical dimension to the analysis of media industries clusters: scale. Of course, the business clustering literature has been rightly criticized for its empirical imprecision and conceptual vagueness on the issue of scale (Martin and Sunley, 2003). This chapter has underlined very clearly that the media industries are acutely variable in scale and scope of operation, a point that has been underlined by Bathelt and his colleagues (Bathelt, Malmberg and Maskell, 2004; Bathelt, 2005).

Another conclusion to be drawn from this chapter under the heading of scale has to be the extreme micro-geographies of the media industries. Even within industries, I have highlighted differential geographies of, say, studios and post production; I have also pointed to the further differentiation within many aspects of post-production companies that are differentially networked and require different skill sets. The prime example is the film special effects industry that is mainly located in one street; elsewhere we have discussed how this extreme clustering is a source of competitive advantage *vis-à-vis* Los Angeles (Pratt et al., 2007), but also how these micro-geographies facilitate production. Underpinning this is the project-based organization of particular media industries (see Grabher 2002a, b, and c).

In this chapter I have not concentrated on the international linkages (but see Pratt, 2008b); instead I have highlighted both the organizational forms and accompanying regulatory and governance changes that have produced clustering, or, as in the case of publishing and music and to a significant extent newspapers, have dispersed existing clusters. This is a third significant point; I have pointed to the role of regulation in the formation or fragmentation of clusters. On one hand, the example of the newspaper cluster is a case in point with union deregulation leading directly to a fragmentation of a hundreds of years old cluster. This was hand-in-hand with technology but was *not* determined by technology; the change occurred to the legal basis and political support. On the other hand, we can see how the massive TV independent production company cluster of Soho was brought into being through legislation in part in the formation of Channel 4, and in part through changes in the BBC.

A fourth point is the importance of organization of work and labour. It can be noted that those industries that require collective labour to make them happen, ensemble pieces, have retained their need to be clustered. In fact they are tightly clustered because they are ensemble projects that are short life, therefore cannot survive unless there are a lot of similar activities in the same proximity; otherwise an individual cannot work on a semi-continuous basis. Arguably, this can be seen in film, advertising, TV and radio and new media. Notably it can be observed under stress in newspapers. However, the new integrated newsrooms of the *Telegraph* and the *Guardian* are located in one space.

Notably, the book publishing industry and the music industry are key media industries that are absent from obvious clustering in London, although the industries themselves are significant. There is an organization-scale spillover issue to be examined here. In both cases contractually artists are not employed but work on a freelance or single contract basis. So, it is questionable to what extent the internet has been the driver of dispersion, or a more systemic form. In the case of music, there is still clustering of consumption spaces, clubs and concert halls.

It is clear that location of media as discussed above is not a simple one of cheap rents. Soho is a very expensive place to operate from. Even where initially new media companies were in marginal locations they have moved to more expensive ones. It is clear that there must be some advantage to such premier locations; the evidence from wider research is that it is the people, or more precisely it is the social information flow that is critical in maintaining an active reputation economy within and across a number of industries: television, advertising, new media and film. Others have referred to this as buzz; I would see it as a far more specific exchange of very specialist time and culturally potent information based on the reputation of the parties involved. Such information can then potentially be deployed in a future situation to gain advantage. The conclusion to be drawn from the above sketches of various prominent examples of the media industries in London is that there is a complex and overlapping presence that does not really constitute a media cluster. It is an overlapping set of activities that share similar activities and forms but are oriented to quite different markets, audiences and outcomes.

NOTES

1. One has only to watch the credits roll at the end of a film to realize the range of non-media workers that are required to produce a film. The notion of a production chain analysis of media industries seeks to capture the whole industry, rather than restrict itself to the on-screen stars. For a wider discussion of this approach in relation to the cultural industries, see Pratt (1997).
2. This was just two years after the miners' strike.
3. These issues are discussed in more detail in Pratt (1997) and (2004).
4. W1 is central London north and south of Oxford Street: roughly bounded in the south by Piccadilly, the west by Park Lane, the north by Marylebone Road and the east by Tottenham Court Road.
5. In this case the FAME business directory.
6. It is this complex organizational form that undermines the notion equating headquarters functions with global importance (as per the 'global cities' paradigm with respect to media and advertising).
7. Programme and channel identifications and introductions.
8. ITV was more fundamentally a federal organization; however, in the 2000s the structure collapsed. The largest programme making residual was Granada TV, based in Manchester.
9. There is an outlier of film production in North London, Camden; see Gornostaeva (2008).

REFERENCES

Adams, P.C. (2009), *Geographies of Media and Communication: A Critical Introduction*, Malden, MA, USA and Chichester, UK: Wiley-Blackwell.

Adorno, T. (1991), *The Culture Industry: Selected Essays on Mass Culture*, London, UK: Routledge.

Bathelt, H. (2005), 'Cluster Relations in the Media Industry: Exploring the "Distanced Neighbour" Paradox in Leipzig', *Regional Studies*, **39**(1), 105–127.

Bathelt, H., A. Malmberg and P. Maskell (2004), 'Clusters and Knowledge: Local Buzz, Global Pipelines and the Process of Knowledge Creation', *Progress in Human Geography*, **28**(1), 31–56.

Blair, H. (2001), '"You're only as Good as Your Last Job": The Labour Process and Labour Market in the British Film Industry', *Work, Employment and Society*, **15**(1), 149–169.

Blair, H., S. Grey and K. Randle (2001), 'Working in Film – Employment in a Project Based Industry', *Personnel Review*, **30**(2), 170–185.

Burns Owens Partnership (2004), *Understanding the Print and Publishing Sectors in the City Fringe*, London, UK: Corporation of London.

Culkin, N., N. Morawetz and K. Randle (2005), *Facing the Digital Future: Digital Technology and the Film Industry*, Industry Report for FDMX, 2nd edn. Harlow, UK: Film Industry Research Group, University of Hertfordshire Business School.

Darlow, M. (2004), *Independents Struggle: The Rise of the New Media Establishment*, London, UK: Quartet Books.

DTI (2001), *Business Clusters in the UK: A First Assessment*, Report by Trends Business Research, London, UK: Deparment of Trade and Industry.

GLA Economics (2002), *Creativity: London's Core Business*, London, UK: Greater London Authority.

Gornostaeva, G. (2008), 'The Film and Television Industry in London's Suburbs: Lifestyle of the Rich or Losers' Retreat?', *Creative Industries Journal*, **1**(1), 47–71.

Grabher, G. (2001), 'Ecologies of Creativity: The Village, the Group, and the Heterarchic Organisation of the British Advertising Industry', *Environment and Planning A*, **33**(2), 351–374.

Grabher, G. (2002a), 'Cool Projects, Boring Institutions: Temporary Collaboration in Social Context', *Regional Studies*, **36**(3), 205–214.

Grabher, G. (2002b), 'Fragile Sector, Robust Practice: Project Ecologies in New Media', *Environment and Planning A*, **34**(11), 1911–1926.

Grabher, G. (2002c), 'The Project Ecology of Advertising: Tasks, Talents and Teams', *Regional Studies*, **36**(3), 245–262.

Herman, E.S. and R.W. McChesney (1997), *The Global Media: The New Missionaries of Corporate Capitalism*, London, UK and Washington, DC, USA: Cassell.

Hutton, T.A. (2006), 'Spatiality, Built Form, and Creative Industry Development in the Inner City', *Environment and Planning A*, **38**(10), 1819–1841.

KEA European Affairs (2006), *The Economy of Culture in Europe*, Brussels, BEL: European Commission DG5.

Kemp, S. (2007), 'Mill Turns on Management Buyout', *The Hollywood Reporter*, 6 February 2007.

Kratke, S. (2003), 'Global Media Cities in a World-wide Urban Network', *European Planning Studies*, **11**(6), 605–628.

Kratke, S. (2006), '"Global Media Cities": Major Nodes of Globalizing Culture and Media Industries', in Neil Brenner and Roger Keil (eds), *The Global Cities Reader*, Abingdon, UK and New York, NY, USA: Routledge, pp. 325–331.

Kratke, S. and P. Taylor (2004), 'A World Geography of Global Media Cities', *European Planning Studies*, **12**(4), 459–477.

Martin, R. and P. Sunley (2003), 'Deconstructing Clusters: Chaotic Concept or Policy Panacea?', *Journal of Economic Geography*, **3**(1), 5–35.

Miège, B. (1987), 'The Logics at Work in the New Cultural Industries', *Media Culture & Society*, **9**(3), 273–289.

Nachum, L. and D. Keeble (2003), 'Neo-Marshallian Clusters and Global Networks: The Linkages of Media Firms in Central London', *Long Range Planning*, **36**(5), 459–480.

Oakley, K. and A.C. Pratt (2010), 'Brick Lane: Community-driven Innovation', in *Local Knowledge: Case Studies of Four Innovative Places,* NESTA Research Report: March 2010, London, UK: National Endowment for Science, Technology and the Arts, pp. 28–39.

Perrons, D. (2003), 'The New Economy and the Work Life Balance. A Case Study of the New Media Sector in Brighton and Hove', *Gender, Work & Organisation*, **10**(1), 65–93.

Porter, M.E. (1996), 'Competitive Advantage, Agglomeration Economies, and Regional Policy', *International Regional Science Review*, **19**(1)–(2), 85–90.

Pratt, A.C. (1997), 'The Cultural Industries Production System: A Case Study of Employment Change in Britain, 1984–91', *Environment and Planning A*, **29**(11), 1953–1974.

Pratt, A.C. (2000), 'New Media, the New Economy and New Spaces', *Geoforum*, **31**(4), 425–436.

Pratt, A.C. (2004), 'Mapping the Cultural Industries: Regionalization; the Example of South East England', in Allen J. Scott and Dominic Power (eds), *Cultural Industries and the Production of Culture*, Abingdon, UK and New York, NY, USA: Routledge, pp. 19–36.

Pratt, A.C. (2006), 'Advertising and Creativity, A Governance Approach: A Case Study of Creative Agencies in London', *Environment and Planning A*, **38**(10), 1883–1899.

Pratt, A.C. (2008a), 'Cultural Commodity Chains, Cultural Clusters, or Cultural Production Chains?', *Growth and Change*, **39**(1), 95–103.

Pratt, A.C. (2008b), 'L'apport Britannique à la Compréhension des Fonctions Créatives dans les Villes Globales (Questioning the Relationship between Advanced Producer Services, the Cultural Industries and Global Cities)', in Frédéric Leriche, Sylvie Daviet, Mariette Sibertin-Blanc and Jean-Marc Zuliani (eds), *L'économie Culturelle et ses Territoires*, Toulouse, FRA: Presses Universitaires du Mirail, pp. 257–267.

Pratt, A.C. (2009), 'Urban Regeneration: From the Arts "Feel Good" Factor to the Cultural Economy: A Case Study of Hoxton, London', *Urban Studies*, **46**(5)–(6), 1041–1061.

Pratt, A.C., R.C. Gill and V. Spelthann (2007), 'Work and the City in the E-society: A Critical Investigation of the Sociospatially Situated Character of Economic Production in the Digital Content Industries in the UK', *Information, Communication & Society*, **10**(6): 922–942.

Pratt, A.C. and G. Gornostaeva (2009), 'The Governance of Innovation in the Film and Television Industry: A Case Study of London, UK', in Andy C. Pratt and Paul Jeffcutt (eds), *Creativity, Innovation and the Cultural Economy*, Abingdon, UK and New York, NY, USA: Routledge, pp. 119–136.

Wintour, C. (1989), *The Rise and Fall of Fleet Street*, London, UK: Hutchinson.

7. Munich's media cluster at the crossroads

Harald Bathelt

In the context of this book, this chapter investigates the case of a large well-established media cluster in Munich, Germany – in particular its TV and film industry – that was shaken by economic crises and restructuring processes at the turn of the millennium. The consequences of these ruptures have had a strong impact on the regional economy and have drawn attention to ways in which the cluster can maintain its importance, regain momentum and reorient itself towards wider networks of media production.

In the post-World War II period, Munich grew into a major centre of media industries in Germany and Europe, with a particular focus on TV and film production. The first goal of this chapter is to document that growth and shed light on the processes and structures underlying the cluster's development. The analysis will focus on the impact of private broadcasters, the role of a supportive institutional infrastructure and the nature of interaction and communication networks. In exploring the developments of the past decade, the chapter will further show that the unprecedented growth in Munich was followed by an unexpected crisis since the turn of the millennium (Bathelt and Gräf, 2008; Zademach, 2009). The second goal of this chapter is to analyse the main factors that led the region to shift from growth to crisis. It will be argued that the combined effects of the recent advertising crisis and the dissolution of the Kirch Group reinforced pre-existing internal weaknesses and rigidities related to the lack of reflexive, interconnected communication and interaction patterns. Although recent restructuring activities have corrected for some of the undesirable structures that were previously established, this study argues that the crisis remains far from being resolved.

After the turn of the millennium, drastic reductions in advertising expenditures, together with the crisis of the Kirch Group – one of the dominant media consortiums in the German TV and film industry – deeply affected the Munich TV and film industry. First, the Kirch Group, which was originally established and controlled by media entrepreneur Leo Kirch, ran into severe financial difficulties related to a variety of structural problems and failures. These were due to false expectations in pay TV, the financial losses of private broadcasting channels, the acquisition of overpriced film rights for sporting events, overly hierarchical decision-making structures centred on Leo Kirch (who died in 2011), and a tendency towards closed, over-integrated group networks (*Frankfurter Rundschau*, 2002a). When the Kirch Group was eventually dissolved in 2002 (*Frankfurter Allgemeine Zeitung*, 2002, 2003a), many people lost their jobs, and bankruptcies, and restructuring activities and management buy-outs became prevalent. Secondly, the media economy suffered a devastating blow as a result of the drastic reduction in advertising expenditures throughout many sectors of the economy (*Frankfurter Allgemeine Zeitung*, 2003b). This advertising crisis (Jentsch, 2004) had far-reaching implications for the media sector (Beck, 2002) and further compounded the impact of the Kirch crisis.

This chapter analyses the structures and processes that left the media economy in Munich vulnerable to such crises, paying particular attention to the internal and external communication and interaction networks of the TV and film industry cluster (Bathelt and Gräf, 2006). The argument presented draws from a broad understanding of a regional value-chain-based cluster definition that emphasizes the importance of combining local networks, or 'buzz', and trans-local and global linkages, or 'pipelines' (Porter, 1990; Malmberg and Maskell, 2002; Bathelt, 2002; Bathelt, Malmberg and Maskell, 2004; Picard, 2008).

The empirical part of the analysis is based on extensive fieldwork conducted between July 2002 and August 2004 in the city of Munich and its surrounding county, which we refer to as the Munich region. This fieldwork includes explorative interviews with experts, unstructured field observations and semi-structured interviews. A total of 65 interviews were conducted with actors from different parts of the TV and film industry value chain (Bathelt and Gräf, 2008). This includes interviews with five TV broadcasters, 24 production firms, 16 post-production and service firms, 16 freelancers and four media organizations/associations. Additional information was acquired through explorative interviews with media experts and planners in the region.

The remainder of this chapter is structured as follows. The next section begins by describing the historical development of the TV and film industry in Munich in the context of the changing media landscape in Germany. The third section analyses the structure and size of today's media economy, and the fourth section identifies the major growth engines of the TV and film industry cluster. The fifth section investigates ownership patterns and associated segmentation in the cluster, while the sixth section focuses on the fragmented networks and communication patterns that have resulted from this. The seventh and eighth sections explore linkages with and potential spillovers to other media clusters in Germany and other countries before the ninth section concludes with a discussion of the likelihood of reinvigorating the Munich media cluster in the future. The tenth section finally draws some policy implications.

HISTORICAL DEVELOPMENT OF THE TV AND FILM INDUSTRY

Favourable conditions for the development of the media industry in Munich were established early on due to the competencies of local industries that were successful in developing fine mechanical and optical products (Biehler, Genosko, Sargl and Sträter, 2003). In fact, by the early 20th century, innovations in these industries had already led to numerous small start-ups in the film industry. Some of these firms, such as Münchener Lichtspielkunst AG (now known as Bavaria Film production/studios) and ARRI (a leading producer of film cameras), became major players in the German film industry during the 'Roaring Twenties'. Munich was initially considered a prime location for shooting Western movies because of the rocky landscape just south of the city. While Berlin, with its famous UFA studios, remained the undisputed centre of German filmmaking until the end of World War II, Munich established itself as an important production site for many high-quality feature films (Horak, 1996).

Following the collapse of Hitler's Nazi regime and the appropriation of Berlin's UFA Studios by the Soviet Union, Munich became the leading location for the film industry in West Germany. This was partially due to the region's well-established infrastructure for film production, left over from the pre-World War II period. When the Allies introduced a decentralized network of public broadcasting stations that were run as regional monopolies according to the British model, Munich became the location of the Bayerischer Rundfunk (BR) (Beck, 2002). Organizations such as the Institute for Broadcasting Technology, the Academy of TV and Film Munich, the Bavarian Academy of Television and the Bavarian Film and TV Fund also created a supportive institutional basis for the industry. Indeed, these organizations represent key elements in Munich's development into the dominant centre of the TV and film industry in Germany (Biehler, Genosko, Sargl and Sträter, 2003).

In the 1960s and 1970s, the Munich region benefited from a steady – albeit moderately paced – growth of the public broadcasting system. The introduction of the so-called dual broadcasting system in 1984, which led to the formation of private commercial TV stations, turned out to be a major impulse for growth in the region (Beck, 2002). Following the introduction of this system, several private broadcasters and production firms were established in the region (van den Berg, Braun and van Winden, 2001). At the centre of these activities was the Kirch group, which quickly grew into a major consortium of media activities in Germany. It included broadcasters such as Sat.1, ProSieben, the pay TV channel Premiere, Kabel1, the sports channel DSF, and the news channel N24, as well as production firms (e.g. ndF – neues deutsches Fernsehen) and other industry-related activities (*Frankfurter Rundschau*, 2002a, 2002b).

With the advertising and Kirch crises in the early 2000s, Munich's long period of steady growth in the TV and film industry ended abruptly. The impact of these crises differed, however, across the various segments of the TV and film industry. Private broadcasting companies were hit particularly hard, many being forced to end their involvement in experiments with new TV formats and to limit the number of contracts signed for the production of new TV films. Instead of seeking out new TV films and programmes with innovative content, low-budget TV series and shows were extended and older productions or licensed films repeated. Of course, the whole supplier sector of the TV and film industry was also affected by the crises. As the number of film-related projects declined, many firms reduced the number of permanent positions and, instead, hired former employees on a contract basis as freelancers. Production firms that were closely associated with the private broadcasters also fell under serious cost-cutting pressures as the number of new productions decreased and budgets for external production contracts dropped – a situation that led to downsizing and reorientation processes. In addition, it became more difficult for independent producers and film distributors to obtain finance for new projects from banks. This was a result of the so-called 'Basel II' accord, in which banks demanded stricter requirements and greater security from firms in exchange for loans – a situation that became even worse with the global financial crisis in 2008/2009 (Bank for International Settlements, 2010).

The historical development of the Munich TV and film industry defies easy characterization; it cannot be simply referred to as a spontaneous, self-generated cluster or as a planned cluster created through industry or government agencies (Picard, 2008). Instead, the Munich cluster exhibits a hybrid structure that combines planned and directed elements with more spontaneous developments. The institutional set-up and original locational choices of broadcasters in Munich were based on political decisions that favoured the Bavarian capital. Provincial and local governments also played an important role in establishing a supportive institutional structure for the industry. Additionally, the development of media centres and greenfield sites in areas such as Geiselgasteig and Unterföhring was

Table 7.1 Number of establishments in selected German media industry clusters, 1998/1999

Media branch	Number of establishments					
	Germany 1998	Munich 1998	Cologne 1998	Hamburg 1998	Berlin 1998	Leipzig 1999
Film	6880	910	502	531	752	31
TV/ radio	2081	168	165	45	165	12
Publishing	15,183	1475	855	744	797	182
Advertising	25,461	1700	1364	1547	1147	278
News agencies/ journalists	2095	273	229	163	144	96
Total	51,700	4526	3115	3030	3005	599

Sources: Based on Deutsches Institut für Wirtschaftsforschung, 1999; Krätke and Scheuplein, 2001; Statistisches Landesamt des Freistaates Sachsen, 2001; Bathelt, 2002, p. 593.

greatly supported by regional policy programmes to develop media parks and support the sector. Shifts in public policy also provided the grounds for private broadcasters, which grew quickly with the rise of the Kirch Group. The growth of the latter was, however, largely spontaneous and not specifically triggered by policy initiatives (Bathelt and Gräf, 2006; Mossig, 2006).

ROLE OF THE TV AND FILM INDUSTRY WITHIN THE MEDIA CLUSTER

The post-World War II economic growth and the crises of the early 2000s both feature prominently in the economic data sets of Munich's media economy. The data clearly demonstrate that Munich is the largest and strongest centre of the TV and film industry in Germany today, challenged only by Cologne, Berlin and Hamburg (Gräf, Hallati and Seiwert, 2001; Ernst & Young, 2006). Of the 51,700 media establishments in Germany in 1999, more than 4500 were located in Munich, followed by Cologne, Hamburg and Berlin with about 3000 establishments each (Table 7.1). A similar pattern emerges when we compare the industry's sales data (Deutsches Institut für Wirtschaftsforschung, 1999; Krätke and Scheuplein, 1999). Altogether, Munich had a fully developed media economy in 1999 with more than 90,000 full-time and part-time employees and 37,000 freelancers, accounting for overall sales of €19.5 billion (Table 7.2).

Table 7.2 Employees and sales in Munich's media economy, 1999

Media sector	Full-/part-time employees		Freelancers		Sales	
	Number	Share (%)	Number	Share (%)	€ million	Share (%)
Print media	44,750	50	8821	24	8272.7	43
Audiovisual media	21,704	24	14,941	40	7426.0	38
Multimedia	5282	6	1457	4	725.0	4
Advertising	17,539	19	11,284	30	2901.6	15
Information services	846	1	604	2	128.8	1
Total	90,121	100	37,107	100	19,454.1	101

Note: The numbers are estimates from a commercial survey conducted on behalf of the Industrie- und Handelskammer für München und Oberbayern and Landeshauptstadt München.

Source: Based on Industrie- und Handelskammer für München und Oberbayern and Landeshauptstadt München, 2003, pp. 8–9.

Although the Munich media economy was dominated by print media (with about 42–43 per cent of overall employment and sales in the sector in 1999), audiovisual media – particularly the TV and film industry – were also important with a share of 29 per cent of total employment and 38 per cent of sales. Table 7.2 demonstrates that the Munich economy hosted a broad range of media activities including a substantial advertising and information services industry, which contributed to a diversified regional media economy. From 1995 to 1999, the number of media firms in the region grew by 32 per cent, with an increase in sales of 40 per cent (Table 7.3). The audiovisual/multimedia industry was the fastest growing segment of this sector, with an increase of 55 per cent and 74 per cent in the number of firms and in sales, respectively.

By the late 1990s, the advertising crisis had already begun to unfold – the effects of which became increasingly apparent after 2000 (Tables 7.3 and 7.4). In fact, by the mid-2000s, the combined effects of both crises were clearly visible. Between 2000 and 2004, sales in the regional TV and film industry (not including advertising) decreased by 19.2 per cent, from €8.0 to 6.5 billion (Table 7.4), while sales in advertising declined by a third. In terms of the number of establishments, however, the effects of the crises were less visible. Although the number of advertising agencies in the region remained almost constant in the early 2000s, the overall number of media establishments increased by about 500 (Table 7.5). This

Table 7.3 Development of firms and sales in Munich's media economy, 1995–1999

Media sector	Number of firms			Sales in EUR million		
	1995	1999	Growth (%)	1995	1999	Growth (%)
Print media/ information services	2074	2489	20	5777.6	7674.5	33
Audiovisual/ multimedia	1545	2392	55	4550.5	7899.4	74
Advertising	3078	3974	29	2505.3	2423.5	−3
Total	6697	8855	32	12,833.4	17,997.4	40

Note: The numbers are estimates from a commercial survey conducted on behalf of the Industrie- und Handelskammer für München und Oberbayern and Landeshauptstadt München.

Source: Based on Industrie- und Handelskammer für München und Oberbayern & Landeshauptstadt München, 2003, p. 10.

Table 7.4 Sales in the Munich TV, film and advertising industry, 2000–2004

Media branch	Sales in € million			
	2000	2001	2003	2004
Broadcasting[1]	2687.3	3475.0[2]	3352.0	3457.9
TV and film production/ post-production	2664.0	2213.9	2194.9	2105.9
Film distribution/other services	2536.7	2626.1	847.3	776.8
Advertising	2118.9	1710.1	1244.0	1404.0
News agencies/journalists	123.7	134.8	128.6	131.0
Total	10,130.6	10,159.9	7766.8	7875.6

Note:
1. Public broadcasters are not included.
2. Due to the merger of the private broadcasters ProSieben and Sat.1 into the ProSiebenSat.1 Media AG, sales in Munich's broadcasting sector increased by ca.€850 million in 2001. Prior to 2001, Sat.1 used to be headquartered in Berlin.

Sources: Computed from Bayerisches Landesamt für Statistik und Datenverarbeitung, 2006; Bathelt and Gräf, 2008, p. 1945.

Table 7.5 Number of establishments in the Munich TV, film and advertising industry, 2000–2004

Media branch	Number of establishments			
	2000	2001	2003	2004
Broadcasting	43	48	54	51
TV and film production/ post-production	953	987	1020	1043
Film distribution/other services	116	105	110	104
Advertising	1980	1979	1973	2084
News agencies/journalists	1391	1409	1494	1647
Total	4483	4528	4651	4929

Sources: Computed from Bayerisches Landesamt für Statistik und Datenverarbeitung, 2006; Bathelt & Gräf, 2008, p. 1945.

was, in part, due to an increase in the number of TV and film production and post-production establishments from 953 to 1043 between 2000 and 2004. Our interviews suggest that this increase was likely due to a tendency towards vertical disintegration and the transfer of permanent employment into freelancing relationships (see also Industrie- und Handelskammer für München und Oberbayern and Landeshauptstadt München, 2003).

In terms of size, the Munich TV and film industry cluster exhibits considerable diversity. On the one hand, it is dominated by large leading media firms such as the private and public broadcasters, major film production firms, important post-production firms, producers of film equipment and leading distributors. On the other hand, most of the media establishments are small in size with only a few employees (Biehler, Genosko, Sargl and Sträter, 2003). This finding is also supported by the size structure of the firms in the survey. Of the firms interviewed, most were small or medium-sized establishments, with 62 per cent having ten or fewer employees and only 12 per cent having more than 100 employees (Table 7.6).

Overall, it can be concluded that the post-World War II growth of the TV and film industry and other media branches has contributed to the development of a major media cluster in Munich. Not only is Munich the largest media cluster in Germany (Table 7.1), it has also developed into a world media city in terms of its size and diversity (Krätke and Taylor, 2004). The substantial agglomeration of media firms in the region, combined with a highly qualified labour market, has enabled TV, film production, advertising and other media firms to quickly assemble their project teams and react flexibly to the challenges of complex project

Table 7.6 Number of firms interviewed in the Munich TV and film industry by size, 2002/2004

Number of employees	Interviews conducted	
	Number	Share (%)
1–10	40	62
11–50	11	17
51–100	6	9
> 100	8	12
Total	65	100

Source: Bathelt and Gräf, 2006, p. 29.

tasks (Grabher, 2002a, 2002b; von Bernuth and Bathelt, 2007). Not surprisingly, a study conducted for the Industrie- und Handelskammer für München und Oberbayern and Landeshauptstadt München (2003) found that media firms emphasized the labour market, proximity to other relevant agents and image factors as key advantages of their location. According to this study, 69 per cent of all media firms were quite pleased with the skill levels in the regional labour market, while 62 per cent emphasized the availability of staff. In terms of identifying Munich's specific regional advantages, 86 per cent of the firms cited proximity to other firms, 78 per cent referred to proximity to suppliers/service firms and 75 per cent mentioned proximity to customers. In sum, 85 per cent thought that the Munich media economy had a very good or good image for their activities.

ENGINES OF THE TV AND FILM INDUSTRY CLUSTER

The TV and film industry in Munich can be characterized as a well-developed cluster along multiple cluster dimensions, namely the horizontal, vertical and institutional cluster dimensions (Gräf, 2005; Mossig, 2006). In terms of its vertical structure, the region hosts almost complete value chains of TV and film production. This offers manifold opportunities to establish local producer–user relationships and select project partners from within the close vicinity. This structure generates opportunities for communication and knowledge exchange in a vertical direction along the value chain. Although the potential for extended horizontal relationships between competing firms with similar capabilities is not equally high in all parts of the value chain, plenty of rivalry exists between local film directors, actors, production firms, lighting and camera specialists, film cutters and post-production specialists. All in all, this provides the basis for learning by interacting, comparison and observation (DeFillippi and Arthur, 1998). Additionally, other media branches, such as advertising, multimedia and print media, offer multiple opportunities for cross-fertilization, the development of new innovative projects, and sector-wide learning. At the institutional level, moreover, the region boasts a wide range of specialized education and training facilities, as well as financial instruments that can be mobilized to support TV and film projects. Despite these advantages, the Munich TV and film industry remains underdeveloped in terms of the global relationships dimension – an issue discussed in more detail below (Bathelt and Gräf, 2008).

Within the Munich cluster, a number of firms and organizations play a dominant role as engines of the growth process. These agents encompass private firms, governmental agencies/programmes and, to a lesser extent, private developers. First, private firms have been the key drivers of economic growth due to their size, expansion strategies and/or networking capabilities. These dominant agents include the former Kirch Group and its various operations and firms, private broadcasters (e.g. RTL II, ProSieben and Sat.1), public broadcasters (especially BR), well-known private and public production firms (e.g. Bavaria Film production, ndF), sophisticated producers of technical equipment (e.g. ARRI), major German distributors (e.g. Constantin) and international post-production networks (e.g. the former Werk Group). Some of the firms have multiple functions within their value chain, such as being a supplier of technical products as well as a film producer. All of them developed strong network linkages with a substantial local basis through which they were able to impact the broader regional development.

Secondly, government agencies, business associations and their specific programmes/activities have also played an important role in the growth of the cluster. Their role was primarily supportive rather than generative. These agencies encompass specialized training facilities, headquarters of national organizations and associations, film festivals and financing programmes, including an important German film fund with explicit local content regulations. Further support was derived from the city's economic development agency, all of which contributed to a favourable local business climate (Industrie- und Handelskammer für München und Oberbayern and Landeshauptstadt München, 2003).

Thirdly, the role of private developers was less prominent and often went hand in hand with municipal policies. It was facilitative in nature and produced opportunities for media developments in former army barracks

(Stetten barracks), older manufacturing cores (the Loden-Frey area) and greenfield sites (e.g. Unterföhring).

In terms of its operational structure, the Munich TV and film industry cluster is characterized by a hybrid nature (Picard, 2008). On the one hand, cooperative modes of interaction are prominent within the cluster through various project endeavours that often have a substantial regional basis. These activities have developed into project networks (Sydow and Staber, 2002), which are partially exclusive and establish particular segments of value chains that do not (or hardly) overlap. This will become clear when analysing segmentation and fragmentation patterns in the next sections. On the other hand, this segmentation leads to practices of inclusion and exclusion that resemble managed networks, especially in the areas of public and private broadcasting. Here, the broadcasters direct and control the performance and outcome of TV-related projects. A similar structure emerges from film projects, which are typically hierarchically structured (DeFillippi and Arthur, 1998).

SEGMENTATION AND OWNERSHIP

As suggested above, the Munich TV and film industry cluster is based on a project mode of interaction and governance with hierarchical, network and market elements (von Bernuth and Bathelt, 2007). Although many projects, especially those centred on TV shows and films, have a strong regional component (Mossig, 2006), this does not imply that communication and interaction patterns are open and diversified, encompassing the whole cluster. In fact, previous research has found that existing value chains are extremely segmented (Gräf, 2005). Through this, exclusive communication channels have become established instead of a region-wide information and communication ecology or broad local buzz (Storper and Venables, 2004; Bathelt, Malmberg and Maskell, 2004). Segmentation tendencies occur along three dividing lines: according to (i) media branches, (ii) TV formats and (iii) broadcasting groups (Bathelt and Gräf, 2006).

(i) Segments of projects and project networks that do not systematically overlap can be found in media branches such as TV, film production and advertising. Although the projects in these branches, at least partially, share similar tasks (e.g. filming, lighting, programming, cutting or post-production), value-chain-specific contexts exist which are associated with different standards, expectations, problem-solving activities and routines. Over time, this has encouraged individuals to become increasingly specialized, resulting in a fragmentation of the labour market between media branches.

(ii) Similar segmentation patterns can be found between different TV formats, such as TV film, documentary, series or shows. Despite the fact that many of the tasks involved are similar, the specific practices of camera and lighting specialists differ in terms of their focus. Different TV formats require specific technical skills and vary in terms of creativity, organization and sequence. This, in turn, leads to exclusive labour market segments.

(iii) A third line of segmentation occurs along the different broadcasting groups and is linked to their ownership status. It leads to a separation between the value chains of private and public broadcasting services due to implicit or even explicit codes of conduct that restrict interaction practices. There are two broadcasting groups in the Munich TV industry which have developed their own producer and supplier networks: on the one hand, private broadcasters that are primarily related to the former Kirch Group, including, for example, ProSieben, Sat.1, Kabel1, Premiere and RTL II and, on the other hand, public broadcasters such as BR, a ZDF branch, and Bavaria Film production/studios. Their networks are mutually exclusive and could be classified as quasi-integrated groups, similar to the configuration of economic networks described by Leborgne and Lipietz (1991). This means that certain script writers, production firms, camera specialists and film cutters almost exclusively work in the context of private TV broadcasters, while others are part of the public broadcasters' networks, with little overlap.

Due to the effects of the advertising and Kirch crises, however, the exclusive character of the project networks of the broadcasting groups has begun to dissolve in recent years. As decreasing advertising expenditures and cost-cutting pressures have led to a reorientation and restructuring of many firms, some have made steps to operate in wider market segments and crossed formerly exclusive value-chain boundaries (Bathelt and Gräf, 2008). Production companies, such as ndF, which was once closely tied to the Kirch Group, aim to conduct business with all broadcasters and cover the entire market. Key actors such as the Bavaria Film studios could play an important role in the process of creating more diversified, variegated project networks in the future because they conduct business with each of the segments. The process of opening up rigid networks has also received support from new financial investors after the Kirch crisis (Zademach, 2009).

CONNECTEDNESS AND LOCAL FRAGMENTATION

Networks of communication and information flows in Munich seem to be stronger and more diversified than in many other German media centres (e.g. Bathelt, 2002; Krätke, 2002; Mossig, 2004, 2006). This is due to the extended vertical and horizontal dimensions of the Munich cluster and the existence of long value chains. In basically every stage of TV and film production, we find a substantial number of firms, suppliers and service providers (Gräf, 2005). Local information and communication practices are not, however, as open and robust as one might expect from this structure. In fact, segmentation tendencies lead to fragmented communication patterns through which knowledge exchange and circulation are hampered.

Overall, the firms in the TV and film industry benefit less from local buzz than expected (Storper and Venables, 2004; Bathelt, Malmberg and Maskell, 2004). Many of our interviewees mentioned that they have relatively little contact with specialists in the region and rarely go to trendy bars or cafes, which are known as important meeting places for the media. Most mentioned that they primarily depend on the personal networks that they or their close colleagues have established over time in order to get new information about their industry and customers. Although information exchange with such colleagues was said to be quite regular, it was neither fully systematic nor ubiquitous. It seemed exceptionally strong within particular 'communication islands' and was usually restricted to such spaces. According to our interviews, industry-related information or knowledge does not easily travel to other localities and networks in the region due to a lack of communication and the fact that unintended, less organized meetings or interactions only rarely occur. As indicated below, this has led to fragmented communication patterns in the region.

(i) Media Park Unterföhring: In Unterföhring – north of the city – there is an important concentration of media establishments consisting of firms such as ProSiebenSat.1 Media AG, BR and parts of the Bavaria Film studios (Figure 7.1). Despite their close proximity to one another, there is hardly any interaction between the employees of these firms. Even during daytime, the area appears almost deserted. The Media Park Unterföhring is characterized by a high degree of anonymity and lacks public meeting places such as street cafes or restaurants where individuals can interact. When employees do meet, it tends to be in the mornings and evenings when they are rushing to or from work with little opportunity to engage with one another. The only local linkages that we detected were between the broadcasters and some of the production firms that were part of their network (e.g. between BR and Megahertz or between ProSieben and SZM).

(ii) Geiselgasteig: The Bavaria Filmstadt in Geiselgasteig is also characterized by a large concentration of TV- and film-related firms, including smaller broadcasters (e.g. RTL II, Tele 5), numerous studios for TV and film production (e.g. Bavaria Film studios), Bavaria Film pro-

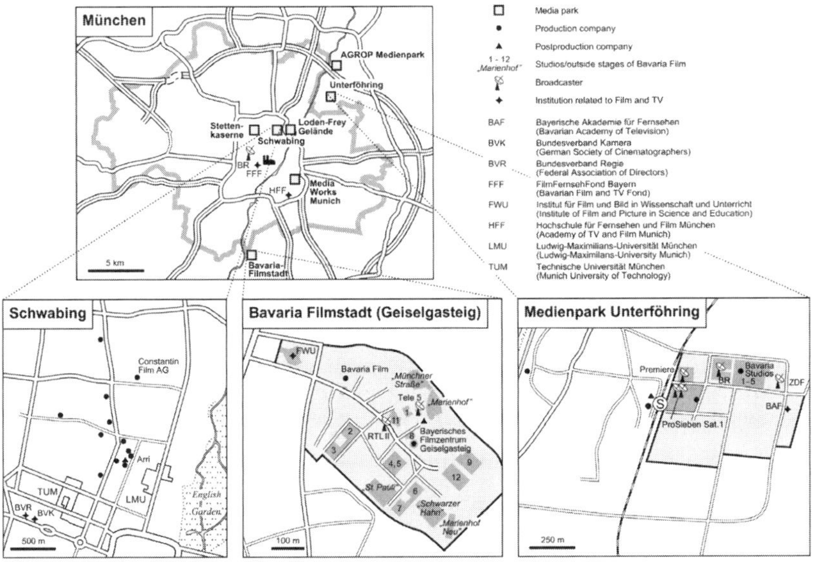

Source: Reproduced from Bathelt and Gräf, 2008, p. 1956 with permission granted by Pion Ltd, London.

Figure 7.1 Location of important firms and organizations in the Munich TV and film industry, 2006

duction and other independent film producers (Figure 7.1). At first glance, Geiselgasteig – south of Munich – appears to be more open than Unterföhring. For instance, there are meeting places such as cafes and places where people from different firms can sit together and have lunch. Our interviewees confirmed that this location was more conducive to interpersonal communication and interaction than Unterföhring. Sometimes, people would meet in the streets, chat and exchange information. Our interviewees also pointed out the limitations to such exchanges, however, as some of the core firms, including RTL II and Tele 5, remained insular in their activities and tended to ignore others.

(iii) Communication islands: In contrast to these sites, we discovered other local communication islands (e.g. TV Werk, parts of Schwabing and, at an early stage, the former Stetten barracks and the Loden-Frey area) (Figure 7.1) where intensive, wider communication patterns existed (Gräf, 2005). Such areas appeared trendy to media people and open to frequent exchange between the people who work there. Based on the interviews conducted, these communication islands were like second homes to employees, some of which would spend extended hours at their workplaces and seemed to be without strong family ties. At the same time, however, it seemed that these locations did not interact intensively with other areas in Munich and were fairly isolated, thus contributing to fragmented patterns in communication.

LINKAGES WITH OTHER GERMAN MEDIA CLUSTERS AND CROSS-SECTORAL SPILLOVERS

Overall, Munich's TV and film industry cluster is mostly dominated by domestic firms, with few branches of global media groups. The dominant groups and large firms typically have sister establishments or subsidiaries in other German media cities, such as Cologne, Berlin and Leipzig, through which important knowledge flows are established and partners for new projects recruited. Within the decentralized network of public broadcasters in Germany, such interaction and exchange have become formalized through agreements about the structure of TV content, a division of labour in content production, the exchange of TV formats and the collaboration with partners in TV projects. According to this research, many of the small firms and freelancers that were not bound to a specific broadcaster were also connected to other domestic media centres through project networks, personal networks and/or acquaintances.

Aside from these patterns of cooperation, however, competition also existed between the media groups headquartered in different cities. Rivalry was especially pronounced between the RTL-Bertelsmann Group centred in Cologne (Mossig, 2004) and the former Kirch Group in Munich. This rivalry also included their respective partner networks. Furthermore, strong competition existed between the private broadcasters and the public broadcasting networks across the German media clusters (Gräf, Hallati and Seiwert, 2001). Relocation tendencies from Munich to Berlin, which were supposedly a threat at some point after the German Reunification, were not very strong at the time of this study. Previous trends to move from Munich to Berlin did not continue and were, in fact, partially reversed, as indicated by the decision of SAT.1 in 2008 to move their headquarters from Berlin to Munich (*Die Welt*, 2008). While some members of the industry are still likely to move to Berlin (e.g. actors, writers or content producers), others have returned to Munich after spending only a few years in Berlin.

Whereas film projects tended to have a systematic interregional component in terms of the recruitment of partners, TV productions and shows often had a stronger regional basis. Intersectoral linkages between different segments of the media economy were also evident but remained fairly weak (for instance between advertising and TV production). While intersectoral linkages have become an important factor in the growth trajectory of the Hollywood media cluster – encouraging the establishment of an integrated entertainment complex (Scott, 2002) – the Munich media cluster does not reveal similar developments. The tendencies that existed in the 1990s of establishing new linkages between different media sectors, such as information technology and audiovisual media in the area of digitalization (van den Berg, Braun and van Winden, 2001), have not developed further.

Despite economic pressures, sources of additional finance through cross-sectoral linkages were not exploited by the Munich TV and film industry (Bathelt and Gräf, 2006). Indeed, with the exception of the Bavaria Filmstadt in Geiselgasteig, merchandising activities were apparently relatively rare. Even successful production firms exhibited a low variety of merchandising products and sold only small quantities of videos or DVDs to the public. One problem, according to our interviewees, was that merchandising rights were rarely in the hands of the production firms. But even the broadcasters did not systematically expand and advertise merchandising products. Such activities were obviously in an infant stage and the potential benefits were widely underestimated. Broader networks that would combine the TV and film industry with music production were also not very strong. Overall, there were no tendencies towards the development of a coherent entertainment complex in Munich.

INTERNATIONAL LINKAGES

As emphasized in the cluster literature, the economic success of clusters often depends on the development of strong international or global linkages, or pipelines, that provide access to international markets and finance (Owen-Smith and Powell, 2004; Bathelt, Malmberg and Maskell, 2004). This suggests that dynamic international linkages and knowledge flows are critical to provide access to new trends and technologies and to become part of international production networks. Although project networks among Munich firms were not restricted to regional actors, our study found surprisingly weak international linkages and market access, which limits the prospects of generating self-sustained growth in the future and reinvigorating media leadership. That being said, the issues surrounding international linkages and networks varied across media segments.

In the area of TV production, for example, there were few linkages with foreign markets, such as networks between the public broadcasters and their Austrian, Swiss and French counterparts. Although joint TV channels such as ARTE and 3sat were not based in Munich, most international linkages were directly related to joint shows or the exchange of TV formats. Successful licensing arrangements with TV programmes, such as the criminal series 'Derrick', were, however, not very common. According to our interviewees, the TV market was primarily viewed as a national market with many 'cultural particularities' (see also De Laurentis, Cooke and Williams, 2003). It also seemed that public broadcasters stopped their earlier efforts to establish international linkages. Very few co-productions were identified by our interviewees and those that were seemed to focus on the joint financing of TV formats. In this respect, the Munich media sector seemed primarily involved in securing co-financing arrangements for joint documentaries and TV films, while the actual production was done elsewhere. An executive of one public broadcaster spoke of the difficulties of international co-productions in general, due to the divergent interests involved.

Similar to the area of TV production, joint international activities in the area of film production were largely focused on co-financing arrangements and did not systematically involve regional suppliers and service firms. German distributors, for instance, carry a substantial portion of the costs of the *Hollywood majors*, which produce 'blockbuster movies' for global markets (Scott, 2000; Kurp, 2004), while actual co-productions are rare. International recognition of Munich's motion picture industry, in turn, remained limited in the post-World War II period. Films such as 'Das Boot' or 'Das Leben der Anderen (The Lives of Others)' were successful in international markets, but they had the character of random successes. Earlier low-budget, high-profile German movies (the so-called Autorenfilme) received some attention through international critics but generally did not sell to a large audience. Overall, linkages with Hollywood's film industry, as well as the film industries in France, the UK and other countries, were weak. To the extent that co-productions were mentioned at all in our interviews, they primarily involved partners in Eastern Europe or Canada. Most of the productions carried out in these countries benefited from cost advantages and tax incentives that were not available in Germany.

In terms of the post-production segment, our study revealed a tendency towards subcontracting to low-cost Eastern European locations, with little interaction or extended knowledge exchange involved. Generally, post-production firms seemed quite passive with respect to the acquisition of contracts and had few external contacts with customers in other countries. The former Werk Group, which had established a large international production network with subsidiaries in Europe and North America, including strong linkages to Hollywood, stood out as an interesting exception to this trend (Krätke, 2002). Due to existing linkages, the group was able to acquire many international contracts. Such linkages brought contracts, expertise and growth to the Munich film industry. Although the Werk Group was recently dissolved and split up, some parts still existed in Munich as independent post-production firms. Due to their small size, however, they found it difficult to establish new international linkages and thus mainly benefited from personal networks previously established by the former Werk Group.

CONCLUSIONS: TOWARDS SELF-SUSTAINED GROWTH AND REINVIGORATED STRENGTH?

By focusing on the Munich TV and film industry, this chapter investigates how a well-established media cluster has experienced a series of crises since the turn of the new millennium reflective of deeper underlying structural problems. Given these problems, the question arises as to how firms in this cluster try to maintain or regain their dynamics faced with shifts in the media industry in Germany. This chapter has analysed the structural effects of the unprecedented growth of the Munich media cluster, as well as the recent economic crises, in order to draw conclusions about the prospects for self-sustained economic growth in the future. It shows that the post-World War II growth of Munich's TV and film cluster was primarily related to shifts in state regulation (especially the introduction of the dual broadcasting system) and expansion processes that went along with the economic recovery after World War II. This was the prerequisite for the introduction of private commercial TV and led to the rise of the Kirch Group. While Munich was originally known as a location for film production, audiovisual media today are primarily dominated by TV production. It is important to note that the post-World War II growth did not involve strong linkages with other international media centres.

This helps us understand why Munich's TV and film industry cluster was severely impacted by the advertising and Kirch crises causing declining sales and substantial job losses. The subsequent orientation towards low-cost TV productions failed to contribute to the knowledge basis of the cluster and has, therefore, limited the prospects of accessing new markets outside of Munich. At present, the effects of these crises are still visible and have not been fully resolved. At the same time, however, restructuring processes driven, in part, by financial investors have corrected some undesirable structures (*Frankfurter Allgemeine Zeitung*, 2003b; *Frankfurter Rundschau*, 2006), especially with respect to opening up formerly closed production networks (Bathelt and Gräf, 2008; Zademach, 2009). In the future, this may help to reduce segmentation and fragmentation tendencies and contribute to a reinvigorated media cluster.

POLICY IMPLICATIONS

The above analysis poses a number of questions regarding public/regional policy: how can policymakers support the reorientation and restructuring processes in Munich's TV and film industry to further its position as an international media centre? And how can policymakers learn from Munich's experience and avoid similar crises in the future? These and related questions draw attention to some broader policy implications.

First, one could speculate whether Munich would be better equipped to develop into a specialized service centre to support media projects done elsewhere or remain a production core itself. The research presented in this chapter indicates that Munich, as a large media centre in Germany, has developed into a world media city with diversified production and service activities (Krätke and Taylor, 2004). Although the city has not emerged as a top-tier media city, it has a substantial home market, involving a broader range of media branches with well-developed value chains. As such, it has the potential to remain an important production *and* service centre. The main question is therefore how to regain momentum and avoid a negative downward spiral of crisis and decline.

Secondly, media policies at the federal and *Länder* levels in Germany to date have not focused on particular regions or urban cores. Urban policy initiatives have primarily provided general infrastructure and positive locational conditions to enable private-sector investments. The different crises in Munich indicate that there is a need to develop a specific spatial perspective towards media policies and integrate all activities at the local, *Länder* and federal levels. In particular, policy should be more actively involved in the design of incubator centres and needs to provide incentives for the emergence of collaborative idea development as well as access to international TV and film projects. Initiatives to improve the institutional settings could include (i) the establishment of media funds that require regional and national collaboration at the producer/director level, (ii) the development of specific policies to improve access to finance (if a potential to stimulate regional economic growth can be identified), and (iii) the provision of incentives for private funds to engage more strongly in local rather than international media financing.

Thirdly, Munich is a media centre that compares favourably in terms of size and diversity with many other media cores. The analysis carried out in this chapter emphasizes, nonetheless, that agents in the Munich TV and film industry need to link up with and systematically seek collaborators outside the regional and national environment at an international level. This could be a decisive step in overcoming existing limitations and rigidities within the media cluster and drawing new growth and innovations to Munich.

Finally, there are several important lessons that policymakers and cluster managers can learn from the Munich case with respect to avoiding regional insulation and lock-in. On the one hand, they should encourage local networking but take steps to ensure that these linkages do not become too tight, too exclusive and too hierarchical. On the other hand, planners and policymakers in the region should be actively involved in the layout of media incubators and media parks to avoid that these become sterile places with little social interaction. In the end, efforts should be made to develop these facilities into attractive meeting points where members of the media community can engage in brainstorming and exchange their 'buzz'.

ACKNOWLEDGEMENTS

Parts of this chapter were presented in a 2004 seminar in the Department of Geography at York University in Toronto, Canada. I would like to thank Rachael Gibson, Armin Gräf and Phil Kelly for stimulating comments in different stages of this research, and the Editors of this volume for their strong support in the preparation. This chapter is based on earlier research on the Munich TV and film industry cluster (Bathelt and Gräf, 2006, 2008).

REFERENCES

Bank for International Settlements (2010), *Basel II: Revised International Capital Framework*, Basel, URL: http://www.bis.org/publ/bcbsca.htm, accessed 9 December 2010.

Bathelt, H. (2002), 'The Re-emergence of a Media Industry Cluster in Leipzig', *European Planning Studies*, **10**(5), 583–611.

Bathelt, H. and A. Gräf (2006), *Internal and External Dynamics of the Munich Film and TV Industry Cluster and the International Entertainment Sector*, SPACES 2006-01, Toronto and Heidelberg: http://www.spaces-online.com.

Bathelt, H. and A. Gräf (2008), 'Internal and External Dynamics of the Munich Film and TV Industry Cluster, and Limitations to Future Growth', *Environment and Planning A*, **40**(8), 1944–1965.

Bathelt, H., A. Malmberg and P. Maskell (2004), 'Clusters and Knowledge: Local Buzz, Global Pipelines and the Process of Knowledge Creation', *Progress in Human Geography*, **28**(1), 31–56.

Bayerisches Landesamt für Statistik und Datenverarbeitung (2006), *Sonderauswertung der Umsatzsteuerstatistik im Stadt- und Landkreis München nach Medienbranchen 2000–2004 (Project-Specific Analysis of Tax Revenue Statistics in the Munich Region by Media Branch 2000–2004)*, München.

Beck, H. (2002), *Medienökonomie: Print, Fernsehen und Multimedia (Media Economy: Print, TV and Multimedia)*, Berlin and Heidelberg: Springer.

Biehler, H., J. Genosko, M. Sargl and D. Sträter (2003), *Standort München – Medienwirtschaft und Fahrzeugbau: Regionale Netzwerke und regionaler Arbeitsmarkt als Erfolgsfaktoren (Media Economy and Automobile Production in Munich: Successes Through Regional Networking and the Regional Labour Market)*, Marburg: Schüren.

DeFillippi, R.J. and M.B. Arthur (1998), 'Paradox in Project-Based Enterprise: The Case of Film Making', *California Management Review*, **40**(2), 125–139.

De Laurentis, C., P. Cooke and G. Williams (2003), *Barriers to the Knowledge Economy: New Media Cluster in the Periphery*, paper presented at the Regional Studies Association International Conference on 'Reinventing Regions in the Global Economy', 12–15 April, Pisa.

Deutsches Institut für Wirtschaftsforschung (1999), *Perspektiven der Medienwirtschaft (Perspectives of the Media Economy)*, Berlin: DIW.

Die Welt (2008), 'Sat.1 muss von Berlin nach München umziehen (Sat.1 Has to Move From Berlin to Munich)', 14 November, p. 14.

Ernst & Young (2006), *Filmbarometer 2006: Berlin, Hamburg, Köln, Leipzig, München und Rhein/Main: Stimmungen und Trends (Film Barometer 2006: Trends in Berlin, Hamburg, Cologne, Leipzig, Munich and Rhine/Main: Moods and Trends)*, München: Ernst & Young.

Frankfurter Allgemeine Zeitung (2002), 'Lange Schatten auf dem Medienstandort München (Dark Shadows on the Munich Media Centre)', 9 April, p. 16.

Frankfurter Allgemeine Zeitung (2003a), 'Kirch Media stößt Unternehmen ab (Kirch Media Gets Rid of Branches)', 4 October, p. 20.

Frankfurter Allgemeine Zeitung (2003b), 'Sparprogramm in Saban-Sendern (Cost-Cutting Measures of the Saban Broadcasters)', 29 October, p. 19.

Frankfurter Rundschau (2002a), 'Aufstieg und Fall im Zeitraffer (Rise and Decline in Time Lapse)', 9 April, p. 10.

Frankfurter Rundschau (2002b), 'Auffanggesellschaft soll den Kern des Kirch-Konzerns retten (Rescue Company Established to Save the Core of the Kirch Group)', 9 April, p. 9.

Frankfurter Rundschau (2006), 'Saban startet Auktion (Saban Starts Auction)', 21 October, p. 1.

Grabher, G. (2002a), 'Cool Projects, Boring Institutions: Temporary Collaboration in Social Context', *Regional Studies*, **36**(3), 205–214.

Grabher, G. (2002b), 'The Project Ecology of Advertising: Tasks, Talents and Teams', *Regional Studies*, **36**(3), 245–262.

Gräf, A. (2005), *München in der Krise? Projektorganisation und Wachstumsprobleme in der Film- und Fernsehproduktion – eine Mehrdimensionale Clusterstudie (Munich in a State of Crisis? Project Organization and Growth Problems in Film and TV Production – A Multidimensional Cluster Study)*, SPACES 2005-08, Toronto and Heidelberg: http://www.spaces-online.com.

Gräf, P., H. Hallati and P. Seiwert (2001), 'Öffentlich-rechtliche und private Rundfunk- und Fernsehanbieter (Public and Private Television and Broadcasting Services in Germany)', in Institut für Länderkunde (eds), *Nationalatlas Bundesrepublik Deutschland: Band 9. Verkehr und Kommunikation*, Heidelberg and Berlin: Spektrum, pp. 118–121.

Horak, J.-C. (1996), 'Munich's First Fiction Feature: Die Wahrheit', in Thomas

Elsaesser (ed), *A Second Life: German Cinema's First Decades*, Amsterdam: Amsterdam University Press, pp. 86–92.

Industrie- und Handelskammer für München und Oberbayern and Landeshauptstadt München (2003), *Der Medienstandort München (Munich as a Media Location)*, München.

Jentsch, C. (2004), *Projektorganisation in der Frankfurter Werbeindustrie (Project Organization in the Frankfurt Advertising Industry)*, SPACES 2004-03, Toronto and Heidelberg: http://www.spaces-online.com.

Krätke, S. (2002), *Medienstadt: Urbane Cluster und globale Zentren der Kulturproduktion (Media Cities: Urban Clusters and Global Centres of Cultural Production)*, Opladen: Leske + Budrich.

Krätke, S. and C. Scheuplein (2001), *Produktionscluster in Ostdeutschland: Methoden der Identifizierung und Analyse (Production Clusters in East Germany: Methods of Identification and Analysis)*, Hamburg: VSA.

Krätke, S. and P.J. Taylor (2004), 'A World Geography of Global Media Cities', *European Planning Studies*, **12**(4), 459–477.

Kurp, M. (2004), *Medienfonds als 'Stupid German Money'. Steuersparmodell unterstützt Hollywood statt deutsche Filmemacher (Mediafonds as 'Stupid German Money'. Tax Saving Model Supports Hollywood Rather Than German Filmmakers*), URL: http://www.medienmaerkte.de/artikel/kino/040502_film-fonds.html, accessed 20 November 2006.

Leborgne, D. and A. Lipietz (1991), 'Two Social Strategies in the Production of New Industrial Spaces', in Georges Benko and Mick Dunford (eds), *Industrial Change and Regional Development: The Transformation of New Industrial Spaces*, London and New York: Belhaven, pp. 27–50.

Malmberg, A. and P. Maskell (2002), 'The Elusive Concept of Localization Economies: Towards a Knowledge-Based Theory of Spatial Clustering', *Environment and Planning A*, **34**(3), 429–449.

Mossig, I. (2004), 'Steuerung lokalisierter Projektnetzwerke am Beispiel der Produktion von TV-Sendungen in den Medienclustern München und Köln (The Governance of Localised TV Production Networks in Munich and Cologne)', *Erdkunde*, **58**(3), 252–268.

Mossig, I. (2006), *Netzwerke der Kulturökonomie: Lokale Knoten und globale Verflechtungen der Film- und Fernsehindustrie in Deutschland und den USA (Cultural Economy Networks: Local Nodes and Global Linkages of the Film and TV Industry in Germany and the USA)*, Bielefeld: Transcript.

Owen-Smith, J. and W.W. Powell (2004), 'Knowledge Networks as Channels and Conduits: The Effects of Spillovers in the Boston Biotechnology Community', *Organization Science*, **15**(1), 5–21.

Picard, R.G. (2008), *Media Clusters: Local Agglomeration in an Industry Developing Networked Virtual Clusters*, JIBS Working Paper Series No. 2008-3, Jönköping: Jönköping International Business School.

Porter, M.E. (1990), *The Competitive Advantage of Nations*, New York: Free Press.

Scott, A.J. (2000), *The Cultural Economy of Cities*, London and Thousand Oaks, CA: Sage.

Scott, A.J. (2002), 'A New Map of Hollywood: The Production and Distribution of American Motion Pictures', *Regional Studies*, **36**(9), 957–975.

Statistisches Landesamt des Freistaates Sachsen (2001), *Umsätze und ihre Besteuerung im Freistaat Sachsen: Ergebnisse der Umsatzsteuerstatistik*

1999 – Sonderauswertung (Tax Revenue Statistics 1999 – Special Analysis), Kamenz.

Storper, M. and A.J. Venables (2004), 'Buzz: Face-to-Face Contact and the Urban Economy', *Journal of Economic Geography*, **4**(4), 351–370.

Sydow, J. and U. Staber (2002), 'The Institutional Embeddedness of Project Networks: The Case of Content Production in German Television', *Regional Studies*, **36**(3), 215–227.

van den Berg, L., E. Braun and W. van Winden (2001), *Growth Clusters in European Metropolitan Cities: A Comparative Analysis of Cluster Dynamics in the Cities of Amsterdam, Eindhoven, Helsinki, Leipzig, Lyons, Manchester, Munich, Rotterdam and Vienna*, Aldershot and Burlington, VT: Ashgate.

von Bernuth, C. and H. Bathelt (2007), 'The Organizational Paradox in Advertising and the Reconfiguration of Project Cooperation', *Geoforum*, **38**(3), 545–557.

Zademach, H.-M. (2009), 'Global Finance and the Development of Regional Clusters: Tracing Paths in Munich's Film & TV Industry', *Journal of Economic Geography*, **9**(5), 697–722.

Section B Clusters expanding or improving their position

8. The transformation of broadcasting and film in Manchester and Liverpool

Gary Cook and Jennifer Johns

This chapter examines the broadcasting sector in the North West of England. The majority of these activities are in Manchester, although the city's scope extends to adjacent cities such as Liverpool. This chapter takes a deliberately broad focus on the sector for a number of reasons. First, broader changes in the regulation and operation of the UK broadcasting sector directly affect the structure and composition of the industry in the North West. Secondly, the boundaries of clusters are indistinct due to high degrees of dependency at a number of geographical scales; for example, the activities in Liverpool are dependent on resources in Manchester while Manchester is similarly dependent on London. The degree of interconnection between broadcasting sites in the region is comparatively high. Thirdly, policymaking in this sector operates primarily at the regional scale with ambitions to support broadcasting across the North West. However, local spaces are competing for resources, and an uneven pattern of policy implementation results.

The cluster of broadcasting activities in the North West has a relatively long – albeit cyclical – history. Independent television production began in Manchester in the 1950s, with film activities locating in Liverpool in the early 1970s. The former was driven by the allocation of regional charters for the newly established independent channel while the latter was a spontaneous response to the availability of empty warehouse space in post-industrial Liverpool. There then followed a period of sustained growth in which both cities increased their reputations for broadcasting activities and became significantly interconnected through accessing shared resources such as labour. This growth was influenced by regulatory processes (such as the 1990 Broadcasting Act, which will be discussed below), which saw an increase in independent firm numbers. However, the success of the cluster primarily resulted from the establishment of a strong reputation for quality content production. This chapter outlines how this existing cluster has changed over time to illustrate how and why it has contracted in size over the last decade. Having reached a situation in which firm failure is the highest and filming activities the lowest in decades, a potential lifeline is being offered by the formation of a global media hub. This is the result of a politically motivated decision that has seen the formation of a carefully planned development financed by private property developers.

The collection of the empirical data on which this chapter is based has been conducted over a number of years, beginning with an examination of Manchester's film and television industry, from which data were collected in 2000–2002 (Coe and Johns, 2004; Johns, 2004, 2010). Studies conducted on other national clusters including Glasgow and Bristol (Cook and Pandit, 2007. 2009) have also been used to provide broader context. The authors have conducted over 40 interviews between August 2009 and May 2010 across all production stages in both Liverpool and Manchester (Manchester is much larger in scale, so proportionately more interviews were conducted there). Policymakers and some firm headquarters in London were interviewed, in addition to property developers responsible for recent cluster development initiatives. Interview questions included topics related to firm size, profitability, nature of activities and competitive dynamics in the region. The availability of data over a decade provides insight into change dynamics. Secondary data are also used to quantify the number, size and profitability of firms.

The chapter argues that while activities in Manchester have always been predicated on finance and distribution connections to London and other key sites, the nature of these connections is changing due to forces originating outside the cluster. The chapter uses Markusen's (1996) industrial district typology to illustrate three phases of cluster development and suggests that the interplay of public service broadcasting, nationally (privately) funded and distributed content and the activities of global media conglomerates has resulted in a 'hybrid agglomeration' (Coe, 2001). The dynamics of change in the North West are still strong, with a number of policy interventions being developed that seek to reshape the structure and nature of broadcasting in the region. The most significant of these is the current construction of MediaCity in Salford (neighbouring Manchester) which has been precipitated by the announcement of five BBC departments being relocated from London. This chapter argues that, just as in the past, the current and future size and form of broadcasting activities in the North West are being determined to a large extent by extra-local forces.

CURRENT SIZE AND STRUCTURE OF THE CLUSTER: CONTEXT

Whilst the broadcasting sector has undergone and still is undergoing change, the North West has traditionally been home to the second largest level of activity outside London. Indeed, the North West is the strongest region for media employment outside London by a considerable margin, according to the most recent Skillset Employment Census (Skillset, 2010a). As Table 8.1 shows, total media employment relevant to the cluster in the North West in 2009 was 170,050, taking employed and freelance workers together, 9.9 per cent of the national total. The next largest region outside London is the South East, with 7.1 per cent of the national total. These figures quite evidently disguise very considerable variation in the strength of particular regions in different lines of activity. The North West emerges as being very strong indeed in interactive media and computer games, in each case accounting for almost one-third of the national workforce. Here it should be observed that figures must be read with some circumspection as, first, figures are rounded to the nearest 50 (which accounts for the zeros entered in various cells of the tables, which are not to be interpreted literally) and secondly, arbitrary allocations have to be made in assigning workers to one category or another where boundaries are often very blurred. The North West is also very strong in television and radio, easily surpassing every region of the UK outside London, including the nations of Wales and Scotland. The strength in independent TV production, very much concentrated in Manchester, is particularly of note. Again, a note of caution is required as the Census shows zero employment (effectively less than 25 people) in commercials and production of pop videos in the North West, whereas compilation of the database of companies by the authors clearly revealed a non-negligible amount of activity in this sector, particularly commercials production.

Table 8.2 examines the employment data in terms of location quotients. These are calculated as, for example, the percentage of national employment in terrestrial broadcast accounted for by the North West divided by the percentage of total national employment accounted for by the North West. A location quotient of 1 would indicate that employment in any given sector was exactly pro rata to the overall share of the North West in total national employment. A quotient above 1 indicates that the North West has a higher level of employment in a particular sector than would be expected based on its share of total national employment. The converse applies to a location quotient below 1. The quotient of 1.36 for independent television in the North West indicates that the region has over one-third more employment than would be expected based on the scale of the

Table 8.1 Total employment (including freelancers) by region in UK media industries (2009)

Totals summary	Total number	North West	Central London	West London	Whole of London	Scot-land	Wales	South East	South West	West Mid-lands	Yorks & Humbs	East Mid-lands	East of England	North East	Nor-thern Ireland
Terrestrial broadcast	15,750	1050	4350	4600	9100	950	1000	450	750	500	650	100	450	200	500
Cable and satellite	12,700	0	7400	5250	12,600	0	*	100	0	0	0	0	0	0	0
Independent production (TV)	21,700	3200	5050	2250	9450	1000	2500	650	1000	500	500	1300	250	150	1150
Radio	20,900	3950	3750	2300	6650	1650	750	1050	350	750	1200	450	1550	450	2050
Post production	7450	200	3400	2150	6000	150	100	300	100	150	50	0	100	250	100
Studios and equipment hire	5900	50	150	1900	2700	250	100	600	900	400	350	0	250	50	200
VFX	6900	0	6250	150	6400	0	*	0	0	0	0	0	0	500	*
Other services for film & TV	22,800	3250	4000	1200	8850	700	450	3350	900	250	2700	800	1250	250	50
Film production**	1300	50	650	*	750	100	50	100	50	50	50	50	50	50	*
Film distribution	1200	0	600	0	850	300	*	0	0	0	0	0	50	0	0

Animation	4300	600	700	50	850	500	400	1650	200	*	50	*	*	*	50
Commercials and pop promos	4100	0	1100	0	1900	0	0	150	900	450	50	0	350	0	300
Corporate production	3950	250	750	700	1800	150	50	400	100	400	250	200	50	300	50
Online content	27,550	800	2750	1750	6400	850	3050	2350	4050	950	6250	900	350	200	1350
Offline multimedia	2750	250	50	0	200	200	450	1050	0	50	100	0	150	0	350
Other interactive media	3950	1200	150	0	150	0	300	200	0	1000	100	50	*	750	200
Computer games	7050	2150	100	0	1350	500	50	250	50	400	200	600	1300	200	0
Archives and libraries	350	50	100	*	150	*	*	50	50	50	0	*	50	0	0
***TOTAL**	**170,550**	**17,050**	**41,300**	**22,350**	**76,200**	**7300**	**9300**	**12,600**	**9350**	**5950**	**12,550**	**4450**	**6200**	**3350**	**6300**

Notes:
* Total does not include cinema exhibition.
** Skillset's Employment Census counted employees in permanent production companies only. A further 9100 freelancers are estimated to be working in the film production sector.

Source: Skillset (2010).

Table 8.2 Location quotients by region for UK media industries for all employment (including freelancers) (2009)

Totals summary	North West	Central London	West London	Whole of London	Scot-land	Wales	South East	South West	West Midlands	Yorks & Humbs	East Midlands	East of England	North East	Northern Ireland
Terrestrial broadcast	0.61	2.11	2.23	4.42	0.72	1.38	0.20	0.56	0.36	0.51	0.09	0.30	0.33	1.21
Cable and satellite	0.00	4.45	3.16	7.59	0.00	0.00	0.05	0.00	0.00	0.00	0.00	0.00	0.00	0.00
Independent production (TV)	1.36	1.78	0.79	3.33	0.55	2.51	0.21	0.54	0.26	0.28	0.84	0.12	0.18	2.03
Radio	1.74	1.37	0.84	2.43	0.94	0.78	0.35	0.20	0.41	0.71	0.30	0.78	0.56	3.75
Post production	0.25	3.49	2.21	6.16	0.24	0.29	0.28	0.16	0.23	0.08	0.00	0.14	0.88	0.51
Studios & equipment hire	0.08	0.19	2.46	3.50	0.50	0.37	0.70	1.78	0.77	0.73	0.00	0.45	0.22	1.30
VFX	0.00	6.93	0.17	7.09	0.00	0.00	0.00	0.00	0.00	0.00	0.00	0.00	1.89	0.00
Other services for film and TV	1.31	1.34	0.40	2.97	0.37	0.43	1.02	0.46	0.12	1.46	0.49	0.58	0.29	0.08
Film production**	0.35	3.82	0.00	4.41	0.91	0.84	0.53	0.45	0.44	0.47	0.54	0.41	1.01	0.00
Film distribution	0.00	3.82	0.00	5.42	2.97	0.00	0.00	0.00	0.00	0.00	0.00	0.44	0.00	0.00

Animation	1.28	1.24	0.09	1.51	1.38	2.02	2.65	0.54	0.00	0.14	0.00	0.00	0.00	0.44
Commercials and pop promos	0.00	2.05	0.00	3.54	0.00	0.00	0.25	2.56	1.25	0.15	0.00	0.90	0.00	2.80
Corporate production	0.58	1.45	1.35	3.48	0.45	0.28	0.70	0.30	1.15	0.78	0.71	0.13	1.99	0.48
Online content	0.27	0.76	0.49	1.78	0.37	2.41	0.59	1.72	0.39	2.80	0.46	0.13	0.19	1.88
Offline multimedia	0.84	0.14	0.00	0.56	0.86	3.56	2.64	0.00	0.21	0.45	0.00	0.58	0.00	4.87
Other interactive media	2.79	0.29	0.00	0.29	0.00	1.65	0.35	0.00	2.87	0.31	0.18	0.00	4.97	1.94
Computer games	2.81	0.11	0.00	1.46	0.84	0.15	0.24	0.08	0.64	0.35	1.19	1.95	0.74	0.00
Archives & libraries	1.31	2.18	0.00	3.28	0.00	0.00	0.99	1.67	1.62	0.00	0.00	1.51	0.00	0.00
***TOTAL**	0.92	1.85	1.00	3.42	0.51	1.19	0.51	0.64	0.40	0.91	0.36	0.38	0.51	1.41

Notes:
* Total does not include cinema exhibition.
** Skillset's Employment Census counted employees in permanent production companies only. A further 9100 freelancers are estimated to be working in the film production sector.

Source: Skillset (2010).

region alone. This is indicative of some form of agglomeration effect, particularly given that much of this employment is concentrated on a fairly compact geographical area in the vicinity of ITV and the BBC around the centre of Manchester. Deconstructing this quotient reveals a quotient of 1.61 when only considering employees and 1.14 when only considering freelancers. The quotient for freelancers is based on the share of the North West in the total of self-employed persons in the UK. Here it should be noted that freelance working is far more common in the media industries (26.8 per cent of the total workforce) than in the economy generally (10.7 per cent of the total workforce).

As Table 8.3 shows, London has a disproportionate share of freelancers in independent television production, accounting for almost half the national total. One plausible explanation for this is that London, being the hub of demand in the independent television sector, is able to offer freelancers greater continuity of work. This is a classic Marshallian labour pooling externality and one to which several interview respondents referred, blaming the talent drain from Manchester in part due to the lack of work. The North West's comparatively low quotients for post production and studios and equipment hire are somewhat harder to explain. Several interview respondents did indicate that they follow a policy of both owning their own equipment and doing as much post production as possible in house in order to keep production costs down. This business model clearly depends on having reasonable continuity of workflow. The North West emerges as having a comparatively low location quotient for film production, behind several other regions of the UK.

Table 8.2 also reveals some other interesting features of the industry. The location quotients for London show how dominant the capital is, not only in film and television, but also in media more generally. Here it must be remembered that the location quotients presented refer to Greater London, whereas much of the industry is concentrated in Central London and, to a lesser extent, in West London. Scotland and Wales both have relatively high location quotients for terrestrial broadcast, which reflects the political imperatives never far from the surface in television broadcasting. There is a marked contrast, given this fact, between the quotients for independent television production, where Scotland emerges as being comparatively weak and Wales as being comparatively strong.

The structure of the broadcasting sector in the North West mirrors that of the UK as a whole. There is a high degree of geographical concentration centred on the major terrestrial broadcasters, the BBC and ITV, in Manchester. There is a very small number of quite large independent production companies and a larger fringe of very small companies. Here it must be noted that the North West is not home to any of the so-called 'super-indies', a small group of very large independent production companies with turnover in excess of £50 million, albeit that Lime Pictures in Liverpool (formerly Mersey TV) is a subsidiary of RDF Media, which is one of the super-indies. Television production companies enjoy a close relationship with both post-production companies and facilities companies that hire equipment (with or without crew subject to requirements). Post-production companies tend to be slightly larger on average and are more capital intensive as they require quite expensive specialized equipment. Post-production is again concentrated geographically on Manchester. Post-production companies tend to specialize to some degree, Sumners and Flix, for example, having more of an orientation towards broadcast television and 422 focusing to a greater extent on commercials. That said, post-production and facilities companies do exploit economies of scope by servicing a broad range of production including that for corporate video, pop videos, radio, music and interactive, web-based and mobile applications (Skillset, 2010b). In many respects this diversification away from broadcasting is as a result of two forces, first, the necessity of maintaining an income to even out the peaks and troughs of broadcasting commissioning, and secondly, as a result of changes in the competitive dynamics in the North West which are discussed further below. Companies which specialize in corporate video generally operate on a different business model from independent television production companies. The former tend to have more stable income streams and therefore tend to maintain larger permanent staffs whom they train to be multi-skilled. They also tend to have more of their own production and post-production equipment as they can ensure fuller utilization rates. Independent television production companies, especially smaller ones, tend to have a very small core staff who will spend much of their time in developing proposals and then in producing those which they are successful in getting commissioned. Once commissioned they will then 'crew up' by bringing in freelance staff and hiring in any necessary equipment. Many will have the capacity to do off-line editing (which involves working a rough cut of the final programme with scenes to be included in the intended sequence), but will generally go to specialist post-production companies for on-line editing (where the final version is produced, incorporating sound, music, titling, colour correction, etc).

Larger production companies, especially those who have returning series, such as Lime Pictures, which makes the long-running soap opera *Hollyoaks*, will be able to maintain more permanent staff and equipment in house, again because they have a more secure income stream. Compared to the national average, the North West appears to be more heavily casualized in terms of television, with 33 per cent of the total workforce in

Table 8.3 Percentage of all freelancers employed in media industries in each region, by industry (2009)

Totals summary	Total number	North West	Central London	West London	Whole of London	Scotland	Wales	South East	South West	West Midlands	Yorks & Humbs	East Midlands	East of England	North East	Northern Ireland
Terrestrial broadcast	100	11.7	23.3	30.0	55.0	3.3	5.0	1.7	6.7	5.0	6.7	0.0	5.0	1.7	1.7
Cable and satellite	100	0.0	55.6	44.4	100.0	0.0	0.0	0.0	0.0	0.0	0.0	0.0	0.0	0.0	0.0
Independent production (TV)	100	11.0	24.1	8.9	48.2	6.8	9.9	4.2	6.8	3.7	3.7	0.0	0.0	1.0	4.2
Radio	100	14.3	13.3	5.1	24.5	10.2	1.0	4.1	1.0	2.0	5.1	2.0	2.0	1.0	32.7
Post production	100	2.8	33.3	41.7	83.3	0.0	0.0	5.6	2.8	2.8	0.0	0.0	0.0	0.0	0.0
Studios and equipment hire	100	0.0	0.0	27.7	44.7	4.3	2.1	2.1	23.4	12.8	2.1	0.0	8.5	0.0	2.1
VFX	100	0.0	100.0	0.0	100.0	0.0	0.0	0.0	0.0	0.0	0.0	0.0	0.0	0.0	0.0
Other services for film and TV	100	22.8	6.6	9.6	29.3	3.6	2.4	4.8	1.8	1.2	28.1	4.2	1.2	0.0	0.0
Film production**															
Film distribution	100	0.0	40.0	0.0	60.0	40.0	0.0	0.0	0.0	0.0	0.0	0.0	0.0	0.0	0.0

Animation	100	10.0	15.0	2.5	20.0	12.5	10.0	45.0	2.5	0.0	0.0	0.0	0.0	0.0	0.0
Commercials and pop promos	100	0.0	11.8	0.0	47.1	0.0	0.0	5.9	14.7	26.5	0.0	0.0	5.9	0.0	0.0
Corporate production	100	7.1	16.7	21.4	50.0	2.4	0.0	11.9	2.4	9.5	7.1	2.4	0.0	7.1	0.0
Online content	100	0.8	5.6	2.4	32.3	7.3	4.0	13.7	4.0	3.2	15.3	7.3	3.2	0.0	8.9
Offline multimedia	100	7.7	0.0	0.0	15.4	0.0	7.7	69.2	0.0	0.0	7.7	0.0	0.0	0.0	0.0
Other interactive media	100	37.5	12.5	0.0	12.5	0.0	0.0	12.5	0.0	0.0	12.5	0.0	0.0	0.0	37.5
Computer games	100	0.0	20.0	0.0	40.0	40.0	0.0	0.0	0.0	0.0	20.0	0.0	20.0	0.0	0.0
Archives and libraries	100	0.0	0.0	0.0	0.0	0.0	0.0	0.0	0.0	0.0	0.0	0.0	0.0	0.0	0.0
***TOTAL**	100	10.2	17.1	12.0	42.2	5.6	4.2	8.3	4.9	4.2	9.6	2.1	2.0	0.8	6.1

Notes:
* Total does not include cinema exhibition.
** Skillset's Employment Census counted employees in permanent production companies only. A further 9100 freelancers are estimated to be working in the film production sector.

Source: Skillset (2010).

terrestrial broadcast being freelance, compared to 19 per cent nationally (which includes the North West). Likewise, taking independent television production and 'other services for film and television' together, 45 per cent of the total workforce in the North West are freelancers, compared to 40 per cent nationally. Taking a dynamic perspective, freelance employment in 2005 was approximately equal at 55 per cent in both the North West and nationally, therefore both have seen a trend of a falling proportion of the workforce that is freelance, but this has happened at a slower rate in the North West. In terrestrial broadcast, 42 per cent of employment in the North West was freelance in 2005, as opposed to 20 per cent nationally, therefore while the North West has been moving closer to the national average, it is still some distance away. Conversely, the proportion of the total post-production workforce that is freelance is almost exactly equal at approximately 25 per cent in both cases. Comparable figures for 2005 are not available. Taken across the entire labour market, the North West has 9.4 per cent of the labour force self-employed, compared to 10.7 per cent for the UK, and therefore the extent of casualization in film and television in the North West cannot be explained on the basis of some general propensity for higher self-employment in the region.

STRUCTURE AND OPERATIONAL CHARACTER OF THE CLUSTER

Currently (and traditionally) this large cluster has been relatively unmanaged with activities supported by agencies operating at a number of geographical scales – local, regional and national. However, these agencies have rarely provided connected and targeted support for broadcasting in the region and have operated with relatively small budgets. The role of institutional support will be discussed in greater detail in the following section.

As indicated above, the cluster is supported by a large – and geographically mobile – labour pool. Recruitment is typically by word of mouth and established reputation or relationship (Johns, 2010). When crewing a production, producers usually attempt to secure the services of those they have worked with successfully before. Where this is not possible, either due to the fact that a given individual is not available or because a specialist skill is required, then almost always producers will seek a personal recommendation from others in the industry they know and trust. When asked what they feared might go wrong if they recruited using more impersonal means, respondents generally found it difficult to articulate the reasons. In part, the reasons were related to how easy a person would be to work with and partly to whether or not they would really be able to deliver the right type of work to the right standard. These reasons are redolent of Ettlinger's (2003) distinction between emotive trust, whether you regard the person as being trustworthy, and capacity trust, whether you believe the person has the required skill to do the job. Clearly these two things are not entirely independent. The distinction between doing the right *type* of work and doing work *to the right standard* is also important. Given the high semiotic content of film and television products, it is essential to have the right look and feel (which applies to sound as much as to visual images). For example, a camera operator might be highly skilled in shooting pop videos, therefore their work will be of high quality from a technical point of view, but might find it very difficult, if not impossible, to adapt their style to camerawork for some other genre, such as period drama or natural history, therefore their skills will be unsuited to such different programme types.

The importance of personal relationships in the operation of the labour market for television production is attested to by the Skillset Labour Market Intelligence Digest (Skillset, 2010b). This reports that, nationally, only 20 per cent of the TV workforce learned about their most recent role via an advertisement. This falls to just 10 per cent in the independent television production sector. Around 39 per cent are approached directly by an employer and 34 per cent hear about job opportunities from people with whom they have previously worked. According to the Digest, a mere 3 per cent of freelancers heard about their most recent role via an advertisement, as opposed to 44 per cent who heard about it from someone with whom they had worked before. Likewise in film production, 87 per cent of the workforce were recruited to their last job by word of mouth (Skillset 2010c) and only 1 per cent secured their job through an advertisement (these proportions being very similar to those identified in Skillset's 2005 census of the film industry). The proportion of freelancers does vary considerably between different lines of activity. Film and television production has a high proportion of freelancers, with 91 per cent of film production crew being freelance. Those who are not freelance are on permanent contracts, yet the duration of these contracts is typically very short and would not conform to any reasonable definition of permanent in most areas of the economy. Among those who have become freelance, having previously had employee status, there has been a rising proportion over time where the primary reason has been redundancy or the threat of redundancy, which stood at 46 per cent in 2009. The desire for greater freedom and more interesting and more remunerative work remains an important, but diminishing, reason for becoming freelance.

The perceived existence of skills gaps is not unique to the North West.

Nationally, around 26 per cent of all employers in the TV industry say they have experienced skills gaps which have impinged on their business (Skillset, 2010a). The gaps occur particularly in camerawork, engineering, producing, commercial awareness, accounting/finance and basic IT.

ENGINES OF GROWTH

The changing dynamics of growth in this cluster have been variable over time, and to a large degree dependent on the impact of broader national flows of capital (particularly broadcaster commissioning levels) and regulation. As suggested above, the cluster is entering into a new era of potential growth that is being driven by government policy and real estate development. This section charts the key factors related to engines of growth for the broadcasting cluster.

National Regulation

Broadcasting has been subject to heavy state regulation for most of its existence and the UK is no exception in this regard compared to other countries. Key regulatory developments have had, and continue to have, a profound impact on the spatial organization of the industry. ITV was created as a regional federation in the 1950s, in part to act as a counterbalance to the London-centricity of the BBC. The regional ITV companies were all to have some input into providing network shows, not simply local and regional news and current affairs, although these were and remain staple parts of ITV's regional operations.

Probably the next major influence on the current regional structure of independent television production was the foundation of Channel 4 in 1982 as a national broadcaster. Channel 4 was significant not only in that it had no in-house production capability and therefore gave rise to the emergence of a large number of independent production companies, but also in that it was required from its inception to give ample airing to minority views and perspectives. The fact that many of these companies set up in close proximity to Channel 4 HQ in Charlotte Street, central London, immediately gave London a significant head-start over the English regions, as well as Wales, Scotland and Northern Ireland, in developing an independent television production and post-production cluster. This was compounded when Channel 5 was launched in 1997 as another London-based national broadcaster which did not have its own in-house programme production operation. Both Channel 4 and Channel 5, now called Five, do commission from the regions, and Channel 4 has an active Nations and Regions office; however, over time both companies have tended to focus their commissions on a small group of trusted suppliers who are almost all large, London-based independent companies. In part to counter this trend, an obligation was placed on Channel 4 in 1998 to spend at least 30 per cent of its production budget in the nations of Scotland, Wales and Northern Ireland and the English regions.

The Broadcasting Act 1990, which took effect in 1993, was a follow-up to the Peacock Report of 1986 (which recommended a 40 per cent independent production quota). It led to a further boost for independent production since both the BBC and ITV companies were required to source 25 per cent of most types of new production from independent sources. Both the BBC and ITV quickly downsized and a number of companies were spun out of both broadcasters, some of which have developed into very large or medium-sized independent production companies, or at least have become parts of the so-called 'super-indies' (e.g. Bazal, which became part of the Endemol group, was founded by ex-BBC producer Peter Bazalgette; Barraclough Carey, which is now part of Television PLC, was also founded by two former BBC producers). Despite the London-centricity of the industry, the independent production quota did lead to more independent companies in the regions. Nevertheless, in 2005, 85 per cent of reported independent production sector turnover was accounted for by London-based production companies. Only nine production companies outside London have a turnover in excess of £4 million (Ofcom, 2006).

Another very important piece of legislation was the Communications Act 2003. This imposed an out-of-London quota for independent production commissions of 30 per cent on the BBC and 50 per cent on ITV. It also brought in requirements for the terms of trade between the major broadcasters and independent production companies. Commissioning contracts had been viewed as unfavourable to the growth of independent production companies, since in many cases they were essentially cost-plus contracts which covered production costs including a small profit margin but required the production company to sign away most, if not all, of the intellectual property rights in the programme to the broadcaster, meaning the production company would be unable to fund growth by developing ancillary revenue streams. The new terms of trade differ between broadcasters and therefore it is tedious to enumerate them in full. The essential thrust of them, however, is as follows: broadcasters get a period of exclusive use on their terrestrial platform which lasts for five years with an automatic extension of two years; there is a limited right to use the content on the broadcaster's new media platforms, e.g. seven days after first transmission for BBC iPlayer; limited use of re-versioned content is allowed, for instance on websites; the holdback on broadcast transmission may be extended to e.g. release on DVD; the broadcaster gets a share in revenues from secondary exploitation from e.g. international sales or merchandise. Ofcom in its Statement on the Review of the Television Production Sector (2006) came to the conclusion that it would not be appropriate to 'micro-manage' regional production quotas at the regional level, since this risked creating too much bureaucracy and militating against a genuine meritocracy between ideas.

Agencies

The largest agency supporting film and TV in the North West is North West Vision and Media. This agency was formed in 2007 from a merger between North West Vision, a screen agency of the UK Film Council established in 2002, and Media Training Northwest. North West Vision and Media operates a range of film offices, the two largest of which are the Greater Manchester Film Office and the Liverpool Film Office, which was the first established in the UK in 1989. The Liverpool Film Office has been particularly successful in attracting film production to the city, whereas the Greater Manchester Film Office has a comparative advantage in attracting television production, particularly for drama. While film and television are important industries supported by North West Vision and Media, the agency also promotes radio, digital media, video games, music, creative services and publishing. North West Vision and Media derives funding from a range of sources, namely the UK Film Council, the European Regional Development Funds for Manchester and Liverpool, the North West Development Agency, Skillset (the sector skills council) and the various local authorities and county councils contained within the North West region. North West Vision and Media is funded with £3 million to deliver the North West Development Agency's Digital and Creative Industries cluster development plan (formulated April 2008 and catalysed by the MediaCity project as well as the Creative Britain strategy articulated by the Department of Culture, Media and Sport), which currently runs to 2012, assuming the role of the single agency with the remit to do this in April 2009. NWDA has identified digital and creative industries as one of the region's priority growth sectors.

NWDA has involvement with a number of cluster development initiatives in the North West, although all have been precipitated by local councils or property developers rather than the NWDA. The NWDA has clearly identified MediaCity (further details below) as a cornerstone of its Digital and Creative Industries cluster development plan. One of the explicit initiatives linked to this is the creation of a Media Enterprise Centre as part of the MediaCity development, project-managed by

NWVM. Media Enterprise Centres are also being developed at other locations in the North West, including one based at the Liverpool Innovation Park. These Media Enterprise Centres will be linked by NorthernNet, a high-speed fibre telecommunications network. NWDA has set the objective of attracting at least one global technology business as an anchor tenant at MediaCity, alongside the BBC. NWVM has itself recently moved to MediaCity (December 2009). These two specific initiatives are part of the ten-point Digital and Creative Industries cluster development plan, the others of which exist as broader statements of intent to support the development of an internationally competitive Creative and Digital Industries sector; to develop higher value-added activity through innovation; to realize opportunities arising from globalization; to develop leadership, management, intermediate and higher skills in the workforce; to increase the size of the workforce; to support the development of major employment sites; to improve access to finance for growth and innovation; to deliver the pilot Regional Creative Economy Framework Strategy (itself arising under the DCMS Creative Britain strategy); and to improve the image of the region to businesses and visitors. The NWDA's strategy clearly envisages MediaCity as being central to its desire to make the North West the innovation hub of the UK's creative industries, with London being identified as the finance and distribution hub. It bolsters this ambition with appeal to Florida's (2005) identification of Manchester as the UK's most creative city and among the top ten creative cities in the world, based on his 'creativity index'. Based on its Gross Value Added of £15.8 billion, Adroit (2005) identified the North West as being the second largest 'creative cluster' in the UK and Europe.

QUANTIFYING THE SIZE AND CHARACTERISTICS OF THE CLUSTER

Ownership of Cluster Firms

Determining the number of firms operating in film and television is notoriously difficult. Many firms are very small and hard to identify from standard sources. There is also a high turnover of firms, so that any snapshot taken will quickly become outdated as new firms arise and existing firms go out of business. In both film and television it is not unusual for a company to be formed for a single production and then either to be wound up or else to lie dormant once production has ceased. The database presented here was assembled using two main sources. The first is the FAME database, which contains details on 2.5 million UK companies. A search was made of the Standard Industrial Classification (SIC) codes relevant to film and television, 92111 motion picture production, 92119 other motion picture and video production, 92120 motion picture and video distribution and 92202 television activities. The Production Guide 2009 (Broadcast, 2009), the principal broadcast industry trade directory, was used to identify firms not found in the FAME database. Many of the firms identified in the Production Guide were found in the FAME database, but classified under different SIC codes. The reasons for this are twofold. First, firms are classified according to their main activity and therefore some firms have other activities besides film or television. Secondly, some firms were misclassified. A thorough scrutiny was performed on the firms that were identified via the FAME database. 718 firms were initially identified by the SIC code search. This was reduced to 412 firms, 317 being eliminated for at least one of the following reasons: the firm was misclassified as belonging to film and television; the firm had ceased active trading; the firm was a 'shell', being a production-specific subsidiary of a production company elsewhere in the database (18 such companies belonging to Red Productions, a major Manchester-based independent TV production company were eliminated with only Red Productions itself being retained); the firm was a cinema. To this were added 102 companies identified via the Production Guide (and in a few cases by the researchers' industry knowledge). Thus, 513 companies were identified as operating in the North West defined as Merseyside, Greater Manchester, Cheshire and Lancashire – Cumbria was excluded as being too distant from the main conurbation in the North West, despite the fact that it is part of the North West Government Office region and thus is included, for example, in the employment figures produced by Skillset (2010a).

The firms in the database were classified into seven main types of activity: broadcasting, television or film production, post-production, facilities and crewing, other production-related activities (includes commercials and corporate video production and ancillary services to production such as casting, model-making and costumes), radio activities and sole traders (companies formed by freelancers acting alone). Firms were also allocated to one of three geographical areas: Greater Manchester, Merseyside and other North West. Both types of classification are arbitrary in important respects and the numbers shown in the following tables must be interpreted as merely indicative and should be treated with caution. Very little information at all was available about some companies; however, at least two sources were identified that associated them with television or film. Some companies had television- or film-related activities as only a small part of their activities; however, no revenue split was available. This means that the figures produced will represent an overstatement to some extent.

Table 8.4 Number of active firms by line of activity and location

	Manchester	Liverpool	Other North West
Television broadcasters	6	3	2
Film and television production companies	68	30	38
Post-production companies	23	0	12
Crewing and facilities companies	20	2	18
Miscellaneous production-related companies	102	17	100
Freelancers trading as sole proprietorships	15	1	7
Radio stations	24	2	26
TOTAL	258	55	203

Source: FAME, Production Guide 2009 (Broadcast, 2009)

To some degree this will be offset by the fact that some firms which are active in film and television almost certainly avoided detection. The extent of that degree is uncertain. Likewise, some classifications by geographic region were arbitrary. For example, one suburb, Altrincham, was associated with Greater Manchester as it is in the borough of Trafford, officially part of Greater Manchester; the nearby commuter town of Knutsford was treated as other North West, as it is outside the official boundary of Greater Manchester. On any sensible definition of a functional city region it is hard to justify treating Altrincham differently from Knutsford. Some boroughs officially part of Greater Manchester were excluded: the northern boroughs of Wigan, Bury, Bolton, Rochdale and Oldham. These boroughs have their main centres some distance away from the City of Manchester and also have particular and separate identities.

The sectoral composition of the Liverpool and Manchester clusters is shown in Table 8.4. This illustrates the extent to which Manchester dominates Liverpool, particularly as a centre for broadcast television and radio. The production sector is not broken down into film and television, but it is important to note that here Liverpool has more film activity than Manchester, yet, Lime Pictures aside, almost no broadcast TV activity. Many of the firms in the 'Other North West' column are in close proximity to Manchester, either in North East Cheshire or in the Northern boroughs of Greater Manchester. Significantly, firm numbers have decreased markedly over the last decade. For example, earlier research indicated that in 2000 there were 138 firms engaged in production (production companies and facilities companies) and 38 post-production companies (Johns, 2004).

Table 8.5 *Age and size of companies*

Variable	Number	Mean	Median	Lower quartile	Upper quartile	Mini-mum	Maximum
Age	480	7.6	6	4	10	1	59
Number of employees	29	57.8	34	8	57	1	431
Turnover £	68	2,803,988	160,707	44,725	2,987,705	2172	36,144,000

Source: FAME.

Age and Size of Companies

Table 8.5 provides summary data on the size and age of companies based on the data collected. These demographics and the figures on financial performance exclude the BBC and ITV (although employment in these two major broadcasters is incorporated in the total employment figures for the region displayed in Table 8.1 and the associated location quotients in Table 8.2). The pattern reveals what is typical of the distribution of company sizes generally; it has a very strong positive skew, with most companies being very small. Directors of companies are not included in the employment totals and very few of the companies in the database were large enough to be obliged to file employment data. The comparatively young age profile reflects the relative recency of the development of independent production in broadcast television and also the high churn of firms in both film and television. Production companies have a similar age profile to all companies in the database, but are typically smaller, with a median size of six employees.

Financial Performance of Companies

The financial data indicate that the median company in the sector is performing adequately, with sound profit margins and liquidity and without excessive gearing. Return on capital figures need to be treated with caution as many companies operate with very low overheads and, particularly in production, hire in equipment, which is then charged as a current expense rather than being a component of long-term capital. Examining the lower quartile does, however, reveal that there is a substantial proportion of companies which are struggling to survive, being both loss-making and lacking liquidity (the conventional 'safe' level of the liquidity ratio is 1, where liquid assets are just equal to current liabilities). Some companies are also highly geared, with those in the upper quartile having substan-

Table 8.6 Financial performance of companies

Variable	Number	Mean	Median	Lower quartile	Upper quartile	Minimum	Maximum
Gross margin %	63	16.0	14.7	−5.2	45.6	−75.0	86.7
Return on capital employed %	78	119.0	48.0	−4.2	163.2	−731.6	845.1
Liquidity ratio	385	1.90	0.96	0.49	1.60	0	94.71
Gearing ratio	139	394.2	22.4	2.96	169.5	0.002	8711.0

Source: FAME.

tially more debt than equity. There is nothing particularly distinctive about profitability of production companies compared to other types of companies in the database.

The profile of companies in the North West may be compared with what is known about independent production companies in film and television nationally (PACT, 2007, 2009). The size distribution has a marked positive skew with nine so-called 'super-indies' with turnovers in excess of £50 million, approximately 20 companies in the £10–£50 million turnover range, just over 100 with turnovers between £1–10 million and around 600 very small companies. The top ten companies account for nearly 60 per cent of all revenue in the sector. The general trend in the sector is for increasing consolidation with a continual high churn of small entrants, many of whom will not survive long. Industry average profit margins are 8.4 per cent (the exact calculation of this figure is not explicitly stated by PACT and as such it is not clear that this can be directly compared with the figures reported in Table 8.6, which is a pre-tax margin). What is clear from the PACT census is that the smallest size class of companies, those with a turnover below £1 million, have far greater variation in profitability, reflecting the hand-to-mouth existence such companies typically endure with periods of feast when they have been commissioned interspersed with periods of famine when they are seeking new commissions.

The most recent PACT Nations and Regions Report (PACT, 2008) puts a different perspective on the precariousness of independent production in the English regions and the nations of Scotland and Wales. The report notes the generally adverse effect of more centralized (in London) commissioning structures among the major broadcasters and also the fact that ITV has essentially downgraded its commitment to the nations and regions. The fortunes of particular regions have been skewed in recent years by the ephemeral popularity of quiz shows. The South East recorded a brief surge in hours commissioned during the relatively short life of *The Mint* (Ludus for ITV; hours of independent production fell by 58 per cent in 2007 when this show was axed), and the North West similarly experienced a short-term surge in hours commissioned associated with two quiz shows which flourished only briefly before being axed, *Make Your Play* (ITV) and *Glitterball* (Ludus for ITV), which together accounted for 1,300 hours out of ITV's total production out of the North West of 1,786 hours in 2007, in which year both quiz shows were axed. Despite the gravitation of ITV towards London, the North West has remained the single largest region for out-of-London production in ITV. The North West has the highest total of hours of independently produced network drama outside London, 143 hours in 2007. 88 per cent of this total was accounted for by *Hollyoaks*, a soap opera produced in Liverpool by Lime Pictures for Channel 4. Channel 4 had 41 per cent of original production (excluding news) in 2007 from the Nations and Regions, Five just 27 per cent.

CONNECTING THE CLUSTER: LOCAL AND EXTRA-LOCAL NETWORKS

Connectedness within the Cluster

The broadcasting sector in the North West, and particularly in Manchester, has been undergoing significant changes in the last 15 years that are radically reshaping and transforming the nature (and quantity) of connections within and between the cluster(s). This section uses empirical data collected in 2001–2002 and 2009–2010 to demonstrate how connectedness within the cluster has changed. Markusen's (1996) work on industrial districts provides a typology to illustrate these changes, although as suggested by Coe (2001) in his examination of film and television in Vancouver, this chapter argues that 'hybrid' districts can be observed. As detailed above, the development of broadcasting in Manchester and the North West was dominated by the presence of two broadcasters – Granada (locally headquartered) and BBC North (a branch of the London-based public service broadcaster). Figure 8.1(a) provides a diagrammatic representation of the cluster before 2003. The broadcasters form central nodes in the cluster, providing financing and distribution. From the mid-1990s the role of BBC North diminished as commissioning shifted to London. The role of Granada strengthened as the North West became strongly associated with the production of high-quality drama, producing a plethora of high profile prime-time productions. For international readers, we can best characterize these successful television pro-

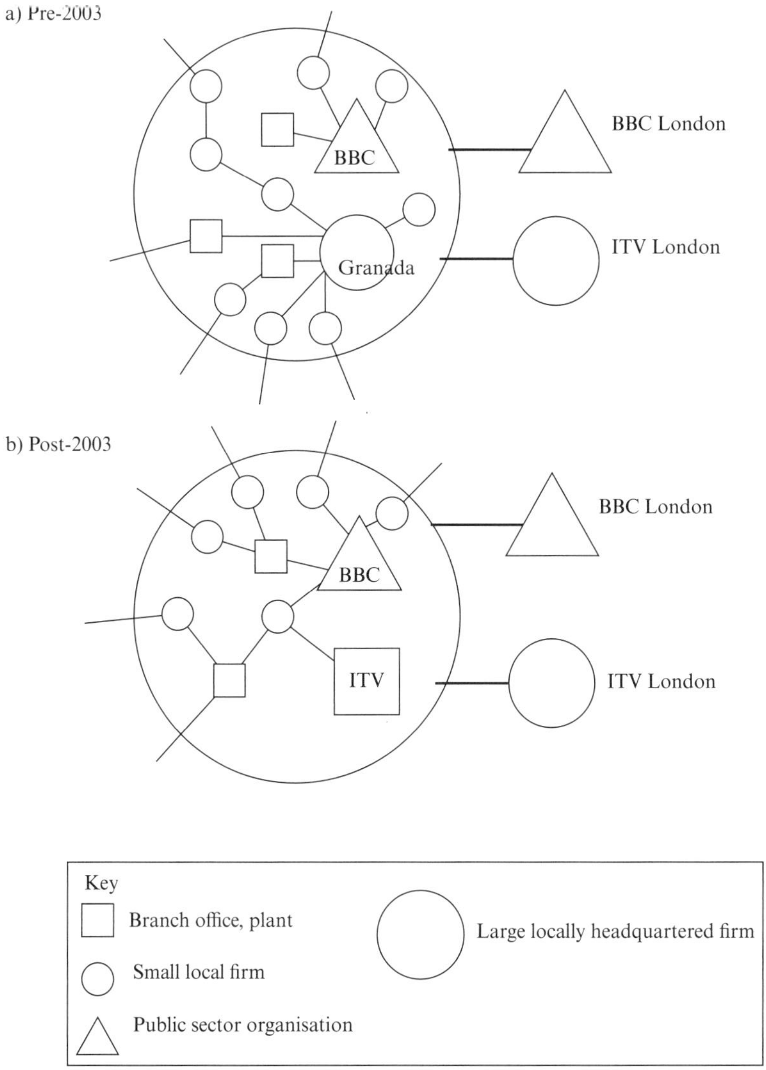

Figure 8.1 Diagrammatic representation of the broadcasting cluster

grammes as gritty and realistic portrayals of life in the North West with messages about crime, poverty and class that resonated across the UK and beyond. The region developed a strong reputation for high quality production standards and story writing. The North West, essentially Manchester, has also established a strong reputation for factual television, which again reflects a particular area of strength of the old Granada, the leading regional ITV franchise for hard-hitting documentaries.

The 1990 Broadcasting Act resulted in the emergence of a multitude of independent production companies, facilities firms and post production companies (many of which were formed by former staff from Granada and BBC North). This spinning out of activities from the core broadcasters resulted in high degrees of connectivity between the independent firms and the broadcasters, and indeed between firms within the cluster generally. These reputational networks were bolstered by high levels of labour turnover and increased levels of freelance staff servicing local firms. In many respects this phase of broadcasting in the region is now seen by many as the heyday of production with a high degree of connectedness within the cluster as independent firms connected in formal business relationships across the supply chain and high levels of informal networks created 'buzz' (Bathelt, Malmberg and Maskell, 2004) in the region.

By 2003 connectedness within the cluster was challenged, as reduced levels of commissioning from the BBC and, significantly, Granada created a substantial rise in competition for declining financial resources. The hollowing out of Granada commissioning and staffing levels in Manchester was part of broader changes in the independent broadcasting sector driven from London. Facilitated by regulatory change, by 2002 Granada had established an effective duopoly of ITC and Carlton, resulting in Granada taking a more national focus and moving their headquarters to London. In early 2004 Granada and Carlton merged, resulting in the end of the brand 'Granada' and signalling a continued – and accelerated – phase of disinvestment in the North West. The reduction in commissioning from within Manchester has resulted in a decline in the total number of firms in the region and has changed the nature and quantity of connections within and beyond the cluster. Since 2003 several national production, post-production and facilities firms have closed their North West subsidiaries. Locally owned firms that continue to survive have done so through the strengthening of network relationships *beyond* the cluster to secure financing and distribution and often through diversification away from the traditional broadcasting sector. Our empirical research has revealed that these extra-local networks are increasingly important and have resulted in an associated decline in connectedness within Manchester. Figure 8.1b shows that the broadcasters are less significant nodes as network actors and that independent locally owned firms across the production chain have increased their connection to outside actors. When asked what proportion of work is in the Greater Manchester area, a locally headquartered facilities firm replied: 'I'll answer that with one word . . . zero and that is really frustrating. There haven't been many productions in Manchester or Liverpool or the North West this year' (Facilities Firm 1, 20 October 2009).

We can therefore observe a cluster that has shifted from one that resembles a hub-and-spoke district (Figure 8.1a) to a more transitory cluster (Figure 8.1b) seeking to survive with a huge decrease in financing and distribution from the hubs. Although the cluster has always been predicated on finance and distribution from London (Johns, 2010), the level of connectedness *within* the cluster has decreased as extra-local connections provide the resources for local firms to continue to compete. We characterize the current structure of the cluster as being in a state of transition due to recent and emerging policy interventions that seek to reclaim and strengthen activities in the North West. These will be discussed below.

Spillovers Within and to Other Clusters

As suggested above, the relationship between broadcasting in the North West and in London has always been uneven. The capital has traditionally been the source of key decision making (both within the industry and in broader policymaking) and finance and distribution. Therefore, the broadcasting sector in the North West has tended to view itself in relation to London and emphasized the challenges of operating in the shadow of London dominance. During 2001–2002 a series of networking meetings were facilitated by a North-West public sector organization that sought to increase communication between firms in each production sector (production, facilities and post-production). Monthly discussions became dominated by evaluation and reevaluation of the cluster's relationship with London and issues of competitiveness (Johns, 2004). Firms debated the merits of offering the North West as a low-cost 'runaway' production site for London firms versus maintaining high production values and services. After just a year the networks failed as conversation veered dangerously close to price-fixing.

This focus on London as the dominant node in national decision making and resource allocation is understandable, but as market conditions in the North West have changed, so too have the perceptions of firms and freelancers.

> The overriding lesson we have learned is quality is key . . . If they [firms] have gone wrong [failed] to be honest they weren't good enough . . . for the market. Some of the production businesses in the North of England just aren't good enough. That is why they don't get the business, it's not about prejudice or policy or allocation of resources or anything. It's just because they aren't good enough (Production Company 2, 8 October 2009).

This characterizes a new attitude within the clusters that seeks to make and maintain connections to other clusters, within the region but particularly to sources of finance and distribution outside the UK. Due in part to the strong presence of sporting activities in the North West, the region is increasingly attracting global advertising agencies seeking sports personalities for their campaigns. Representing a source of diversified income, the region is now attracting US, European and Asian advertising agencies that use the North West as a production facility, but all other parts of the production chain (finance, post production and distribution) are conducted outside the region.

This illustrates that extra-local connections to London and other global cities are still based on uneven power relationships in which the North West seeks to compete but is unable to extract maximum value from the sourcing of non-local financing. As this chapter will go on to argue, the nature of connections to other clusters is evolving as a variety of policy interventions are seeking to reshape the broadcasting sector through the development of several clusters that aim to connect together in and beyond the region at the global scale.

RECENT CLUSTER DEVELOPMENT POLICIES

As part of broader cultural economy policymaking, the North West is seeking to re-establish the region as a significant site of broadcasting. Until recently, policy intervention in the region consisted of business support (although not necessarily specific to the sector), small-scale funding of individual projects and the networking initiative cited above. The announcement of the relocation of five BBC departments to the North West has provided a catalyst for more concerted efforts to support the sector. A more coherent set of objectives is beginning to emerge, with the clearest being attempts to connect the broadcasting sector with the strong IT cluster in Manchester. This section presents the four key cluster initiatives currently emerging in the region, of which the development of MediaCity in Salford is the largest in size and level of investment. Each cluster has different objectives and ambitions and in combination may radically change the nature of broadcasting in the region.

Table 8.7 shows the four key sites of cluster development in the region. All have emerged since 2009 and are in various stages of development. With the exception of MediaCity, the physical spaces selected are a pragmatic response to the availability of brownfield sites (often containing warehousing) that are characteristic of post-industrial cities. As one interviewee suggests, '. . . in the countries that do have a "media city", places

Table 8.7 A comparison of the four key cluster developments in the North West

	The Pie Factory	MediaCity	The Sharp Project	The Baltic Triangle
Location	Salford	Salford	Manchester (East)	Liverpool (City Centre)
History	Brownfield development of existing warehousing	Brownfield site; all new build	Brownfield development of vacated manufacturing site	Brownfield development of historic port area
Ownership	**Private** property development	**Private** property development with public and private tenants	**Publicly** owned (Manchester City Council) with private sector engagement with local property developers	Liverpool Vision (a **public/private** economic development agency)
Government funding levels	Unknown	£30 million facilitated by NWDA (for infrastructure development, i.e. roads and tram connection)	£5 million (Manchester City Council) followed by £6.3 million (NWDA and ERDF)	NWDA and ERDF funding; amounts unknown
Size	15,000 sq. ft. of office and warehouse accommodation	700,000 sq.ft. office space; 250,000 sq.ft. studio space; 60,000 sq.ft. retail and leisure; 378 apartments; 218-bed hotel	200,000 sq. ft. of office and warehouse accommodation (modular offices built as required from converted containers)	40,000 sq. ft. of office and warehouse accommodation

Table 8.7 (continued)

	The Pie Factory	MediaCity	The Sharp Project	The Baltic Triangle
Cluster aims	**Broadcasting studios** 'Providing freedom and flexibility for TV and film productions, photo shoots and advertising campaigns. With three sound stages, make-up rooms, green rooms, flexible office space, workshop space, and 24/7 security The Pie Factory boasts the finest ingredients all under one roof. It is also home to specialist "on-the-lot" companies, from casting agencies to camera and lighting hire, so you can decide how big a slice of "The Pie" you want to take' http://www.thepiefactory.co.uk/.	**Global Media City/Hub** 'MediaCityUK will be a vibrant waterside community of workers, residents, students and visitors. We're developing a bespoke environment, designed around the specific needs of the creative and digital industries; somewhere like-minded people can develop content and find new ways of working. But MediaCityUK won't just be an innovative place to work – it'll also be a great place to live, study and visit' www.mediacity.co.uk.	**Digital Media Cluster** 'The independent hub for the creative and digital industries and entrepreneurs in the Manchester City region. The project is part of the City's vision to drive forward the digital economy and help it achieve the critical mass it needs to make an impact on the world stage. The aims of The Sharp Project are: to strengthen the existing cluster of industries in this sector, many of which are already world class; to attract a larger volume of production; to expand the freelance talent pool in the city; to develop a pipeline of young people with the range of skills required to meet the industry's needs' http://www.thesharpproject.co.uk/about/.	**Cultural Quarter** 'Imagine an area where musicians rub shoulders with photographers, artists, fashion designers, digital agencies, architects, film-makers, young entrepreneurs, recording studios and there's a bunch of drinking holes and eateries, nightlife venues, internationally acclaimed arts festivals and galleries to drop-by on. That's us . . . Quietly, under the radar, just getting on with our stuff' http://www.baltictriangle.co.uk/about/.

Types of company present	**Broadcasting** Casting agencies, crew, camera and kit hire, lighting and grip hire, production services, outside broadcasting and software development.	**Mixed** Still in development. Confirmed tenants: broadcasters (BBC anchor tenant; discussions with ITV ongoing), University of Salford, supermarket, radio production company; others to be confirmed.	**Broadcasting and multi-media** Studios used for TV and commercial production including a large drama for the BBC. Cluster still in development. Confirmed tenants include a camera company, a design agency and a digital content production company. Exhibition of cultural content has taken place including art exhibitions. Plans to house Manchester's IT Disaster Recovery Centre.	**Mixed** Business support, logistics, retail, online content production and distribution, web design, fashion design, animation.
Cluster differen-tiator/USP	**Proximity to MediaCity** Flexible office and warehouse space with close proximity to MediaCity. Aims to develop into a more cutting-edge multi-media facility including a visitor centre, conference facilities and to operate as a live music venue.	**State-of-the-art facilities** Technologically advanced, high-definition broadcast studios with high connectivity. Broadcaster(s) (and commissioning) onsite. Aims to attract global media and internet firms. A platform for content production, distribution and exhibition.	**Low cost, large capacity** Low cost, flexible office accommodation for start-up companies and SMEs. Largest studio space in region (studios are larger than those at MediaCity).	**Unique in Liverpool** Low-cost office accommodation for start-up companies and SMEs.

like Seoul, Korea, places like Dubai, Barcelona, there is a whole range of them. The difficulty is comparing apples with apples because again, the reality is that most of them offer something different' (Property Developer 1, 17 March 2010).

All four clusters are seeking to attract firms that will combine to make a unique offering. In the cases of The Pie Factory, The Sharp Project and The Baltic Triangle, these are offerings that are distinctive at the national scale, while MediaCity aims to be globally competitive. This section builds on the information contained in Table 8.7 and discusses the possible implications for the wider broadcasting cluster in the North West.

The four cluster initiatives all involve – to a greater or lesser degree – the North West Development Agency. This raises questions surrounding the consistency and broader vision of media policymaking in the region as the current situation implies that the regional government supports *four* clusters within a relatively small and highly competitive industry. Possibly as a result of this, each cluster aims to serve a different purpose within the sector.

The MediaCityUK development is the most substantial development in a regional television centre since the creation of ITV in the mid-1950s. A catalyst to the development was the announcement in 2004 by the BBC that it was looking to create a centre in the North associated with the move of five BBC departments from London. The MediaCity development at Salford Quays was selected ahead of a rival proposal based around development of the Granada Studios complex in Manchester in 2006; construction started on phase 1 of the development in January 2007 and MediaCity is scheduled to open in Summer 2011 at a cost of £500 million (although our interview data reliably inform us that spending has already reached over £600 million). The key anchor tenant (thus providing the impetus for the creation of the 'city') is the BBC. The five BBC departments moving to the site are: Children's Television, Sport, Learning, Radio 5 Live and Future Media and Technology. The existing BBC operations on Oxford Road in Manchester will also move to MediaCity. In all, some 1400 new BBC staff will be located at MediaCity, joining the 800 staff who already work in Manchester. A little under half of this additional 1400 will be staff relocating from London within the affected departments. There has been considerable uncertainty regarding whether or not ITV will also be relocating to MediaCity.

The vision is for MediaCity to be the largest purpose-built creative and digital content media hub in Europe and thus to be a major media centre globally. The BBC has committed to 40 per cent of the studio capacity at MediaCity in addition to office space, and the property developers are seeking global media conglomerates to locate in Salford. The presence of the BBC is considered to be an asset in attracting investment:

> . . . the BBC . . . is going to be a very powerful partner for them, it's an attractive partner for them, it's a powerful brand nationally and internationally so what I'd say is that there is tremendous potential to be realized and if I was a truly global media organization, why would I go there rather than Dublin, Singapore, Abu Dhabi? (Broadcaster 2, 19 November 2009)

Indeed, the MediaCity property developers have not been actively networking with local businesses to offer them space, as this is considered to be a 'robbing Peter to pay Paul' mentality (Property Developer 1, 17 March 2010). Therefore, the vision of the MediaCity is to attract global sources of finance and distribution through subsidiaries located on-site. This conforms to a 'global pipelines' (Bathelt et al., 2004) conceptualization of industrial spaces, although at this stage it is unclear how and where 'local buzz' will contribute beyond the boundaries of MediaCity.

The cluster is struggling to overcome the tension between attracting international organizations while not excluding local firms:

> Some people have been wary of Ascent [a US-based media company which owns a substantial proportion of post production in central London] coming into the region and are wondering if that means that it is all buttoned-up. We have been getting out and talking to businesses. If we can do this well we can bring in CBS or Disney or Microsoft or Google or Yahoo . . . You have to have something to have a proposition, but there is a fine line between putting too much in and squeezing out opportunities for anyone else. And you want it to be a cluster. It's about finding a balance, putting in the minimum that you need. And leave opportunities for others to come in and develop unique propositions. Developing businesses around here and using us as a platform (Property Developer 1, 17 March 2010).

Figure 8.2 shows an interpretation of the MediaCity cluster based on interview data collected from local property developers and prospective and confirmed tenants including the BBC and local broadcasting firms. The presence of a second national broadcaster (ITV) is still in question, and if MediaCity is successful in attracting international firms then more 'branch plant' subsidiaries will be present. The central role of the publicly-owned BBC in this cluster may suggest this cluster is moving towards a 'state-anchored' industrial district model. However, the whole MediaCity site is privately owned, somewhat obscuring the applicability of this type. Over the next decade it will be possible to chart the development of this cluster and to re-evaluate the nature and composition of the broadcasting sector. The key question of the degree of *local* firm presence and integration in the supply chain remains.

Doubt has been cast on whether any but well-established independent production companies will be able to afford to rent space in MediaCity by

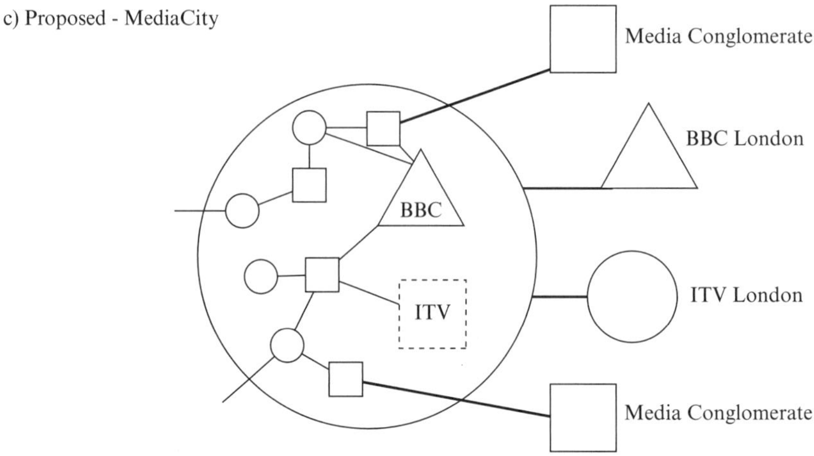

Figure 8.2 Possible cluster structure following completion of MediaCity

some interview respondents and Stuart Cosgrove, Head of Nations and Regions at Channel 4. Many Manchester independents, even if they were able and willing to pay MediaCity rents, may be constrained by the terms of their existing leases. Peel Holdings have been courting major London-based independent production companies and post-production houses, including major US-based media company Ascent Media. Some London-based independents have established outposts in Manchester such as Shine North, Zig Zag North, October North and Channel K. Some have come and gone, with Objective North and Scarlet TV (owned by Motive Television) being recent closures (Scarlet is currently in administration at the time of writing, but appears destined to be wound up).

Possibly in response to this perceived need for more realistic rental and studio space in the region, three alternative sites have emerged. One part of the MediaCity development, The Pie Factory, opened in January 2007. The Pie Factory is a flexible office and production space, including three sound stages, which is adjacent to the main office complex, part of which will be occupied by the BBC when it makes its move north. At present The Pie Factory has 15 tenants, including production companies, crewing and facilities companies and a casting agency. However, the vision for this site is to reconfigure the space to be more 'funky', housing design-intensive industries rather than facilities firms. The 'low-cost' alternative is The Sharp Project. This development has resulted from Manchester City Council's purchase of the abandoned Sharp electronics factory. It aims to offer cheap office accommodation, with individual modular offices constructed from recycled containers, and very low cost studio space (with a larger, but less technologically advanced, capacity). This explicit cost differentiator is an outcome of perceived demand, local council ownership and pragmatic response to industry uncertainty. While rhetoric and discourse surrounding broadcasting in the region has become more positive as a result of the MediaCity development, those on the coal face remain more pessimistic:

> Our rent at The Pie Factory has gone up again so we're looking to move. We won't even consider MediaCity . . . it's not our kind of place and there isn't room anyway. The Sharp Project may be a good idea because it's cheap and we aren't sure what will happen over the next few years (Facilities Firm 4, 14 May 2010).

Finally, The Baltic Triangle is a cluster initiative with much broader ambitions to attract any new media, media- or design-intensive industries to an historical, but rundown, port area of the city. It is a collection of buildings rather than an integrated site but has already attracted a number of different firms including those in the broadcasting sector. Significantly, this cluster's differentiator is its geographical location in Liverpool, rather than viewing itself in comparison to MediaCity. This raises questions about the geographical scope of the MediaCity project and the degree to which North West, or indeed Northern, firms feel they will be able to engage with this 'global node'.

SUSTAINABILITY OF THE CLUSTER

As acknowledged by Impacts 08, which has investigated the impact of the European Capital of Culture in Liverpool in 2008, the concept of sustainability is both hard to conceptualize and to measure empirically. It is very difficult to track the pattern of births and deaths of firms over time as available statistics on, for example, VAT registrations are not classified in sufficient detail to identify firms in the film and television industries (or the creative industries more widely defined). As regards the television industry in Manchester, there is evidence that it does have some properties of sustainability. It has been and remains the second largest broadcast TV region outside London. What is significant is that it has managed to retain this status despite the significant downscaling of ITV (Granada), which now only maintains the long-running soap *Coronation Street* as a major production activity. Independent production companies have had the capacity to compete for and win commissions from broadcasters outside the region, and the scale of production activity maintained in Manchester has retained a large and diverse talent pool and a network of associated firms providing goods and services to the core activities of broadcasting, production and post-production. It is a moot point how much of the current scale would be maintained (net) if a similar run-down were also to occur in the BBC. The fortunes of the BBC in Manchester have fluctuated over the years, but not on the scale either of the recent downsizing of ITV, nor of the imminent influx of BBC staff with the MediaCity project. Film in Manchester has not seen anything akin to the waxing and waning of key hub firms, and film activity remains on a smaller scale than television.

Different considerations apply when examining the case of Liverpool. Mersey TV, now Lime Pictures, is an exceptional firm and one whose success was based on a combination of a novel and effective business model combined with a high level of creative talent. Lime's success was not really attributable to any clustering effect in Liverpool, nor does it appear to have generated significant externalities. That said, many individuals do pass through Lime, albeit that many do so on fairly limited internships and work experience schemes. Liverpool has never had a large television broadcasting presence. It was home to TV-AM for a few years, yet this cannot be compared in scale to the combined operations of the BBC and ITV at their apex in Manchester. Liverpool can claim to have demonstrated greater sustainability in film, where independent filmmaking survives at a higher scale than in Manchester. The city has also been successful in promoting itself as a location for filming.

The Impacts 08 evaluation of the Capital of Culture identified a number of particular opportunities and threats facing the creative industries generally in Liverpool. Among the opportunities were the enhanced image of Liverpool as well as its ability to benefit from greater activity within the North West, with potential linkages with Manchester being identified in particular. It was also felt there were identifiable networks forming in the creative industries in Liverpool which might provide the basis for leadership to arise from within to guide the creative industries. Conversely, among the threats, it was identified that this leadership has yet to emerge, leading to the danger that the creative industries be perceived as incoherent. There was also felt to be an inadequate institutional basis for bringing the public and private sectors into productive cooperation. Finally, there was a perceived risk that gentrification in the city might lead to a lack of affordable workspaces, necessary for the incubation of new creative businesses. The report found (Impacts 08 2009, p. 48):

> Key priority areas have been outlined . . . These include: the need for specialist and tailored professional development support for growth businesses; the need to bring more work into the city; the value in fostering new connections; strategic sector profile raising and development and the relationship between universities and industry, in particular around graduate retention and student development.

The tenor of these findings from the Impacts 08 assessment accords with remarks made by interview respondents from Liverpool. All felt there had been a boost to the image of the city and to morale within it but did not articulate any direct benefit for their business.

CONCLUSIONS

This chapter has presented the case of broadcasting in the North West with a focus on the agglomeration of activities in Manchester. Broadcasting in Manchester and Liverpool has traditionally suffered from national inequalities in the distribution of finance and distribution resources. However, both cities have been able to carve niches – drama in Manchester and film production in Liverpool – in spite of these challenges. National legislation has impacted the North West in a variety of ways, most recently with the relaxation of regulation of independent broadcasting. The consolidation of ITV in London has exacerbated the centralization of decision making (and resources) in the capital city. As a consequence, levels of production and firm numbers across the production chain have declined in both Manchester and Liverpool.

Using Markusen's (1996) typology, this chapter has attempted to illustrate a cluster undergoing significant transition. The politically motivated decision to relocate five BBC departments has provided the impetus to create a media city that can act as a global hub of content production. This represents the most ambitious media cluster development project in UK history. The chapter makes the following points in relation to this development. First, the cluster is a privately-funded initiative in which the publicly-owned BBC is an anchor tenant. This raises questions about the applicability of Markusen's state-anchored industrial district model. Secondly, the focus of MediaCity is on attracting investment from large global media conglomerates. The role of local firms is as yet unclear and given the high rental cost of locating at MediaCity it seems unlikely that many firms will locate there. The owners of MediaCity are not constrained by local development criteria as the only public funding has contributed to infrastructure development in public spaces and to educational facilities. Thirdly, MediaCity sits alongside other, albeit smaller, cluster initiatives that are more limited in ambition and scope. Nonetheless these may offer a more realistic environment for local and national firms to engage in networking activities and the creation of 'local buzz' (Bathelt et al., 2004).

As the other chapters in this section reveal, media clusters in second cities face particular challenges in relation to continued existence (and growth). The geographical concentration of media activities (and sources of financing) in key global cities such as London and Los Angeles results in second-tier clusters often being predicated on connections to these sites. The broadcasting cluster outlined in this chapter is both dependent upon accessing financial resources from London and influenced by political decision making in the capital. As illustrated by the Hilversum chapter, the drain of creative capital to larger clusters presents a serious threat to the continuation of secondary clusters. London, just as with Amsterdam, continues to attract investment (both national and global) and skilled media labour. Traditionally institutional support in the North West has tended to be weak and is not supported by tax incentives as in the case of Toronto.

This chapter has thrown into sharp relief also the considerable challenges facing policymakers at regional and local level outside the capital. The fortunes of the film and television industry in the North West, and elsewhere in the UK, have been dominated by policy developments at national level. The development of Manchester as a major regional centre is rooted in the system of regional franchises laid down in the 1950s as part of the template for independent television broadcasting. The creation of Channel 4 and Five in London and more recently the relaxation of competition policy permitting the merger of Granada and Carlton, which catalysed the significant winding down of Granada's operations in Manchester, were both developments which significantly weakened the industry in Manchester. Local policy has been comparatively weak in mitigating the effects of these national policy changes. The MediaCity development, which will be a substantial boost to the industry in the NorthWest, particularly Manchester, is fundamentally driven by a London-based locus of decision making. This has arisen internally within the BBC and also within the regulator Ofcom and political imperatives towards greater regional spending within the BBC expressed in the Houses of Parliament. The policy challenge in the North West is how to capitalize on this major shift in UK broadcasting to the benefit of local companies and in a way which will create a sustainable industry.

The development of MediaCity is significantly changing the landscape of broadcasting in the North West. The decentralization of some BBC departments from London has been received positively by many in the North West. However, this new 'global media hub' is essentially a private property development in which the BBC is just one (albeit very large) tenant. The development includes retail and consumption spaces, which seeks to make MediaCity a busy, vibrant location for all. This is driven by the demands of commercial return on the investment of capital and represents a particular model for cluster development. The embryonic status of MediaCity makes reflection on its potential for success problematic. At present benefits have been realized by the construction sector but those connected to broadcasting remain ambivalent regarding the potential for real benefits reaching the *whole* cluster in the North West. Many are sceptical of the degree to which they will be able to engage with production activities at MediaCity. It will take a number of years to evaluate the impact of cluster developments and to conceptualize the emerging shape and form of the broadcasting sector in the North West.

REFERENCES

Adroit (2005), *North West Economy Regional and Sub Regional Cluster Analysis: Internal Briefing Document for the EI&S Directorate, NWDA*, Adroit Economics Ltd.

Bathelt, H., A. Malmberg and P. Maskell (2004), 'Clusters and Knowledge: Local Buzz, Global Pipelines and the Process of Knowledge Creation', *Progress in Human Geography*, **28**(1), 31–56.

Broadcast (2009), *The Production Guide 2009*, Hampton UK: RunningMan Publishing.

Coe, N.M. (2001), 'A Hybrid Agglomeration? The Development of a Satellite-Marshallian Industrial District in Vancouver's Film Industry', *Urban Studies*, **38**(10), 1753–1775.

Coe, N.M. and J. Johns (2004), 'Beyond Production Clusters: Towards a Critical Political Economy of Networks in the Film and Television Industries', in Dominic Power and Allen J. Scott (eds), *Cultural Industries and the Production of Culture*, London, UK: Routledge, pp. 188–204.

Cook, G. and N. Pandit (2007), 'Service Industry Clustering: A Comparison of Broadcasting in Three City Regions', *Service Industries Journal*, **27**(4), 453–469.

Cook, G.A.S. and N.R. Pandit (2009), 'Clustering and the Internationalisation Strategies of SMEs in the Media Industry', *International Journal of Globalisation and Small Business*, **3**(3), 306–330.

Ettlinger, N (2003), 'Cultural Economic Geography and a Relational and Microspace Approach to Trusts, Rationalities, Networks, and Change in Collaborative Workplaces', *Journal of Economic Geography*, **3**(2), 145–171.

FAME (Financial Analysis Made Easy), Bureau van Dijk Electronic Publishing, Amsterdam: Netherlands (online database, access via subscription only, accessed 18/9/09).

Florida, R. (2005), *Cities and the Creative Class*, New York, NY, USA: Routledge.

Impacts 08 (2009), *Liverpool's Creative Industries: Understanding the Impact of Liverpool European Capital of Culture 2008 on the City Region's Creative Industries*. Available at: http://www.impacts08.net (accessed 3/11/09)

Johns, J. (2004), *Tracing the Connections: Manchester's Film and Television Industry*, PhD thesis, Manchester, UK: University of Manchester.

Johns, J. (2010), 'Manchester's Film and Television Industry: Project Ecologies and Network Hierarchies', *Urban Studies*, **47**(5), 1059–1077.

Markusen, A. (1996), 'Sticky Places in Slippery Space: A Typology of Industrial Districts', *Economic Geography*, **72**(3), 293–313.

Ofcom (2006), *Review of the Television Production Sector: Statement*, available at http://www.ofcom.org.uk/consult/condocs/tpsr/statement/review_tv.pdf, accessed 12/08/09.
PACT (2007), *The Production Trend Report for Out of London*, London, UK: PACT.
PACT (2008), *Nations and Regions*, Report produced for PACT by Attentional.
PACT (2009), *Pact Policy Survey and Financial Census 2009*, A report by Oliver & Ohlbaum Associates Ltd for PACT.
Skillset (2010a), *Skillset Employment Census*, available at http:// www.skillset.org, accessed 19/2/10.
Skillset (2010b), *Television Sector – Labour Market Intelligence Digest*, available at http://www.skillset.org, accessed 19/2/10.
Skillset (2010c), *Film Sector – Labour Market Intelligence Digest*, available at http://www.skillset.org, accessed 19/2/10.

9. Sydney's media cluster: continuity and change in film and television

Tom O'Regan, Ben Goldsmith and Susan Ward

Sydney is Australia's largest city and hosts its largest media concentration. A significant media city globally, Sydney is the production and design centre for the Australian media system and a subsidiary node of larger international systems principally headquartered in Los Angeles and London (Mould, 2007, 2008; Krätke, 2003; Krätke and Taylor, 2004). Its media cluster has long been important in Australia. The cluster is undergoing transformations to solidify that position and to improve its position internationally by increasing capabilities and ties to other Australian and international production clusters. Sydney's media cluster is not organized in the precinct-like manner of the Netherlands' Hilversum with its demarcated broadcasting city. Nor is it akin to the cluster of post production houses found in London's Soho on a grid of several streets. Rather, it is a collection of suburbs forming an arc along major transport corridors stretching from Macquarie Park in the north to Sydney airport in the south. As a dispersed rather than tightly bound cluster, it is defined by the functional proximity provided by automobile and telecommunication networks.

Sydney's media cluster is considered here along two dimensions – that of Sydney's place within the ecology of Australian and international media and that of its internal organization within the geographical space of metropolitan Sydney. The first examines Sydney's media cluster at the level of the metropolitan area of Sydney within its state, national and international contexts; the second digs below this level to explore its working out in urban space. The media cluster identified in this chapter produces TV programmes, TV advertisements and feature films and to a lesser extent corporate video and documentary. We will be using here the definitions of the Australian Bureau of Statistics (ABS), which differentiate among 'TV services (TV station and network production, income and employment)', film, video and television production and post-production companies' (independent production and post production companies producing for film, TV and advertising), and the 'advertising and marketing' industries (associated with commercial production and corporate video).

SYDNEY'S AUSTRALIAN PLACE

With 4.4 million people, Sydney has 21 per cent of Australia's 21.4 million people (ABS 2009; June 2008 figures). As the state capital of New South Wales (NSW), Sydney's scale and capacity is further boosted by having within a 150 kilometre radius two of Australia's four largest regional cities in Newcastle and Wollongong. Like other Australian state capitals, Sydney is not only the political and administrative hub of the state, but also its most important commercial and business centre (Gibson, Murphy and Freestone, 2002, p. 179). This pattern is pronounced in the media industries with Sydney's share of state screen production employment standing at 89 per cent in film and 88 per cent in TV services in 2006[1] and its share of film and TV production companies standing at 91.5 per cent in 2009. These state shares have remained consistent with comparable results for production employment in both 2001 and 2006, and for production companies with an average 94.5 per cent of NSW companies for 1987–2009 (see Table 9.1). The decline from nearly 100 per cent to a little over 90 per cent in this period was largely the result of companies locating to fringe areas around Sydney.[2]

The national prominence and stability of Sydney's media cluster is evident from its 409 production companies in 2009 making up half of the Australian total. As Table 9.1 shows, this national share has remained constant averaging 56.3 per cent over the 22 years and moving mostly in the 50–59 per cent range with an average of 429 companies ranging from 385 to 487 companies. The 73.7 per cent share in 1990 was due to a steep decline in Melbourne's share; when its numbers recovered, longer-term relativities were restored. Other Australian media centres exhibit much less stability. Further evidence of Sydney's depth is provided by levels of Australian expenditure on feature films where in the 11 years to the 2008/2009 financial year NSW accounted for 59 per cent of the national total production at 'almost AU$1.85 billion' (Screen Australia, 2010).

Sydney's commanding national position is due to a combination of the scale of its film and TV production capacity and its dominance of command and control and design functions. Indicating Sydney's role as Australia's media design centre, NSW-based companies were responsible in the five years to 2008/2009 for 71 per cent of the total expenditure on Australian film and TV production spending, 46.5 per cent of this in NSW (Screen Australia, 2010). In 2008/2009 NSW companies were

Table 9.1 Sydney's NSW and national share of film and TV production companies

Year	Number	State share %	National share %
1987	406	98.8	58.6
1990	439	98.9	73.7
1992	411	96.5	56.8
1995	406	95.5	57.4
1998	487	93.5	55.3
2001	486	93.5	53.5
2004	385	91.9	50.2
2007	428	90.5	50.4
2009	409	91.5	50.6
Average	429	94.5	56.3

Source: *Encore Directories 1987–2009.*

responsible for AU$497m or 69 per cent of the AU$720m spent nationally on feature film and TV drama production (Screen Australia, 2010). In post-production services where considerable capital, equipment and skills are required, a similar pattern is evident. In 2006 there were approximately 364 NSW companies employing 1668 people generating an income of AU$288.1m and representing 56.1 per cent of the national workforce and 65 per cent of national income (ABS, 2008, p. 26). In TV commercial production NSW had 62 per cent of employment and income and 64 per cent of the national businesses in 2002/2003 (Australian Film Commission 2007, p. 75), and in documentary filmmaking NSW companies produced 55 per cent of titles and 61 per cent of total broadcast hours between 1996/1967 and 2006/2007 (Screen Australia, 2009, p. 7).

Sydney's national media leadership is underscored by its housing the head offices of all five free-to-air TV networks (three commercial and two public service), the leading pay-TV provider, Foxtel, and most pay-TV channels and the major provider of TV and radio ratings, AC Nielsen. Sydney also hosts the national training institutions, the Australian Film, TV and Radio School and the National Institute of Dramatic Arts. It is the headquarters for the national screen agency, Screen Australia, and the media and communications regulatory body, the Australian Communication and Media Authority. All these institutions are 'in part locally and in part nationally constituted' (Cook and Pandit, 2008, p. 276). They develop 'institutional proximity' by creating 'shared norms, conventions, values, expectations and routines arising from the commonly experienced frameworks of institutions' across the nation and within Sydney.

Sydney's media cluster is enhanced by the size of related industries. In Australian market and audience research – a good proxy for command and control functions in a TV system still dominated by free-to-air broadcasting – most companies and most of the leading companies are either headquartered in Sydney or have Sydney offices (see B&T Directory 2009). Sydney hosts over a third of Australia's major performing arts companies, the majority of large (book) publishers (DSRD, 2008, p. 66) and a third of creative industries businesses. The creative industries' share of Sydney's workforce is the highest of any capital city at 6.5 per cent (Higgs, Hagaman and Freebody, 2008, p. 2), and its creative workers are better paid with mean income across creative industry segments 10 per cent higher in Sydney than in the nation as a whole.[3]

Sydney's national position is also expressed in consumption and demand. It commands the highest premium for TV advertising. In 2003/2004 it was AU$214 per capita, compared with Melbourne's AU$184, Brisbane's AU$161 and regional markets' AU$102 per capita (Australian Film Commission, 2005, p. 46). This allowed Sydney with just 21 per cent of the population to command 28 per cent of free-to-air TV advertising revenue. Sydney also has the highest level of pay-TV penetration. In 2004 35 per cent of Sydney households subscribed to a pay-TV service, compared with 28 per cent in Melbourne and Brisbane and the then national average of 22 per cent (Australian Film Commission, 2005, p. 66).

Sydney not only hosts a disproportionate concentration of creative talent and activity, but also of other service industry functions of broader benefit to its media cluster. As West (2006, p. 15) notes, Sydney 'dominates . . . software development, advertising, and industrial and virtual design sectors, with reported firm density for these activities in key inner-city Sydney locations significantly above rival centres'. It is Australia's major tourist and logistics hub as well as its principal finance and business services centre (West, 2006, p. 14; Daly and Pritchard, 2000).

After Sydney there is only one media city of significant capacity. Melbourne, Australia's second largest city, has 18.2 per cent (3.9 million) of the national population and, depending on the measure chosen, has a media industry one third to one half the size of Sydney's. While Melbourne is usually cast as Sydney's 'rival', it is best thought of as its junior partner. These two cities account for the lion's share of film and TV production with three quarters of Australia's film and TV production companies based there in 2009 (602 companies) and a 22-year average to 2009 of 78.6 per cent. Production expenditures for feature films and TV point to a similar pattern with NSW and Victoria's combined share of expenditures at 76 per cent between 1994/1995 and 2008/2009 (Screen Australia, 2010).

These cities combine their dominance of production with an even greater role in media design. Over the same 1994/1995 to 2008/2009 period NSW and Victorian companies generated 92.7 per cent of the total budgets (with highs of 94 per cent and lows of 80 per cent in the period) (Screen Australia, 2010). This collective dominance of production and design extends to the media-related segment of Advertising and Marketing where CCi customization of ABS statistics shows Sydney and Melbourne having 63 per cent of its employment in 2006 (breaking down to 37 per cent and 27 per cent each). These figures point to a longstanding relationship between Sydney and Melbourne companies, agencies and individuals, in organizing Australian film and TV production.

In a TV network system with head offices in Sydney, Melbourne is the logical production location after Sydney. But in an era of branded drama content, Sydney-based networks look not only to Sydney and Melbourne but also more widely for 'hero locations'. Just as the police drama series *Water Rats* featured Sydney's harbour in the lead up to the 2000 Olympics and the gangster series *Underbelly* featured Melbourne then Sydney inner-city locations, *McLeod's Daughters* in the early 2000s featured South Australian 'outback' landscapes close to Adelaide while *Sea Patrol* used Gold Coast and Whitsunday Islands locations in Queensland to provide the required tropical islands and sea settings. With the availability of quality production infrastructures in Adelaide and Brisbane/Gold Coast particularly, Sydney-based design interests were increasingly able to operate on the same Australia-wide canvas as had international producers in their Australian location decisions.

Paradoxically the increasing integration of national markets while centering head office functions in Sydney and contributing to Sydney's production share, has also decentralized some production functions. More integrated national markets in free-to-air broadcasting and pay-TV require production to be based, at least in part, outside Sydney and Melbourne particularly for staple genres such as sports and infotainment programming. The establishment of national sporting competitions in rugby league and Australian rules football and international competition in rugby union created regional teams requiring substantial associated stadia and TV production infrastructure.

Sydney's international significance is underscored by the size and scope of Australia's media market. In 2006, for instance, Australia was ranked 4th in cinema admissions with 4.1 visits per capita per year, 11th for total box office revenue (US$653m; AU$867m), 12th for number of domestic films released, and 18th for production investment in feature films (Screen

Australia, 2010). It sustains large DVD and computer games markets: in 2006 retail DVD sales were AU$1045m and games were AU$596m. As a medium-sized audio-visual market Australia is an importer more than an exporter of cultural goods. In 2005/2006 Australian companies paid AU$869.0 million in royalty payments for imported films, TV programs and video products and a further AU$213.3m in recorded audio-visual media imports – making up combined film and TV imports of AU$1082.3m. This dwarfed the export figure of AU$271m (Screen Australia, 2010).

With this profile, multinational companies set up regional headquarters in Sydney to distribute and produce their goods and services to Australian and adjacent New Zealand, Pacific and some Asian markets. With the expansion of pay-TV from the mid-1990s, global brands such as the BBC set up Australian operations. There is also a longstanding interest by Hollywood majors, international producers and distributors, exhibitors, video store chains and multinational media production companies in the Australian market. Hollywood, British and to a lesser extent German and more lately Dutch companies have been longstanding production partners with Australian companies. This now extends to company ownership. Local market leader Grundy was taken over by Pearson TV in 1995 (and later acquired by Bertelsmann's RTL Group in 2000 to become part of the FremantleMedia brand) and Southern Star by the Dutch-based Endemol in 2009 (part-owned by Silvio Berlusconi). The Ten Network was from 1992 to 2009 majority-owned by the Canadian group CanWest while the regional pay-TV provider AUSTAR is majority-owned by the US-based Liberty Media group. There is also a long history of TV co-productions and partnerships with the BBC, Granada and the German TV network ZDF. Since 1998 UK's Granada has had separate Australian operations and currently produces over 120 hours of TV a year across all genres with production primarily for the Australian TV market. In their turn local companies have grown from their Australian base to become global media companies – most notably Rupert Murdoch's News Corporation but also the mid-sized mini-major Village Roadshow (Goldsmith, Ward and O'Regan, 2010, pp. 120–151).

This combination of international interest in accessing Australian talent, companies and markets when combined with the scale and complexity of Australia's domestic media markets endorses Krätke's identification of Sydney as a second-rung Beta Media city to be seen alongside Copenhagen, Madrid, Hamburg, Stockholm, Milan, Oslo and Toronto (Krätke, 2003). While obviously not of the scale of the Alpha World Media Cities of New York, London, Paris, Los Angeles and Munich, Sydney met Krätke's criteria of classification: more than 30 enterprise units of global media firms and more than 11 global media firms.

O'Connor, Stimson and Daly (2001, p. 173) usefully see Sydney achieving its status as Australia's global city through the combination of increasing national integration, its domestic dominance of 'knowledge-based services and industry' (including the creative industries), and globalization. Rather than seeing Sydney as becoming disembedded from its national territory so as to better participate in a globally linked production, distribution and exhibition system (cf. McGuirk, 2005, p. 63 and Connell, 2000), Sydney appears to be participating globally through its command of a national economy which has begun to operate as a single economic unit (O'Connor et al., 2001; O'Connor, 2002, p. 254).

GEOGRAPHY OF SYDNEY MEDIA CLUSTER(S)

Sydney's media cluster is primarily located in what has been called Sydney's 'global arc' stretching from Macquarie Park, through North Sydney, the central business district (CBD), inner Sydney and ending at Sydney airport. Firm and facility proximity is measured here, not in streets or blocks, but in kilometres and suburbs. Macquarie Park, the business park which houses the leading pay-TV provider Foxtel and the broadcast ratings agency A.C. Nielsen, is 12 kilometres to the north of the Sydney CBD. Moore Park, site of Fox Studios and more lately the Australian Film, TV and Radio School, is 5.4 kilometres south-east of the CBD. There are production precincts in this arc, notably Fox Studios, providing a one-stop shop of facilities and firms to service high budget film and TV production (Jensen, 2009a, p.27; Goldsmith and O'Regan, 2003, pp. 45–46). But such tightly bounded – and in Fox's case gated – production spaces are not the norm. Typically there are more loose aggregations of firms and facilities such as those on the lower North Shore in North Sydney and in the area immediately adjacent to Sydney's CBD in Pyrmont-Redfern-Moore Park evident in Figure 9.1 (see also Gibson, Murphy and Freestone, 2002; Jensen, 2009b, pp. 13–15). Figure 9.1 shows the location pattern of Sydney's film and TV production companies drawn from the 2009 *Encore Directory* (which provides the largest and most comprehensive listing of film, TV production and documentary producers and service providers in Australia).

Sydney's media are defined by the interplay and changing balance between the industry on the two sides of Sydney Harbour. Today's dominant element is the inner city on the southern side of the harbour, but firms and facilities on the lower North Shore (North Sydney and Willoughby in Figure 9.1) make a significant contribution. Until the 1990s the lower North Shore was dominant with its TV stations, facilities, production

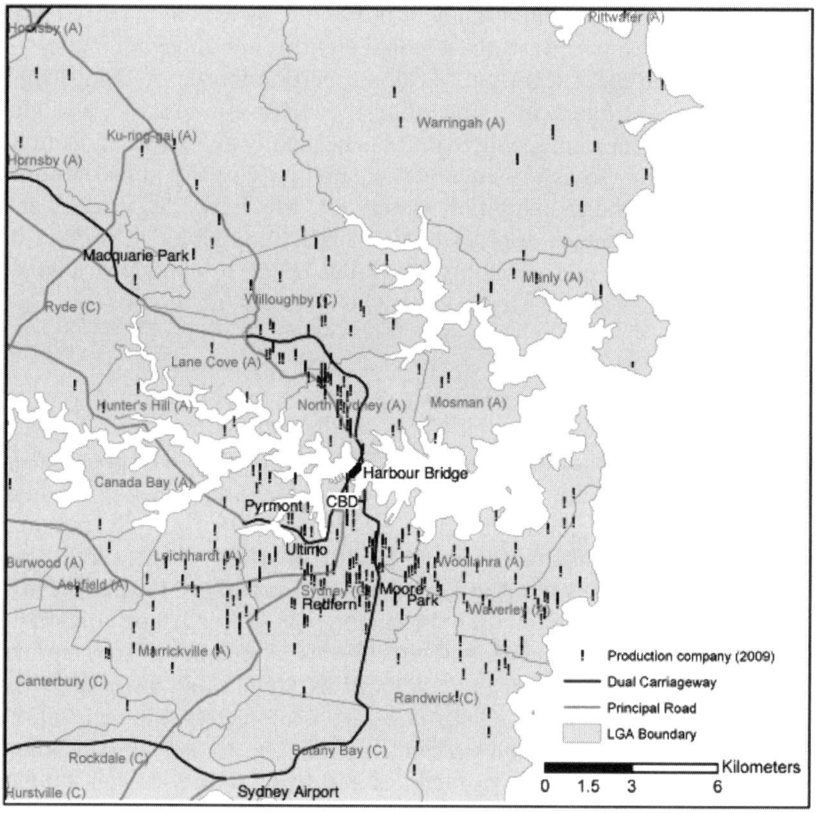

Figure 9.1 Production companies (Encore Directory 2009)

companies, advertising agencies, marketing firms, screen agencies and broadcasting regulators. From the 1990s this mix started to change with the progressive relocation to inner city sites of three of the five free-to-air broadcasters, the screen agencies, the major screen training institution, broadcast regulators and major TV studio providers. In the mid-1990s important new facilities were also established in the inner city with the Fox Studios. These relocations and new infrastructures were both preceded by and coincided with a growing number of companies, service providers and creative workers locating in the inner city and immediately adjacent inner western, eastern and southern suburbs.

This arc-like pattern of media firms and infrastructure follows the urban and industrial pattern of dispersal characteristic of the 'city of cities' urban form developed after World War II and are now a feature of Sydney's regional planning (McGuirk, 2007, p. 187). The pattern for head offices, R&D functions and production infrastructures to be established in various edge-city, middle-ring suburbs and purpose-built environments like business parks 'proximate to leafy residential suburbs' (Searle and Pritchard, 2005, p. 146) was repeated in a number of industries in Sydney and elsewhere (O'Connor, Stimson and Daly, 2001, p. 147).

The media industry's contemporary move back to the inner city in Sydney is also part of equally familiar urban processes. As Hutton (2004, p. 104) observes more generally, 'growing concentrations of employment within the inner city constitute an important new spatial division of labour' connected with new economy industries and globalization. Certainly, large-scale inner-urban regeneration processes have recast Sydney's inner city areas (O'Connor et al., 2001, pp. 143–144).

THE 'TV CLUSTER' ON THE NORTH SHORE 1956–1990

Before TV was introduced in Australia in 1956 Sydney's centre of broadcasting was the CBD with radio stations, major advertising agencies and independent radio drama packagers all in streets close to the Post Office (GPO). By being downtown, radio stations were close to retail and other advertising sponsors and accessible to the news services of print media firms. By contrast the TV stations built their own studios and transmission towers between 1956 and 1965 on ridgelines stretching from the lower North Shore to Macquarie Park and Epping further to the north west. The ABC, Nine and Seven stations and studios were built between 1956 and 1964 on land almost within the shadow of their transmission towers on elevations high enough to either serve most parts of the greater metropolitan area or to provide line-of-sight links to their transmission tower. This co-location of station offices, studios and transmission created self-contained 'TV cities' for the in-house production of news, variety, drama and the coordination of sports broadcasting. TV stations became significant employers owning their own facilities and equipment.

Sydney's commercial free-to-air TV stations were, for the most part, located some distance apart (see Figure 9.2). Each station undertook significant amounts of in-house production. This encouraged largely separate operations and sometimes suppliers with businesses occasionally signalling station proximity through their advertising. As competitive businesses, commercial TV networks do not want their competitors to know their business, so relations of a silo-like character developed among stations in programming genres such as sports, news and current affairs. Drama and quiz show programming were partial exceptions here as contracting out to independent producers grew alongside in-house production

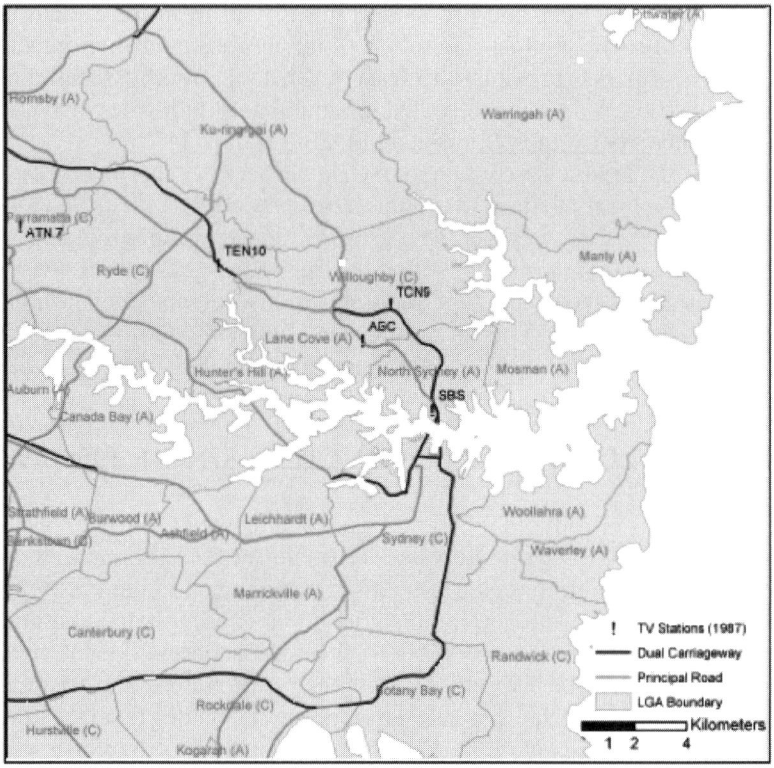

Figure 9.2 Sydney's TV stations, 1987 (Encore Directory 1987)

(Moran, 1985; Moran and Keating, 2003). After Australian TV drama production was put on a more secure footing in the mid-1960s, a pattern was established where four to seven companies had the requisite scale, capability and financial depth to work as independent producers of long-running series and serials (Moran, 1985). This encouraged rival stations, later networks, to enlist the same company to produce TV programming for different networks. But even here all but the largest firms tended to work for only one station/network at a time.

There was one part of the industry, however, where silos were non-existent: advertising. Advertising agencies and market research firms typically located on the North Shore between the TV stations to the north, and the head offices of national and large regional companies in the CBD. Advertising played a major role in the cluster's development. Its need for 'branded' images and sounds capable of bearing repeated exposure helped renovate film and TV production infrastructure at the higher end.

The scale and scope of advertising ranging as it did from the low to the very high budget created service providers across a wide spectrum. The short-term project character of advertising production with its assembling of teams of people for a wide variety of clients contributed in no small way to the development of 'contracting in' and 'contracting out' logics in other areas of film and TV production. Furthermore, there were no barriers to the circulation of the same advertising across commercial channels. Advertising production therefore had significant localization benefits as the Sydney media cluster thickened along the major road corridors connecting the CBD to the emerging business centres of North Sydney, and to the immediate north. This dispersed cluster of related film and television businesses also had the benefit of being in the general vicinity of the different stations allowing advertising agencies and production companies to reliably transport programming or advertising to stations for broadcast.

Until the 1970s the media cluster was defined by TV programme and advertising production. The industry was enlarged after 1970 by the re-establishment, with government support, of continuous feature film production and in the 1980s by a mini-series and feature film production boom financed through tax concessions (O'Regan, 1989). With these developments some of the TV stations' control over programming and enthusiasm for in-house production waned. Independent production companies started to locate further away – on the northern beaches and in the inner city in gentrified areas near the CBD.

Right up until the end of the 1980s the clustering north of the harbour bridge grew. The federal government documentary film production unit, now named Film Australia, moved there in 1962. In 1973 the Australian Film and TV School was set up first on the lower North Shore before moving to Macquarie Park in 1988. In the 1970s the federal film agency, the Australian Film Commission, the federal government's Department of the Media, the industry's trade association, the Federation of Australian Commercial TV Stations, and a new broadcasting regulatory body, the Australian Broadcasting Tribunal, were all established in North Sydney. In 1980 a new public service multicultural broadcaster, SBS TV, also set up its headquarters there.

Some of the dimensions of this cluster can be grasped from 1987 data on film and TV production companies drawn from both the *Encore Directory 1987* and the *B&T Yearbook 1987*. The *Encore Directory* with its film industry focus shows an evenly balanced cluster with slightly more companies on the North Shore (183) than in the inner city (173); while the *B&T Yearbook* with its focus on marketing, advertising, TV and PR industries shows North Shore dominance (148 or 58.3 per cent) with the inner city playing the supporting role (78 or 30.7 per cent of companies).

This balance of location demand indicates the enduring character of Sydney's media 'arc' just as it reflects a production industry defined by free-to-air television programming needs, feature film production and TV advertising.

TV and film were here part of the familiar post-war story of dispersal and the diminishing importance of the CBD as a place to work, live and play. Sydney's North Shore suburbs were seen as attractive, modern locations to both work and live in. They became 'wealth belt' suburbs of advantage with significant concentrations of high-income earners, executives, managers and professionals (Baum, O'Connor and Stimson, 2005, p. 03.9). The North Shore also became the preferred location for new high-tech industries, business services, information, communication and information technology (ICT) businesses and research facilities. TV, advertising and marketing industries were among a number of industries extending the focus of their operations beyond the inner city.

Yet it is also clear from the 1987 data that the inner city was becoming an increasingly important zone of film and television production. The urban regeneration and gentrifying processes generating this change accelerated in the 1990s and 2000s. The event that signalled the beginning of this process for major infrastructure was the Ten Network's 1990 decision to move its corporate offices and news production to the inner city. Ten continued, however, to produce other in-house programming in North Ryde-Macquarie Park up until its old TV Studios were demolished in 2007. During this time its facilities were spun off to a facilities provider, known today as Global Television, in which Ten retained an interest.

The ebb and flow of TV station locations and infrastructure decisions is evident from the Network Seven-Channel 7 site in Epping. Seven began broadcasting from there in December 1956 with the facility still incomplete. By 1961 the site had all essential services and amenities on-site. In the early 1970s the site underwent further expansion so that by 1975 it was a six-studio facility and it had been equipped for colour-TV broadcasting. After that alterations and additions were carried out to buildings, and new buildings were constructed on a needs basis. By 1983 satellite dishes were installed with further satellite dishes installed in 1986 for programme distribution via the domestic satellite. Seven began its move to the inner city in 2004. First its corporate offices, sales departments and news shifted to the inner city. The final move was in early 2010 when it relocated to a purpose-built facility in Australian Technology Park in Redfern (Graham Brooks and Associates, 2008, p. 6).

Despite the contemporary loss of TV infrastructure and film and TV production companies, much TV infrastructure and many companies remain on the North Shore. This includes the Nine and SBS Network head offices and facilities and two of Australia's largest TV production companies, Fremantle Media Australia and Southern Star. St Leonards (in Willoughby in Figure 9.1) boasts a significant post-production and digital visual effects cluster (Jensen, 2009b, p. 15), despite its loss of Animal Logic, a major post-production company, to the Fox Studios. Macquarie Park has grown its media-related offerings with leading firms' head offices in market research (A.C. Nielsen), pay-TV (Foxtel) and telecommunications (Optus). North Sydney-Macquarie Park corridor's ICT concentration has prompted its media identification as 'Australia's Silicon Valley' (Searle and Pritchard, 2005, p. 145) while its growing multimedia industry is focused on both the lower North Shore and the inner city (Searle and De Valence, 2005, p. 239) close to corporate clients, advertising agencies, suppliers and service providers and ICT expertise. North Sydney is Sydney's IT marketing hub and its advertising services centre (Searle, 2009, p. 123). The North Shore remains an attractive residential area with its 'higher amenity suburbs' and 'large professional and managerial workforces' (Searle, 2009, p. 127) including many working in film and TV production. In a media cluster defined by functional proximity the North Shore remains important.

THE INNER CITY

The now dominant cluster on the edge of the CBD in Pyrmont-Ultimo-Redfern-Moore Park emerged gradually through the relocation of key infrastructure. As we have seen, both Ten and Seven moved their operations gradually. Ten's broadcast facilities – including its head office and studios – are now in Pyrmont on the western edge of the CBD having moved there from Ultimo in 1997. These facilities produce Ten's national and local Sydney news bulletins and broadcast to other cities. Non-news production is outsourced to studio providers including Fox Studios and Global Television Studios. The ABC relocated its TV and radio operations to a purpose-built site in Ultimo in 2003. In 2010 Global Television Studios, by then the major provider of TV studio space for the TV industry, co-located with the Seven Network in Australian Technology Park. The other major infrastructure completing the architecture of this new media hub was the Fox Studios. This purpose-built Hollywood standard film and TV production studio and associated film services precinct was designed to service both international production and the higher ends of Australian feature film and TV production. For Jensen, Fox Studios was critical in that it 'shifted the balance of location demand, pulling many of the lower North Shore businesses into the new complex or into nearby premises' (Jensen, 2010, p. 8). It also facilitated a high-tech capability in post-production and digital visual effects, with international production now joining advertising as the major drivers of technological renewal of higher-end film and TV production infrastructure of benefit to the entire sector.

At the same time as this shift towards the inner city was occurring, the film and TV industries increasingly 'contracted in' services for in-house production and 'contracted out' productions to independent producers. Whereas 'in-house' productions had once meant productions in the TV stations' own studios using their own equipment and facilities, it now meant producing in someone else's space and leasing their equipment. The scale of this work is evident in Australian TV broadcasters accounting for 65.1 per cent (AU$889.3m) of total production costs for productions made primarily for television (ABS, 2008, p. 7).

The dimensions of this change are evident in the changing business of Global Television Studios. Global began by providing production services and facilities for Ten's in-house productions. Over the intervening years it expanded its client base to all three commercial free-to-air networks and independent TV production companies. It increasingly facilitated all kinds of production including sport, concerts, awards, drama and reality TV. In late 2006 a private equity firm, Catalyst, acquired Global Television Studios from its then majority owners Nine and Ten Networks for AU$40m. At that time Global was describing itself as 'Australia's leading provider of TV studio facilities and digital outside broadcast services' (it had nationally ten TV studios, six digital production outside broadcast vans and one high definition portable outside broadcast unit). With Global needing a significant capital injection to upgrade for high definition television, responsibility for the upgrade fell to its new owners (Quay Capital, 2010) who invested on the expectation of a growing demand for high definition TV services and a continuing trend for TV stations to 'contract in' services for in-house productions. 'Contracting in' allowed TV stations to 'improve profitability by reducing the capital tied up in production equipment and facilities' (Quay Capital, 2010). When it announced its move to new premises in 2007, Global claimed it would be employing 120 staff and a further 500 freelancers working on studio projects at various times.

Meeting the need for technological renewal is a consistent theme in these station and facility relocations. ABC's, Seven's and Global's moves were all related to the need for broadcasting to become digital in all its operations as online services progressively became part of the broadcasting mix (see Balding, 2002). There was, however, no intrinsic necessity for broadcasters to move. They could have rebuilt studios and facilities on their existing sites as they had done in 1974–1975 when the conversion to colour TV required changes in technology, organization and work practices. There were also advantages in staying put as broadcasters had nearby a film and TV cluster of considerable size and complexity which had grown up to service their operations. Many executives and employees also lived on the North Shore. Why then did some move out and others stay in the 1990s and 2000s?

There were certainly tax advantages in moving from ownership towards the long-term rental of premises. But this does not in itself explain this shift, as selling off and then renting back a space is a familiar pattern in business and government. Similar financial reasons are often advanced for both the contracting in of services and facilities and the contracting out of programming to independent production companies. But as the example of Nine, SBS-TV and Foxtel shows, this need not imply inner-city premises.

A key driver of TV and film production company location decisions is the availability of affordable production spaces. Film and TV productions require large amounts of space – a traditional reason for film studios to be located in peri-urban areas (Hall 1999, pp. 173–185). The availability of accommodation in the inner city helps explain the move there by TV stations, film producers and service providers. As port-related infrastructure, warehousing and manufacturing moved out of Pyrmont and Ultimo, the rag trade out of Surry Hills and rail-related infrastructure out of Redfern, warehouse space and development sites became available in the inner city. There were thus no large cost disadvantages to moving. Initially Foxtel located there and a number of important Fox pay-TV brands such as Fox Sports continue to be located in Pyrmont. Similar considerations of rents and available space led Seven and Global to locate to what had been a struggling inner city business park, Australian Technology Park, as its anchor tenants in 2010. Sometimes governments took an initiating role in making a prime site available on favourable lease and rental terms as when NSW and federal governments used the former Sydney Showgrounds at Moore Park to attract a Hollywood major, Fox, to set up film studios. However, in a move suggestive of the potential for inner city costs to rise beyond those able to be afforded by film production companies and broadcasters, Foxtel relocated from its Darling Harbour waterfront address in 2008 as the cost of maintaining a presence in what had become a premier waterfront address had become prohibitive.

Inner city location decisions of firms have also been connected with firms seeking to locate to epicenters of creative activity and cultural amenity where 'creatives' live, work and play. The Sydney inner city exhibits many of the characteristics identified by Hutton (2004, 2008). Certainly the relocation of stations and, most particularly, the Australian Film, TV and Radio School to the Fox lot was made on the basis of securing greater proximity to and therefore capacity to involve top talent in the School's activities.

Yet another reason advanced for industry location decisions is changing urban planning and policy priorities. State and federal government policy actors have been significant players in shaping developments with a media component in inner city Sydney through their control of key land assets, zoning and preparedness to work with private sector investors through special authorities (Searle, 2007). McGuirk (2005, p. 60) contends that in the 1990s and 2000s there was an 'institutional reconfiguration and a rescaling and refashioning of policy mechanisms, governance practices and planning strategies' towards 'the coordination of private sector investment' as a means of securing Sydney's 're-positioning on the world stage' as Australia's global city. This encouraged what she (McGuirk, 2005, p. 64) calls 'planning by exception' involving the creation of special purpose authorities for particular spatial targets, judged important to securing 'key global consumption and market opportunities that would catapult the city into global city league tables' or being critical to 'determining national economic competitiveness'.

While we can observe different uses of brownfield sites in the former Sydney Showgrounds, the port and manufacturing spaces of Pyrmont and Ultimo, and the rail workshop yards of Redfern – all are centrepieces of a consistent Sydney City Council, NSW and federal government strategy to use control of land and the incentive of state and federal funds to redevelop each for various place making, national cultural policy, 'competitive' and 'global city' strategic ends. Sometimes the imprint of government was through direct funding: the federal government supported the relocation of the principal public broadcaster, the ABC, to state-of-the-art digital facilities in new purpose-built buildings in Ultimo as a part of its cultural and digital economy policies. Mostly, however, it took the form of a federal-state-private partnership as in the remediation of Pyrmont-Ultimo and the Sydney Showgrounds (Searle and Cardew, 2000, pp. 371–372; Goldsmith and O'Regan, 2003, 2004). Within this policy thinking, ironically, clustering is widely touted as a benefit of these developments (even if these moves involve disrupting already existing clusters to achieve new ones legitimated on 'clustering logics'!).

The Pyrmont-Ultimo-Redfern redevelopment was initially handled by the NSW government agency, City West Development Corporation, which was established in 1992 to oversee the redevelopment of the area towards a mix of medium to high density housing, entertainment and cultural facilities, and knowledge-based industries (Searle, 2007, pp. 5–13). This redevelopment was co-funded with the federal government and was, at the time, touted as 'an urban redevelopment project of a scale never before undertaken in Australia' (Sydney Harbour Foreshore Authority, 2004, p. 11). Alongside TV networks and radio stations were a range of new events and entertainment facilities including a casino, a new museum and an entertainment precinct including new performance spaces and a theme park. Opening in November 1996 the Australian Technology Park was initially part of the City West Development Corporation portfolio. In 2000 its management was taken over by the Sydney Foreshore Authority and in 2005 by a new Redfern-Waterloo Authority to manage and promote the development of Australian Technology Park and its surrounding suburbs.

The governmental action taken to secure Network Seven for Australian Technology Park and Fox Studios for Moore Park indicates the importance of film and television to the place-making ambitions of governments in this period. Fox Studios is also an example of how governments are now active participants in 'locational tournaments' for signature production infrastructure and company locations as places vie with each other nationally and internationally across a range of industries (Dicken, 2007, p. 238). For its part, Fox Studios was designed to secure an immediate Sydney advantage over both its local (Gold Coast) and international competitors by offering an inner city studio strategically close to the city and Sydney's iconic beaches. Typically such public-private projects provide ample scope for the place-making ambitions of local, state and national governments alike (Searle and Bounds, 1999, p. 171).

Sydney city's media hub strategy – if the loosely connected projects making it up can be called such – has been defined by both Global Sydney strategy foregrounding Sydney as the nation's 'sole globally competitive city-region' (McGuirk, 2007, p. 182) and the absence of any strategic governmental interest in the North Shore media cluster. The inner city push was formidable and North Shore location interests had few defences. There was no equivalent governmental agency to those overseeing the 'new media cluster' in the inner city, no larger national cultural policy and national economic ends to be served, no high profile place-making purposes to be promoted, no large slices of government land on offer to use as arbitrage for high profile public-private partnerships and no funds to remediate and reposition land use. There was no compelling state or federal interest to support the retention, capture and extension of the 'old media cluster' on the lower North Shore. Unlike the inner city where there was one large strong local government authority covering not only the CBD but also surrounding suburbs, the North Shore had several smaller local councils with limited strategic planning capability and resources to partner in industry development and regional planning. The exception here was the

Ryde Council and State Government's management of Macquarie Park as Australia's premier business park (see Planning NSW, 2002).

FOXTEL AND MACQUARIE PARK

Confounding the accelerating trend towards the inner city, the leading pay-TV provider, Foxtel, moved in 2008 from Darling Harbour to 'campus accommodation' in Macquarie Park. While we can observe large differences between Foxtel's relocation and the location decisions of Network Seven and Fox Studios, they have much in common. All are moves to planned business parks. Both Macquarie Park and Australian Technology Park have a technology and ICT focus while Fox Studios was part of planning for the transition to digital in high budget film and TV production. Macquarie Park was planned in the 1960s to be Sydney's version of Stanford's technology business park, while Australian Technology Park was to be a late 1990s and 2000s inner-city version of Silicon Valley. Both business parks house a variety of firms with media-related businesses as one component. The Fox Studios precinct, by contrast, is a restricted access film services and film studio business park.

When Robert Freestone studied Macquarie Park in 1996 he found little evidence of synergy or clustering among its companies. Its typical business unit 'served national and offshore markets, was foreign owned, and was a strategic unit of a larger corporation vertically integrated across state and national boundaries' (Freestone, 1996, p. 25). Macquarie Park had 'evolved into a prestigious suburban corporate "branch plant" address' with economic activity revolving around 'administration, sales, storage and distribution rather than dynamic product research and development' (Freestone, 1996, p. 27). Its main links were international to foreign headquarters while its product links were 'generally restricted to the importation of goods' and to corporate entities 'acting in the capacity of Australian sales/distribution outlets' (Freestone, 1996, p. 26). It was, Freestone contended, more 'an economic agglomeration' characterized by 'the physical juxtaposition of businesses' rather than their 'functional interaction'.

Foxtel's relocation of its head office functions and many of its pay-TV brands to Macquarie Park suggests, however, advantages of such a location. Real estate agents promoting Macquarie Park rentals claim a move to Macquarie Park from the CBD and North Sydney could cut rentals by up to 67 per cent and 50 per cent respectively on comparable premises (van Grootel quoted in Cummins, 2009, p. 18LA). Macquarie Park had become by the late 2000s Sydney's third CBD after the Sydney CBD and

North Sydney, so Foxtel was locating to an ICT, head office and marketing and distribution 'hub' consisting of telecommunication companies, leading market research companies and head offices of major multinationals. Macquarie Park also combined railway access and attractive parking provisions with cost-effective rentals (van Grootel in Cummins, 2009, p. 18LA). This combination was not always available in inner-city locations, which have increasing restrictions on parking. And just as the inner city offered lifestyle amenity, Macquarie Park was offering the North Shore and the northern beaches.

Like its counterparts at Seven, the ABC and Fox Studios, Foxtel was making the transition to high definition digital TV in a new state-of-the-art facility which not only provided a better space to work, but left room for expansion. Its stand-alone 'campus location' had the benefit of being located away from its free-to-air TV competitors. This fitted Foxtel's self-identity and corporate ambitions to be the 'underdog new player' changing the ground rules for Australian media. In this Foxtel had shades of its part-proprietor Rupert Murdoch's location of Sky TV operations in the UK away from the traditional spaces and places of the TV industry to better shape an alternative identity based on a different business culture (Horsman, 1998). So too Australian pay-TV is not a large producer of local programming – although local production is likely to grow in size and importance. In mostly distributing and marketing 'foreign' branded networks whose schedules are international not local, Foxtel is like many of the businesses operating out of Macquarie Park.

Foxtel's move to Macquarie Park is the highest-profile example of a countervailing tendency towards the dispersal of production spaces away from the inner city. With higher rental prices and processes of gentrification in inner urban areas, inner-city locations are showing signs of becoming unaffordable and difficult to negotiate as both film production and living spaces. This has had the consequence that 'many individuals committed to cultural production as part of their immediate self-identity have since moved to peri-metropolitan areas where rents are comparatively lower and where amenable lifestyles could be pursued' (Gibson et al., 2002, p. 186). This drift is evident in the 2009 data on the location of film and TV production companies cited earlier showing companies locating to peri-metropolitan areas around Sydney and to the far north coast of NSW.

CONCLUSION

As a media centre dominating its national territory, Sydney is situated between London with its dominance of the UK market and Toronto which shares design and production functions with Montreal and has serious rivals as a production centre in Vancouver and Montreal. Australia's media and design centre is the principal but not the only place through which global connections need to pass. While Sydney shares many characteristics with Toronto, not least a second city with significant creative industry and financial capability, Australia's second and third production spaces cannot readily bypass Sydney in the way that Montreal and Vancouver actors can Toronto given their geographic proximity to American producers.

Sydney's leadership in market coordination, command and control functions is being extended with increasing shares of media planning and buying, market research, occupations related to the networking of TV programming and the location of production companies undertaking production. But on other measures such as its proportion of film and TV production companies, employment in occupational categories like producer and director, share of overall industry employment and the location of production expenditure, Sydney is maintaining a national share it had achieved by the mid-1980s.

Sydney is both Australia's design centre and its major production centre. In a globalizing world, the 'design interests' – whether in Sydney or Los Angeles – increasingly have a range of options available when deciding on the location of higher budgeted film and TV production (see Goldsmith and O'Regan, 2005). With location decisions now the product of a variety of factors including cost and the need for production designs and locations that stand out, Sydney-based location interests could no longer rely on proximity to the design centre for work. They increasingly had to work on becoming as film friendly and focused on attracting production, as had their counterparts internationally and locally. Out of this was born the strategy to make NSW more 'film friendly' (Department of Premier and Cabinet, 2008; Jensen, 2009a, p. 28).

Sydney's media cluster evolved gradually, and while the policies and planning regimes of three levels of government – federal, state and local council – have helped to shape the geography and make-up of the cluster, its growth has largely been spontaneous rather than the result of top-down planning. The cluster is largely unmanaged. Sydney's media cluster is not a specific precinct of the city like Hilversum, but rather is dispersed across the city with different centres of gravity emerging at different points in history, in part in response to location incentives provided by the different levels of government.

The transformation of the old Sydney Showgrounds site at Moore Park into a modern studio complex for film and television production owed much to the federal and state governments' desire to develop and strengthen international linkages and to regenerate a neglected inner-urban area. As in Montreal, London and Toronto, Australian policymakers embraced adaptive re-use strategies that expanded both the amenity and competitiveness of Sydney's inner-city areas. Inner-city renewal was expected to give these cities a distinctive edge as cultural tourism destinations, as multifaceted entertainment and leisure precincts and as 'global city' hubs for the creative industries, IT and financial and other services (see Hannigan, 2002; McGuirk, 2007). Sydney's inner-city film studio and business technology park have their parallel in similar studios and precincts in Montreal and Toronto (see Goldsmith and O'Regan, 2005). Other drivers for the shifting geography of Sydney's media cluster are industrial and financial. The availability of affordable space was a key factor in the initial location of television broadcasting stations, along with a need to be in close proximity to transmission facilities located in elevated positions in outer-urban areas. The recent move of most of these stations and network headquarters closer to the centre of the city was also in part motivated by the availability of large and relatively cheap spaces in inner-urban areas like Pyrmont, Ultimo, Moore Park and Redfern. Similarly, Foxtel's move from a harbour-side location in the inner city to Macquarie Park was determined to a great extent by financial considerations. In short a combination of factors are driving change and continuity in Sydney's media cluster. After a long period of leaving the industry to get on with its business, federal and state governments have played a much more activist role in shaping the places and spaces of film and TV production, but the particular industrial and financial needs of media production and distribution have also been significant factors in the evolution of Sydney's media cluster.

NOTES

1. These figures are drawn from customized tables generated by the ARC Centre of Excellence for Research in Creative Industries and Innovation (CCi) from 2006 ABS census data for this research. The researchers wish to thank Peter Higgs and Stuart Cunningham for making this data available.
2. The other growth area was some distance away in Northern NSW closer to the Gold Coast and Brisbane than Sydney – although this activity is rendered functionally proximate to Sydney by virtue of regular flights from the Gold Coast to Sydney (Henkel, 2000).
3. This figure is drawn from customized tables generated by CCi from 2006 ABS census data for this research.

REFERENCES

Australian Bureau of Statistics (2008), *Television, Film and Video Production and Post-Production Services, Australia, 2006–07*, catalogue no. 8679.0, Canberra, AUS: Australian Bureau of Statistics.

Australian Bureau of Statistics (2009), *Australian Demographic Statistics*, catalogue no. 3101.0, Canberra, AUS: Australian Bureau of Statistics.
Australian Film Commission (2005), *Australia's Audiovisual Markets: Key Statistics on Australia's Cinema, Video, Television and Interactive Media Markets*, 1st edn 2004, updated 2005, a 'Get the Picture' publication, Sydney, AUS: Australian Film Commission.
Australian Film Commission (2007), *Audiovisual Production in Australia: Key Statistics on Australia's Audiovisual Production Industry and Australian Films and Programs in the Marketplace*, 1st edn, August, a 'Get the Picture' publication, Sydney, AUS: Australian Film Commission.
Balding, R. (2002), 'ABC Ultimo Centre Opening Speech by Managing Director, Russell Balding', Sydney, AUS: Australian Broadcasting Corporation, available at http://www.abc.net.au/corp/pubs/speeches/s736778.htm.
Baum, S., K. O'Connor and R. Stimson (2005), 'Suburbs of Advantage and Disadvantage: The Social Mosaic of our Large Cities', in *Fault Lines Exposed*, Clayfield, Melbourne, AUS: Monash University ePress.
B&T Directory 2009 (2009), Chatswood, Sydney, AUS: Reed Business Information.
B&T Yearbook 1987 (1987), Chippendale, Sydney, AUS: Thompson Publications.
Connell, J. (2000), 'And the Winner is . . .', in John Connell (ed), *Sydney: The Emergence of a World City*, Melbourne, AUS: Oxford University Press, pp. 1–18.
Cook, G.A.S. and N.R. Pandit (2008), 'Clusters in the Broadcasting Industry', in Charlie Karlsson (ed), *Handbook of Research on Cluster Theory*, Cheltenham, UK and Northampton, MA, USA: Edward Elgar, pp. 274–291.
Cummins, C. (2009), 'Macquarie Park the New Hot Spot', *Sydney Morning Herald*, 31 October 2009, p. 18LA.
Daly, M. and B. Pritchard (2000), 'Sydney: Australia's Financial and Corporate Capital', in John Connell (ed.), *Sydney: The Emergence of a World City*, Melbourne, AUS: Oxford University Press, pp.167–188.
Department of Premier and Cabinet (2008), *Making NSW Film Friendly*, Sydney, AUS: NSW Department of Premier and Cabinet.
Department of State and Regional Development (DSRD) (2008), *NSW Creative Industry Economic Fundamentals*, Sydney, AUS: Department of State and Regional Development.
Dicken, P. (2007), *Global Shift: Mapping the Changing Contours of the World Economy*, London, UK: Sage, 5th edn.
Encore Directory 1987, Manly, Sydney, AUS: Chekeven.
Encore Directory 2009: the Essential Business Resource for the Film and Television Industry (2009), Chatswood, Sydney, AUS: Reed Business Information.
Freestone, R. (1996), 'The Making of an Australian Technoburb', *Australian Geographical Studies*, 34 (1), 18–31.
Gibson, C., P. Murphy and R. Freestone (2002), 'Employment and Socio-spatial Relations in Australia's Cultural Economy', *Australian Geographer*, **33**(2), 173–189.
Goldsmith, B. and T. O'Regan (2003), *Cinema Cities, Media Cities: The Contemporary International Studio Complex*, Sydney, AUS: Australian Film Commission.
Goldsmith, B. and T. O'Regan (2004), 'Locomotives and Stargates: Inner-City Studio Complexes in Sydney, Melbourne and Toronto', *International Journal of Cultural Policy*, **10**(1), 29–45.

Goldsmith, B. and T. O'Regan (2005), *The Film Studio. Film Production in the Global Economy*, Lanham, MD, USA: Rowman & Littlefield.

Goldsmith, B., S. Ward and T. O'Regan (2010), *Local Hollywood: Global Film Production and the Gold Coast*, St Lucia, Brisbane, AUS: University of Queensland Press.

Graham Brooks and Associates (2008), *Channel 7 Site, Mobbs Lane, Epping: Epping Park Preliminary Interpretation Strategy*, December.

Hall, P. (1999), 'The Future of Cities', *Computers, Environment and Urban Systems*, **23**(3), 173–185.

Hannigan, J. (2002), 'Cities as the Physical Site of the Global Entertainment Economy', in Marc Raboy (ed), *Global Media Policy in the New Millennium*, Luton, UK: University of Luton Press, pp. 181–195.

Henkel, C. (2000), *Imagining the Future: Strategies for the Development of Creative Industries in the Northern Rivers Region of NSW*, Lismore, AUS: Northern Rivers Regional Development Board.

Higgs, P., S. Hagaman and S. Freebody (2008), *Strong Attractors and Lily Pads: How Putting Numbers to the Drift of Creative Talent in the Creative Economy through the Concentration Effect can Reveal the Impact of Local Factors.* Presented at the International Forum on the Creative Economy, Gatineau, Quebec, CAN, 17–18 March 2008.

Horsman, M. (1998), *Sky High: The Amazing Story of BSkyB – and the Egos, Deals and Ambitions that Revolutionised TV Broadcasting*, London, UK: Orion Business.

Hutton, T.A. (2004), 'The New Economy of the Inner City', *Cities*, **21**(2), 89–108.

Hutton, T.A. (2008), *The New Economy of the Inner City: Restructuring, Regeneration and Dislocation in the Twenty-first-century Metropolis*, New York, NY, USA and Abingdon, UK: Routledge.

Jensen, R. (2009a), 'Planning for Creative Cities', *Australian Planner*, **46**(3), 22–31.

Jensen, R. (2009b), 'The Sustainability of Australia's Visual Entertainment Industry', Institute of Australian Geographers 2009 Conference, Cairns, 28th September to 1 October. Lodged at https:/respubs.online.unsw.edu.au/ Publication ID: 201023214.

Jensen, R. (2010), 'Sydney Media on the Move', *Cityscape Creative Cities*, vol 40 (March), p.8. Available at http://cityscape-news.com/MAR-2010.pdf.

Krätke, S. (2003), 'Global Media Cities in a World-wide Urban Network', *European Planning Studies*, **11**(6), 605–628.

Krätke, S. and P.J. Taylor (2004), 'A World Geography of Global Media Cities', *European Planning Studies*, **12**(4), 459–477.

McGuirk, P. (2005), 'Neoliberalist Planning? Re-thinking and Re-casting Sydney's Metropolitan Planning', *Geographical Research*, **43**(1), 59–70.

McGuirk, P. (2007), 'The Political Construction of the City-Region: Notes from Sydney', *International Journal of Urban and Regional Research*, **31**(1), 179–187.

Moran, A. (1985), *Images and Industry: Television Drama Production in Australia*, Sydney, AUS: Currency Press.

Moran, A. and C. Keating (2003), *Wheel of Fortune: Australian TV Game Shows*, Nathan, Brisbane, AUS: Australian Key Centre for Cultural and Media Policy.

Mould, O. (2007), 'Mission Impossible? Reconsidering the Research into Sydney's Film Industry', *Studies in Australasian Cinema*, **1**(1), 47–60.

Mould, O. (2008), 'Moving Images: World Cities, Connections and Projects in Sydney's TV Production Industry', *Global Networks*, **8**(4), 474–495.
Planning NSW and Ryde City Council (2002), *Macquarie Park Corridor Structure Plan, Part 1 – Background Report*, Sydney, AUS: Planning NSW.
O'Connor, K. (2002), 'Rethinking Globalisation and Urban Development: The Fortunes of Second-Ranked Cities', *Australasian Journal of Regional Studies*, **8**(3), 247–260.
O'Connor, K., R. Stimson and M. Daly (2001), *Australia's Changing Economic Geography: A Society Dividing*, Melbourne, AUS: Oxford University Press.
O'Regan, T. (1989), 'The Enchantment with the Cinema: Film in the 1980s', in Albert Moran and Tom O'Regan (eds), *Australian Screen*, Ringwood, AUS: Penguin, pp. 118–145.
Quay Capital (2006), 'Catalyst to take over Television Studios'. Extract from Private Equity Media article December. Available at http://www.quaycapital.com.au/news_details.php4?news_id=28. Accessed 19 June 2010.
Screen Australia (2009), *Documentary Production in Australia, 2009: A Collection of Key Data*, Sydney, AUS: Screen Australia.
Screen Australia (2010), *Get the Picture*, Sydney, AUS: Screen Australia. Available at http://www.screenaustralia.gov.au/gtp/default.html. Accessed 12 June 2010.
Searle, G. and M. Bounds (1999), 'State Powers, State Land and Competition for Global Entertainment: The Case of Sydney', *International Journal of Urban and Regional Research*, **23**(1), 165–172.
Searle, G. and R. Cardew (2000), 'Planning, Economic Development and the Spatial Outcomes of Market Liberalisation', *Urban Policy and Research*, **18**(3), 355–376.
Searle, G. and B. Pritchard (2005), 'Industry Clusters and Sydney's ITT Sector: Northern Sydney as "Australia's Silicon Valley"?', *Australian Geographer*, **36**(2), 145–169.
Searle, G. and G. De Valence (2005), 'The Urban Emergence of a New Information Industry: Sydney's Multimedia Firms', *Geographical Research*, **43**(2), 238–253.
Searle, G. (2007), 'Sydney's Urban Consolidation Experience: Power, Politics and Community', Urban Research Program Research Paper 12 March 2007, Griffith University, Brisbane AUS.
Searle, G. (2009), 'The Spatial Division of Labour in the Sydney and Melbourne Information Technology Industries', *Australasian Journal of Regional Studies*, **15**(1), 115–129.
Sydney Harbour Foreshore Authority (2004), *Ultimo + Pyrmont: Decade of Renewal*, Sydney, AUS: Sydney Harbour Foreshore Authority.
West, J. (2006), *A Strategy to Accelerate Innovation in NSW: Outline for Policy Development*, Hobart, AUS: Australian Innovation Research Centre, commissioned by NSW Department of State and Regional Development.

10. The Toronto media cluster: between culture and commerce

Charles H. Davis

In North America, the media industry is highly agglomerated in two 'alpha' media cities, Los Angeles and New York City (Krätke, 2003; Krätke and Taylor, 2004). Only one 'beta' media city has emerged – Toronto, the historical media capital of English-speaking Canada.[1] Beta media cities are far more common in Europe, where they developed much as the Toronto cluster did, as the principal centre of corporate and public media serving a national market. Montreal and Vancouver, Canada's other major media metropoles, are smaller and more specialized, the former serving the national French-speaking market and the latter providing production services and other inputs to transnational firms in the film, television and games industries.

As the principal media centre for English-speaking Canada, Toronto benefits from the numerous programmes and policies put in place by the federal government to ensure cultural sovereignty by keeping telecommunications, broadcasting and newspapers in Canadian hands. Toronto also benefits from federal and provincial policies and programmes that ensure the production and distribution of indigenous media content and are motivated by the ongoing challenge of sustaining Canadian English-language media alternatives in the face of the US cultural industries' market power. 'Publishing Canadian books is a high-risk, low-margin business conducted on the fringes of empire' observes MacSkimming (2006), and the same could be said of many other media content industries in Canada's small domestic market.[2] Domestic market share for many categories of indigenous media products – notably those major carriers of culture, feature films and television drama – is very low. At the same time, open networks may provide opportunities to deliver media products to global audiences. Many observers believe that the Toronto media industry is well placed to make the transition from a largely domestic-oriented media cluster to one that is more successfully outward-looking, without loss of its role of informing and entertaining Canadians. In other words, concern about jurisdictional advantage – place-specific strengths that support enhanced industry performance and that are not easily imitated by competitors – has joined concern about cultural sovereignty as a rationale for public investment in indigenous media capabilities in Canada. This evolution of media policy rationale has major implications for the Toronto media cluster.

This chapter focuses on the Ontario Entertainment and Creative cluster, most of the firms of which are located in the greater Toronto region.[3] The core components of this cluster are the book, magazine, film/television, music and interactive digital media industries. After briefly reviewing the economic and social characteristics of Toronto, I assess the strengths and weaknesses of the Toronto media cluster and its constituent subsectors, and I analyse the principal structural characteristics of the Toronto cluster, including its industrial dynamics, market orientation and extent of regional agglomeration in the Toronto urban area. I then examine the cluster's growth processes, noting that its overall orientation to the domestic English-language market is its primary *raison d'être* as well as a major constraint to further development. However, unlike 'satellite' production clusters, which provide low-cost services to Hollywood, the Toronto cluster possesses a full range of well-developed higher-order media business, creative and technological capabilities across a range of media industries, providing a potential advantage. A second potential advantage of the Toronto cluster is its co-location with strong technology, finance and business service clusters. A third potential advantage is Toronto's multicultural population, whose entry into the mainstream of Toronto's media industries could improve the cluster's (and the country's) global outlook and enhance the city's branding as a cosmopolitan place. This configuration of assets and capabilities provides a range of potential growth pathways that concurrently meet Canada's needs for cultural sovereignty and jurisdictional advantage.

SITUATING TORONTO'S MEDIA INDUSTRIES

Over the past four decades Toronto has emerged as a significant population and economic centre in North America, in the process becoming one of the most culturally diverse cities in the world. Half of Toronto's population is foreign-born, and Toronto has one of the largest urban Aboriginal communities in Canada. With a population of 2.5 million, Toronto is the fifth largest city in North America. Toronto's regional population (the Golden Horseshoe region, straddling the western end of Lake Ontario) of around eight million represents about a quarter of Canada's population and makes Toronto the fourth largest urban region in North America and the largest in Canada.

The GTA's Gross Domestic Product of CA$327 billion is comparable to that of Argentina, Venezuela, South Africa, Ireland or Finland. Toronto's economy encompasses 12 industrial clusters (defined as higher than average industrial location quotient among Canadian population centres): textiles and apparel, food, automotive, plastics and rubber, biomedical, ICT manufacturing, ICT services, finance, business services, creative and cultural industries, higher education and logistics (Spencer and Vinodrai, 2009). In the North American context, Toronto's top 12 areas of relative specialization are publishing and printing, financial services, building equipment and services, power generation and transmission, business services, apparel, information technology, jewellery, entertainment and automotive manufacturing (Martin and Florida, 2009).

Toronto and Ontario business and political elites aspire to move Toronto up in the ranks of world cities alongside London, New York, Hong Kong, Paris, Sydney, Tokyo, Singapore, Beijing and Shanghai.[4] A key component of Toronto's globally oriented economic development strategy is to compete on creativity. In 2003 Toronto City Council adopted a ten-year *Culture Plan for the Creative City* enacting a 'Cultural Renaissance' strategy to guide investment in cultural infrastructure and events, including ongoing waterfront development and eight large iconic architectural projects in the downtown core (Jenkins, 2005; Lehrer and Laidley, 2008). In addition to the built environment the city has fostered a variety of popular cultural festivals such as Nuit Blanche, Caribana, Luminato, Pride and the Toronto International Film Festival, which has become a widely recognized element in Toronto's 'brand promise'. To mentor Toronto's creative upgrading and help make the city attractive to the footloose creative class, in 2007 the city and province helped to recruit the prominent urban development thinker Richard Florida to the University of Toronto, where he directs his own think tank. Florida's message is that if the city region does the right things now, it can be outstanding and will be rewarded: 'Toronto is at an inflection point, to strive for greatness as one of the world's creative cities or to be a really good second-tier city. All the ingredients are here' (as cited in AuthentiCity, 2008).

The Toronto media cluster is not the product of unbridled market forces, nor is it the result of cluster policies or creative city policies (each of which is a relatively recent development). It is instead an outcome of decades of Canadian media, telecommunications and cultural policies that have shaped the evolution of the Canadian media and telecommunications industries and their locational dynamics. The Toronto media cluster probably would not have developed in the absence of longstanding federal policies that ensure Canadian control of telecommunications and broadcasting and, along with provincial programmes, provide support to various indigenous cultural industries.[5] Canada has not allowed the domestic broadcasting and telecommunications sectors to follow many other industries into continental integration through trade and investment liberalization. Adhesion to the UNESCO Convention on Cultural Diversity and claims of exemption for cultural products in trade agreements are additional measures Canada and other countries have taken to ensure latitude for governmental support of indigenous cultural industries (Acheson and Maule, 2004; Puppis, 2009, 2008). The Canadian broadcasting and telecommunications industries are subject to national ownership and other regulatory provisions, and indigenous media content industries – film/television, book, magazine, music and interactive digital media – receive various kinds of public support and protection on the grounds that they constitute an important expression of national cultural identity.[6] Public support measures for 'Canadian' content (in the context of screen-based media and music) are based primarily on the nationality of owners of intellectual property and the key creative and executive positions in the production.

Broadcasting receives much greater regulatory attention than other media industries. This is because of broadcasting's historical cultural and political salience and also because of its policy tractability: the federal government can regulate the broadcast distribution system to ensure investment in, and distribution of, Canadian content in ways that are less feasible in the case of theatrical exhibition of films, retail distribution of recorded music or film, or distribution of content over the internet.[7] Approximately half the cost of every certified Canadian television programme is provided by federal and provincial tax credits and subsidies (Murray, 2002).

Toronto serves as the headquarters for English-speaking Canada's major book, magazine, music and newspaper publishers, many of its major screen production houses, its principal English-language public broadcasters and many of its private broadcasters. Of the dozen principal Canadian media conglomerates (Astral, Bell Canada, CanWest, Cogeco, Newcap, Shaw, Quebecor, Telus, Corus, CTVglobemedia, Rogers and TorStar), the latter four are headquartered in Toronto.[8] Two important public broadcasters are also located in Toronto: the Canadian Broadcasting Centre of the CBC (Canadian Broadcasting Corporation) and TV Ontario, the provincial broadcasting network. All three levels of public policy and programme agencies are strongly represented in Toronto, and the cluster encompasses the country's largest concentration of independent screen content producers, specialty broadcasters, supporting institutions and multitudinous suppliers of 'humdrum' services and inputs such as sound recording studios, law firms, post-production services, media marketing and publicity agencies, financial and insurance services, theatrical exhibitors, internet publishing firms, technical service suppliers, advertising agencies, below-the-line crews and their craft unions, and public and private post-secondary educational programs.

Rankings based on various combinations of industries in the Ontario Entertainment and Creative Cluster put the city in third place in North America for core copyright industries, artists and film and video, in fourth place for aggregate entertainment and creative industries and music, and in fifth place for publishing, usually following New York and Los Angeles and in some cases Chicago (A-Line Consultants, 2006). Of greater significance is the comprehensive set of horizontal and vertical media capabilities present in the Toronto cluster, ranging from abundant below-the-line production crews to executive producers and from screenwriters to media marketers, financiers and distributors. These capabilities distinguish Toronto from the satellite or 'edge' media cities that have emerged to capture outsourced production business (Lukinbeal, 2004; Storper and Christopherson, 1987). Satellite production centres lack creative business capabilities and are unable to create and exploit intellectual property to create value. Canadian media capitals Toronto and Montreal are instead full-function media centres that are comparable to Los Angeles and New York, but smaller.

Measurements of the economic and demographic size of the Ontario Entertainment and Creative Cluster vary widely because of differing definitions of the cluster's composition and boundaries. Nordicity (2008a) calculates the economic size of the Ontario creative sector to be CA$12.2 bn, about two-thirds the size of the Ontario automotive sector, one-third the size of the ICT sector and one-ninth the size of the Ontario financial sector. The Ontario creative sector is about the same economic size as the Ontario energy sector and much larger than the Ontario agricultural and forestry or mining sectors.

Table 10.1 compares the book, magazine, film and television, music and digital media industry subsectors of the Ontario entertainment and media cluster. Based on various published assessments of these five subsectors in Ontario and the percentage of firms in each subsector that are located in the Toronto region, I estimate aggregate revenues of the content-producing segments of the Ontario media industry at CA$6.2 bn in 2006–2007, of which around CA$4.5 bn in the Toronto region. The six subsectors employ about 56,600 people in Ontario, of which about 40,400 in the Toronto region. The industry supports about 4500 firms in the six subsectors, roughly 70 per cent of which are located in the Toronto region. The above numbers do not take into account many

Table 10.1 Size and composition of the Ontario media cluster

Media industry	Revenues of Ontario firms	Profit margin in industry	Ontario employ-ment	# of firms and agencies in Ontario	% of firms / agencies in GTA	Exports as % of revenues	Self-identifi-cation as part of a cluster
Book publishing	CA$ 1.362bn[a]	10%–12%[f]	4729[k]	479[p]	80%[u]	22%[z]	95%[ee]
Magazine publishing	CA$ 1.2bn[b]	10.9%[g]	9389[l]	416[q]	61%[v]	6%[aa]	86%[ff]
Film-tv	CA$ 2bn[c]	8%[h]	23550[m]	2214[r]	71%[w]	27%[bb]	80% and 74%[gg]
Music	CA$ 498m[d]	8.6% and 19%[i]	3030[n]	393[s]	72%[x]	16%[cc]	65%[hh]
Interactive digital media	CA$ 1.1bn –1.2bn[e]	un-known[j]	16000[o]	950–1050[t]	75%[y]	36%[dd]	73% and 47%[ii]
Total	CA$ 6.21bn		~56800	~4500	71.8%	21.4%	74.3%

Notes:

a. 2007 data from Statistics Canada (2009), Table 1.

b. Statistics Canada data cited in 'The Daily', March 19, 2008, as reported in HAL (2009).

c. Coish (2004) as reported in HAL (2009).

d. Number refers to record label operating revenues, from the OMDC-funded *Strategic Study of the Magazine Industry* (TCI 2008), citing Statistics Canada data. Ontario music publishers had 2007 revenues of around CA$95 million and Ontario sound recording studios had 2007 revenues of around CA$41.6 million (Ibid.).

e. The number refers to revenues attributed to interactive digital media. OMDC, *Industry Profile: Interactive Digital Media*.

f. Statistics Canada, 'Annual Survey of Service Industries: Book Publishers, 2004', Catalogue no. 87F0004XIE, Tables 3 and 6, June 2006, as reported in OMDC (2010), *Industry Profile: Book Publishing*. Ontario book publishers had an operating profit margin of 12.5% in 2007 (ibid.). Nordicity (2004) reports book publisher profit margins of .5%–6.9% in 2000–2001 based on Statistics Canada data. The lower range refers to SMEs and the higher range refers to larger firms

g. Statistics Canada, The Daily: Periodical Publishing, 2006, March 19, 2008, as cited in OMDC (2010), *Industry Profile: Magazine Publishing*.

h. Nordicity (2006), p. 14 (regarding Canadian film and television production companies). Coish (2006) reports 2.8%.

i. Profit margins of music publishers in Canada in 2007 were 8.6%. Profit margins of Ontario sound recording studios were 19% in 2007. OMDC (2010), *Industry Profile: Music*. Profit margins of record labels are not indicated.

j. No official data or reporting of profit margins are currently available.

k. Statistics Canada, 'Survey of Service Industries: Book Publishers 2005', Table 1, 29 March 2007 as reported in OMDC, *Industry Profile: Book Publishing*.

l. Average number of direct and indirect jobs in the industry in Ontario between 1997 and 2005 according to Informetrica Ltd et al., *Economic Contribution of the Canadian Magazine Industry*, December 2006, as cited in OMDC, *Industry Profile: Magazine Publishing*.

Table 10.1 (continued)

m. FTE direct and indirect jobs. Estimated from OMDC (2010), *Industry Profile: Television.*
n. This figure refers to the number of persons employed in sound recording (NAICS 5122) in the Toronto Census Metropolitan Area (average 2003–2007). *Source*: Toronto Economic Development (2009) which is based on Statistics Canada's Labour Force Survey.
o. OMDC (2010), *Industry Profile: Interactive Digital Media.*
p. Statistics Canada, 'Annual Survey of Service Industries: Book Publishers, 2004', Catalogue no. 87F0004XIE, Tables 3 and 6, June 2006, as reported in *OMDC, Industry Profile: Book Publishing*. http://www.omdc.on.ca.
q. Number of periodical publishers (NAICS 511120) in Ontario in December, 2008 according to the *Business Register* (Statistics Canada, 2008). Excludes indeterminate firms (i.e. those without employees).
r. Estimated from the *Ontario Production Guide* (OMDC, 2009).
s. As reported in HAL (2009).
t. DC (2010), *Industry Profile: Interactive Digital Media.*
u. As reported in HAL (2009).
v. Periodical publishers (NAICS 511120) in the Toronto Census Metropolitan Area as percentage of periodical publishers in Ontario in December, 2008 according to the *Business Register* (Statistics Canada, 2008). Excludes indeterminate firms (i.e. those without employees).
w. Estimated from the *Canada Film and Television Production Guide* (2007).
x. HAL (2009).
y. HAL (2009), p. 130.
z. This number refers to the percentage of export revenues in firm revenues among book publishing firms surveyed. HAL (2009), p. 119.
aa. This number refers to the percentage of export revenues in firm revenues among GTA magazine publishing firms. HAL (2009), p. 99.
bb. This number refers to the percentage of export revenues in firm revenues among film/television production and post-production firms. HAL (2009), p. 83.
cc. This number refers to the percentage of export revenues in firm revenues among music firms surveyed.HAL (2009), p. 51.
dd. This number refers to the percentage of export revenues in firm revenues among music firms surveyed. HAL (2009), p. 139.
ee. The number refers to book publishing firms. HAL (2009), p. 122.
ff. The number refers to GTA magazine publishing firms. HAL (2009), p. 101.
gg. The numbers refer to production and post-production firms respectively. HAL (2009), p. 84.
hh. The number refers to music firms in GTA. HAL (2009), p. 51.
ii. The numbers refer to IDM firms in downtown Toronto and the rest of the GTA, respectively. HAL (2009), p. 140.

thousands of microenterprises or self-employed individuals registered as firms without employees, most of which are located in the Toronto region.

STRENGTHS AND WEAKNESSES OF THE CLUSTER'S CORE SUBSECTORS

Ontario's media industries face a number of common challenges – notably the transition to digital platforms and audience development in an environment of proliferating channels and choices – but they also display significant differences in their strengths and weaknesses.

The Ontario *magazine (periodical) publishing industry* is stable and viable, successfully retaining 41 per cent of the domestic market – a much higher share than other domestic English-language media industries (TCI, 2008). The industry is confident that it can hold its audience in the face of competition from the internet, and magazine readership is growing. Furthermore, magazines are discovering an affinity for web publishing. This industry, however, while benefitting from income from subscriptions, is largely dependent on advertising revenues. Convincing advertisers that 'Canadian magazines remain a successful way to reach Canadian consumer and business communities of interest' is proving a challenge (TCI, 2008, p. 7). The barriers to growth of the indigenous English-language magazine industry are (1) the industry's very slender profit margins, especially amongst the smaller publishers (profits are highly concentrated among the larger magazine publishing companies); (2) dependence on advertising; (3) the small size of the domestic market; (4) vulnerability to rising costs; (5) limited access to capital; and (6) the relative low salience of the indigenous magazine industry in provincial creative industry support programmes.

The strengths of the Ontario *book publishing industry* are government support programmes and the presence of a strong pool of players in the publishing business ecosystem (authors, domestic producers, multinationals, agents and distributors). Success factors of average strength are exports, professional development capabilities and intra-industry cooperation. Success factors of below average strength have to do with migration to digital platforms: online marketing, sales and distribution; innovation in business models; private investment; and copyright protection (Nordicity, 2008b).

The Toronto Film Board's *Strategic Plan for Toronto's Screen-based Industry* (2007) sees the cluster's *film and television production industry* as 'seriously wounded' by the 35 per cent decline in production spending since 2001 due largely to competition in the foreign location production business and the regionalization of Canadian audiovisual production spending for political purposes. The report notes that Toronto has been 'caught in the downdraft of globalization of the screen-based industry' in which six factors have come together to form a 'perfect storm': a paradigm shift in forms of production, distribution and finance; the hollowing out of Toronto-based screen industry by provincial and federal incentives to regionalize production; intense tax-based competition for service production in many jurisdictions; improvements in purpose-built studio infrastructure in many locations that draw productions away from Toronto;

the rising value of Canada's dollar which has undermined Toronto's cost-based competitiveness; and the unavailability of 'new methods of financing' which are 'required for a digitized screen world'. The Toronto Film Board recommends that 'Toronto . . . focus on becoming the English speaking world's foremost screen arts centre of excellence', 'the best place in the world to practise screen arts in the digital age' and urges governments to align their interventions to develop Toronto as the 'national centre of screen-based industry excellence'.

Most of the Ontario *music industry's* key success factors are at average strength or below (Nordicity, 2008a). Strengths are government support programmes, business ecosystem capabilities, well-developed production collaboration and stronger export capabilities than those of other Canadian English-language media sectors. Success factors of average strength are physical retail distribution, online innovation, the live music scene and capabilities for entry-level training. Weaknesses are digital distribution, absence of a media-driven star system, radio airplay support for emerging artists, professional development for mid- and senior-level personnel, cross-industry collaboration, access to private investment and copyright protection.

The Ontario *interactive digital media industry* encompasses games designers and developers and interactive software, content developers, distributors and service providers for education, entertainment, advertising/marketing and social networking. This industry is very heterogeneous, encompassing several specialities including digital games, computer animation/visual effects, and mobile media, which are discussed below.

The Ontario *digital games industry* consists almost entirely of indigenous firms – a small number of console game developers and around 800 developers of games for personal computers and mobile platforms, with estimated revenues of CA$70 million in 2006 (SECOR, 2008). Nordicity (2008d) assesses GTA's potential in digital games as merely average on the basis of its population of smaller games firms and development studios, labour pool of around 1450 employees and modest levels of conference buzz, co-located hardware manufacturers, product lines, access to financing and capacity for collaboration. In recent years, Ontario policymakers considered that the GTA digital games industry was suffering from lack of critical mass and low international traction due to the absence of a domestic or international market-leading firm in the cluster. Consequently, Toronto was seen to compare unfavourably with rivals Montreal and Vancouver as a site for the expansion of a digital games industry. Unlike Canada's protected media sectors, digital games are not regarded as carriers of domestic culture and are largely unregulated. Therefore, foreign direct investment is an option. Noted a consultant,

> [a]ttracting a multinational publisher to open a studio in Ontario in the short term would be highly beneficial; in particular, the greater scale, capital influx, and legitimacy that a large publisher would bring to Ontario could considerably shorten the industry's development timeline to achieve critical mass. Ultimately, the spillover effects would contribute to organic growth in the rest of the game community (SECOR, 2008)

In 2009 the Government of Ontario announced that Ubisoft, the French video game publisher, had agreed to establish a studio in Toronto that would create 800 jobs over a decade, in exchange for a grant of CA$263 million.

The Ontario *computer animation and visual effects industry* services the domestic and international film, television and advertising industries. Approximately three-quarters of its revenues come from customers in these industries, and roughly half its revenues are earned outside Canada (Nordicity, 2008d). The industry consists of approximately 40 firms employing 1600 to 1900 people and generating CA$170 to 200 million annually (Nordicity, 2008c). Most are small indigenous firms with around two dozen employees and revenues from $1 to $4 million, but the sector also includes a few larger firms, including some under foreign control. Firms in this subsector mainly provide services for fees and most do not originate intellectual property. The subsector is very sensitive to rising competition from animation and special effects industries in low-wage Asian countries, and Ontario firms increasingly outsource production to these countries. Nordicity (2008e) rates the quality of the GTA animation and special effects cluster as good. Toronto is the national leader in animation for television, but its post-production sector is not noticeably strong in animation and visual effects services, although Seneca and Sheridan Colleges are recognized internationally as post-secondary animation and visual effects centres of training excellence.

Oligopoly among wireless carriers in Canada has kept the cost of Canadian wireless data rates among the highest in the world, dampening consumer demand for wireless data services and associated content until recently.[9] A 2008 wireless spectrum auction enabled new entrants into the Canadian wireless industry, creating competition and lowering prices. This is expected to create significant consumer demand for mobile media in the near term. Players in the Toronto wireless industry are positioning themselves to take advantage of this anticipated acceleration of uptake of mobile services among Canadian consumers. The Toronto mobile media subsector consists of a complete business ecosystem: Canada's three major carriers (Rogers, TELUS and Bell), network operators, content providers and application developers (of which there are hundreds), services, advertisers and marketers, mobile device manufacturers and equipment suppliers, mobile platform providers and distribution and content creation tool providers (MEIC, 2009). Following the recent spectrum auction, the Canadian government overruled a CRTC decision and will allow greater foreign investment in the wireless sector.

The overall competitive position of the Ontario Entertainment and Creative Cluster is assessed in Table 10.2. Briefly, the cluster's strengths are its deep pools of creative, technical and business talent, its fine public cultural and educational infrastructure and the high potential for variety creation and innovation due to the range of co-located media subsectors along with the co-location of strong IT, financial and business service clusters. The weaknesses of the Toronto cluster are its embeddedness in the relatively small domestic English-language market, weak export performance, undercapitalization of most indigenous media firms, difficulties experienced by content producers in earning revenues with digital technologies and poor ability to commercially exploit intellectual property. The threats to the Toronto media cluster are the splintering of consumer and advertising markets, competition for service and production business from low-cost production centres, the development of alliances between foreign technology and content leaders and major media conglomerates and the undermining of the Canadian broadcast-based domestic content regulation regime by open networks. Growth opportunities for the Toronto media cluster are believed to lie in the emergence of creative convergent media that will shift markets toward multitudes of niches serviced by direct distribution of digital content.

THE TORONTO MEDIA AGGLOMERATION'S CLUSTER PROPERTIES

Recent research on the Ontario media and entertainment cluster investigates eight 'cluster' properties of the agglomeration: (1) extent of agglomeration in the Toronto region; (2) areas of localization in specific areas of the city; (3) size composition of the subsectors; (4) industrial dynamics; (5) market orientation; (6) self-awareness and shared identity; (7) digital distribution of content; (8) governance (Davis, 2010; Davis et al., 2009; HAL, 2009).

Extent of Agglomeration in the Toronto Metropolitan Region

About 70 per cent of the Ontario cluster's principal media firms are concentrated in the Toronto region (Table 10.1). The degree of concentration in the Toronto region is much higher when the smaller firms, associated firms and support institutions are included. Of the 2214 firms and

Table 10.2 Ontario entertainment and creative cluster: strengths, weaknesses, opportunities and threats

Strengths	Weaknesses
• High-quality creative talent and technical skills • High cluster density: #1 in Canada, #3 in North America • Optimal mix of sectors represented • World-class educational institutions • 'Indie' niche content creators and producers with global market potential • Excellent infrastructure (healthcare, public arts institutions, telecom) • High-quality related clusters: Information Technology and Financial Services	• Undercapitalized firms • Small domestic market • Poor technology adoption by traditional content firms • Generally poor global market performance • Poor ability to develop and retain intellectual property • Loss of top tier talent to more vibrant clusters • Lack of star system for creative talent • Public funding dependency
Opportunities	**Threats**
• Technology disruption of mass consumer media • Digital technology lowering barriers to entry for innovative new companies • Market shifting towards niche content delivered through multiple channels • New models for direct distribution or one-to-one web advertising relationships	• Global players are taking the technology lead: Yahoo, Google, Apple and Microsoft partnering with the multinational media conglomerates • Open network technologies threaten CRTC content regulation regime • Innovative competitor firms can be from anywhere: USA, Europe, Asia • Low-cost production centre status is under threat from currency • Fluctuations and competing jurisdictions globally • Traditional domestic mass consumer market is splintering • Advertising dollars are splintering with the consumers

Source: A-Line Consultants (2006).

organizations in Ontario listed in the *Ontario Production Guide* (OMDC, 2009) the greater Toronto region encompasses 85 per cent of the 337 film commissions and production companies, 83 per cent of the 97 investment, insurance and funding organizations, 86 per cent of the unions, guilds and

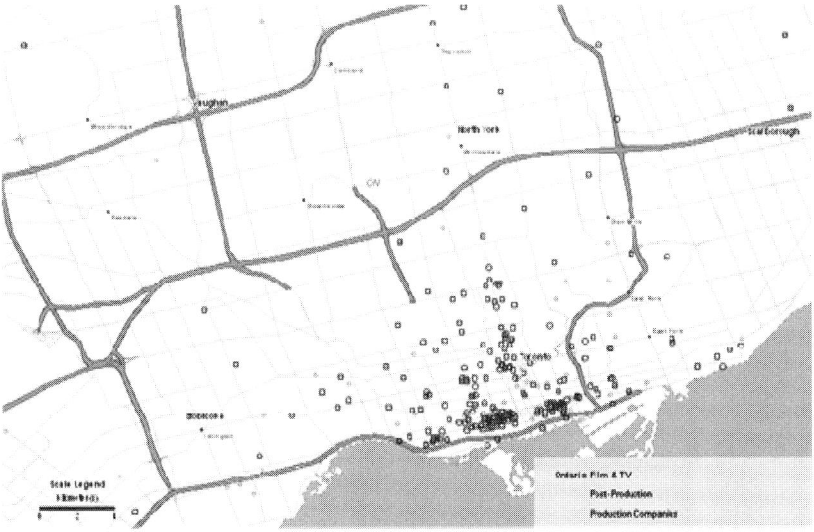

Source: HAL, 2009.

Figure 10.1 Location of film and TV production and post-production firms in downtown Toronto

professional and training organizations, 91 per cent of the 113 production services, 88 per cent of the 222 post-production services and 89 per cent of the 120 organizations in the distribution segment. Segments and specialties of the film and television industry that are least susceptible to clustering are government agencies, exhibitors, indoor and outdoor cinemas and training and educational institutions. These actors are unaffected by the project-based networking typical in the production segment of the film, television and interactive digital subsectors of the media industry.

Concentration in Specific Areas of the City

The Ontario Entertainment and Creative Cluster displays the mononucleated central city-led pattern of clustering typical of art, culture and media agglomerations (Currid and Connolly, 2008). Many of the firms in the cluster are located in three central neighbourhoods in downtown Toronto: Liberty Village/Queen West, the Distillery District and Yonge Street north of Bloor, as shown in the case of film and television production and post-production firms in Figure 10.1. These three districts can be characterized respectively as the hip new media scene, the night-time entertainment district and the upscale celebrity district.

Size Composition

Approximately 10,000 entities were registered as firms in the Toronto CMA in the NAICS 51 series of industry sectors (Information and Cultural Industries) in December 2008. The pinnacle of the Toronto media cluster is occupied by about 30 large firms, each with more than 500 employees, and by about 140 medium firms with between 100 and 499 employees. This group of about 170 firms includes information service providers, programme distributors, broadcasters, wireless and wired telecommunications carriers, internet hosting services, video and motion picture producers, post-production service providers and news, book, periodical and software publishers. The middle of the size spectrum consists of about 800 firms with 10 to 99 employees. At the low end of the size spectrum, the cluster is alive with about 9000 firms with fewer than ten employees, many of which are in fact self-employed individuals who are registered as firms to comply with Canadian tax regulations (Davis, 2010). Like micro-enterprises in other industries, most of these tiny firms are neither oriented towards nor resourced for growth. Small size does not imply small production capability, however, since production firms can manage large projects, and even tiny firms partner with larger firms to engage in translocal media production that spans continents (Davis et al, 2008; Davis and Nadler, 2009).

Nearly half of the firms in the Toronto CMA in the NAICS 51 series of industry sectors are in the motion picture and video production segment (NAICS 512110), of which 95 per cent are micro-enterprises (firms with fewer than five employees, including firms without employees). This fluid pool of video production micro-enterprises serves the film and television, advertising, corporate, real estate, wedding and other industries. Toronto also has pools exceeding 400 firms in the software publishing, periodical publishing, post-production and data processing segments, and in each case micro-enterprises constitute 70 per cent or more of the firms. If we include graphic and computer design services (NAICS 5414 and 5415), advertising firms (NAICS 5418) and independent artists, writers and performers who are registered as firms (NAICS 7115), the number of registered media firms in the Toronto Census Metropolitan Area (CMA) in December 2008 exceeds 42,000.

Industrial Dynamics

The cluster displays an apparent low rate of new firm formation via spinouts and spin-offs. The proportion of firms that have spun out of another firm ranges from a low of 8 per cent in film and television production to a high of 18 per cent in interactive digital media (HAL 2009). Apparently most of the firms in the Toronto media cluster did not originate in other firms, although their founders may have had previous contractual relationships with other firms. The process of *ab ovo* firm genesis through self-employment has important implications for the development of firm-level capabilities in the media industry, since key initial advantages typically are inherited from pre-entry resources and capabilities (Helfat and Lieberman, 2002). For example, most successful production firms in Toronto's children's television industry were established by individuals with extensive prior experience in the industry at senior executive levels, not by recent graduates of post-secondary institutions (Davis et al., 2008).

Market Orientation

Most Canadian technology-based clusters display highly extraverted forward market linkages to distant regions (Davis et al., 2009). In contrast, the Toronto media cluster is quite oriented towards customers in the domestic English-language market. Firms in the five media subsectors in question earn from 94 per cent (books) to 64 per cent (digital media) of their income in the domestic market. Two factors help explain the introversion of the Toronto media cluster: (1) Toronto is headquarters to many corporations, so the national English-language market can be served by Toronto-based content producers with local corporate clients, and (2) indigenous broadcasting and telecommunications conglomerates are generally content importers, not content exporters. Improvement of export capabilities of English-language Canadian media content is a challenge that the Toronto media cluster must learn to meet.

Self-identification among Firms as Members of a Cluster

Most of the firms in the core subsectors of the cluster believe that they belong to an Ontario media cluster (Table 10.1). This suggests some capacity for collective action and collective branding, a sense of untraded interdependencies among cluster actors and some shared understanding of parameters of public policy for the industry.

Digital Distribution of Content

With the exception of some areas of the music and interactive digital media subsectors, most subsectors of the Ontario Entertainment and Creative Cluster are not yet strongly affected by digital distribution of content. This is in spite of much policy exhortation and many programme incentives to promote production and distribution of cross-platform content. It is true that new technologies, as well as unfamiliar aesthetic conventions of interactive media, can present challenges to traditional content creators. The basic problem, however, is that in many cases digital content does not return sufficient revenue to cover its cost of production, and so must be subsidized by other business activities. Firms that produce films or television programmes are increasingly expected by broadcaster clients and funding agencies to prepare complementary cross-platform content. In the Ontario film and television production industry, cross-platform interactive media production provided around 2 per cent of the total volume of CA$897 million in 2007–2008 (Nordicity, 2009). Around 20 firms in the Toronto cluster produce only cross-platform content for film or television.

Governance of the Cluster

The cluster does not lend itself to straightforward policy actions or monitoring with a small number of indicators (Davis et al., 2009), and the strategic management of the cluster is a challenging proposition.

The governance of the Toronto media cluster is organized largely on sub-sectoral lines. Coordination and steering of activities in the Toronto media cluster take place via a governance network centred around industry associations, federal and provincial agencies, educational institutions and certain key firms. Horizontally, the cluster encompasses a range of sub-sectors whose principal common features (reliance on copyright and increasing use of digital platforms to distribute cultural content) do not overpower older sectoral patterns of organization. Thus each industry or subsector has its own industry association and often its own sub-sector-specific programmes, legislation and training institutions. The interactive digital media sub-sector is exceedingly heterogeneous. Its components (web 2.0 applications, games, advertising, animation and special effects and mobile applications) mainly have in common the use of broadband and digital technologies. When a new sub-sector such as mobile media emerges, it establishes its own networks and support infrastructure. The result is a very diverse and dynamic local industrial environment that constantly challenges the monitoring, coordination and institutional capabilities of associations, governments and service providers.

Furthermore, although the three major Canadian communications conglomerates (Telus, Bell and Rogers) earn the majority of their revenues from telecommunications services, each is also increasingly involved in broadcasting and other forms of content delivery. The economic and political power of these players is considerably greater than that of content-producing subsectors.

Vertically, the Ontario Entertainment and Creative Cluster falls under the jurisdiction of all three layers of government: metropolitan, provincial and federal, with the latter responsible for broadcast and telecommunications regulatory matters, tax incentives, R&D support, intellectual property legislation, international trade, immigration and national industry policy such as it is. The provincial government is largely responsible for education and training, active promotion of priority industries through programmes and tax credits and overall policy leadership in the area of creative industries. The Toronto metropolitan government provides land use planning and real estate development coordination, local promotion, advocacy, certain cultural programmes and various services to industrial actors. Of the three levels, the Ontario Government is the principal architect of the idea that the various cultural, creative and media industries form an Entertainment and Creative Cluster, and is by far the principal policy champion for the development of a regional cluster for purposes of regional economic expansion (McKinnon, 2008). The core policy and programme agency, the Ontario Media Development Corporation (OMDC), an arm of the Ontario Ministry of Culture, has adopted the McLuhan maxim 'culture is our business' as its own.

A relatively small number of educational institutions, public policy and programme agencies, trade associations and private firms are network nodes in the Toronto media cluster. In a recent survey, several hundred firms in the Ontario film, television, interactive media, books and magazine segments were asked to mention specific institutions with which they discuss R&D, marketing, human resources, partnering or economic development issues. The top ten institutions, accounting for about 27 per cent of mentions, include two public funding agencies (the OMDC and Telefilm Canada), two trade associations (the Canadian Film and Television Production Association and Interactive Ontario), three institutions of higher education (Ryerson University, Humber College and Sheridan College) and three broadcasters (CBC, CTV and CanWest).

SPECIALIZATION, SPILLOVERS AND GROWTH PROCESSES IN THE TORONTO MEDIA CLUSTER

The Toronto media cluster's development opportunities involve an innovation landscape and growth processes that go well beyond the model of industrial upgrading that has attracted much attention in research on North American media clusters: induced development through film and television production service linkages. This line of research focuses on the emergence of satellite production centres that have attracted 'runaway' or outsourced production from Hollywood (Lukinbeal 2004; 1998; Miller et al., 2005;

Scott, 2002; Scott and Pope, 2007). Canada pioneered the production services business based on tax incentive in the 1980s as a way to bring revenues into the domestic film and television production and post-production sectors and raise the quality of Canadian film and television production crews and infrastructure (Davis and Kaye, 2010). The foreign location production business boomed in Canada in the early 2000s but has since become very crowded. Presently Toronto and other Canadian cities compete with many new entrants around the world, most of which offer attractive tax and infrastructure benefits for outsourced film and television production and post-production business from Hollywood (Christopherson and Rightor, 2010; Davis and Kaye, 2010; Miller et al., 2005).

Film and television production outsourcing is motivated primarily by cost considerations and it engages mainly local 'humdrum' inputs: below-the-line crews and various infrastructure and service providers, not the principal above-the-line creative talent or high-level business functions. Thus satellite production centres are entry-level clusters, the media equivalent of maquiladoras. Of theoretical as well as practical interest is how satellite centres can evolve from contract production centres to more autonomous creative media clusters by developing higher-order creative, business, marketing, financing and distribution capabilities. The Vancouver film and television cluster, which depends in majority on foreign location production, is the most closely analysed case of evolution of a satellite production centre (Coe 2000, 2001; Davis and Kaye, 2010; Gasher, 2002; Scott and Pope, 2007; Tinic, 2005). Foreign location production declined substantially in Ontario in the last early years of the decade, returning film and television production spending in 2008 to its level of ten years earlier (Figure 10.2) although the next year spending picked up again considerably. Prestige infrastructure projects like the state-of-the-art downtown Filmport studio have been transferred to foreign management. Indigenous production, not foreign location production, is the mainstay of the Toronto film and television industry.

Investigation of media production outsourcing and other international business linkages helps counter the tendency in much cluster research to attribute competitiveness to local externalities (see e.g. Aksoy and Robins, 1992; Coe and Johns, 2004; Miller et al., 2005). Few authors have examined Toronto's global-local linkages in the media industry, however. Notable among these is Vang and Chaminade's (2007) application of an analytical framework drawn from international business theory to the Toronto feature film industry. They show that innovation cluster analysis using Marshallian and Jacobs frameworks (which emphasize local externalities) cannot explain the failure of the Toronto cluster to leverage its involvement as a production services provider to grow a viable indigenous feature film industry. They rec-

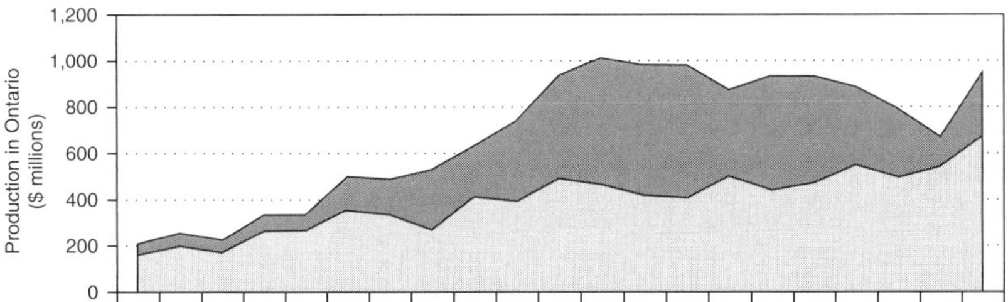

	1989	1990	1991	1992	1993	1994	1995	1996	1997	1998	1999	2000	2001	2002	2003	2004	2005	2006	2007	2008	2009
Total Foreign	42.0	56.8	54.1	72.0	68.9	142.0	157.0	252.8	220.8	347.0	442.7	543.0	561.1	574.4	369.9	486.3	458.8	338.7	292.4	126.6	272.1
Total Domestic	167.4	203.0	174.3	267.0	269.0	359.0	339.0	277.4	414.3	396.2	491.3	468.2	420.5	410.1	504.2	448.2	475.1	549.4	498.6	544.6	674.4
Total Production	209.4	259.8	228.4	339.0	338.0	501.0	496.0	530.2	635.1	743.2	934.0	1011.2	981.6	984.5	874.1	934.5	933.8	888.1	791.0	671.2	946.4

The chart above represents productions shot in Ontario which have received facilitation services and/or applied for tax credits from the OMDC.

Source: http://www.omdc.on.ca/Page3417.aspx.

Figure 10.2 Film and television production in Ontario – foreign vs. domestic, 1989–2009

ommend a strategy of distinctive differentiation (using the Danish film movement Dogma as an example) as a way to avoid price-based competition. This is an important theoretical improvement, but it needs to focus on more than leveraging service linkages. The Toronto media cluster did not originate as a satellite centre and is not organized primarily to provide production services. In Toronto's model, service production complements indigenous production. Toronto already possesses very well-developed higher-level media creative, business and distribution capabilities. The Toronto media cluster has considerably stronger absorptive capacities than those of a satellite production centre, and in principle these absorptive capacities should facilitate the development of successful media products, including feature films. Yet service production, not media content, remains the major source of Toronto's – and Canada's – audiovisual export revenues. Of the nearly CA$ 2 billion in export revenues earned by the Canadian film and television production industry in 2007–2008, nearly 90 per cent were earned through service production, not through licensing of intellectual property (CFTPA, 2009). Most of this export revenue is earned by production services firms, not by independent film and television production firms (Davis and Kaye, 2010; Nordicity, 2009). Most of Toronto's export revenues from Canadian-owned IP in film and television are earned in specialized niches, especially children's and youth programming (Nordicity, 2009).

Economics and politics provide the best explanation of how Toronto came to develop strong higher-order media capabilities while experiencing difficulty in climbing the ladder in the international division of cultural labour to positions of higher value-add and more effective value capture in export markets. Canadian producers of English-language content face the economic reality that the relatively small domestic market does not support investment in screen media product development on a scale comparable to the USA (Grant, 2008; Puppis, 2009). Linguistic and cultural proximity to the USA means that American products are, in many cases, legible and appealing to English-speaking Canadian audiences (Olson, 1999). American products enjoy a significant competitive advantage in English-speaking Canada because of their much higher production and marketing budgets, visibility through the star system and consequent attractiveness to advertisers and exhibitors, and availability for licensing in Canada at far below production cost (Grant, 2008). Given the availability of American media products, domestic broadcasters and exhibitors have little economic incentive to screen English-language Canadian feature films or television drama, let alone invest in production of indigenous content. Canadian broadcasters invest less in Canadian content production than in acquisition of programmes in Hollywood, where their arrival in town with generous acquisition budgets during the programme purchasing season is duly noted in the trade press (Vlessing, 2007).

Survival of Canadian film and television content producers would be problematic without subsidy of indigenous production and a regulatory framework that reserves air time for Canadian media content. Even with considerable public support and protection, Canadian English-language television drama attracted just 14 per cent of peak-period viewing of all drama programming on Canadian TV in 2008. Canada produces around 70 feature films annually, but Canadian feature films captured just 1.1 per cent of the English-language market box office in 2008 (CFTPA, 2009). Canada does not impose national origin quotas on theatrical exhibitors, a policy which is directly attributable to pressures and threats from the US film industry and its domestic Canadian allies, the exhibition industry (Magder, 1993; Mills, 2009). Consequently, most of the time Canadian feature films can hardly be found in theatres even by eager cognoscenti. That Canadian feature films are not more readily obtainable on domestic broadcast television, however, is a shortcoming of Canadian television policy (cf. Grant and Houle, 2009).

CONCLUSION: CULTURAL SOVEREIGNTY, JURISDICTIONAL ADVANTAGE AND THE TORONTO MEDIA CLUSTER

Over time, American entertainment products have shaped preferences and expectations among English-speaking Canadian audiences to such an extent that American products do not suffer much of a 'cultural discount' or loss of economic value when crossing the cultural boundary between the USA and English Canada (Hoskins and Mirus, 1988). Thus it is now perfectly normal for Canadians to consume large quantities of American film and television products, especially drama. But the relationship is asymmetrical, and most media content – especially screen content – produced for Canadian English-language audiences does not export well to the USA. Frequently US distributors require the removal of Canadian markers and signifiers from media products imported from Canada. For example, the film *How She Move*, which was written, located and shot in Toronto, was edited for distribution outside Canada to portray a generic mid-west American city. International co-productions, a favoured internationalization pathway for Canadian production companies, are particularly prone to cultural discount in the US market. The Canada-France co-produced youth comedy *Family Biz* would have been more appealing to Hollywood distributors had it included fewer Canadian cultural markers, more American comedic conventions such as a laugh track, and greater product placement and merchandising opportunities (Davis and Nadler, 2009). Toronto's involvement in the production services business has led it to specialize in 'placelessness' – a nondescript, shapeshifting locale that can represent other places, especially New York City, Chicago and Washington, D.C. (Matheson, 2004). For example, the film *Chicago* was shot in Toronto. A *Hulk* film was recently shot on Yonge Street made to look like New York City. The downside is that Toronto rarely gets to play itself. In nearly 700 film and television productions between 1999 and 2006, Toronto played itself only about 5 per cent of the time (Davis and Kaye, 2010). This strategy works for foreign location shoots but it does not help Toronto to develop place-specific advantages based on 'look and feel' that brand the city in creative products such as tourism experiences, fashion, cuisine and live performance (cf. Currid and Connolly, 2008). It is also regarded as a major constraint on storytelling by Canadian screenwriters (Kaye and Davis, 2010).

What is the potential for Canadian content to satisfy American and other audiences? Canadian English-language television producers have known periods of strong demand from cable and syndication markets in the USA, mainly for inexpensive generic fare (Tate, 2007). But some well-known Ontario media products do appeal to American audiences. The award-winning teen drama television series *Degrassi: the Next Generation*, produced and shot in Toronto, has a distinctive style in its category and has proven attractive in the USA. The show, which 'successfully negotiates the tension between national specificity and universality' (Levine, 2009), was proclaimed by a *New York Times* critic to be 'tha Best Teen

TV N da WRLD!' (Neihart, 2005). The television police drama series *Flashpoint*, produced and shot in Toronto and featuring views of the city's recognizable skyline, aired in a primetime CBS slot in 2008–2009. Another example of an internationally successful Ontario cultural product is Lynne Johnston's comic strip *For Better or For Worse,* which is read by hundreds of millions of people worldwide. It portrays life in a fictitious small city near Toronto and contains abundant Canadian references and signifiers.

A contrasting business model for cultural production in Canada is provided by Harlequin Enterprises, the world's largest publisher of romance novels and Canada's most successful indigenous book publisher. Harlequin romances are not intended to showcase Toronto, make significant contributions to Canadian cultural sovereignty or even make profound artistic statements, and they are dismissed by cultural nationalists, discounted by literary theorists and ridiculed by feminists. An analysis of more than 15,000 Harlequin titles finds the eight most prevalent themes to be marriage, reproduction, Western (as in cowboys and ranches), wealth, medicine, Christmas, royalty and professional or corporate life (Cox and Fisher, 2009). Harlequin sold 130 million books in 2008. The Toronto-based company (owned by TorStar) publishes 110 romance titles per month in 28 languages and has offices in 17 cities around the world. Ninety-five per cent of the firm's revenues are generated outside Canada. Harlequin has led the adaptive diffusion of mass-market romance publishing around the world not by exporting from its mothership in Canada but by establishing separate publishing companies to produce books in local languages, using a network of over 1000 authors (McWilliam, 2009). The romance genre is the product, and the Canadian value-add is to organize the creation of extensive variations on the genre to appeal to tastes in a specific demographic segment.

A tension between policy objectives aiming at cultural sovereignty and those promoting jurisdictional advantage is now an inherent feature of Canadian English-language media policy. Multiple assessments of the Toronto media cluster's subsectors, reviewed above, demonstrate that the cluster's core market in English-speaking Canada provides limited scope for further growth. Further, the main policy arrangement ensuring jurisdictional advantage, the Canadian content provisions in the broadcast regime, is losing traction. The defining characteristic of the Toronto cluster is, however, its 'across-the-board strength in all cultural industries' (Government of Ontario, 2010) – a unique mix of assets and capabilities that provide scope and variety, a strong basis for innovation and expansion. The Toronto new media sector has proven especially resilient (Britton, 2007). Foreign location production spending in the Ontario screen industry, after nearly a decade of stagnation, increased dramatically in 2009 (Figure 10.2), suggesting to industry insiders that Ontario's value proposition has become clearer. Migration to digital platforms and distribution systems, development of specializations, spillovers within the urban cultural economy, entry of persons from Toronto's multicultural population into the media industry, extensive translocal and transcluster personal linkages, access to a variety of global production networks and abundant creative, technical and financial talent provide potential for many new combinations and growth pathways for this promising media cluster.

ACKNOWLEDGEMENTS

Portions of the research reported in this chapter were supported by a Major Collaborative Research Initiative grant from the Social Sciences and Humanities Research Council of Canada on 'Innovation and Creativity in City Regions'. This support is gratefully acknowledged. I also thank Irene Berkowitz, Robert Picard, John Schoales and Jeremy Shtern for useful comments on earlier drafts.

NOTES

1. The world hierarchy of media cities is defined by the number of corporate headquarters in each city across a range of media industries.
2. In media and many other matters, Canada and the United States 'may be the most extreme case of the "big nation, small neighbour" syndrome' (Mulcahy, 2000). Canada's location on the northern periphery of the British Empire, adjacent to the powerful United States, has made English-Canadian political and cultural theorists acutely sensitive to the ways media power underpins political and economic power. Deployment of communication systems in the service of empire is the central theme of foremost Canadian economic historian and founding father of institutionalist political economy of media, Harold Innis, and English-Canadian political-economic theorizing consistently displays a preoccupation with themes of cultural dependence, inauthenticity and commodification (Kurasawa, 2003).
3. Although branded as part of the *Ontario* Entertainment and Creative Cluster, approximately three-quarters of Ontario's media firms and supporting institutions are in the Greater Toronto Area (GTA) or a somewhat larger highly urbanized area in southern Ontario that includes small cities adjacent to Toronto, notably Hamilton and the Guelph-Kitchener-Waterloo region an hour west of Toronto. In this chapter, I refer to the urban region at the western end of Lake Ontario as the 'Toronto region' with the understanding that depending on the particular issue at hand, smaller adjacent urban regions find inclusion in, or exclusion from, the Toronto metropolitan region attractive or unattractive.
4. Many scales for ranking cities are available. According to the Globalization and World Cities Study Group and Network (GaWC), Toronto is already an alpha city, but is subordinate to seven alpha+ and two alpha++ cities.
5. In this chapter, the term 'indigenous' refers to media firms in Canada owned by Canadians or media content produced by them. 'Domestic' refers to location in Canada. 'Aboriginal' refers to First Nations.

6. On Canadian cultural policy and the programmes that support it, see Dowler (1996), Grant and Wood (2004) and Vance (2009).
7 On the Canadian broadcast-based domestic content regulation regime, see Armstrong (2010) and Hunter, Iacobucci and Trebilcock (2010).
8. No single Canadian city, however, predominates as a telecommunications headquarters. Telus is headquartered in Vancouver, Shaw is in Calgary, CanWest is in Winnipeg and Bell Canada and Quebecor in Montreal. Decentralization of telecommunications headquarters in Canada represents a major difference between Toronto's profile as a dominant city in the Canadian economy and New York's in the US economy (Rice, 2006).
9. Most consumers in Canada have been exposed to mobile applications only since mid-2008. The BlackBerry, produced by RIM in Waterloo, Ontario, originally served mainly business customers.

REFERENCES

Acheson, K. and C. Maule (2004), 'Convention on Cultural Diversity', *Journal of Cultural Economics*, **28**(4), 243–256.

Aksoy, A. and K. Robins (1992), 'Hollywood for the 21st Century: Global Competition for Critical Mass in Image Markets', *Cambridge Journal of Economics*, **16**(1), 1–22.

A-Line Consultants (2006), *Entertainment and Creative Cluster Strategy for Ontario. Final Report*, Toronto, CAN, report prepared for the Ontario Ministry of Culture.

Armstrong, R. (2010), *Broadcasting Policy in Canada*, Toronto, CAN: University of Toronto Press.

AuthentiCity (2008), *Creative City Planning Framework: A Supporting Document to the Agenda for Prosperity: Prospectus for a Great City*, Toronto, CAN: AuthentiCity for the City of Toronto.

Britton, J.N.H. (2007), 'Path Dependence and Cluster Adaptation: A Case Study of Toronto's New Media Industry', *International Journal of Entrepreneurship and Innovation Management*, **7**(2)–(5), 272–297.

CFTPA (2009), *09 Profile. An Economic Report on the Canadian Film and Television Production Industry*, Ottawa, CAN: Canadian Film and Television Production Association.

Christopherson, S. and N. Rightor (2010), 'The Creative Economy as "Big Business": Evaluating State Strategies to Lure Filmmakers', *Journal of Planning Education and Research*, **29**(3), 336–352.

Coe, N.M. (2000), 'On Location: American Capital and the Local Labour Market in the Vancouver Film Industry', *International Journal of Urban and Regional Research*, **24**(1), 79–94.

Coe, N.M. (2001), 'A Hybrid Agglomeration? The Development of a Satellite-Marshallian Industrial District in Vancouver's Film Industry', *Urban Studies*, **38**(10), 1753–1775.

Coe, N.M. and J. Johns (2004), 'Beyond Production Clusters: Towards a Critical Political Economy of Networks in the Film and Television Industries', in Dominic Power and Allen J. Scott (eds), *Cultural Industries and the Production of Culture*, Abingdon, UK and New York, NY, USA: Routledge, pp. 188–204.

Coish, D. (2004), *Census Metropolitan Areas as Culture Clusters*, Ottawa, CAN: Statistics Canada. Catalogue no. 89-613-MIE, No. 004.

Coish, D. (2006), *Profile of Selected Culture Industries in Ontario*, Ottawa, CAN: Statistics Canada, 81-595-MIE2006038.

Cox, A. and M. Fisher (2009), 'The Texas Billionaire's Pregnant Bride: An Evolutionary Interpretation of Romance Fiction Titles', *Journal of Social, Evolutionary, and Cultural Psychology*, **3**(4), 386–401.

Currid, E. and J. Connolly (2008), 'Patterns of Knowledge: The Geography of Advanced Services and the Case of Art and Culture', *Annals of the Association of American Geographers*, **98**(2), 414–434.

Davis, C.H. (2010), 'New Firms in the Screen-Based Media Industry: Startups, Self-employment, and Standing Reserve', in Mark Deuze (ed), *Managing Media Work*, Thousand Oaks, CA, USA: Sage, pp. 165–178.

Davis, C.H., T. Creutzberg and D. Arthurs (2009), 'Applying an Innovation Cluster Framework to a Creative Industry: The Case of Screen-based Media in Ontario', *Innovation: Management, Policy & Practice*, **11**(2), 201–214.

Davis, C.H. and J. Kaye (2010), 'International Production Outsourcing and the Development of Indigenous Film and Television Capabilities – the Case of Canada', in Greg Elmer, Charles H. Davis, Janine Marchessault and John McCullough (eds), *Locating Migrating Media*, Lanham, MD, USA: Rowman and Littlefield, pp. 57–78.

Davis, C.H. and J. Nadler (2009), 'International Television Co-productions, Clustering and the Cultural Discount: The Case of *Family Biz*, a Comedy', in Iréne Bernhard (ed), *Revised papers presented at the 12th Uddevalla Symposium: the Geography of Innovation and Entrepreneurship*, 11–13 June, Bari, Italy, Trollhattan, SWE: University West, pp. 359–378.

Davis, C.H., F. Vladica and I. Berkowitz (2008), 'Business Capabilities of Small Entrepreneurial Media Firms: Independent Production of Children's Television in Canada', *Journal of Media Business Studies*, **5**(1), 9–40.

Dowler, K. (1996), 'The Cultural Industries Policy Apparatus', in Michael Dorland (ed), *The Cultural Industries in Canada: Problems, Policies and Prospects*, Toronto, CAN: James Lorimer, pp. 328–346.

Gasher, M. (2002), *Hollywood North: The Feature Film Industry in British Columbia*, Vancouver, CAN: UBC Press.

Government of Ontario (2010), *Ontario's Entertainment and Creative Cluster: A Framework for Growth*, Toronto, CAN: Ministry of Tourism and Culture.

Grant, P.S. (2008), *Stories Under Stress: The Challenge for Indigenous Television Drama in English-Language Broadcast Markets*, report prepared for the International Affiliation of Writers Guilds, December.

Grant, P.S. and M. Houle (2009), *Broadcaster Support for Feature Film: Expanding the Audience with Television Platforms*, Toronto, CAN: report prepared for Telefilm Canada.

Grant, P.S. and C. Wood (2004), *Blockbusters and Trade Wars: Popular Culture in a Globalized World*, Vancouver, CAN: Douglas & McIntyre.

HAL (2009), *Ontario's Creative Cluster Study*, Ottawa, CAN: HicklingArthurs Low, report prepared for the Ontario Ministry of Culture.

Helfat, C.E. and M.B. Lieberman (2002), 'The Birth of Capabilities: Market Entry and the Importance of Pre-history', *Industrial and Corporate Change*, **11**(4), 725–760.

Hoskins, C., and R. Mirus (1988), 'Reasons for the US Dominance of the International Trade in Television Programmes', *Media, Culture and Society*, **10**, 499–515.

Hunter, L.A.W., E. Iacobucci and M.J. Trebilcock (2010), *Scrambled Signals:*

Canadian Content Policies in a World of Technological Abundance, Toronto, CAN: C.D. Howe Institute Commentary No. 301.

Jenkins, B. (2005), 'Toronto's Cultural Renaissance', *Canadian Journal of Communication*, **30**(2), 169–186.

Kaye, J. and C.H. Davis (2010), '"If it ain't on the page, it ain't on the stage": Screenwriting, National Specificity and the English-Canadian Feature film', *Journal of Screenwriting*, **2**(1), 61–83.

Krätke, S. (2003), 'Global Media Cities in a Worldwide Urban Network', *European Planning Studies*, **11**(6), 605–628.

Krätke, S. and P.J. Taylor (2004), 'A World Geography of Global Media Cities', *European Planning Studies*, **12**(4), 459–477.

Kurasawa, F. (2003), 'Finding Godot? Bringing Popular Culture into Canadian Political Economy,' in Wallace Clement and Leah Vosko (eds), *Changing Canada: Political Economy as Transformation*, Montreal & Kingston, CAN: McGill-Queen's University Press.

Lehrer, U. and J. Laidley (2008), 'Old Mega-projects Newly Packaged? Waterfront Redevelopment in Toronto', *International Journal of Urban and Regional Research*, **32**(4), 786–803.

Levine, E. (2009), 'National Television, Global Market: Canada's *Degrassi: The Next Generation*', *Media, Culture & Society*, **31**(4), 515–531.

Lukinbeal, C. (2004), 'The Rise of Regional Film Production Centers in North America, 1984–1997', *GeoJournal*, **59**(4), 307–321.

Lukinbeal, C. (1998), 'Reel-to-reel Urban Geographies: The Top Five Cinematic Cities in North America', *The California Geographer*, **38**(1), 64–78.

MacSkimming, R. (2006), *The Perilous Trade: Book Publishing in Canada, 1946–2006*, Toronto, CAN: McClelland and Stewart.

Magder, T. (1993), *Canada's Hollywood: The Canadian State and Feature Films*, Toronto, CAN: University of Toronto Press.

Martin, R. and R. Florida (2009), *Ontario in the Creative Age*, Toronto, CAN: Martin Prosperity Institute.

Matheson, S. (2004), 'Projecting Placelessness: Industrial Television and the "Authentic" Canadian city', in Greg Elmer and Michael Gasher (eds), *Contracting Out Hollywood: Runaway Productions and Foreign Location Shooting*, Lanham, MD, USA: Rowan and Littlefield, pp. 117–139.

McKinnon, S.E. (2008), 'From Cultural Nationalism to Regional Development: Examining the Growing Role of Canada's Provincial Cultural Agencies in the Support of the Nation's Cultural Industries During the Era of Globalization', Toronto, CAN: research paper, Ryerson University.

McWilliam, K. (2009), 'Romance in Foreign Accents: Harlequin-Mills & Boon in Australia', *Continuum Journal of Media & Cultural Studies*, **23**(2), 137–145.

MEIC (2009), *Innovation and Insight: Mapping Ontario's Mobile Industry*, Toronto CAN: Mobile Experience Innovation Centre.

Miller, T., N. Govil, J. McMurria, R. Maxwell and T. Wang (2005), *Global Hollywood 2*, London, UK: British Film Institute.

Mills, N. (2009), *In Limited Release: The Political Economy of the Canadian Motion Picture Distribution System*, Toronto, CAN: Unpublished MA thesis, Ryerson University.

Mulcahy, K.V. (2000), 'Cultural Imperialism and Cultural Sovereignty: U.S.-Canadian Cultural Relations', *American Review of Canadian Studies*, **30**(2), 181–206.

Murray, C. (2002), *More Money Blues: Review of Financial Support for Canadian Television Production*, Vancouver, CAN: School of Communication, Simon Fraser University, report prepared for the Standing Committee on Canadian Heritage, House of Commons.
Neihart, B. (2005), 'DGrassi Is tha Best Teen TV N da WRLD!', *New York Times*, 20 March.
Nordicity (2004), *Profile of Small and Medium-sized Enterprises in the Canadian Cultural Industries*, Toronto, CAN: report prepared for Department of Canadian Heritage.
Nordicity (2006), *Analysis of Canadian Broadcaster Financial Performance and Programming*, Toronto, CAN: Report prepared for the Canadian Film and Television Production Association.
Nordicity (2008a), *A Strategic Study for the Music Industry in Ontario. Final Report*, Toronto, CAN: Report prepared for the Ontario Media Development Corporation Music Industry Advisory Committee.
Nordicity (2008b), *A Strategic Study for the Book Publishing Industry in Ontario. Final Report*, Toronto, CAN: Report prepared for the Ontario Media Development Corporation Book Industry Advisory Committee.
Nordicity (2008c), *Economic Profile of the Ontario Computer Animation and Visual Effects Industry*, Toronto, CAN: Report prepared for the Computer Animation Studios of Ontario.
Nordicity (2008d), *The Greater Toronto Area's Potential for Innovation in the Screen-Based Industries: International Position, Market Opportunities, and Critical Success Criteria*, Toronto, CAN: Report prepared for CONCERT.
Nordicity (2009), *Ontario Profile 2009: An Economic Profile of Domestic Film, Television and Cross-platform Interactive Media Production in Ontario*, Toronto, CAN: Nordicity for Ontario Producers' Panel of the Canadian Film and Television Production Association.
OECD (2008), *Competitive Regional Clusters. National Policy Approaches*, Paris, FRA: Organisation for Economic Co-operation and Development.
OMDC (2009). *Ontario Production Guide*, Toronto, CAN: Ontario Media Development Corporation, http://www.omdc.on.ca/.
OMDC (2010), *Industry Profile: Book Publishing*, Toronto, CAN: Ontario Media Development Corporation, http://www.omdc.on.ca.
OMDC (2010), *Industry Profile: Interactive Digital Media*, Toronto, CAN: Ontario Media Development Corporation, http://www.omdc.on.ca.
OMDC (2010), *Industry Profile: Magazine Publishing*, Toronto, CAN: Ontario Media Development Corporation, http://www.omdc.on.ca.
OMDC (2010), *Industry Profile: Music*, Toronto, CAN: Ontario Media Development Corporation, http://www.omdc.on.ca.
OMDC (2010), *Industry Profile: Television*, Toronto, CAN: Ontario Media Development Corporation, http://www.omdc.on.ca.
Olson, S.R. (1999), *Hollywood Planet: Global Media and the Competitive Advantage of Narrative Transparency*, Mahwah, NJ, USA: Lawrence Erlbaum.
Puppis, M. (2008), 'National Media Regulation in the Era of Free Trade: The Role of Global Media Governance', *European Journal of Communication*, **23**(4), 405–424.
Puppis, M. (2009), 'Media Regulation in Small States', *International Communication Gazette*, **71**(1)–(2), 7–17.
Rice, M.D. (2006), 'Dominant National Centers: A Comparative Analysis of

the Headquarters Communities of New York and Toronto', *The Industrial Geographer*, **4**(1), 29–51.

Scott, A.J. (2002), 'A New Map of Hollywood: The Production and Distribution of American Motion Pictures', *Regional Studies*, **36**(9), 957–975.

Scott, A.J. and N. Pope (2007), 'Hollywood, Vancouver, and the World: Employment Relocation and the Emergence of Satellite Production Centers in the Motion-picture Industry', *Environment and Planning A*, **39**(6), 1364–1381.

SECOR (2008), *Ontario 2012: Stimulating Growth in Ontario's Digital Game Industry*, Montreal CAN: SECOR Consulting.

Spencer, G. and T. Vinodrai (2009), 'City-Region Profile: Toronto', unpublished manuscript prepared for the Innovation Systems Research Network, June.

Statistics Canada (2008), *Business Register*, Ottawa, CAN: Statistics Canada. Semi-annual list of businesses engaged in the production of goods and services in Canada.

Statistics Canada (2009), *Book Publishers 2007*, Catalogue no. 87F0004X, April.

Storper, M. and S. Christopherson (1987), 'Flexible Specialization and Regional Industrial Agglomerations: The Case of the U.S. Motion Picture Industry', *Annals of the Association of American Geographers*, **77** (1), 104–117.

Tate, M.A. (2007), *Canadian Television Programming Made for the United States Market: A History with Production and Broadcast Data*, Jefferson, NC, USA: McFarland & Co.

TCI (2008), *A Strategic Study of the Magazine Industry in Ontario*, Toronto, CAN: Final Report by TCI Management Consultants for the Ontario Media Development Corporation Magazine Industry Advisory Committee.

Telefilm Canada (2007), *Directory of the Canadian Film, Television and Video Industry*, Montreal, CAN: Telefilm Canada.

Tinic, S. (2005), *On Location: Canada's Television Industry in a Global Market*, Toronto, CAN: University of Toronto Press.

Toronto Economic Development (2009), *Toronto CMA 2008 Industry Profiles*, Toronto, CAN: City of Toronto.

Toronto Film Board (2007), *Bounce Back to Fast Forward: Strategic Plan for Toronto's Screen-based Industry*, Toronto, CAN: Toronto Film Board/ Economic Development, Culture & Tourism.

Vance, J.F. (2009), *A History of Canadian Culture: From Petroglyphs to Product, Circuses to the CBC . . .*, Oxford, UK: Oxford University Press.

Vang, J. and C. Chaminade (2007), 'Cultural Clusters, Global–Local Linkages and Spillovers: Theoretical and Empirical Insights from an Exploratory Study of Toronto's Film Cluster', *Industry & Innovation*, **14**(4), 401–420.

Vlessing, E. (2007), 'Canada on Shopping Spree for U.S. Dramas', *Hollywood Reporter*, 24 May.

11. Vancouver as media cluster: the cases of video games and film/TV

Trevor Barnes and Neil M. Coe

If ever Joseph Schumpeter's (1942) notion of 'a gale of creative destruction' has applicability it is to Vancouver, British Columbia. Over the course of the last 25 years, immensely powerful gusts of economic change, cyclonic in their energy, have destroyed Vancouver's old urban economy based on processing natural resources like lumber and fish. In their place, a 'new economy' has been erected resting on creative, weightless industries like those in the new media. Consequently, the old inner city where resource activities happened, and where resource-processing workers lived, has been torn up and remade. Even some of Vancouver's suburbs, particularly the oldest, Burnaby, lying directly to the east of the city, have experienced a radical makeover as former light industrial and warehouse spaces were reconstructed as movie studios and 'dream factories' for the manufacture of video games. The purpose of this chapter is to analyse the gale of creative destruction that has touched down in Vancouver, transforming the city into, among other things, a media cluster. In particular, we focus on two of the city's media industries, both of which generate over a billion Canadian dollars in revenue each year: video games and film and TV production.

The chapter is divided into five substantive sections followed by a brief conclusion. Firstly, we outline the recent historical transformation of Vancouver from a staples-producing local metropole to a world city that is now one of the termini on the global media industry's international circuit of labour, capital and ideas. Secondly, we discuss the origins, development and geography of the video games and film/TV clusters within Vancouver. Thirdly, we describe the particular critical institutional contexts that differentially have borne upon and shaped the development of the two clusters, and which include the role of the state, labour organizations and non-profit institutions. Fourthly, we identify the internal dynamics propelling each of the two industrial clusters, setting their respective future trajectories and constraints. Finally, we speculate about the two industries' future prospects, which include the blurring of the boundaries that so far have kept them distinct.

Our analysis is based for the most part on semi-structured interviews. We completed 20 interviews in the film/TV industry and 35 in the video games industry. Interviewees were typically key corporate and institutional informants. The interviews were carried out in the summer and autumn of both 2008 and 2009.

THE TRANSFORMATION OF VANCOUVER AND THE RISE OF NEW MEDIA

For the first 100 years of its existence, Vancouver functioned as what Harold Innis (1956), the preeminent historian of Canada, called a 'local metropole' within the larger British Columbia (BC) staples (resource) economy. That economy rested on the extraction, processing and export of natural resources, most prominently in forestry, fishing and mining. The prime functions of the city as a local metropole were as a decision-making centre, and as a storage and export entrepôt. It also carried out a small amount of manufacturing and processing especially within the inner city areas around False Creek and Burrard Inlet.

The corporatization of the provincial resource sector after World II War was an important benchmark. It reorganized the economy along Fordist lines, creating general affluence and bringing 'the good life' to BC. It also solidified an internal core-periphery regional relation between Vancouver and the rest of the province. Vancouver undertook the local control function, as well as physical distribution, while the rest of the province undertook the grunt work of extraction and processing.

More specifically, Vancouver's central business district (CBD) in the downtown peninsula was the site of corporate resource offices, especially for branches of firms whose headquarters were often located elsewhere. The downtown also provided ancillary producer services, such as in finance, including a penny stock exchange specializing in generating venture capital for speculative resource operations (particularly mining). To the north of the CBD was the harbour linked to warehouse and transportation functions for staple distribution (not all of which were produced in BC). To the south lay False Creek, a hub for warehousing and transportation but intermingled with some resource-processing activities (e.g. saw-mills and fish packing plants), heavy industry (e.g. iron and steel foundries and concrete plants) and working-class boarding houses, apartments and houses. East of False Creek was more warehousing along with light manufacturing and the principal working-class residential neighbourhoods.

From the late 1970s, all three of BC's staple industries – fishing, mining and forestry – experienced serious economic difficulties stemming from diminishing resource stocks, environmental conflicts, falling prices, plateauing markets and various disputes with the USA over jurisdiction and market access. Corporate resource firms, previously the backbone of Vancouver's economy, went bankrupt, were radically downsized or left the city altogether. Consequently, Vancouver in effect decoupled from the rest of the province, cutting its ties to the staples hinterland to which it was formerly tethered (Davis and Hutton, 1989). In the process the urban economy fundamentally reorganized. Vancouver lost 30 per cent of its head office jobs between 1999 and 2005, falling from 16,894 to 11,983 employees (and the only major Canadian city to lose jobs in this category: Statistics Canada 2006). Only four new office blocks were constructed in downtown Vancouver between 1991 and 2009. Former office towers were even converted into condominiums. For example, the first ever modernist skyscraper built in Vancouver (1955–1957), the head office for BC Hydro, was in 1998 transformed into a residential complex, the 242 strata suite 'The Electra'.

The new economy that emerged in Vancouver was post-staples, post-corporate and post-industrial. Moreover, it was wired in complex ways to global circulations of talent, money and technology. Beyond the video games and film/TV industries that form the focus of this chapter, new firms were to be found in a wide range of 'new economy' sectors including software design, animation, graphic design, music production, wireless technology, remote sensing, pharmaceuticals, biotechnology and fuel cell research. The resulting new economy has thus taken various forms, but an increasingly important constellation of activities is in the area of the new media. The new media is defined by Britton et al. (2009, p. 211) as 'the interrelated set of economic activities that produce digital, text, audio, or computer graphic material that can be accessed through the internet, films, kiosks, and related communication channels'.

In 2004 a large survey was undertaken of Vancouver's new media firms of which there were 569, representing more than 14,000 employees (Britton et al., 2009). Employment in those firms was divided roughly equally between suburbs, especially the municipalities of Burnaby, Richmond and the North Shore, and the central city (Figure 11.1). And within the central city, there were pronounced clusters of new media in former warehousing and working-class residential inner-city neighbourhoods: Yaletown, Gastown and along Hastings Street (Victory Square) (Barnes and Hutton, 2009). The size distribution of the firms fitted very much with the post-corporate designation, with three-quarters of new media companies in Vancouver having less than ten employees, and with only 2 per cent with more than 100 (Britton et al., 2009).

The basis of Vancouver's economy had thus profoundly shifted. It

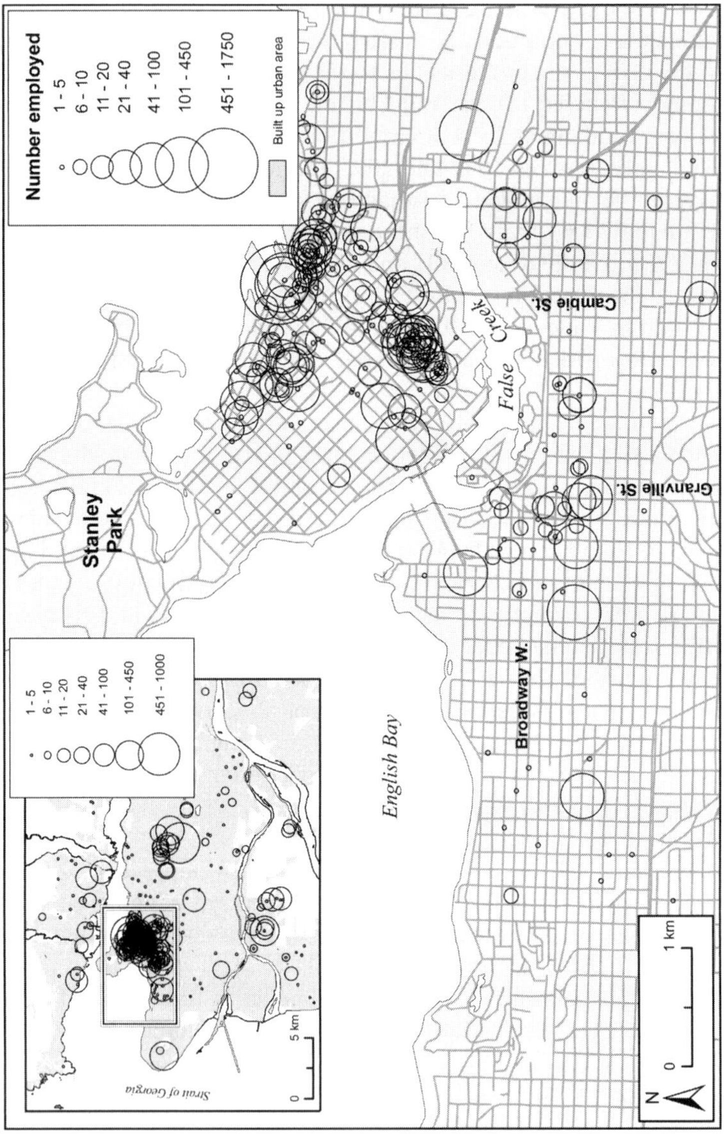

Source: Britton et al., 2009, reproduced with permission.

Figure 11.1 Vancouver's new media economy, 2004

was no longer a city based on the processing and distribution of staples resources. Its central products were now weightless, digital, requiring not brawn and muscle from workers but mental agility and creativity. Employees of the new economy were not high-school dropouts, but graduates of the Vancouver Film School and the Emily Carr School of Design. Moreover, as this new economy emerged, the city changed geographically to accommodate it, actively egged on by the Vancouver City Planning Department. Former resource-processing and warehouse spaces in the inner city were zoned for residential development, as homes for the creative class. And intermingled with the high-rise condominiums were workplaces and commercial spaces – converted offices, loft studios, bars and cafes, faux piazzas and the full spectrum of retail bric-a-brac associated with the consumption of the new class (Hutton, 2008, Ch. 8).

But Vancouver's new economy is not a homogeneous block. There is considerable sub-sector variation that affects industrial organization, sources of funding, relationships to technological change, institutional support and the form and segmentation of the talent that works in it. Such variation is seen clearly in our two case studies: video games and the film/TV industry.

ORIGINS, DEVELOPMENT AND GEOGRAPHY OF VANCOUVER'S VIDEO GAMES AND FILM/TV CLUSTERS

The Video Games Industry

The first video games ever produced were in the 1950s, a result of bored Cold War Pentagon researchers playing around on a cathode-ray tube (Dyer-Witheford, 2004). It took another good decade for the first commercial game to be sold, *Computer Space* in 1971 (Kline et al., 2003, Ch. 4). But from that moment the industry grew exponentially with global revenues in 2007 reaching US$41.9 bn, with estimates that by 2012 sales will be US$68.4 bn (Caron, 2008).

The origins of Vancouver's video games industry are in the early 1980s, with two suburban Burnaby schoolboys, Don Mattrick and Jeff Sember. They began designing and selling digital games out of the basement of Mattrick's parents' house, producing their first published game, *Evolution*, in 1982. They formed the company Digital Software Incorporated (DSI) in 1985, and with Accolade, an American publisher, developed and distributed a series of racing and sports games such as the *Test Drive* series. By 1988 Mattrick had bought out Sember, and DSI had moved to an old warehouse in the inner city Yaletown district (over a pub). Rents were cheap, there was ample room for studio space, and the neighbourhood was already acquiring chicness as the first gentrifiers moved in. Between 1985 and 1991, DSI produced 20 games.

This success led Electronic Arts (EA), a giant California-based multinational producer and publisher of video games, to buy out Mattrick. It acquired DSI in 1991 for CA$11m, with Mattrick hired in a key executive position within the new company, EA Canada. Not all the former DSI employees acquired by EA Canada were happy with the new arrangements, however. The same year that DSI was bought out, a disgruntled group of them formed a new firm, Radical Entertainment. But within six years some of those same employees were moving on again, starting yet two more companies, Barking Dog and Relic (both in 1997). This process of new firm creation through splitting we will call 'firm fission': one firm begetting another firm through the mechanism of employees leaving and setting up a new company (Kyllo, 2009). Figure 11.2 represents the entire family tree of Vancouver game developers produced by firm fission. The city is now on its fifth generation of firms, with the original firm Mattrick and Sember's DSI (Kyllo, 2009).

At the end of 2008, the total revenue of Vancouver-based video games firms was around CA$1.5 bn (EA Canada made close to a billion dollars). There were approximately 3500 jobs and 145 firms. The firms ranged in size from the very large – EA Canada had roughly a thousand employees – to several SMEs like Hothead Games, Slant 6 and United Front each employing between 100 and 150 workers, to a large number of very small companies that included many single-person start ups.

Central to the fission process undergirding the Vancouver video games industry was the presence of EA Canada. It was the anchor for the whole sector, providing the prime source of new entrepreneurs of new firms, a lure for urban talent and capital and the buyer of subcontractor services. In a well-known paper, Anne Markusen (1996) drew up a four-fold typology of forms of cluster development. Vancouver's video games industry best fits her 'hub and spoke' type. This is where a single key firm is in the centre and around which smaller firms rotate. In Vancouver's case, EA Canada is the hub and the SMEs and start-ups are the spokes.

In terms of the geography of the video games cluster, Figure 11.3 shows the geographical distribution of video games firms within the Vancouver metropolitan area. As one would expect, the map shows broad similarities to the earlier one of the new media (Figure 11.1). Within the inner city, the main cluster is in Yaletown, especially along a single road, Homer Street. In the larger metropolitan area, apart from the inner city, the greatest concentration is in Burnaby around where EA Canada is based. In 1999, they

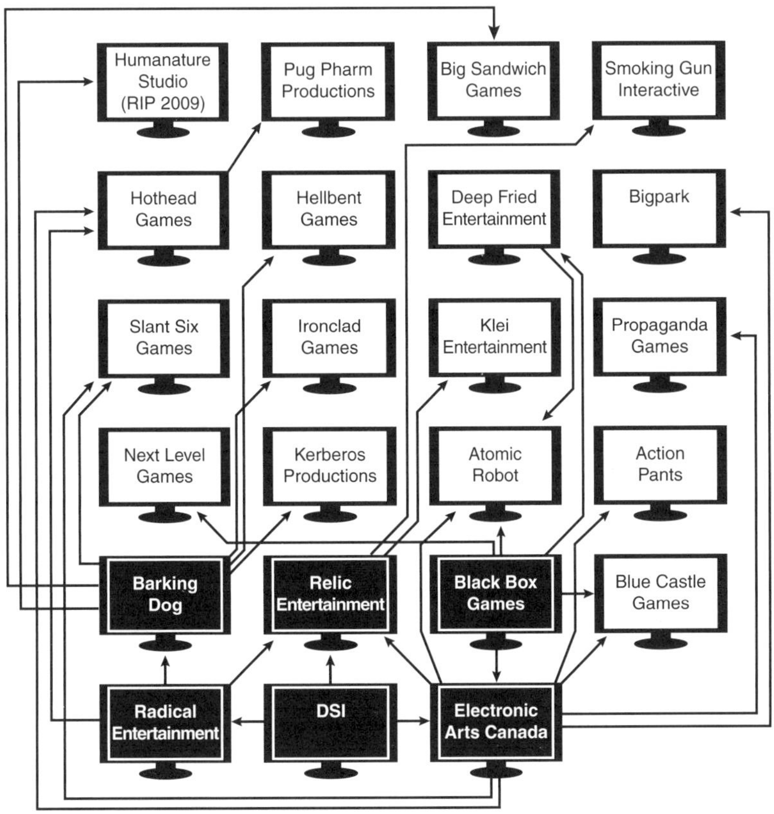

Source: Redrawn from Kyllo, 2009.

Figure 11.2 Firm fission in Vancouver's video game industry

moved into a purpose-built facility, dubbed the 'Dream Factory', opened by the then Canadian Prime Minister, Jean Chretien.

The Film/TV Industry

The development of Vancouver as a film/TV production centre is intimately related to the post-war organizational restructuring of the Hollywood studio system and the concomitant rise of location shooting on a large scale (Christopherson and Storper, 1986; Gasher, 1995; Elmer and Gasher, 2005). Although filmmaking in British Columbia dates back to the turn of the 20th century (e.g. Browne, 1979), a significant film industry only emerged from the late 1960s.

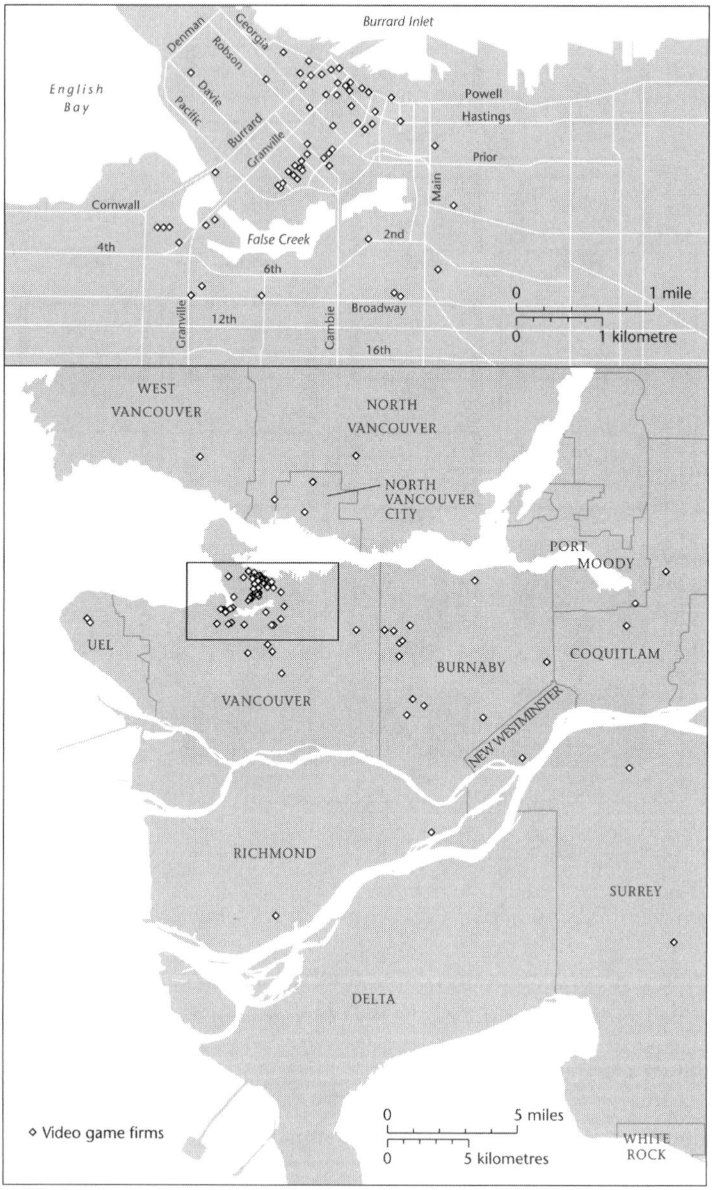

Source: Authors' research.

Figure 11.3 Video games companies within Vancouver's metropolitan area

As a location, Vancouver has been, and remains, extremely well placed to benefit from the opportunities created by the vertical disintegration of the Hollywood studios. The city is close to Los Angeles (2½ hours flying time), is in the same time zone (thereby allowing easy coordination of activities between the two centres), has a mild climate which allows year-round filming, and offers a large range of different scenic locations within one or two hours' drive of central Vancouver. It has also benefited enormously from the low value of the Canadian dollar against the US dollar, which has held uninterrupted since 1976 (except for a brief four-month blip in 2007). In 2002, the Canadian-US dollar exchange rate reached an all-time low of US 63 cents before slowly climbing. When lower Canadian wage rates and government incentives are also included – an issue we will return to shortly – savings of 20–30 per cent can be realized by shooting productions in Vancouver as opposed to Hollywood.

This last point indicates another advantage held by Vancouver, namely the proactive role of both the provincial government and the labour unions (Gasher, 2002). We discuss both institutions in more detail in the next section, but their formative function should be recognized here. With respect to government, the BC Film Commission was inaugurated in 1978. Its main task has been to facilitate film production for Hollywood, a one-stop shop for prospective producers, smoothing production and investment. Likewise the key labour unions involved in film/TV production – the Teamsters and two locals of the International Alliances of Theatrical Stage Employees (IATSE) (Local 669 camera operators, and Local 891 technicians) – have gone to great lengths to meet the needs of Hollywood producers. Murphy (1997) argues that the technical unions in particular have played a pivotal 'entrepreneurial' role in the development of the industry in Vancouver.

Finally, also important were key individuals who made a difference just as Don Mattrick did in the video games industry. Early on in the film industry it was Stephen Cannell, a Hollywood TV writer, producer, creator and actor, who came to Vancouver in the early 1980s to shoot his new TV series *21 Jump Street*. To cut costs he opened new studio facilities, the North Shore Studios (formerly Lion's Gate Studios), and the first of five major studio spaces to be built in the metro area. The second was the Bridge Studios, converted from an old bus depot and financially underwritten by the provincial government.

The combination of these factors has now made Vancouver one of the leading 'cinematic cities' of North America (Lukinbeal, 1998). Over the 30-year period 1978–2007, British Columbia's film and television industry generated some CA$15 bn in revenues. Annual revenues first passed CA$1 bn in 1999 and have hovered around and in some years significantly exceeded that mark ever since (see Figure 11.4). The industry – widely

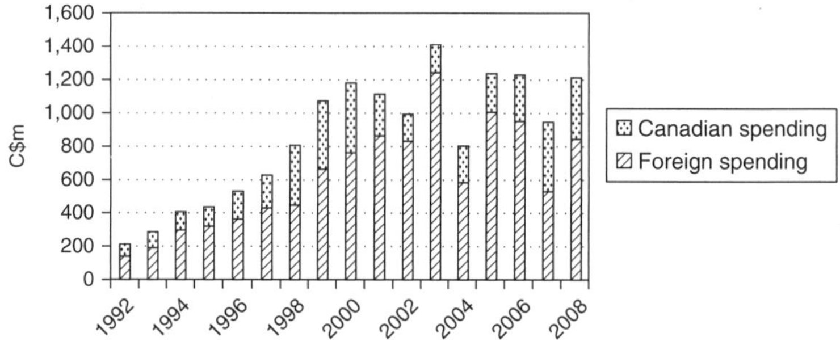

Source: http://www.bcfilmcommission.com/about_us/stats.htm

Figure 11.4 BC film/TV industry revenues, 1992–2008

considered to be the third largest in North America after Los Angeles and New York – accounts for an estimated 23,900 full-time equivalent jobs in BC (13,200 in direct employment, 10,700 indirect) and an average wage that is around twice the provincial average.

As its nickname 'Hollywood North' indicates, Vancouver's fortunes are closely connected to those of the Los Angeles film and television complex, with inward investment accounting for between 60 and 80 per cent of total spending each year. In Lukinbeal's (2004) terminology, Vancouver is an 'edge center' – a Hollywood satellite location that benefits from cost-based 'runaway' production. Moreover, Vancouver is perhaps best described as a *television* production cluster, with TV accounting for 75 per cent of production expenditure in 2007 (cf. Tinic, 2005). Table 11.1 breaks down the production data for 2008, showing an unusually strong year for feature film production (44 per cent of the total) but a more typical split of foreign to domestic production in budget terms (70 per cent to 30 per cent). Overall, BC accounts for fully two-thirds of Canada's foreign location and service production (CFTPA, 2009).

As an industry it is constituted by a mass of independent small firms – Scott and Pope (2007) estimate there may be around 2000 – which then articulate with labour provided by the various union locals on a project-by-project basis. Given the distances between Vancouver and the nearest large-scale production centres (Toronto and Los Angeles) most firms are highly locally embedded, with many undertaking all of their business within the Vancouver metropolitan area.

That said, the genesis and emergence of the Vancouver film industry has largely depended on the spending decisions of a small group of large US

Table 11.1 Breakdown of spending in BC film/TV industry in 2008

Genre	Canadian (CA$ m)	No.	Foreign (CA$ m)	No.	Total (CA$ m)	No.
Features	83.7	25	441.5	40	525.2	65
TV series	82.8	42	320.8	14	403.6	56
TV movies, pilots and mini-series	92.3	46	53.3	16	145.6	62
Documentaries, shorts and animation	106.8	61	25.6	16	132.4	77
Totals	365.6	174	841.2	86	1206.8	260

Source: BCFC (2009).

studios and media conglomerates ('the eight giants' as they are sometimes called: Fox, Paramount, DreamWorks, Sony, MGM, NBC Universal, Time Warner, Disney). The studios often have complete financial and creative authority over the projects filmed in Vancouver, with control exercised indirectly through subcontracting networks rather than through direct ownership. In some instances, key production personnel are sent to Vancouver to oversee or manage particular projects through a temporary subsidiary. In others, the complete production process is subcontracted to a Vancouver production company. The small-firm networks of the Vancouver film industry thus rely ultimately on funding from US studios and TV networks. The key group that engages with financial decision-makers in Los Angeles are Vancouver-based producers. Over the past 30 years, many have built strong personal relationships with Hollywood studio executives. In this sense, they, along with studio managers and a few government officials, are crucially embedded in extra-local personal relationships that facilitate the continued flow of capital from Los Angeles to Vancouver (Coe, 2000a).

In contrast to Markusen's hub-and-spoke cluster type that fits Vancouver's video games industry, the film and TV sector perhaps represents a hybrid of her Marshallian and satellite types (Coe, 2001). On the one hand, key investment and creative decision making come from outside the cluster, in this case from Hollywood. On the other hand, that investment creates a locally formed Marshallian industrial district, in this case Scott and Pope's cluster of some 2000 independent small firms operating within the Vancouver metro area.

As for the video games industry, the geographical distribution of film and TV firms can be plotted (see Figure 11.5). There is clustering in the old inner-city industrial areas like Yaletown, Victory Square and Gastown, as well as in

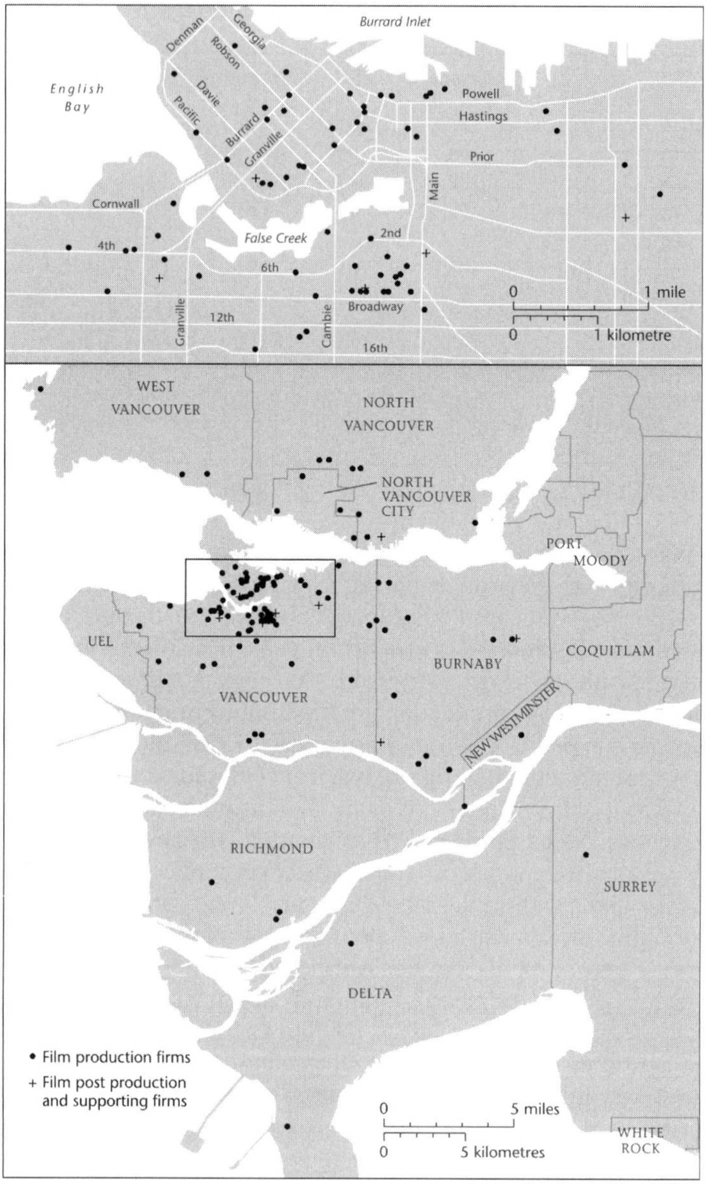

Source: Authors' research.

Figure 11.5 Film/TV production companies in the Vancouver metropolitan area

Mount Pleasant (nicknamed 'video drive' by one of our informants), but the clustering is more suburbanized than for the video games industry. Pulling the industry to the suburbs, to North Vancouver and especially to Burnaby, are the major studio spaces. There are five major studios in the metro area: North Shore Studios in North Vancouver, Vancouver Studios on the boundary with Burnaby, and three Burnaby studios, Bridge, Mammoth and the latest, which opened in 2008, Canadian Motion Pictures Park.

INSTITUTIONAL CONTEXTS

As many studies have made clear (see Chapter 2), the coherency and development of an industry cluster is often tied to a set of formal and informal institutions. This is no different in our study. Both the video games and film/TV clusters in Vancouver are regulated and shaped by a set of interrelated institutions that give each a distinctive form, providing geographical advantages in attracting capital and achieving a strong bottom line.

The State

The first of the institutions is the state, in particular the local state, the provincial government of British Columbia. Until very recently, the state treated the video games and film industries quite differently. The BC government gave the video games industry almost nothing, fomenting bitterness among video games firm owners. Until 2010, the sole state subsidy for the video games industry was a 30 per cent tax credit but given only to the providers of venture capital, and even then up to a maximum of only CA$60,000. There was nothing for operating costs, contrasting with various generous subsidies offered by other provincial jurisdictions in Canada. In Quebec, for example, Dyer-Witheford (2004) estimates that the local state provides a subsidy of 25 per cent for every game produced in that province mainly through the provision of tax credits on labour costs. In Ontario, which has had only a minimal video games industry, the provincial government announced in July 2009 that it had attracted Ubisoft to Toronto with the lure of a CA$263 m grant that need not be paid back provided the firm stayed in the province for five years. Ubisoft agreed to invest CA$500 m and create 800 jobs in Toronto (Ebner, 2009). It was precisely these kinds of financial subsidies given out by other provinces that led the BC provincial government in early 2010 to implement a tax credit of 17.5 per cent on labour costs in the development of video games. One firm owner, Doug Tronsgard of Next Level Games, thought this change would be extremely beneficial. In an interview he said the tax credit 'will do two things. It will stop job losses that have been happening now, and it will prepare us properly for future growth in Vancouver. Before the tax credit it didn't make sense to grow your business in Vancouver. I know that we will be adding people to our company now' (Andrew, 2010). It is important to note, however, that this still falls significantly below the 35–40 per cent offered by Ontario's Interactive Digital Media Tax Credit (OIDMTC).

In contrast, state subsidies were from the beginning generous in the film/TV industry of BC, provided not only by the province but also by the Canadian federal government. In 1978 the BC government inaugurated, and has since then continuously funded, the BC Film Commission (now a branch of the BC Ministry of Tourism). The Commission provides a range of services for producers including location scouting and surveys, immigration advice, script breakdown, an extensive photo library of potential locations and community and business liaison services. In addition, the province offers a series of tax credits on labour costs, which increase with the distance away from Vancouver that filming occurs. The basic credit is 33 per cent on top of which can be added up to another 12 per cent if production is carried out at a 'distant location' outside the city. Additionally, the Federal government offers a tax credit of another 16 per cent on labour costs. Although the basic BC tax credit rates for labour increased in 2010 (from 25 per cent to 33 per cent), some in the industry still do not think it is sufficient. This is because other jurisdictions in Canada – in what may be a race to the bottom – have instigated greater subsidies. For example, the Ontario government in June 2009 announced that they would cover 25 per cent of *all* movie or TV production costs, a move quickly matched by Quebec. In response, some local BC movie production companies – for example Bright Light Films – announced that they would be moving to Ontario. That said, none of the Hollywood studios have yet suggested that they are ready to move on. The representative in BC of these Hollywood producers, Don Cott (Vice-President, Canadian Affiliate, Alliance of Motion Picture and TV Producers (AMPTP), personal interview, September 2009), told us that the sheer density of infrastructure and trained labour in Vancouver has created its own inertia, anchoring Hollywood North in Vancouver.

Across both industries, the setting of incentive levels somewhat below those of competitor jurisdictions reflects two interrelated issues. First, in political terms, there is an element of hubris on the part of the provincial government that BC has sufficient natural advantages in these sectors, a viewpoint sharpened in recent times by the increasingly parlous state of the province's public finances. Secondly, the depth and quality of the labour pool in Vancouver acts as a significant counterweight to interprovincial disparities in incentives level.

Industry Associations and Labour Unions

A major difference between the video games and film/TV industries is that the latter is heavily unionized while the former is not. The video games industry does have a strong industry association, the non-profit DigiBC with a mandate 'to promote, support and accelerate the growth, competitiveness and sustainability of BC's digital media and wireless industry' (http://www.digibc.org/executive.html; accessed 5 December 2010). DigiBC was founded in October 2009, the result of two former industry associations merging: New Media BC (established in 1998) that dealt primarily with the video games industry and electronic publishing, and the Wireless Innovation Network of BC (established in 2001) concerned with wireless and mobile technology. DigiBC continues the function found in both of the previous organizations by acting as a clearinghouse for labour which it fulfils by offering a 'job board' and organizing networking meetings and job fairs. Unions, though, have never been let into the industry.

In contrast, following the tradition of the former Fordist model of film production, unions are a vital component of the Vancouver motion picture industry. Key to their successful involvement has been the ability to secure autonomy from their respective national umbrella organizations allowing them to focus on the particular needs of the inward investors that dominate spending in the BC industry (Coe, 2000b). Significantly, in 1996 the three unions representing the Teamsters and two IATSE locals formed a coalition that negotiates collectively on a single master agreement on a three-year rolling basis (the current master agreement runs from March 2009 to March 2012). There is no similar inter-union agreement anywhere else in North America, and it is a major incentive for Hollywood producers to invest in Vancouver. It provides certainty around wage rates, guarantees uninterrupted, stable production and for Hollywood producers means they deal with only one labour bargaining unit. That bargaining unit, the BC Council of Film Unions, also offers differential labour rates to attract independent producers and actively solicits new outside business.

In addition, the three unions along with the BC Council of Film Unions are members of what is in effect a super committee, the Motion Picture Production Industry Association (MPPIA),which acts as 'the voice and vision of the motion picture industry in BC' (http://www.mppia.com/). Consisting of 80 members, including representatives from industry (studios, producers, equipment suppliers and post-production firms), government and organised labour, MPPIA settles internal and external disputes and also acts as a vehicle for promoting the industry to potential investors. Again, there is nothing like this organization – in essence a form of cross-class alliance – anywhere else in North America. It ensures that all the institutional parts necessary for the reproduction and growth of the movie industry in BC are talking to one another and acting in concert to promote the full interests of the sector.

Talent and Training

At the core of both industries is the talent base of creative labour, spilling over to the issue of the institutional infrastructure of education and training. Of course, much of that education and training is internal, organic and cumulative. There is much learning on the job and learning from others. Certainly, the fission process described earlier of new firm formation in the video games industry contributes to this development by transferring skills from one firm to another through the movement of key creative personnel. Likewise, the project-based character of work contributes by ensuring that labour movement across firms is continually sustained and is the norm. More generally, there is a culture of restlessness within the two industries that promotes recurrent flux and movement. The only constant is change. As Don Mattrick said in a recent interview: 'If you look at the innovation and growth [in Vancouver's video games industry] that comes from that cross-pollenization [of people changing jobs], that sharing of ideas, that new experience, it's an accelerant. We have that culture here. It's what the industry is' (quoted in Kyllo, 2009).

Both in film/TV and video games there was a similar pattern where initially in the early history of both industries specialized labour and services were brought and bought to Vancouver. But in both cases that is generally no longer true. Much of the talent is now local, indeed locally trained, or comes on its own volition to Vancouver, drawn by the critical mass and reputation of the creative industries cluster. There are exceptions, but not many. In the film and TV industry, star actors come from outside, but there is a phalanx of local extras and supporting cast members. The upper echelons of production – directors, producers, writers – tend also to be non-local (either from Hollywood or, if it is Canadian TV, Toronto), but technical production staff are from Vancouver. There is a sense in the industry that the city has crossed a threshold: it now possesses sufficient depth and breadth of talent to undertake the full array of pre-production, production, and post-production services necessary for the delivery of major motion pictures and TV programmes. The same is true, perhaps even more so in the video games industry. Talent is brought into the city by HR departments, sometimes from distant places – the collapse of the industry in London has led to some significant high-end game designers moving to Vancouver. But in general, it is outside firms that move into Vancouver to tap into its established talent pool. As noted earlier, our research suggests that this is a highly significant factor which buffers any temporary economic disadvantages compared to other localities – either due to exchange rate shifts or changes in fiscal incentives – allowing the city to retain stable or growing levels of inward investment in these two industries. At the opening of its Vancouver studio in April 2010, for example, Pixar managers were very explicit that it was the combination of talent base and government incentives that made the city the ideal location for the new venture (scheduled to employ 75 staff by the end of 2011) (CTV News, 2010).

Contributing to the growth of that talent pool have been various educational institutions operating in the city, both public and private. The public side includes the two universities, University of British Columbia (the Film and Theatre Department and Computer Science) and Simon Fraser University (the Centre for Contemporary Arts), as well as the community college, British Columbia Institute of Technology, and the Emily Carr Institute of Art and Design. On the private side is the Vancouver Film School (VFS). Opened in 1987 and currently ranked 5th in the world it now offers 13 different programmes – including acting, video game design, animation, writing – and spread over six buildings in downtown Vancouver with its centre in the old inner-city neighbourhood of Victory Square. The School's establishment was a direct response to Hollywood runaway productions. The latest addition to the educational pantheon has been the Great Northern Way Campus, a unique collaboration among the four publicly funded educational institutions in the city: University of British Columbia, Simon Fraser University, Emily Carr Institute of Art and Design and British Columbia Institute of Technology. The four have combined to create on False Creek Flats, an old inner-city industrial site purposely cleared in the 1990s for new economy activities, what the Great Northern Way Campus's website calls a 'digital village destined to change the way people think about art, science, learning and commerce' (http://mdm.gnwc.ca/). It might not do quite that, but it offers a radical curriculum where studies of the visual arts, industrial arts, writing and literature, technical expertise in computer hardware and software, and business studies are blended together, preparing the next generation of workers for Vancouver's Brave New World of the New Economy.

INDUSTRY DYNAMICS AND FUTURE PROSPECTS

The advent of a severe global recession in 2008–2009 makes the current juncture a difficult one for gauging industry dynamics and the growth prospects of the two industries. It is important – though sometimes difficult – to distinguish the shorter-term effects of economic downturn from longer-term developmental trends.

In terms of video games, since the autumn of 2008 there are changes that possibly are shifting the industry to a new configuration. Partly this has been prompted by the financial crisis of 2008 and the ensuing recession, but also by industry reorganization and technological change. Such changes are most manifest in Vancouver's cluster becoming increasingly corporatized, with former independent SMEs bought up and in some cases closed down. Thus, Microsoft and Disney are now both found in the city, with Disney operating under the name of Propaganda Games in Yaletown (although it announced layoffs in early 2009), and in 2008 Microsoft located in the suburb of Richmond. Radical Entertainment, the original fission firm, was bought in 2005 by the French multinational Vivendi, which in 2007 merged with Activision Blizzard. In February 2009 another French multinational video games publisher, Ubisoft, came into the city by buying the locally owned SME Action Pants. As these new large multinational companies entered Vancouver, the anchor firm EA Canada began experiencing difficulties. Those began in early 2009 with EA cancelling the proposed opening of a boutique studio in Yaletown, later followed by the closing down of its downtown Vancouver subsidiary that it had bought in 2002, Black Box Games. In December 2009 EA further announced it was laying off 1000 workers worldwide from a staff of 10,000. It is unclear exactly how these changes will make a difference long term, but so far they primarily represent a consolidation of the video games industry in the city through the investments of a series of large international corporations.

While concerns about the lack of labour costs subsidies have been answered initially at least by the advent of the BC Interactive Digital Media tax credit in February 2010, two other challenges arguably face Vancouver's industry. The first relates to future platforms for games development in the industry. Several of our respondents felt that the standard format of big set piece games may be coming towards the end of its natural life and that in future there would be more use of the internet for downloading games on an ongoing basis, either for a fee or for free, and with users being charged for various avatars, accessories and the like. The second challenge relates to the shifting landscape of international competition in games production. Industry participants were concerned that the sector should not go the way of the London industry, which has struggled to cope with the high costs of labour and property. This is particularly a concern for the larger transnational companies in Vancouver, who have to make tradeoffs between the quality of the city's workforce and the cheaper programmers and designers on offer in other locations,

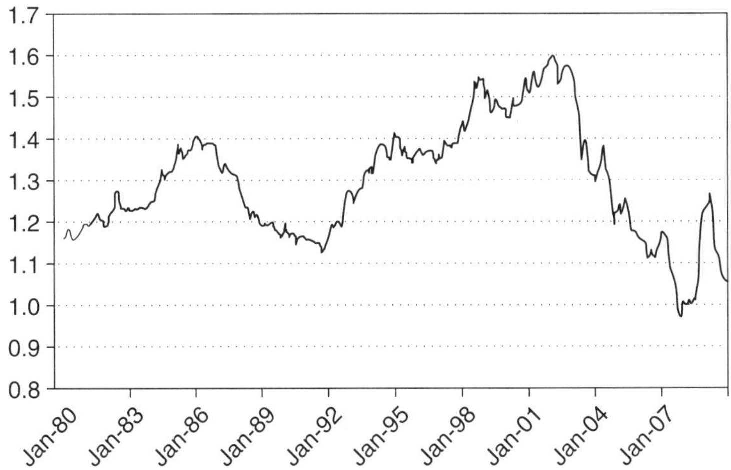

Source: derived from Pacific Exchange Rate Service (http://fx.sauder.ubc.ca).

Figure 11.6 CA$/US$ exchange rates, 1980–2009, monthly averages

most notably Eastern Europe and Asia. Singapore in particular was noted as an emerging hotspot in this regard.

The picture in film/TV is somewhat different. In large part, the basic production model of servicing US productions has stayed the same for several decades now. For some commentators on the 'new map of Hollywood' (Scott, 2002), Vancouver is simply a satellite production location dependent on maintaining its exchange rate and incentive cost advantages. The view is summarized nicely by Gasher (2002, p. 109) when he argues that 'the BC film industry is overly dependent on Hollywood, rendering it vulnerable to such factors as the Canada-US currency-exchange rates and shifts in labour costs among competing jurisdictions. There is nothing to prevent Hollywood producers from leaving British Columbia as suddenly as they arrived should any elements of British Columbia's competitive position change'.

And yet they have not, at least in aggregate terms, and sustaining business levels at or around the CA$1 bn a year during the 2000s is a significant achievement in itself given the increasing number of locations seeking to tap into this market, both elsewhere in Canada and the USA (e.g. Ontario, North Carolina and Florida in addition to initiatives to retain production in long-established centres of Los Angeles and New York), and beyond (e.g. the UK, Ireland, Czech Republic, Australia, New Zealand etc; see Goldsmith and O'Regan (2005) on global studio provision). Comparing Figures 11.4 and 11.6 suggests that while there may be some relationship between exchange rates and production volumes, it is not a strong signal. While the 'tapering off' from 2000–2004 detected by Scott and Pope (2007) is broadly in line with exchange rate movements, the rebound in production levels in 2005 and 2006 is not, and the writers' strike in 2007–2008 was a significant contributor to the fall in revenues in 2007. Exchange rate variations are far from all determining, and our interviews suggested that the ability of Vancouver to supply up to 30 high quality crews at any one time within a stable and predictable labour relations environment – in addition to the broad range of other locational and fiscal attractions of the city – had served to maintain its position as North America's preeminent 'full service' production location for Hollywood in the medium term. The main impact on the ongoing recession, it seems, has been to alter the balance of Vancouver's revenues, with a relatively small number of foreign-funded features in 2008 and 2009 making up for a slump in TV production as both Canadian and US networks have struggled to deal with a collapse in advertising revenues.

That being said, despite strenuous efforts, Vancouver has not been able to break out of this basic model of growth (cf. Coe, 2001). The indigenous industry continues to struggle to get off the ground, caught between the difficulties of fulfilling Canadian content requirements and tapping into TV networks based primarily in Toronto and Montreal on the one hand, and the need to develop more generic content to secure distribution deals beyond Canada on the other. Technological change has meant that Vancouver's attempts to break Los Angeles' hold on high value-added post-production activities have largely been stymied – digitization means daily footage can easily be beamed to US studios and networks. Moreover, foreign ownership of support services such as camera supply, lighting services and postproduction has steadily increased. The past decade, it seems, has served to entrench the Hollywood service production model yet further in Vancouver. Breaking free of Hollywood control simply does not seem possible given the stranglehold of the US studios over the critical (and interlinked) activities of finance and distribution (Coe and Johns, 2004; De Propris and Hypponen, 2008).

BLURRING THE BOUNDARIES?

It seems likely that the futures of the video games and film/TV sectors in Vancouver will become increasingly intertwined. Currently, in institutional terms at least, the industries are distinctive with separate trade associations (DigiBC and MMPIA, respectively) and different provincial incentive schemes. And yet, as Figure 11.7 suggests, growth in activities in

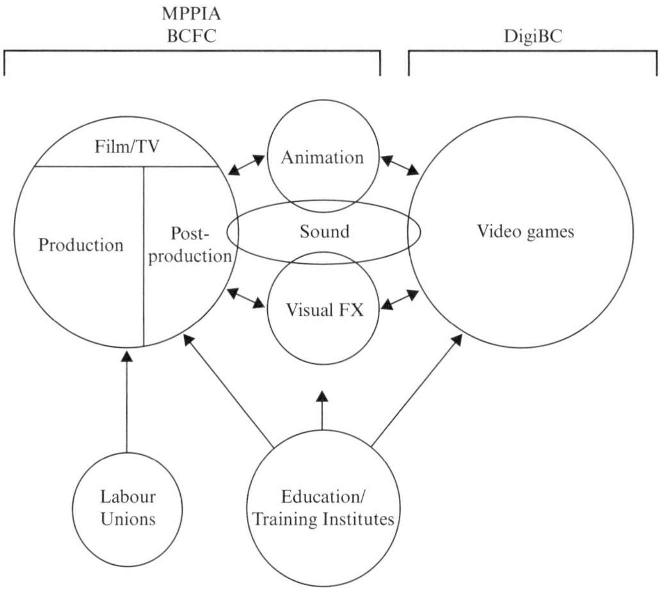

Source: authors' research.

Figure 11.7 Reconfiguring Vancouver's media sector – old meets new?

between the two sectors has been strong over the past decade. While animation has long been an important subcomponent of the film/TV industry, its relative importance has increased, expanding from 4.5 per cent of total revenues in 1998 (CA$36.6 m) to 10 per cent in 2008 (CA$122.2 m). The decision of Pixar to open a Vancouver studio in 2010 can only add impetus to developments in this area.

Alongside this, the city has seen significant expansion of its visual effects industry in the past decade. These firms are not simply involved in adding visual effects to productions shot in Vancouver but are plugged into wider international divisions of labour, and many operate at the cutting edge of the industry. There are at least 30 visual effects firms in the city at the present time, and as one respondent described, 'You've got all these visual effects companies up here, which are quite creative, and they don't have to be anywhere near the editorial process or the finishing process. And they're doing quite well, and with various forms of remote review and approval, it's quite manageable . . .' (personal interview, September 2009). The sector contains a number of local firms, but in employment terms it is dominated by the Vancouver branches of large international post-production and visual effects houses such as Technicolor and Deluxe.

The drivers of growth in these areas are at least threefold. First, and as described earlier, Vancouver's educational infrastructure appears to be adept at supplying workers with the right combination of technical and creative skills to work in the areas of animation and visual effects, supported by the livability and lifestyle offered by the city. Secondly, as with video games, there have undoubtedly been 'push' factors in operation elsewhere, with wage and property issues in other jurisdictions increasing the relative desirability of Vancouver at the international level. And, once again, public subsidies are important. The DAVE – Digital Animation or Visual Effects – tax credit was introduced in 2003, offering a 15 per cent tax credit on labour spending on animation and visual effects activities in BC. For many industry observers this has been a key development, perhaps reflected in the fact that the credit was increased to 17.5 per cent in February 2010 as the inter-provincial competition for jobs in this area ramped up further (Ontario's Computer Animation and Special Effects (OCASE) tax credit currently stands at 20 per cent of eligible labour costs).

Our tentative suggestion here is that strong growth in these activities is increasingly acting as a bridge connecting the film/TV and video games clusters in functional terms. We are not alone in making this assessment: according to Vancouver's Economic Development Commission, '[d]igital media has a strong symbiotic relationship with the established film and TV sector, making Vancouver a creative force in North America' (http://www.vancouvereconomic.com/page/digital-media, accessed 5 December 2010), and the BCFC expresses similar sentiments on its website. This convergence can be seen in different ways. On one level animation, visual effects and video games are increasingly drawing on a common labour pool, a feature enhanced by the flexible, project-based nature of employment relations in all these sectors. On another, there are a range of emerging functional connections between firms in these different areas. Sound engineering, for example, has for a while now been an area of expertise that straddles film, cartoon and video games projects. Technological trajectories are also at play here, such as the increasingly interactive nature of television programming. One respondent spoke to both these aspects when he described how 'Electronic Arts is now thinking about getting into the movie business. So . . . you can have somebody working on a visual effect in Stage 17 and then going to Electronic Arts and working on a game. Or now . . . the movie, it's integrated with animation and integrated with a video game. And so . . . we're just sort of starting to see that convergence model really happening: before we just talked about it' (personal interview, October 2009). A final area that may promote convergence relates to speculation among our respondents that financial incentives – particularly at the Federal level – may increasingly be tied to cross-platform activities (e.g. film, website and video games) as 'the Harry Potter economy' (*The Economist*, 2009) of strong cross-branding which continues to develop apace.

CONCLUSION

Our story of Vancouver's video games and film/TV clusters has been one of similarities, differences and, increasingly, interconnections. In terms of similarities, the industries are of comparable size in revenue terms, have similar geographies in terms of an inner-city concentration along with suburban outposts, are highly dependent on inward investment and foreign capital, draw upon a large and successfully reproducing pool of creative and technical labour, are supported by provincial fiscal incentives and are loosely coordinated by strong and effective industry associations. International linkages and processes of firm fission are crucial to the growth and ongoing renewal of both clusters. Both can be thought of as *spontaneously generating* clusters – rather than being pre-planned – and are broadly *unmanaged clusters*, with management being collective and dispersed across a range of public and private sector actors.

In terms of differences, the film/TV industry has a longer history in BC, is significantly larger in employment terms, has a deeper and more long-standing reliance on fiscal subsidies, is characterized by strong trade union influence and does not exhibit large corporate entities in the production sphere at least – although the support segments such as post-production, lighting and cameras have become increasingly concentrated and externally owned. By contrast, the 'big' corporate actors in the film/TV industry – the US studios and TV networks – act at a distance and simply invest on a project-by-project basis. As the previous section has suggested, strong growth in the animation and visual effects areas in Vancouver seems to be leading a convergence between the industries, primarily in terms of the common labour pool being drawn upon, but also increasingly in tangible connections between firms. Moving beyond the broad characterization of both clusters as unmanaged, there is a somewhat greater degree of central coordination within the film/TV sector, a feature that has developed over time and has been cemented by the formation of the industry association MMPIA.

What is clear is that both industry clusters have become highly significant components of Vancouver's media sector and, indeed, wider economy. We can point to three interrelated issues that are pertinent to both sectors as they move forward and raise interesting theoretical issues.

First, as noted above, both the film/TV and video games industries have become heavily reliant on non-local sources of capital. While the long-term trajectory of the film/TV industry suggests this is not necessarily an impediment to success, it remains a somewhat precarious position, particularly in industries that invest in little fixed capital and are project-based in nature. In conceptual terms, it raises the intriguing question as to whether these industries can be seen to represent another version of Vancouver's old staples economy, albeit one based on a strong pool of talented and highly specialized labour. Secondly, the forms of both industries in Vancouver are different from those found in Canada's political and cultural urban heartlands of Toronto and Montreal, where both the state and Canadian corporate capital are more active participants (Vang and Chaminade, 2007). Clearly, this taps into wider debates surrounding Vancouver's arguably marginal place in the national cultural and political imagery (e.g. Pendakur, 1990). Thirdly, both the film/TV and video games industries are now propped up by significant government subsidies and tax breaks as BC has become involved in ratcheting up rounds of tit-for-tat retaliation with other jurisdictions. This seemingly irrational 'quiet war' is premised on the assumption that the benefits of new spending and job creation will outweigh the expenditure, despite the evidence on the fiscal efficacy of incentives at the provincial level being somewhat mixed (e.g. InterVISTAS, 2005). In theoretical terms, it will be important to unpack the extent to which the geography of media industry production is increasingly 'finance following' (Morawetz, 2009) as producers seek to wrest maximum benefit from the dynamic landscape of public incentives (both within Canada and beyond).

In conclusion, what might be learned from the Vancouver experience? Three broad policy lessons stand out. First, Vancouver's success has rested on the productive interplay of three sets of factors: basic locational attributes (e.g. close to Los Angeles, general appeal of the city), financial incentives (e.g. exchange rate differentials, fiscal incentives) and labour market attributes (not only the breadth and depth of the talent pool, but also the medium-term stability of labour costs). Policy interventions that focus on just one or even two of these pillars are not likely to yield success, as evidenced by the broad range of localities that offer tax incentives but have no significant games or film/TV industries. That same combination of factors has enabled Vancouver to sustain its position as a leading North American centre in both sectors for the past two decades, providing a resilience that has maintained business levels despite increased competition and external shocks (e.g. exchange rate shifts, Hollywood writers' strike, global recession). Hence, and secondly, Vancouver shows the medium-term viability of clusters built primarily on inward investment, suggesting that policy initiatives should be as much about fostering connections to key external sites of funding and creative influence as generating local 'buzz'. Thirdly, recent developments show the potential for policy interventions that deliberately target the intersections of these sectors – particularly in the areas of animation and special effects – as the multi-platform media world continues to develop apace.

ACKNOWLEDGEMENTS

Trevor Barnes's portion of the research for this paper was supported by an MCRI SSHRC grant on the 'Social dynamics of innovation systems' held at the University of Toronto, David Wolfe, Principal Investigator. At UBC, Barnes was a co-investigator on that project with Tom Hutton whose ideas, knowledge and support are gratefully acknowledged. Barnes would also like to thank his various RAs who worked for him including Jessica Dempsey, Kean Fan Lim, Guanming Low, Tyler Pearce, and Ted Rutland, as well as all the many industry representatives who spoke to him. His part of the chapter was written while he held a fellowship at the Peter Wall Institute of Advanced Studies, UBC, 2009–2010. Neil Coe would like to thank the Media Management and Transformation Centre at Jönköping International Business School for funding a research visit to Vancouver in September/October 2009 and Ted Rutland for research assistance during that trip.

REFERENCES

Andrew, M. (2010), 'BC Boasts Film Production Tax Credits', *Vancouver Sun*, February 3.

Barnes, T.J. and T.A. Hutton (2009), 'Situating the New Economy: Contingencies of Regeneration and Dislocation in Vancouver's Inner City', *Urban Studies*, **46** (5)–(6), 1247–1269.

BCFC (2009), *British Columbia Film Production Statistics 2008*, Vancouver, CAN: BCFC. http://www.bcfilmcommission.com/database/rte/files/Published_Package_2008.pdf accessed 5 December 2010

Britton, J.N.H., D-G. Tremblay and R. Smith (2009), 'Contrasts in Clustering: The Example of Canadian New Media', *European Planning Studies*, **17**(2), 211–234.

Browne, C. (1979), *Motion Picture Production in British Columbia, 1898–1940: A Brief Historical Background and Catalogue*, Victoria, CAN: British Columbia Provincial Museum, Heritage Record No. 6, Victoria.

Caron, F. (2008), 'Gaming Expected to be a $68 Billion Business by 2012', *Ars Technica* (arstechnica.com/gaming/news/2008/06/gaming-expected-to-be-a-68-billion-business-by-2012.ars).

CFTPA (2009), *Profile 2009: An Economic Report on the Canadian Film and Television Production Industry*, Ottawa, CAN: CFTPA.

Christopherson, S. and M. Storper (1986), 'The City as Studio, the World as Back Lot: The Impact of Vertical Disintegration on the Location of Production of the Motion Picture Industry', *Environment and Planning D: Society and Space*, **4**(3), 305–320.

Coe, N.M. (2000a), 'The View from out West: Embeddedness, Inter-Personal Relations and the Development of an Indigenous Film Industry in Vancouver', *Geoforum*, **31**(4), 391–407.

Coe, N.M. (2000b), 'On Location: American Capital and the Local Labour Market in the Vancouver Film Industry', *International Journal of Urban and Regional Research*, **24**(1), 79–94.

Coe, N.M. (2001), 'A Hybrid Agglomeration? The Development of a Satellite-Marshallian Industrial District in Vancouver's Film Industry', *Urban Studies*, **38**(10), 1753–1775.

Coe, N.M. and J. Johns (2004), 'Beyond Production Clusters: Towards a Critical Political Economy of Networks in the Film and Television Industries', in Dominic Power and Allen J. Scott (eds), *Cultural Industries and the Production of Culture*, Abingdon, UK: Routledge, pp. 188–204.

CTV News (2010), 'Buzz Lightyear Ushers in Pixar's First Canadian Studio', 20 April. Available at: http://www.ctv.ca/servlet/ArticleNews/story/CTVNews/20100420/ pixar_canada_100420/20100420? hub=EntertainmentV2, accessed 5 December 2010.

Davis, H.C. and T.A. Hutton (1989), 'The Two Economies of British Columbia', *BC Studies*, **82**(Summer), 3–15.

De Propris, L. and L. Hypponen (2008), 'Creative Clusters and Governance: The Dominance of the Hollywood Film Cluster', in Philip Cooke and Luciana Lazzeretti (eds), *Creative Cities, Cultural Clusters and Local Economic Development*, Cheltenham, UK and Northampton, MA, USA: Edward Elgar, pp. 258–286.

Dyer-Witheford, N. (2004),'Mapping the Canadian Video Game and Computer Industry', paper given at *Digital Poetics and Politics Summer Institute*, Queen's University, Kingston, Ontario, 4 August 2004. http://publish.uwo.ca/~ncdyerwi/Mapping-Queens.pdf; accessed 5 December 2010.

Ebner, D. (2009), 'The Next Level: Redrawing the Video Game Map'. *Globe & Mail, Report on Business*, 3 August.

Economist, The (2009), 'The Harry Potter Economy', 19 December, 123–125.

Elmer, G. and M. Gasher (eds) (2005), *Contracting out Hollywood: Runaway Productions and Foreign Location Shooting*, Lanham, MD, USA: Rowman and Littlefield.

Gasher, M. (1995), The Audiovisual Locations Industry in Canada: Considering British Columbia as Hollywood North', *Canadian Journal of Communication*, **20**(2), 231–254.

Gasher, M. (2002), *Hollywood North: The Feature Film Industry in British Columbia*, Vancouver, CAN: University of British Columbia Press.

Goldsmith, B. and T. O'Regan (2005), *The Film Studio: Film Production in the Global Economy*, Lanham, MD, USA: Rowman and Littlefield.

Hutton, T.A. (2008), *The New Economy of the Inner City: Restructuring, Regeneration and Dislocation in the 21st Century Metropolis*, New York, NY, USA: Routledge.

Innis, H.A. (1956), *Essays in Canadian Economic History*, Mary Q. Innis (ed), Toronto, CAN: University of Toronto Press.

InterVISTAS (2005), *British Columbia Film and Television Industry Review*, prepared for the Ministry of Economic Development (http://www.tted.gov.bc.ca/Publications/ Documents/FilmandTVIndustryReview.pdf), accessed 5 December, 2010.

Kline, S., N. Dyer-Witheford and G. de Peuter (2003), *Digital Play: The Interaction of Technology, Culture, and Marketing*, Montreal and Kingston, CAN: McGill–Queen's University Press.

Kyllo, B. (2009), 'Vancouver's Video Game Family Tree', *The Georgia Straight*, 29 January, http://www.straight.com/article-198534/video-game-family-tree.

Lukinbeal, C. (1998), 'Reel-to-Real Urban Geographies: The Top Five Cinematic Cities in North America', *The California Geographer*, **38**, 64–78.

Lukinbeal, C. (2004), 'The Rise of Regional Film Production Centers in North America, 1984–1997', *GeoJournal*, **59**(4), 307–321.

Markusen, A. (1996), 'Sticky Places in Slippery Spaces: A Typology of Industrial Districts', *Economic Geography*, **72**(3), 293–313.

Morawetz, N. (2009), *The Rise of Co-Productions in the Film Industry: The Impact of Policy Change and Financial Dynamics on Industrial Organization in a High Risk Environment*, Unpublished PhD thesis, University of Hertfordshire Business School.

Murphy, D.G. (1997), 'The Entrepreneurial Role of Organized Labour in the British Columbia Motion Picture Industry', *Relations Industrielles/Industrial Relations*, **52**(3), 531–552.

Pendakur, M. (1990), *Canadian Dreams and American Control: The Political Economy of the Canadian Film Industry*, Toronto, CAN: Garamond Press.

Schumpeter, J. (1942), *Capitalism, Socialism and Democracy*, New York, NY, USA: Harper and Brothers.

Scott, A.J. (2002), 'A New Map of Hollywood: The Production and Distribution of American Motion Pictures', *Regional Studies*, **36**(9), 957–975.

Scott, A.J. and N.E. Pope (2007), 'Hollywood, Vancouver, and the World: Employment Relocation and the Emergence of Satellite Production Centers in the Motion-Picture Industry', *Environment and Planning A*, **39**(6), 1364–1381.

Statistics Canada (2006), *Head Office Employment in Canada, 1999 to 2005*, Ottawa, CAN: Statistics Canada.

Tinic, S. (2005), *On Location: Canada's Television Industry in a Global Market*, Toronto, CAN: University of Toronto Press.

Vang, J. and C. Chaminade (2007), 'Cultural Clusters, Global-Local Linkages and Spillovers: Theoretical and Empirical Insights from an Exploratory Study of Toronto's Film Cluster', *Industry and Innovation*, **14**(4), 401–420.

Section C Start-up clusters

12. Dubai Media City: creating benefits from foreign media developments

Robert G. Picard and Leon Barkho

Dubai Media City (DMC) is a start-up media cluster in a location previously unknown for media production; it represents an attempt to benefit from the globalization of media activities by serving media companies from other countries. It is one of several free zone clusters designed to help alter the economic bases of the Emirate of Dubai, which is using two major financial resources – income from oil revenue and trade – to lessen its overall financial dependence on oil and to diminish the effects of oil price gyrations.

Its leaders, keen to copy the success of Hong Kong and Singapore in Southeast Asia, pioneered the idea of free-trade zones in the Middle East, and Dubai Media City (DMC) is an initiative that crowns a series of free zones in which the emirate has invested oil revenues and developed various economic and commercial activities. This chapter looks at the economic vision behind DMC, its benefits to resident firms and the organizers, the business model it employs, the structure on which it is built, its density and intensity as well as its participants, operations and rivals.

Dubai Media City is one of a growing number of media-related clusters developing in the Middle East. At present eight media cities are operational – one each in Egypt, Jordan and Oman and five in the United Arab Emirates – Dubai Media City and Dubai Studio City, Abu Dhabi's twofour54, Ras Al Khaimah Media City and Creative City Fujairah.

BRIEF DESCRIPTION AND HISTORY

Dubai Media City (DMC) was established in January 2001 as a free-trade zone for media. It embraces a variety of activities, ranging from broadcasting, publishing and printing to music, leisure and film companies.

It is unique from other clusters in that its purposes are designed to promote neither local employment nor local media production. Created through specific planning, rather than the spontaneous development of local media, its organization and function are distinct from most other media clusters. Its advantages are achieved through unique financial benefits, a free trade zone and real estate projects rather than through the traditional economic benefits from agglomeration and significant employment of local labour. It is primarily designed to attract and serve the interests of foreign firms rather than domestic firms, and then to achieve local benefits primarily through facilities and services such as business services, housing and retailing to serve the needs of expatriate employees. According to Abdulhakim Karmostaji, a DMC senior manager, once clients walk in, they

> are provided with everything they need, from A to Z. It is one shop show. They (firms) have nothing to do. We do everything for them. They just need to care about their business. We do their legal papers, we take care of everything else apart from their business (interview with authors).

Kamal Nasser, chairman of the highly successful Conservus, a community portal firm, concurs. He thinks of DMC as an ideal locality for a media firm. 'When I wanted to get established here, I did not deal with a single official. I just delivered the papers and things were done for me', he says. Nasser's firm started with two people and currently he employs a dozen. He started with a paid-up capital of 1 million Emirati dirhams (approx. US$270,000). When Intel came with an offer, Conservus was valued at US$7 million. Nasser says his firm is now worth up to US$12 million.

In the eight years since its inauguration, the city has developed from a real-estate entity into a one-stop business development locale, offering clients more than merely office space in which to operate. Its officials handle visas and process work permits, help with travel bookings, etc. Besides its state-of-the-art infrastructure, it offers the kind of business milieu that has widely served customers, ranging from media companies to a large number of individual freelancers.

DMC has achieved its original aim of helping media companies use Dubai as a basis for operations in the Middle East, South and Southeast Asia. Operating inside a free zone park allows companies to benefit from a package of incentives, including keeping 100 percent foreign ownership, net-of-tax income and permitting 100 percent repatriation of capital. It has lured more than 1400 companies to the single location and created networking opportunities that are promoted with events and activities involving as many residents as possible. By 2009, DMC had reached and even surpassed the original target it had set for itself in terms of number of companies and employees. Ostensibly, the park seems to have weathered the global financial crisis, despite media business press reports voicing concerns that Dubai, after seeing one of the most ambitious and fastest economic growth rates in the world, is on the verge of economic collapse (Armitstead, 2008; Worth, 2009).

But not all clients are happy with the status quo. Thomas Ovesen of AEG, a leading international entertainment presenter, says while 'it is easy to set up a business, DMC rates and rentals are fairly high. The difference between the rates between the free zone and the surroundings are significant. There is one power provider and only two IT providers and the rates are very high, particularly for data' (interview with authors).The average phone bill is US$2000 and US$1000 for six gigabyte downloads.

DUBAI AND ITS FREE TRADE ZONE INVESTMENTS

One of the seven emirates, or states, that make up the United Arab Emirates (UAE), Dubai has invested heavily in free trade zones. Authority in the UAE is decentralized with each emirate enjoying a large degree of autonomy. UAE's supreme council – which decides on essential matters like foreign policy, education and defence – consists of the heads of the seven ruling families in the seven states. But each emirate, including Dubai, has its own executive council, headed by the ruling family's eldest son. The all-powerful ruling families hold both legislative and executive powers in their emirates, and involvement even in judicial affairs is not unusual. The monarchs rule by decree and are heavily involved in the economic affairs of the states. This situation has created a unique and rather unusual economy where it is difficult for economists to separate between ruling family (government) finances and those of the private sector.

This state of affairs has also in a short time catapulted UAE royals – particularly those of the emirates of Dubai and Abu Dhabi – into the top lists of the richest individuals and families in the world (Serafin, 2008). Money was never a problem for Dubai until perhaps the global financial crisis of 2008. Dubai's economic priorities are determined by the royal family and euphemistically referred to as 'government policy or action'. Dubai Media City is a reflection of the government's economic priorities, which mostly rest on an especially designed business model based on the notion of free-trade zone ventures characterized by the type of extravagance that is not confined to the lifestyles of the royalty but overlaps to their property projects. This creates an attractive location for foreign businesses.The cluster has several hundred acres of manicured parks and gardens, which are maintained clean and tidy by low-paid Pakistanis and Indians who also look after the tidiness and cleanliness in its scores of buildings. Some of DMC's lawns are even bigger than football grounds. Its lake on the slopes of which international performances are held is twice as big as a football pitch.

The country's constitution, like all legal codes in the Middle East, guarantees freedom of expression, but that always comes with one important caveat. Normal behaviour of individuals, groups and companies should not contradict Islamic ethics and morals, and criticism of 'national symbols', the ruling family, is prohibited. The caveat is used to censor the internet, the press and media operations, for example. There is no direct internet access, as all wireless traffic must pass through a proxy that Etisalat, Dubai's sole communications company, monitors. However, the degree of relative freedom in Dubai is unmatched in the region. At least 90 faiths and denominations are freely practised in the emirate, and publications originating in DMC would be banned or heavily censored in other areas in the Middle East.

At the turn of the 21st century, Dubai had so diversified its economy that non-oil income constituted about 90 per cent of its GDP estimated at US$54 billion in 2008 with a per capita of US$ 40,000 if split between Dubai's population of nearly two million (John, 2008; Armitstead, 2008). Dubai is one of the few oil-producing states whose economy has moved beyond petrodollars, with most of its income currently derived from real estate, trade, tourism and financial services. It is one of the most favourable locations for multinationals and it is considered the world's third most important re-export hub after Hong Kong and Singapore.

But Dubai's GDP figure must be viewed with caution due to demographic imbalances where the native population is a tiny minority in proportion to the expatriate population, mostly foreign labourers. Of Dubai's nearly two million people, it is estimated that only about 10 per cent are nationals who alone reap the benefits of economic prosperity while most of the expatriate labourers are not equally compensated. Critics argue that the emirate's high-rises, boulevards, supermarkets, upscale residential quarters and free zones are a showcase for a shining economy that hides abject poverty and exploitation particularly of foreign expatriates from developing countries like India, Pakistan and the Philippines. Behind the ostensible affluence lies a grim picture of illiteracy, poor working conditions and denial of women's rights. Its behaviour towards and treatment of its expatriate workforce falls short of UN or international standards (Walters et al., 2006; Quinn et al.,2004; UNDP, 2002a).

DMC SIZE AND DENSITY

Cluster density refers to the number of participants and the extent and range of their activities. Clusters with high density means a wide range of participants who are involved in a variety of media operations. Clusters with low density have a lower number of participants and fewer activities. DMC belongs to the former category within the Middle East context. Its only rivals, the media cities in Jordan and Egypt, are classic examples of low density with far fewer participants, a much lower range of activities and far less technically advanced infrastructure (cf. Quinn, Walters and Whiteoak, 2004).

If the number of participants and their standing in international media is a measure, DMC can rightly be described as one of the top global bases for broadcasting, print and audiovisual media. Media companies have found the city very attractive and within nine months after its inauguration more than 300 firms with global reach had pitched their tents in its premises. Sullivan (2001), one of the first scholars to write about DMC a year after its launch, held interviews with major participants' executives who said they were pleased with its services. The list of residents has substantially grown since then. Besides major international broadcasters and news agencies, it includes an impressive list of publishers, graphic artists, writers and others. The city is now the base for CNNArabic.com, which though located in Dubai Internet City (DIC), is run from DMC. DMC had lured more than 550 media companies by the end of 2005, including global giants such as CNN, Reuters, Sony Broadcast & Professional, McGraw-Hill Publishing, Bertelsmann, MBC, CNBC and the Associated Press along with regional companies and new start-ups (Walters, Kadragic and Walters, 2006).

By 2006, DMC more than doubled its list of tenants to an impressive 1213 companies. The figure does not include the additional arrivals of freelance print journalists, writers, designers, publishers and IT experts operating in the Media Business Center. Officials estimate annual growth at 30–40 per cent in number of registered companies and gross leasable area and they predict this impressive growth to continue through to 2013 (absent the current crisis). Its current 30 buildings were reported to be fully occupied before the onslaught of the world financial crisis, with a waiting list of more than 400 firms. Some 450 tenants (about half the resident population) are magazine and other publishing firms in addition to 160 satellite TV channels. By the end of 2007 there were 27 more buildings under construction in an ever-growing free-trade zone that is served by three hotels while another ten are scheduled for completion by 2010. Currently, all real-estate phases are completed offering 1.1 million square feet of which 99 per cent are leased, according to Abdulla Al-Mohaisin, director of business development. He says DMC's inventory currently includes more than 1400 firms.

PHYSICAL STRUCTURE

The builders of DMC had originally envisaged two phases. A large portion of phase one was ready when the city was inaugurated in 2001. Shortly after the launch, the space was sold out. The precincts also included an adjacent housing complex ranging from luxury villas to reasonably priced flats. As part of the Dubai Holding, DMC fits under the TECOM Investments technology, e-commerce and media free zone authority umbrella, which also includes Dubai Internet City and Dubai Knowledge Village (see Figure 12.1). Dubai Holding is an umbrella or holding company created by the Dubai government and the royalty to develop large infrastructure projects in Dubai. The regulatory environment is governed by TECOM, which oversees a number of other free-trade zones in Dubai. The DMC Authority is licensed to establish companies in the areas of

1. Broadcasting
2. Consulting
3. Electronic media and media support services

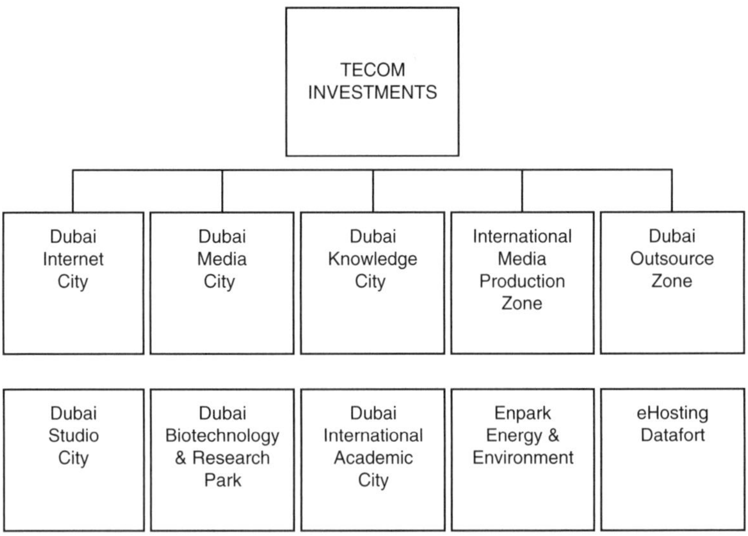

Figure 12.1 TECOM and its eight knowledge-based free-trade parks, which include DMC. TECOM is a member of Dubai Holding

4. Film distribution, management and production
5. Information agencies
6. Media and marketing services
7. Music and entertainment
8. News agencies
9. Publishing
10. Support service providers
11. Web design and management.

In 2004 the first phase of DMC had been completed providing about 33,000 m^2 of space. The authorities had then said they would soon embark on the second phase that will include significant property development of DMC (Quinn et al., 2004). DMC space is provided with thousands of housing units and accompanying infrastructure. Most of phase one was built in one year, a signal of what massive wealth can do. It was estimated to have cost up to US$1 billion (Schleifer, 2000; Sirri, 2003). DMC was forecast to have the second phase of additional 46,450 m^2 completed by the end of the decade and, according to a report in WAM, Emirates News Agency, MDC and its sister free-zones were to employ more than 75,000 people by the end of the decade (WAM, 2002). DMC has launched a third phase specifically designed to accommodate increasing demand from media freelancers. John Brash, founder and CEO of Brash FZ-LLC, says that when he wanted to establish in DMC in 2008 there was no space left. He adds:

> TECOM let us start and do trade from a special address without physically being established in the zone. In other countries the free-zone area is first marked and then companies move in and the real-estate boom follows. Here it is the opposite. First you have the real-estate boom and then the influx of tenants (interview with authors).

Dubai's MDC and other free-trade zones are unique in the sense that they only come into being once state-of-the art infrastructure and the flurry of the real-estate boom are in place. Spending lavishly on real estate is an indication of the wealth of the royal family. Most of TECOM investments, estimated in billions of dollars, are part of the private wealth of the royal family.

SERVICES AND CHARGES

A minimum start-up capital of AE$50,000 (US$13,600) is needed to set up shop in DMC. Besides offering lucrative financial benefits, the DMC has built a reputation for processing start-up requirements quickly and easily with regard to residence permits, visa work permits, and so on. Residents have the right to have 100 per cent foreign ownership, while outside free-zone areas companies are required to have a local sponsor and maximum foreign ownership should not exceed 49 per cent. Moreover, DMC offers a guaranteed 50-year tax exemption status.

But set-up costs vary depending on activities and operations. Freelancers are normally charged at least AE$20,000–30,000 (US$5400–8160). The sum covers freelance permit and trade licence, hot desk space (shared desk space) in DMC and visa costs for the first year. Part of DMC's success is due to the attention it pays to media freelancing activities as will be shown later. Benefits to residents vary but they mostly emanate from synergies and easy shopping for skills and services due to freelancing activities and the presence of giant media firms. The Arab world is extremely poor when it comes to intellectual property rights and very little of value is produced in this regard. According to UNDP (2002b), the 23 Arab countries produced a paltry 20 patents in total.

The city's state-of-the-art infrastructure has assisted media-related enterprises dealing with broadcasting, publishing, advertising, public relations, research, music and postproduction activities to also operate globally, thanks to the working environment the city offers. DMC officials assist media companies willing to relocate there. For example, the MBC, an Arab media giant, moved its broadcasting facilities from London to Dubai without having to go off air for a single minute. DMC authorities provided all the intermediate equipment for a smooth and uninterrupted move.

DMC is not a spontaneous cluster and therefore charges, services and most other activities are determined by the organizers. It is managed and operated by the Dubai government and driven by the flurry of real-estate boom that has been one of the main drivers of the emirate's economy. Most of Dubai's financial benefits are drawn from leasing property offices and flats and overhead charges. But it is not clear how far the latest financial crisis has impacted the city as business press reports speak of housing slumps of up to 50 per cent in late 2008 and 2009 (Worth, 2008, 2009; PropertyWire, 2008).

DMC is a classic example of what Picard (2009) calls 'parallel networks of virtual clusters' in which media firms flock to a particular geographical region, the location of which furnishes very little of the benefits associated with traditional clusters such as transaction cost savings and availability of local labour.

DMC theoretically ensures that resident media businesses have the 'Freedom to Create' (Dubai Media City official website, 2009) though there have been instances of interference on the part of the authorities with regard to content (Arabian Business.com, 2007). DMC theoretically provides for freedom of expression but issues of freedom in general have always been sensitive to religion and cultural norms in the Middle East. Constitutions of almost all Middle East states provide for the freedom to communicate. But in reality the situation is different. Middle East media revolve around political regimes that are mostly autocratic (Johnston, 1998; Tawella, 2002; Walters and Quinn, 2003; Worth, 2009).

Tenants have mixed feelings about restrictions. Russell Frame, director of operations at the Media Factory, a Dubai-based publishing house, says the absence of clear-cut rules is in a sense beneficial to his firm. 'The lines are blurred for the people who want them to be blurred. It is a challenging environment and the rules are clearer about what you can do than about what you cannot.' Frame's company publishes airways magazines with monthly copies in hundreds of thousands. It has its own Middle East launch of renowned international monthlies such as *FourFourTwo*, an international football magazine.

CONNECTEDNESS, INTENSITY AND SPILLOVER

Picard (2009) argues that clusters are not equal particularly in terms of intensity and density. We have discussed DMC's density above. In this section, we focus on DMC's intensity, which is an important tool to measure the cluster's activity and strength. Our empirical investigation reveals a low degree of intensity, and the DMC managers are aware of the shortfall in this area. When queried about how much the park helps tenants network, inter-connect and work to spill over their creative knowledge, DMC's officials retorted by saying that they were about to issue 'a new book' on talents available within the cluster to give tenants – firms and freelancers – the opportunity to know about skills within their reach. Established under the rules guiding Dubai's other free-trade areas, DMC is a highly organized and managed entity with regular activities on the part of the administering authority and resident companies. Our observations and first-hand information point to dedicated staff, joint promotions and awards but rather negligible interdependence. Location and highly advanced infrastructure have hitherto failed to boost transactions between participating companies for both products and services. However, there are some signs of links between DMC and institutions in the UAE such as universities and related businesses, but the park has still a long way to go to act as a knowledge-generating cluster such as those found in biotechnology and information and communication technologies.

However, the intensity is worthwhile when viewed within the regional context. And since DMC and its sister clusters are established mainly to serve the larger Middle Eastern region, the tenants say they face problems when taking their services and products outside the UAE. Cijo Varghese, director of B.E. International with nearly 200 employees, complains about the lack of standardization of rules guiding business operations in the region:

> We need common regulations. As it is you are not safeguarded. It is just trust what counts. There are so many legal loopholes and here we are far away in that respect from Europe and a long way to go on litigation. Each country have [sic] their own agenda and laws and regulations keep changing (interview with authors).

Despite the complaints, since setting foot in DMC with a handful of employees seven years ago, Varghese's company has achieved nearly 100 per cent growth annually and revenues in the range of $¼ billion before the onslaught of the financial crisis which despite its severity 'has not affected business but caused problems in recovering money from the market', he says. But the crisis has been a learning lesson to Dubai. Varghese says: 'This place was awash with money. The people did not think about how to manage it. The crisis is a lesson teaching them how to learn to spend their money.'

As for newly developed products, industries and services, the city has so far failed to create skilled domestic staff pools due to almost total reliance on expat skills with negligible domestic participation. Joint learning activities, if they take place, are mainly among the participants but rarely spill over into the local environment. Noticeable has been the lack of cultural interaction due to the huge demographic imbalance between the national and expatriate population. But if personal relations, as Picard (2009) tells us, are an important indicator of intensity, then DMC can be considered a success story. Dubai as a new economic phenomenon mostly relies on the vision and wealth of its royalty, whose members have built up wide-ranging networks of relations based on trust. Such relations have been found to be of crucial importance to cluster stability, sustainability and growth (cf. Kaiser and Liecke, 2007; Krätke, 2002; Nachum and Keeble, 2003; Vang and Chaminade, 2007; Turok, 2003).

Of the important density-related issues to investigate is how far Dubai and subsequently its free-trade zones are integrated into the global economy. Dubai's economy, as evidenced by the latest financial crisis, is extremely reliant on and very sensitive to international market gyrations. Dubai has been adversely affected by the financial crisis, signalling functional integration with international banking and global majors. Though there are studies providing evidence that foreign global relations might not be a guarantee of success (cf. Ward and O'Regan, 2007), without such integration DMC would not be there. Dubai was once reputed for having the world's largest number of cranes adorning its skylines. Today, the city has more idle cranes and half-completed buildings than any other place in the world. Another important aspect is DMC's almost total reliance on markets beyond its immediate vicinity, the UAE. The knowledge-based free-trade areas have been established specifically to serve the needs of countries other than the UAE.

There are a few signs, albeit dim, of networking with the immediate environment. DMC authorities are keen to boost contribution to the local environment, whenever possible. For example, the city has launched a programme to cooperate with universities in the UAE in a bid to cultivate local talent and provide future job opportunities to media students. At least one university, Sheikh Zayed University, has an office in DMC. Such synergies are on the increase. DMC has close relations and cooperation with Dubai Internet City, which has its own programme of working with UAE universities.

DENSITY AND BENEFITS

Clusters have a variety of benefits, but generally governments have three major aims in mind when setting them up: (1) economic benefits, (2) spillover benefits and (3) inter-cluster benefits. In the case of DMC, economic benefits come at the forefront, and the UAE authorities are internationally renowned to dump projects that spin no money (Grant, Golawala, Fatema, McKechnie and Donelda, 2007). With economic advantages comes the broader aim of innovation advancements from high-tech parks which normally transfer their skills to the communities they serve. This spillover is not always easy to detect in the case of DMC due to demographic imbalance in the proportion of nationals to foreign labour.

The density of media firms in DMC, apart from its economic benefits to the government, has been most beneficial to the residents themselves. Interaction among members and their organizations is reported to have sparked close cooperation between companies carrying out more or less similar activities such as news agencies and broadcasters and the way they have been organized. Grouped together, it is usually hard for members to hide their specialized services and keep their technological edge under wraps for a long time. Clustering encourages cooperation among members and in the case of media firms, 'pooling' – rivals agreeing to do things together instead of competing – is not an unusual activity. Within a media cluster, firms find it easier to share and lease equipment and services to each other. Dubai's free-trade zones make it easy and even cheaper to provide the requisite resources and equipment to companies establishing themselves by attracting hundreds of highly specialized and skilled freelancers.

However, there are signals of spillovers among the high-tech free zones in Dubai. For instance, the neighbouring media, internet and knowledge cities coordinate services and it is possible for firms to have a foot in more than one city. One example of such synergy is CNNArabic.com which has its regional office and administration at MDC but launches its website from Dubai Internet City (DIC). DMC's Business Center provides the kind of incubation where freelancers synergize and cooperate and there are instances of two or three of them starting up new businesses and then moving to special precincts in one of the buildings. DMC has launched the Ibda'a (innovation) Awards for the winners of a competition in which university students from India and the Middle East take part. It has special internship programmes for UAE students and graduates. Cooperation agreements have been signed with several UAE universities, particularly those offering media and communication courses. DMC authorities say they have recently expanded such programmes to cover other countries in the Middle East, such as Egypt (DMC official website, 2008).

A case in point is Vortex Studios, a gaming company, whose Managing Director Saleh Al Nobani, says some local universities and institutes have started seeking internships and help with training:

> While we have no local expertise in the kind of business we are doing, we have started some small training programs for students and have contributed with our skills and talent to a couple of universities. We now try to help in setting up a new department about the gaming industry in Dubai (interview with authors).

Showtimearabia, one of the largest DMC firms, has established good ties with the community in the larger Middle East, proving the authors' idea that DMC functions like a 'terminal' rather than an 'anchor', where skills, talents and products are unloaded and where they are remolded and shuffled and then shipped once again to other regions. Showtimearabia has also functioned as an 'incubator' for other regional media organizations 'to come here for training and expertise as interns from across the region', according to the company's Vice-President Colin Smith (interview with authors).

DMC management has drawn up a plan to help knowledge and expertise of firms spill over to the community. 'We have a plan of talent competition and rewards under which firms working with universities may get scholarships', said Abdulla Al-Mohaisin, director of business development (interview with authors).

Some 'extra-curricular' benefits for the UAE and the larger region are in the offing. The region, which for long has shunned international advertisers and markets for lack of proper metering, is on the threshold of integrating with metering standards prevalent internationally. Says DMC's Executive Director Jamal Al Sharif: 'People's metering is in a working process thanks to DMC. The companies have invested a lot in it with of course many inputs from the cluster' (interview with authors).

ROLE OF NATIONALS

Employing young nationals is a UAE government's priority. But lack of verified statistics makes it hard to assess the so-called 'Emiratization' drive. Still, it is reported that Emiratization is making some progress, particularly in the banking and finance sectors, where 50 per cent of the workforce was expected to be national by 2007 (Jarrah, 2006). Moreover, nationals are only interested in white-collar, well-paid jobs, which normally require skills and education levels that the locals can obtain in order to avoid labour/menial jobs (National Bank of Dubai, 2004, 2006). The government has set different quotas for different industries, but as said earlier the demographic reality of the country makes their fulfilment almost impossible (Golawala, Ganesh, Grant and McKechnie, 2006). Under current rules, some companies are required to increase their Emirati employees by 4 per cent a year. But in a country where nationals make up less than 15 per cent of a population of 6.4 million, there are simply no Emiratis to fill the vacancies and many of the local graduates who apply to get such jobs lack the required skills (AFP, 2008; Glass, 2008).

However, there is little sign in DMC of progress in the country's Emiratization policy. The tenants and the top management (executives and managers of free zone areas are mostly nationals) agree that there is a long way to go for the country's nationals to enter into real business and turn into company owners and operators. 'The locals will not learn', said Russell Frame of The Media Factory firm when asked whether he had any Emirati among his over 100 employees.

> People (company owners) do not hire Emiratis. You know why? First, Emiratis enter into business deals outside free-trade zones where no businesses can be established without a 51% Emirati ownership. Second, Emiratis do not want to work in the private sector and prefer the public sector where wages are higher, working times very flexible and the skills required very low (interview with authors).

Frame publishes about 50 magazine titles, some of them in Arabic. Arabic writing and editing is mainly done by Lebanese, Egyptian and

Tunisian nationals. However, Emiratization rules do not apply to free-trade zones such as DMC though its management is trying hard to develop local talent. As it stands now, there are only two Emirati firms among the 1400 companies in DMC.

ECONOMIC VISION

Vision and Structure Geared Towards Moneymaking

The economic vision behind the launch of DMC is not very much different from the numerous multi-billion dollar free zones in Dubai where royal family members and private entrepreneurs invest their riches. On inauguration, officials heralded DMC as a zone 'for free-thinking talent . . . a place where the media around the region and the globe will bring their productive and creative talent home . . . [a] city to help facilitate both the networking among regional Arab talent and the joining and integration of such talent with the rest of the media world' (Sullivan, 2001).

But on close examination the economic vision behind DMC and other free zone ventures is mainly geared to serve the interests of Dubai property developers for whom public and national interests are rarely among top priorities. Dubai's real-estate developers are internationally known to be very skilful and generous with space. The buildings they have dedicated for DMC are spacious enough to accommodate production precincts oriented towards audio and television. The whole point of building a new Media City was to accommodate international and regional media firms engaged in multimedia activities and cash in on rents, leases and other overheads.

Established mainly to maximize property developers' profits, DMC has structured itself in a way to engage in different media activities. The structuring and the economic vision, bent on moneymaking, have produced the kind of park that combines all the differences Krätke (2002) and Goldstein and O'Regan (2003) identify as distinguishing media cluster categories and where the contrasting media cluster distinctions mentioned by the authors are blurred. DMC brings together not only broadcasters, its list of participants currently includes publishers, IT experts, writers, print journalists and designers. Even the 'four distinct compositions' of media clustering Picard (2009, p. 10) identifies – 'print media clusters, audiovisual clusters, new media clusters and creative clusters' – do not hold in DMC where agglomeration of distinct media compositions is seen as a strategic advantage to maximize profits for cluster builders and boost networking, synergies and spillovers for the tenants – a goal DMC has yet to achieve. Media industries in general have fragmented and synergized at the same time. News businesses like the AP and Reuters, for example, are not mainly concerned with the dissemination of news. They are involved in a variety of economic and media activities that bear some of the traces that are a characteristic of clusters dealing specifically with print, audiovisuals, the internet and media.

Free-trade zones have been at the heart of Dubai's economic boom, which the authorities have viewed as a means to diversify the emirate's economy (Moore, 2004). The foundations of Dubai's free-zone economy are the government's no-tax policy and relaxation of ownership rules for foreigners within and outside these zones. The emirate is strategically located as a commercial launching pad mainly for countries in Asia and Africa. The location has made it possible for Dubai to transform itself into something like the Hong Kong or Singapore of the Middle East, albeit with significant structural differences. And it seems there is no limit to Dubai's free-trade economy ventures. Besides DMC, the emirate today boasts a host of other clustering economies, namely the Internet City, Media City, Healthcare City, Sports City, Aviation City and Academic City, among others (see Figure 12.1. above). These high-tech free zones are jointly administered by the government-owned TECOM, signalling the rush for money by Arab Gulf property developers. However, TECOM makes no statistics available on its profits and revenues. Asked about DMC profits, Abdulla al-Mohaisin, director of business development said: 'Our profits are in the success of our business partners (companies). If they are happy business partners, it means our profits are very high' (interview with authors).

BUSINESS MODEL

'Anchor Stores' or 'Terminal Concept'

The few researchers investigating DMC have found that it pursues the business model of 'anchor stores' (Quinn, 2004). A common shopping mall idea, entrepreneurs initially recruit one major anchor for both differentiation and positioning in order to lure other anchors or businesses (Smiley, 2002; Fernie, Fernie and Moore, 2003). But the authors' investigation shows that DMC pursues the type of business model that is closer to the 'terminal concept'. DMC has elements similar to a 'circuit' or 'device' that media firms can use to facilitate and establish connections and is thus like an electricity terminal where power pours in from original plants and is distributed elsewhere. Simultaneously it is a terminal where media firms do not anchor but rather pour operations, skills and activities which are unloaded and then reloaded to other destinations, much like petroleum and finished goods terminals (Mulcahy, 1993; Tusiani, 1996; Rushton, Croucher and Baker, 2006; Mattfeld, 2006). This differs from anchoring stores that serve clients within a small radius or rather in the immediate vicinity. DMC has very little to do with its immediate vicinity. When the BBC, Reuters, CNN and MBC relocated their services in DMC, their aim was to take advantage of its incentives to better serve clients in the larger Middle East and countries in both Asia and Africa.

The terminal concept seems to have been the business model that the rulers of Dubai have been pursuing in their drive to attract international majors of different orientations. It is a concept that is familiar in Dubai because of its long history in the petroleum industry and as a trans-shipment point for goods and services from the East and West and throughout the region. In the case of DMC, they first started by providing a world-class environment for every kind of media business, focusing mainly on media and marketing services, printing and publishing, music, film, new media, leisure and entertainment, broadcasting and information agencies (DMC official website, 2008).

The Dubai government's major aim for DMC as well as other free-zone ventures is the creation of a clustering terminal in which participating firms can have access to a variety of services such as logistics, multimedia, telecommunication, software, remote services, etc which no other zone in the region can provide. This terminal brings within easy reach an economic critical mass whose major aim is 'to line the pockets of the ruling families and their friends' (Quinn et al., 2004) who own the property and the infrastructure.

Geographical location is one of the pivotal factors in the success of any cluster, and location is of significant importance for the success of terminals. It entails easy access to requisite resources and the availability of amenities such as transportation and other necessary services. Dubai is a suitable place for companies to set businesses. Besides economic and commercial incentives, its Dubai International Airport is now the aviation and cargo centre of the Middle East and one of the world's busiest emerging aviation hubs. In 2008 it opened its Terminal 3, the world's largest terminal. Despite global economic downturn and high oil prices, the airport handled a throughput of 37,441,440 passengers and 1,824,991 tons of cargo in 2008 against 34,348,110 passengers and 1,668,505 tons of freight in 2007. Its airport has numerous daily scheduled flights to major international destinations such as London, Cairo, Paris, etc (Dubai International, 2009).

Dubai is currently the world's ninth largest container port. Its terminals are witnessing major expansions that are to result within less than a decade in a gigantic port with 82 berths, 125 portside cranes and capacity to handle more than 21 million containers per year (Logistics Insight Asia, 2008). The company handling the ports, the state-owned DP World, was embroiled in a furious controversy in 2006 following its multibillion-dollar acquisition of the British firm Peninsular and Oriental Steam Navigation Company which managed a number of US ports. But the acquisition met strong opposition from the US Congress, and DP World, under US political pressure, was forced to sell off its US operations to an American owner (Weisman and Graham, 2006).

DMC'S FREELANCING BUSINESS MODEL

Media clusters have traditionally thought very little of freelancers. But in DMC they are given priority and the required sponsorship as the authorities believe they can attract media firms since their presence and availability reduces costs in terms of both content and creation. Moreover, the presence of freelancers provides the skills, technical expertise and highly efficient staff that Dubai is not in a position to make locally available. DMC sees freelancing as an industry with the potential to lure media firms and prevent migration.

DMC's freelancing project has been described as the park's most successful. DMC's freelancing business model is based on the notion that cost has always been a key factor for the media industry and the presence of freelancers in a region with poor media-proficient labour is certain to reduce costs for companies willing to reside in the park. The freelancing industry had been unknown to the Middle East before DMC introduced it as a main component of the cluster. In the presence of so many freelancers, broadcasters and other media firms are supposed not to have long lists of employees on their payroll since a certain portion of content creation can be performed with part-time labour. But unfortunately many of the firms have yet to learn how to utilize the pool of freelancing talent in their vicinity. DMC management is putting up a new community portal and issuing a new book specifically to make tenants aware of what exists just a stone's throw from their precincts.

Initially, 150 open slots were available to individuals and these were immediately snapped up shortly after inauguration. For a price of about US$5000 each freelancer gets a trade licence, resident visa, desk, phone, computer, a shared secretary and other business services. Freelancing has resulted in innovative networking. There are several instances in which freelancers involved in different activities – a music producer, a TV producer, a print journalist, a presenter, a cameraman, etc – have formed their own companies. Such networking is not unusual for knowledge economies but it may rarely have been as normative as in DMC where talent, money, skill and ideas are combined to create a new company. A case in point is Eng. Milo Torres which had originally been established at DMC as a freelancer in 2004 but since then has been successfully engaged in providing comprehensive IT services in fields of website development, digital imaging, CD presentation, email marketing solutions, online database solutions and other professional designs.

In 2006, DMC authorities launched DMC's third phase especially dedicated to expand the park's business centre where the city's then 366 freelancers were based. The new phase has significantly expanded the centre, which has emerged as an auxiliary business model – DMC's freelancing business model – and as the Middle East's and perhaps the world's largest media freelancing pool and one of the main reasons for large and small companies to stay put in the cluster. Called Business Centre III, the phase provides an additional 8382 m^2 of space, featuring, as is the case with almost all free-zone infrastructure in Dubai, sleek executive offices and state-of-the-art technology and communications systems, conference and meeting rooms and a lounge area specially designed for professionals to display their work. The DMC business centre housing the freelancers has virtually served as an incubator for many business ideas. Since 2004, over 35 companies have scaled up their business operations to set up their own commercial offices. A 2006 report in AME Info, Middle East business and financial news quotes the then DMC director Mohammed Al Mulla as saying:

> Our Media Business Centre has today developed into a large resource of talent that the industry can tap for their needs. Over the years, the Business Centre has supported the growth of many enterprising media professionals. We hope to give wings to the dreams of many more talented individuals (http://www.ameinfo.com/103343.html).

In the meantime, many of the major services, such as studios, cameras and recording equipment, are made available by DMC at reasonable prices. The possibility to set up a one-man company has turned DMC into a hub for highly skilled freelancers – reporters, editors, directors, lighting technicians, sound editors, designers, etc – whose services companies can hire for shorter periods of time and thus reduce costs. The technology trajectories the government provides in the form of highly advanced infrastructure and lucrative financial incentives are important, but DMC member firms mainly rely on expat skills due to the lack of a skilled local labour force, and the business centre's freelancers are a good pool.

Saleh Al Nobani of Vortex Studios says he seeks freelancers with qualified skills for his gaming company, which currently employs up to

20 people. This pool of freelancers, and the easy access of cluster firms to them, falls in line with one of the significant benefits attributed to clusters – namely access to specialized contract labour.

How did the freelancing concept start? Jamal Al Sharif, DMC's Executive Director, says when the management looked closely at the media industry and the idea of a media cluster, it found a freelance factor to it. 'It is the industry itself. It is the need of the industry. Freelancing was part of our strategy.'

SUSTAINABILITY, RENEWAL AND ADAPTATION

DMC's story of success is not without limitations and cultural issues come at the forefront. Moreover, Dubai's business environment despite its ostensible stability is easily influenced by the volatility and gyrations of international markets, as has been the case with the latest financial crisis hitting the world economy. Exacerbating Dubai's vulnerability is the official persistence on concealing economic weaknesses and highlighting only what the rulers see as economic 'feats'. A case in point is the official attempt to hide the worsening conditions of an economy that has been in free fall due to the world financial crisis. Transparency is a word that may take a long time for the Middle East's economics lexicon to have as an independent entry. *New York Times*' Robert F. Worth in a 12 February 2009 report from Dubai writes:

> Instead of moving toward greater transparency, the emirates seem to be moving in the other direction. A new draft media law would make it a crime to damage the country's reputation or economy, punishable by fines of up to 1 million dirhams (about $272,000). Some say it is already having a chilling effect on reporting about the crisis (Worth, 2009).

The pinch from the financial crisis is felt at DMC but it has not led to large-scale migration or mortality. For instance, John Brash, founder and CEO of Dubai branch BrashFZ-LLC, an international brand strategy and design firm, has laid off one-third of its highly paid and qualified 23 staff since the crisis. 'After the crisis and particularly in November 2008 everything almost stopped. Our operations used to generate half a million dollars a month and we had started with a capital of 100 000 dollars but suddenly we could only make 600 dollars a month.' Brash had to dip into his US$1 million dollar reserve cash deposits to make ends meet, however, he said things were improving. 'If you survive this year, it will be great', he said.

Although there are no exact figures on migration or mortality rates, officials confirm that the effect of the financial crisis 'is not that severe'. Jamal

Al Sharif, DMC's Executive Director, says it is not clear that all segments have been hit. 'If there are companies that are moving, we have companies which are just landing. Yahoo came to DMC during the crisis.'

For some firms Dubai is only a base with operations, activities and products aimed at the larger Middle East region. For instance, Colin Smith of Showtimearabia has many of his clients in Egypt, Saudi Arabia and Kuwait, where he says 'there is no recession'. But his business in Dubai, he adds, has been affected because 'there have been economic pressures on expatriates to leave' (interview with the authors).

For some media firms, like AEG, the leading sports and entertainment presenters in the world, business is as usual. The managing director of the company's Dubai subsidiary, Thomas Ovesen, says his business has nothing to do with the crisis and lax regulations make it easy for him to hold performances. 'If I put an event, there are no regulations about scaffolding or terracing.' But there are drawbacks. He says 'jobless people in the region are no longer part of the buying power while in Europe they still earn something and play a role in the society's buying power' (interview with the authors).

But taxes in Dubai are increasing. The authorities have slapped 10 per cent on all tourism tickets and Ovesen now avoids theatres outside the free-trade zone area and prefers to have them within the DMC precincts to evade the tax.

The authorities' aim of diversifying benefits from their free-trade zone adventures beyond purely financial advantages is hard to realize. They have been good money spinners but have so far failed to create jobs for the locals as staffing is still dominated by foreigners as well as the activities these companies carry. Training and education of locals is still at a minimum. DMC remains a potential revenue stream but has not helped much in creating jobs and graduates capable of coping with a high-tech economy.

And there is the issue of 'responsible journalism', a term that surfaces whenever talking about media in the Middle East. The term is extremely hard to define in the absence of clear regulations and transparent administration. However, it is difficult to see any Middle East state, including Dubai, accepting content that will be seen as violating basic Islamic tenets. The official religion in the UAE is Islam, and Muslim culture and traditions have to be respected even within the confines of free-trade zones. Therefore, the social behaviour and business activities of MDC residents will have, to a large extent, to comply with the prevalent religious practice and cultural norms. Having said that, many firms, particularly broadcasters, advertisers and magazine publishers have learned what they cannot do, which in a nutshell is related to how much 'skin' can be exposed.

Nudity, particularly of women – albeit restricted – is not a big issue in Dubai, but almost a taboo in Saudi Arabia. What is surprising is that while many women parts can be exposed today, male nudity is almost tantamount to blasphemy.

But the lack of regulatory standards has been a blessing for Colin Smith, vice president of Showtimearabia, a pay TV firm. The company, currently running 42 channels, was based in London but only decided to make Dubai a venue when it obtained guarantees 'that we were not regulated any more than in London'. But the DMC is, for Smith, even better than London:

> The place is not more stringent than Ofcom (the statutory duties as set down in the UK Communication Act of 2003). There are a few regulatory issues here but they are not formal. Ofcom regulates beer and sponsorship. TECOM is even more liberal in some areas than Ofcom (interview with the authors).

Showtimearabia is one of the largest firms in DMC with 600 employees, 400 of them housed in its own headquarters in Dubai, which the company built with a 50-year lease from TECOM.

Constitutionally, the UAE enshrines freedom of speech but within a context that respects the country's values, traditions and religion. 'Ethical behaviour', which is hard to define and delineate, is a prerogative for all media firms inside and outside free-trade zones to follow. There is also the regulatory framework of the Gulf Cooperation Council (GCC), of which the UAE is a member and which makes it incumbent on member states to 'uphold the cultural order of the region' (Chaker, 2003).

Growth seems to have so far been a characteristic of DMC. The regulatory framework and licensing procedures are set in a manner that they promote dynamic growth and accommodate both small and large firms, and the clustering facilities provide good access for both skilled staff and technology. But this has not been without drawbacks. Unlike similar clusters in advanced countries like Britain and Canada, for example, where the promotion of national and local firms is one of the priorities, DMC is dominated by foreign organizations, with only two Emirati tenants (cf. Britton and Legare, 2005; Cornford and Robins, 1992).

DISCUSSION

The development and operation of Dubai Media City follows a different model from that of most other media clusters in that its establishment and operations are strategically driven as part of broader national economic but not cultural goals. It is a real-estate driven cluster, planned by real-estate developers inseparable from government planners, designed to diversify the sources of revenue and income generation in the emirate.

Development of the cluster was not designed to meet the needs of local companies, but specifically designed to attract foreign firms to locate in the cluster for their own benefit. In doing so it has become one of the largest clusters operating worldwide with more than 1200 companies and players that have co-located.

The cluster is managed and supported by real-estate and business service staffs to improve its effectiveness and appeal to participants and designed to provide all necessary services and facilities within the cluster. Although a managed cluster, the management does not significantly focus on promoting cooperation and connectiveness among its firms, but mainly on providing relevant services for a fee.

Its spillover effects appear limited to economic effects due to expenditures by cluster company staff because it does not create intellectual property whose benefits accrue to Dubai and it does not promote knowledge transfer to Dubai citizens. Some interaction and spillovers are occurring with participants in similarly developed telecommunication and information and communication technology cities, but few of the spillovers to educational, cultural and social institutions that are found in other clusters are evident. The cluster can thus be seen as helping to promote globalization goals of media firms but not development of domestic media and content.

The impact of the global financial crisis has had a significant effect on Dubai because its economy is strongly connected to financial markets. It has deeply felt the harm of the recession (*Economist*, 2008; Worth 2009). The crisis has slammed the brakes on Dubai's surging property development. This glittering metropolis still has more cranes than any other place in the world – but most of them are now idle. Hundreds of development projects, both public and private, have been abandoned halfway through. The authorities strive to give the impression of 'life-as-usual' but the adverse impact of the crisis cannot escape the most casual look of any visitor, with half-built and abandoned towers, residential quarters and buildings dotting the outskirts of the city reaching into the desert. It is estimated that projects worth US$582 billion have either been put on hold or cancelled.

REFERENCES

AFP (2008), 'UAE Nationals make up One-seventh of Population', 17 December 2008.

Arabian Business.com (2007), 'Dubai Deals Blow to Pakistan TV', 18 November 2007. Retrieved 5 January 2009 from http://www.arabianbusiness.com/504209-dubai-silences-pakistan-tv.

Armitstead, L. (2008), 'Dubai Finally Reveals its Financial Position', *Daily Telegraph*, 25 November 2008. Retrieved 8 January 2009 from http://blogs.telegraph.co.uk/louise_armitstead/blog/2008/11/25/dubai_finally_reveals_its_financial_position.

Britton, J.N.H. and G. Legare (2005), 'Clustering and the Digital Economy: New Media in Toronto', *Canadian Journal of Regional Science*, **28**(2), 329–349.

Chaker, M.N. (2003), 'The Impact of Globalization on Cultural Industries in United Arab Emirates', paper accepted for presentation at the 2003 Hawaii International Conference on Business 18–21 June 2003. Retrieved 29 January 2009 from http://www.hicbusiness.org/biz2003proceedings/Mohammad%20Naim%20Chaker.pdf.

Cornford, J. and K. Robins (1992), 'Development Strategies in the Audiovisual Industries: The Case of North East England', *Regional Studies*, **26**(5), 421–435.

Dubai International (2009) (official website). Retrieved 21 December 2009 from http://www.dubaiairport.com/DIA/English/MainMenu/Airport+Guide/.

Dubai Media City (official website). Retrieved 3 February 2009 from http://www.dmc-communityguide.com/dmc/.

Dubai Media City expands Business Centre for media entrepreneurs. Retrieved 4 February from http://www.ameinfo.com/103343.html.

The Economist (2008), 'The Credit Crunch: World on the Edge', 2 October 2008. Retrieved 11 January 2009 from http://www.economist.com/opinion/displaystory.cfm?story_id=12341996.

Fernie, J., S. Fernie and C. Moore (2003) *Principles of Retailing*, Oxford, UK: Butterworth-Heinemann.

Glass, A. (2008), 'Foreigners pose "Risk" to UAE Security', Arabianbusiness.com, 16 April 2008. Retrieved 6 January 2009, from http://www.arabianbusiness.com/foreigners-pose-risk--uae-security-50657.html?parentID=336881.

Golawala, F., P. Ganesh, J. Grant and D. McKechnie (2006), 'Non Emaratis' Perception of Emaratis Entering Education Careers', Proceedings of the Women as Global Leaders Conference, Abu Dhabi, UAE, p. 38.

Goldstein, B. and T. O'Regan (2003), *Cinema Cities, Media Cities: The Contemporary International Studio Complex*, report, Screen Industry, Culture and Policy Research Series, Sydney, AUS: Australian Film Commission.

Grant, J., F. Golawala and D. McKechnie (2007), 'The United Arab Emirates: The Twenty-first Century Beckons', *Thunderbird International Business Review*, **49**(4), 507–533.

Jarrah, F. (ed) (2006), *United Arab Emirates Knowledge Economy 2006*, Dubai, UAE: Madar Research Knowledge Economy Series, Madar Research.

John, I. (2008), 'Dubai set to Sustain 11pc GDP Growth', *Khaleej Times*, 28 March 2008. Retrieved 8 January 2009 from http://www.khaleejtimes.com/DisplayArticleNew.asp?xfile=data/business/2008/March/business_March865.xml&section=business&col=.

Johnston, C.B. (1998), *Global News Access: The Impact of New Communications Technologies,* Westport, CT, USA: Praeger.

Kaiser, R. and M. Liecke (2007), 'The Munich Feature Film Cluster: The Degree of Global Integration and Explanations for its Relative Success', *Industry and Innovation*, **14**(4), 385–399.

Krätke, S. (2002), 'Network Analysis of Production Clusters: The Potsdam/Babelsberg Film Industry as an Example', *European Planning Studies*, **10**(1), 27–54.
Logistics Insight Asia – Industry News (2008), 'International Intralogistics Trade Fair – January 19 to 21, 2010 Dubai'. Retrieved 30 January 2009 from http://www.logasiamag.com/article-884-internationalintralogisticstradefairjanuary19to212010dubai-LogisticsAsia.html.
Mattfeld, D.C. (2006), *The Management of Transshipment Terminals: Decision Support for Terminal Operations in Finished Vehicle Supply Chains*. Berlin, DEU: Springer.
Moore, P.W. (2004), *Doing Business in the Middle East: Politics and Economic Crisis in Jordan and Kuwait*, Cambridge, UK: Cambridge University Press.
Mulcahy, D.E. (1993), *Warehouse Distribution and Operations Handbook*, London, UK and New York, NY, USA: McGraw-Hill.
Nachum, L. and D. Keeble (2003), 'Neo-Marshallian Clusters and Global Networks: The Linkages of Media Firms in Central London', *Long Range Planning*, **36**(5), 459–480.
National Bank of Dubai (2004), 'Factors impeding emiratization in the insurance industry', *Economic Report*, **8**(2). Retrieved 28 November 2009 from http://www.pdfchaser.com/pdf/UAE-Dubai-Modern-Education-School.html.
National Bank of Dubai (2006), 'Trade Barriers in the UAE: National Versus Foreign Perspective', *Economic Report*, **10**(3), 2–3.
PropertyWire (2008), 'Prices fall up to 50% in prestigious Dubai development', *PropertyWire*, 12 November 2008. Retrieved 3 January 2009 from http://www.propertywire.com/news/middle-east/prices-fall-prestigious-dubai-development-200811122048.html.
Quinn, S., T. Walters and J. Whiteoak (2004), 'A Tale of Three (Media) Cities', *Global Media Journal*, **3**(5). Retrieved December 14, 2009, from http://lass.calumet.purdue.edu/cca/gmj/fa04/gmj-fa04-quinn-waters-whiteoak.htm.
Picard, R.G. (2009), 'Media Clusters: Local Agglomeration in an Industry Developing Networked Virtual Clusters', *JIBS Working Paper Series No. 2008-3*. Downloadable at: http://www.ihh.hj.se/mmt/documents/WP-2008-3%20Picard-Publ.pdf (accessed 2009).
Rushton, A., P. Croucher and P. Baker (2006) *The Handbook of Logistics and Distribution Management*, London, UK: Kogan Page.
Schleifer, S.A. (2000), 'The Dubai Digital Broadcasting Miracle', *Transnational Broadcasting Studies*, **5**, Fall/Winter 2000. Retrieved 12 November 2009, from http://www.tbsjournal.com/Archives/Fall00/Schleifer_Dubai.html.
Serafin, T. (2008), 'The World's Richest Royals', *Forbes.com* 20 August 2008. Retrieved 6 January 2010 from http://www.forbes.com/2008/08/20/worlds-richest-royals-biz-richroyals08-cz_ts_0820royalintro.html.
Sirri, O. (2003), 'The Oracle in the Desert: Can Dubai's Media City Deliver on its Promise of Freedom of the Press?', *Cairo Times*, **6**(43), 9 January 2003. Retrieved 29 December 2009 from:http://www.cairotimes.com/content/archiv06/dubai media 0643.html.
Smiley, D.J. (ed) (2002), *Sprawl and Public Space: Redressing the Mall*, New York, NY, USA: Princeton Architectural Press.
Sullivan, S. (2001), 'Dubai Media City Prepares for Next Phase', *Transnational Broadcasting Studies*, **7**, Fall/Winter 2001. Retrieved 14 January 2010, from http://www.tbsjournal.com/Archives/Fall01/dubai.html.

Tawella, W. (2002). 'New Media in the Arab World: The Social and Cultural Aspect', New Media and Change in the Arab World conference. Amman, Jordan, 27 February through 1 March 2002 http://www.media-arabia.org.

Turok, I. (2003), 'Cities, Clusters and Creative Industries: The Case of Film and Television in Scotland', *European Planning Studies,* **11**(5), 549–565.

Tusiani, M.D. (1996), *The Petroleum Shipping Industry Vol 2: Practices and Operations*, Tulsa, OK, USA:Pennwell Books.

UNDP (2002a) *The Arab Human Development Report*, New York, NY, USA: United Nations Publications.

UNDP (2002b) *The Arab World: Let the Numbers Speak*, New York: United Nations Publications. Retrieved 20 January 2010, from http://www.undp.org/rbas/ahdr/PR2.pdf.

Walters, T.N., A. Kadragic and L.M. Walters (2006), 'Miracle or Mirage: Is Development Sustainable in the United Arab Emirates?', *The Middle East Review of International Affairs*, **10**(3), Retrieved 16 December 2009, from http://meria.idc.ac.il/journal/2006/issue3/jv10no3a6.html (accessed 2009).

WAM (9 September 2002), 'Dubai palm island traffic plan under study', http://www.wam.org.ae/2002/Sep/04/707734.htm, also available https://www.worldhighways.com/news/article.cfm?recordID=2963.

Ward, S. and T. O'Regan (2007) 'Servicing "The Other Hollywood": The Vicissitudes of an International Television Production Location', *International Journal of Cultural Studies*, **10**(2), 167–185.

Weisman, J. and B. Graham (2006), 'Dubai Firm to sell U.S. Port Operations', *The Washington Post*, Friday, 10 March 2006, p. A01. Retrieved 29 January 2009 from http://www.washingtonpost.com/wp-dyn/content/article/2006/03/09/AR2006030901124.html.

Worth, R.F. (2008), 'Boomtown Feels Effects of a Global Crisis', *New York Times*, 4 October 2008. Retrieved 5 January 2009 from http://www.nytimes.com/2008/10/05/world/middleeast/05dubai.html?pagewanted=a.

Worth, R.F.(2009), 'Laid-Off Foreigners Flee as Dubai Spirals Down', *New York Times*, 12 February 2009. Retrieved 12 February 2009 from http://www.nytimes.com/2009/02/12/world/middleeast/12dubai.html?_r=1&hp.

13. Media industry clustering in South Africa: prospects for economic development and spatial reconfiguration

Harry Dugmore and Johanna Mavhungu

The media industry in South Africa is very concentrated both in terms of ownership and in terms of close geographical proximity in South Africa's two leading cities, Johannesburg and Cape Town. Despite South Africa having no national strategy to encourage or enhance the geographical clustering of the media industry, more than 90 per cent of media companies cluster a short distance from each other in these two cities.

This would at first glance appear to be somewhat of an anomaly. Despite the opportunities presented by the 2010 FIFA World Cup, South African cities historically and currently have shown little interest in attracting media companies to their regions or incentivizing existing companies to stay and grow. But this has not inhibited media clustering or media development more generally from taking place. Almost all current growth fits into the 'traditional agglomeration' notion of private-sector driven, 'organic' geographically based clustering developed by Picard (2008). Media organizations are almost all historically concentrated in Johannesburg and Cape Town. In these cities, a great deal of clustering has taken place, particularly in the last few decades. This reflects in turn South Africa's concentrated levels of media ownership, which is itself partly a legacy of apartheid-era patterns of accumulation and exclusion.

This chapter outlines how in South Africa clustering continues and, in some places, has even been accelerated recently with limited involvement from government. In this way, the growth and spatial configurations of the media industry in South Africa are different from, for example, the start-ups in Dubai, Singapore and Trollhattan. There is no doubt that South African media would welcome more state support at any level, but for various reasons explored in this chapter, that is seldom forthcoming.

Three of the four of South Africa's largest print media companies – Avusa, Caxton and Independent Newspapers – are located in Johannesburg. The fourth and largest conglomerate, Naspers, is based in Cape Town.[1] The national TV and radio broadcaster, the SABC, is based in Johannesburg, as are the vast majority of South Africa's private TV and media production companies. Book publishers, 'new media' firms, PR and advertising companies, etc are all mostly headquartered in Johannesburg, with a small minority based in Cape Town and the occasional outlier located in other cities, such as Durban. The city of Johannesburg can confidently claim that it is 'the headquarters of the South African media industry, [boasting] a lively and remarkably diverse range of media' (Johannesburg News Agency, 2010a).

In both Johannesburg and Cape Town, there is significant geographical proximity among media companies, even across different media platforms. Clearly, some areas have developed because of their proximity to larger firms or state institutions, such as the large cluster of media companies around the South African Broadcasting Corporation (SABC) in Auckland Park and Melville/Richmond in Johannesburg. Other companies, particularly those in film production, have chosen what were peri-urban areas for their locations to obtain cheaper rentals. Many of these once outlying areas are now fully within the urban area of greater Johannesburg.

There is also some 'virtual' clustering, of the kind described by Picard (2008), where firms cooperate closely over wider distances across cities, using digital connectivity or physical couriers to, for example, post-produce a TV show.

More recently, there have also been some private-sector driven attempts to 'cluster' and attract media companies or, more broadly, 'creative' companies in Johannesburg and, more assertively, in Cape Town, particularly around digital media and the film industry. This has also happened to a lesser extent in Stellenbosch, near Cape Town.

While these initiatives could be considered media-related in a much broader sense, at least where they include encouragement for information and communication technology related companies and various 'creative' industries (such as web/mobi design houses), the inducements rarely extend to 'legacy' media. Johannesburg, for example, supports the fashion design and jewellery manufacture sectors as key 'creative industries', going as far as trying to set up physical clusters in Johannesburg known as 'Jewel City' in Johannesburg East (Johannesburg News Agency, 2010b) and the so-called 'Fashion Kapitol' district.

Likewise, although focusing on different areas of 'creativity', Cape Town aspires to market itself as a hub of 'creative industries' and, in particular, as a design centre. Its biannual Design Indaba, which started in the late

1990s and featured, for example, American design guru Martha Stewart as keynote speaker in 2010, continues to make a case for Cape Town playing a role as an important part of the international design circuit.

Despite these kinds of initiatives, or perhaps in contrast to the official support for design, jewellery, clothing manufacture (and design) and some support elsewhere for 'tech start-ups', two key questions remain: Why is there lack of interest by local, provincial or national government in South Africa to develop strategies to attract or even keep media companies in their locales? Why is there seemingly so little of the kind of public/private partnerships that have caused a degree of media sector clustering – and the variety of benefits that often flow from thoughtful city and local economic development planning – elsewhere in the world?

Although these questions can only be answered obliquely and somewhat speculatively in this chapter, they are particularly sharp-edged, as the post-1994 democratic South Africa has embraced both media diversity and pluralism as key ambitions. In addition, South African cities are eager to stake their place in the 21st century by attracting 'new industries' and developing their attractiveness to 'creative industries' more broadly. Furthermore, the ruling African National Congress (ANC), by far the largest political party in parliament, espouses an overtly interventionist 'developmental' approach to the role of the state in the economy. Why then, to put those questions in slightly different words, in the plethora of national, provincial and local economic developments plans and within major City planning strategies, are strategies for encouraging media development and clustering so underdeveloped, even in the context of the massive stimulus of the 2010 FIFA World Cup?

It is only by attempting to answer this question of context that some sense can be made of the few initiatives to encourage the clustering of media and/or 'creative' industries that have emerged in the past decade and are outlined later in this chapter. Getting a better grasp of this official reticence also provides a framework for assessing whether current or future interventions to foster media development and geographic or 'virtual' clustering, post the catalytic event of the FIFA World Cup, might be successful.

MEDIA IN POST-1994 SOUTH AFRICA

Prior to 1994, there was a cosy if complex relationship between large media organizations and the apartheid government. Despite pockets of liberal expression through certain media titles, most of the commercial print, television and film industry was pliant and collaborative, while the apartheid state carefully controlled state media, which included all television and radio broadcasting. South Africa only started TV broadcasts in 1975, due to fears by the apartheid leaders that TV could undermine white minority rule. Three oligopolists dominated the print industry. Very little media for the majority of the African population existed, South Africa's majority sharing the lack of 'media density' that characterizes much of Africa (Berger, 2006).

After the 1994 elections, the new democratic South African government set about igniting growth in an economy nearly bankrupted by apartheid and, as part of this, creating the kind of media that might give greater voice to the majority of South Africans. It also set out, at least at the level of rhetoric, to create a regulatory regime that would enhance consumer options, increase the diversity of media, give citizens access to mobile phones and cheap broadband and allow community radio and print to flourish (Berger, 2009).

But 16 years later very little of this has happened.

Private, previously white-owned media companies have flourished, and their ownership is still largely in institutional and white hands.

State media have been expanded, particularly in radio, but under the logic and limitations of 'commercialization' that has often crowded out the public education and public trust mandates of the national broadcaster in particular.

As many writers point out, post apartheid media development – or underdevelopment – needs to be located in an analysis of the nature of transition away from apartheid South Africa (Barnett, 1999; Horwitz, 2001a; Berger, 2006). Most make a compelling case that the ANC-led government has pursued a surprisingly conventional neoliberal approach to economic development. By putting the emphasis largely on 'de-racializing' capitalism, rather than pursuing more participatory or equalitarian development paths, patterns of accumulation and development have not changed much in the post-apartheid era. This has been particularly true of media.

The commercial sector – particularly print, TV and radio – is lightly policed. While there is often criticism from government and ruling party sources of established private media's supposed 'anti-transformation' agenda and even periodic threats of starting a state-controlled newspaper to counter-balance these perceived biases, these threats have never amounted to much.

The public sector, and in particular the national radio and TV broadcaster the SABC, continues to exhibit clear ruling-party bias, despite myriad policies to ensure greater editorial freedom, impartiality and fairness.

Since 1994, the state has forced the official broadcaster, the SABC, to 'commercialize' further, and this logic extends in different ways to all media in South Africa. Media are expected to 'pay their way' regardless of any notion of public good. State subsidies are meagre where they exist at all, and regulations that place restrictions on ownership, cross-ownership and even foreign ownership are relatively mild when compared to other countries.

In terms of the media's role in de-racializing the South African economy, despite various 'empowerment charters' specifying, for example, minimum desirable levels of black ownership of private enterprises, little has changed in terms of ownership structures. So-called 'Black Economic Empowerment' (BEE) and, more recently, 'Broad-Based Black Economic Empowerment' (BBBEE) has attempted to transfer some ownership to so-called 'previously disadvantaged individuals' through transfer of ownership of shares in larger businesses.[2] While this has shifted some fractions of ownership at the margins, real shifts of either managerial power or meaningful ownership have not occurred.

'Community Media'

By contrast to the relative stasis in the private sector over the past few decades, despite government efforts to broaden and de-racialize ownership and control, smaller 'community media' have been a much more fluid field. The state has contributed substantial strategic and financial resources to create smaller-scale 'community media', sheltered from at least some commercial pressures. The establishment of the Media Development and Diversity Agency (MDDA) and the creation of a large-scale community radio-licensing regime are the two best-known and most successful initiatives led by the government since 1994.

In operation since 2002, the MDDA is a public-private partnership, with large media companies contributing funds based on their income. Government then matches these funds (Media Development and Diversity Agency, 2008).

This model has had some success. Upwards of 200 projects have been funded by 2010, and about ZAR80 million (approximately US$10 million) has been spent (Media Development and Diversity Agency, 2008).

But the model has also attracted criticism, particularly of underfunding and lack of interest from the government. In addition, the logic of commercial sustainability, coupled with the imperative of racial transformation, complicates the development of community media and the MDDA's mission in interesting ways. As Guy Berger, MDDA board member, writes:

> Also at stake in this is the strategy of transforming media ownership by expansion of the sector, as distinct from interventions to dispossess the existing proprietors. Unlike businesses like banks, which agreed under pressure to adopt industry charters to redistribute share-holdings, the country's media companies are offering the success of the MDDA as a way to grow new owners alongside them.
>
> Unbundling the mainstream would produce more owners (at least amongst the usual BEE players) – but it would not necessarily expand the industry in the way the MDDA seeks to do. In this sense, the agency is an experiment that has a broader significance than just the projects it supports (Berger, 2009).

Partly because of the MDDA's work, and taken together with deregulation of the radio and to a much lesser extent the TV sector, there is now more diversity of media for most South Africans compared to 1994. New media owners have appeared: 126 community radio stations and about 200 local community newspaper titles have been established[3] as well as four community TV channels.

Despite these successes, community media have struggled to win audience share and create viable and sustainable business models. Although ICASA has granted 126 community radio stations, only 87 stations were still on air in 2010. Many of these survivors are in precarious financial situations. According to recent All Media Product Survey (AMPS) data, community radio audience represents only 4.6 per cent of total radio audience in South Africa.[4]

It is common cause in South Africa that community newspapers have also battled financially, almost without exception (see, for example, Hadland and Thorne, 2004). Most of the 200 titles known to exist either publish erratically or else are advertising-driven to the extent of carrying very little journalism.[5]

South Africa has a few community television stations but high set-up and production costs deter players in this market.[6]

Digital Media and Cellular Telephony

Access to the internet and to the World Wide Web, email and other wonders of the digital world has been ill-served by the post-1994 government. Despite repeated promises, it took the government 12 years to create any form of fixed line competition to the apartheid monolithic telecoms operation, Telkom. This has been a key reason why, in 2010, only about 10 per cent of the South African population has access to the internet through fixed line broadband and for a large percentage of this population this access takes place exclusively through places of work or study (MyBroadband, 2009). Broadband costs are high in absolute and relative terms, almost entirely because of the excessive Telkom charges (IOL Technology, 2010).

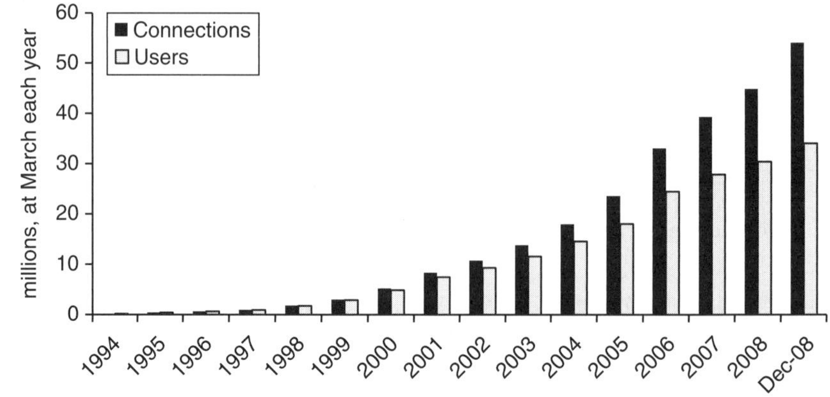

Figure 13.1 Mobile connections vs users in SA 1994 to 2008

By contrast, mobile phones have been a standout success story, with almost 100 per cent of South African families owning a cell phone or having easy access to a cell phone. Actual penetration, as shown in Figure 13.1 from research firm World Wide Worx, is approaching 100 per cent of South Africa's adult population (South Africa's total population is about 50 million people, with a large percentage under the age of 14). There is currently a rapid uptake of the 'mobile web', as tens of thousands of South Africans are discovering the power of the internet each month for the first time, mostly over their cell phone. Instant messaging is a huge success, as is Facebook (World Wide Worx Research Notes, May 2010).

But despite this rapid uptake, high costs relative to average incomes limit the use of phones for data services, even if handsets are ubiquitous. Although defined as a middle-income country, South Africa income levels are extremely unequal. About 34 per cent of the population live on US$2 per day or less (Population Reference Bureau and African Population and Health Research Center, 2008). A one-minute phone call routinely costs about 20 US cents, 10 per cent of a day's income for many South Africans. Even a single SMS can cost 10 US cents (Duncan, 2009). The majority of South Africans find that much more than US$10 a month on a cell phone is a luxury they cannot afford (Duncan, 2009).

All this has meant that while there is growth and good profits for two dominant cell phone companies, Vodacom and MTN, new content providers, i.e. media companies that provide phone content, are still thin on the ground because of the low level of demand for data-driven services. Some music downloads and ringtones are provided by off-shore sites and appear to be successful. There are no data as to the exact breakdown of local versus international content providers. Other than MXit, the instant messaging service based in Stellenbosch, there are few local cell phone oriented media companies of any scale outside the news and information services provided by the traditional media houses Avusa, Naspers and the Independent Group.

The South African Media Industry in 2010

It is perhaps more than a little surprising that after 16 years of democracy, while there is a greater plurality of voices, particularly in terms of dozens of new community radio stations and print titles, their 'share of voice' is so minuscule. The large apartheid-supporting monopolies of the pre-1994 era have, a little ironically, grown larger and stronger. The SABC lurches from very public crisis to crisis, often in sync with intra-party machinations within the ruling ANC. It offers little by way of participatory or critical journalism.

Off this base of hyper-concentration and, in the SABC's case, ineptitude, the world recession of 2008–2010 has impacted on South African media. The three oligopolists battled to maintain their previously market-topping margins, while the SABC has had to rely on the government for extraordinary financial bailouts. But community radio and print publications have seemingly been even harder hit, and many operations have closed. Very few new initiatives have been announced, even in the more fluid digital and cellular arenas, where financial barriers to entry are lower.

Many have asked and hoped: Might the massive investment – upwards of ZAR40 billion (US$6 billion) – in the FIFA World Cup not have provided some impetus for the South African media landscape?

MEDIA DEVELOPMENT AND CITY PLANNING: THE PROSPECTS FOR PLANNED MEDIA CLUSTERING AS A SPUR TO MEDIA DEVELOPMENT IN SOUTH AFRICA

Johannesburg and Cape Town provide two contrasting examples of city approaches to encouraging media development and promoting clustering both in general and within the context of the FIFA 2010 World Cup. A brief overview of media development in the two cities usefully illustrates their differences of emphasis.

An Overview of Media in Johannesburg

Johannesburg hosted the Football World Cup Final in June 2010, probably the largest media event in the world, being host to not only the

International Broadcast Centre (IBC) for the month of the finals, but also the vast majority of visiting media crews.

Johannesburg, as outlined in the introduction, is home to the national public service broadcaster, the SABC, with its three 'free-to-air' TV stations and national radio channels.[7] Caxton, Avusa and the Independent Group's print media assets are housed in Johannesburg, which is also the HQ for many foreign broadcasters.

The small downtown area of Johannesburg was the commercial and financial hub of South Africa for most of the 20th century. Only in the early 1990s did commercial companies start to move towards the north, to newer commercial areas such as Sandton and Midrand. There are many explanations for this recent and comprehensive move away from the downtown area, not uncommon in many cities in the world. In Johannesburg, at least part of the explanation for this 'flight to the north' is the rapid influx of black South Africans and Africans from further afield after the abolition of influx control laws. Proximity to (largely white) staff has also played a factor in the suburbanization of the media industry out of the city centre and towards the north of Johannesburg (Rogerson and Rogerson, 1997).

Over a decade, most large companies relocated their headquarters north of Johannesburg's downtown area, and even the iconic Johannesburg Stock Exchange (JSE) moved from its headquarters to the upmarket and 'whiter' Sandton area in the late 1990s. Very few media companies are currently still operating in downtown Johannesburg.

By 2010, media companies in Johannesburg cluster in four areas of close geographical proximity in suburbs such as Melville, Auckland Park (home to the SABC), Richmond, Rosebank and, a little further away, in Sandton, where a great many advertising agencies, for example, have their headquarters. Given the vast area of Johannesburg metropolis, this clustering is very clear and distinctive. The west, south and eastern sides of Johannesburg have very little media company presence, a small area to the north of the city centre houses almost 100 per cent of media companies.

While there is no indication in the urban-planning literature as to why such distinctive clustering has taken place in Johannesburg, it is clear that the location of the SABC in Auckland Park is a key reference point for at least TV-related companies in Johannesburg (and South Africa). Major radio stations are also based at and run by the SABC. Most foreign media have rented office space within 2 km of the SABC, while many major TV studios like Red Pepper Productions, Ochre Media and Endemol South Africa are also close by. DStv, the large satellite broadcaster in Africa, owned by Naspers, is based in Randburg, about 5 km away from the SABC.

All of this clustering has been 'spontaneous' or 'organic', i.e. driven by autonomous decisions by private players. There has been no local government encouragement of this patterning at all.

In an interview, Rashid Seedat, Head of Strategy for the Johannesburg Metro Council explained, 'There's never been any real impetus for developing the media sector in Johannesburg. We have been spoilt by the sector's obvious enthusiasm to be here and to stay here. Most of the big companies are doing pretty well, and we've never thought we are in any danger of losing them' (Seedat, interview, 2010).

Lael Bethlehem, until recently head of the Johannesburg Development Agency (JDA) largely agrees with Seedat's views and provides an explanation as to why this might be the case:

> There have been some efforts to make part of the Newtown redevelopment a home for media, and a few important media companies moved in there. But I think there is scepticism in government about how many jobs media can create. Some parts of the media industry would be seen as 'sunset' industries, and while others are obviously industries of the future, or 'sunrise' industries, there is not the sense that attracting such media should be a high priority for the City (Bethlehem, interview, 2010).[8]

Johannesburg as a city accounts for, by various estimates, 30 per cent of the GDP of South Africa. The city contributes about 48.2 per cent of the provincial economy and 18.1 per cent of the national economy (Mayor of Johannesburg, 2008). Both the province and the national government have a variety of economic development frameworks and paradigms, none of which have any focus on media.

As Bethlehem says, 'With South African unemployment so high, we (i.e. development agencies) have to focus on the kind of city development that will not only redress the spatial geography of apartheid, but also promote development and job creation. I'm not sure how government helping large media companies would accomplish that. But helping smaller companies, like (digital) start-ups, web design and internet companies – perhaps that is something we could have been doing more of in the past few years' (Bethlehem, interview, 2010).

There have in fact been attempts by Johannesburg to promote digital access through the Blue IQ project and to upgrade municipal infrastructure to provide public access to the internet, but neither of these have brought any notable success.

The Legacy of the 2010 FIFA World Cup

Johannesburg Executive Mayor Amos Masondo said, at the opening of the almost ZAR 1 billion International Broadcast Centre (IBC), that the edifice would help the city to meet its developmental objectives and attract investment long after the 2010 FIFA World Cup and would 'go a long way towards ensuring that our developmental objectives become a reality and attract investment to the city' (SouthAfrica.info, 2010). But later in the same speech, the Mayor added that the greatest benefit of hosting the IBC for the city has been the catalytic effect it has had on the development of the Nasrec area.

This latter statement betrays the reality of the legacy of the World Cup: the opportunities of the FIFA World Cup, including the IBC and the temporary influx of 10,000 journalists, have not been seized by the authorities in Johannesburg. The most trenchant example of this is that the IBC has been built on rented ground and is to be entirely deconstructed after the World Cup (Acuna, interview, 2010). While this would be better judged after the World Cup, and is clearly an area that requires further research, there is nothing to indicate that there will be any future direct media benefit from the IBC development, or indeed from any other FIFA World Cup activity. There is no doubt that there will be some benefit for all business from the additional ICT infrastructure that the 2010 World Cup has helped spawn, both in terms of locally-laid cable, and increased international bandwidth (Alfers, interview, 2010). But because it appears that no one at a city, provincial or national level has focused on media development strategies, there was consequently no thinking or planning for a permanent World Cup legacy, at least in terms of media development.

The government's failure is largely due to a lack of planning and, at some levels of government, a lack of execution of the few plans that were developed to implementable levels. The opportunities of the FIFA World Cup, for example, were recognized well before 2010. However, the emphasis has been on staging the World Cup successfully and every effort has been directed towards stadia construction, security and tourism facilities. Much more could have been done to secure the longevity of other resources such as the fibre optic cable at the MTN Nasrec Expo Centre to benefit media sector development.

MEDIA INDUSTRIES IN CAPE TOWN

Cape Town has had a very different development trajectory when compared to Johannesburg (Boraine, 2006). As a much older city, its spatial geography has been deformed by decades of segregation and then, from 1948, by apartheid, in particular ways. African South Africans were barred almost completely from Cape Town until the 1980s, and are still a minority in the city. 'Coloured' South Africans were given preference

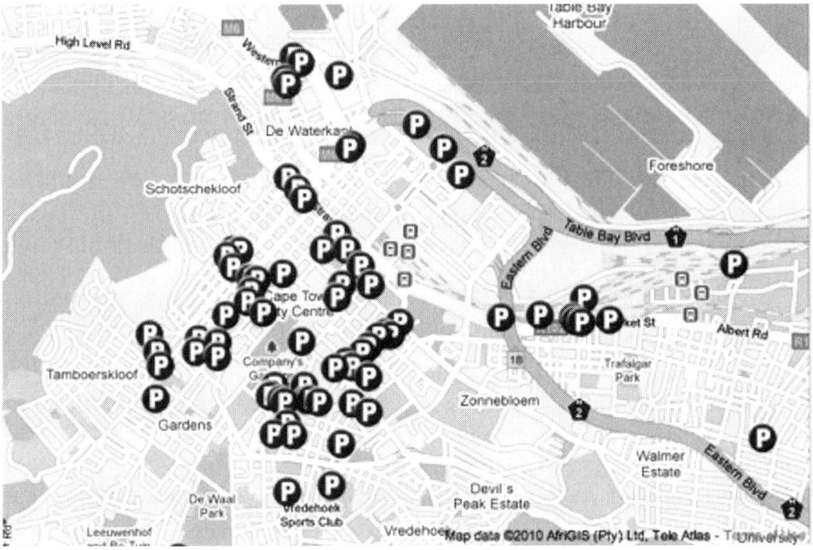

Source: Creative Cape Town website, 2010

Figure 13.2 Cape Town media industry clustering. P = Publishing, Media and Film

after whites in terms of access to resources and space, although coloureds were also subjected to forced removal, segregation and the multi-layered discrimination that was apartheid.

More recently, the City Council has been controlled by the Democratic Alliance, the official opposition party in South Africa, which espouses a more 'pro-business' set of policies, some of which appear to be shaping spatial developments in Cape Town.

Cape Town also already exhibits a high degree of existing and historical physical clustering of media companies (see Figure 13.2). It is estimated that about 90 per cent of all Cape Town's media companies are located within 4 km of each other.

Cape Town has been very proactive in seeking to use the World Cup for development. Its iconic stadium is as impressive as that of Soccer City in Johannesburg. The City also managed to lure the BBC away from Johannesburg and away from using the IBC as a base for their operations during the World Cup by offering a rent-reduced building in Cape Town, with a majestic backdrop of Table Mountain.

In addition to this existing concentrated physical media clustering, Cape Town is host to a number of other promising media initiatives, including the creation of a large-scale film studio and various initiatives to encourage the clustering of 'creative industries'. Unlike Johannesburg, Cape Town projects, while driven by private businesses, do appear to have at least some overt local government support and infrastructure investment.

Three examples illustrate the vision and energy that are going into these initiatives: the development of the Cape Town Film Studios (CTFS), the Cape Town Partnership's Creative Cape Town Cluster and the Bandwidth Barn.

The Cape Town Film Studios

The Cape Town Film Studios – named 'Dreamworld' in their initial stages of development – are envisaged as a major new venture to take root in the area of Faure on the outskirts of Cape Town. The first phase was anticipated to be complete in April 2010 with four sound studios built on 300 hectares of land. According to the development company's literature, it is envisaged that this will be 'Africa's leading digital media hub and telecommunications centre. It will link with studios in North America and Asia via broadband highways' (*Cape Times*, 2008).

The development of Cape Town Film Studios is a collaborative effort among filmmakers, business, government and the City of Cape Town. According to CEO Nico Dekker, more than 80 businesses in film production and related industries have expressed a commitment to move to the site.[9] The film studio is primarily aimed at the overseas movie business as Cape Town has gained prominence with overseas filmmakers as a prime location for shooting over the past decade. About 30 international feature films and 300 commercials are shot in South Africa every year, according to a recent newspaper article, but filmmakers have always had to travel elsewhere in the world to find established, state-of-the-art studios.[10]

Should this initiative succeed, it would create significant physical clustering of media firms. Businesses moving to the site do not and will not receive any incentives; instead if they 'apply early' they may stand a chance of being able to buy the premises at a good price.

CEO Nicco Dekker says: '[We offer] cheaper rates for South African producers when major films are not in the making – the whole idea is that the studio becomes a hub from where local filmmaking grows' (*The Star*, January 2009).

The Cape Town Film Studios do aim to boost the local film industry by enabling the shooting of local films. Dekker predicts that South Africa should be able to produce at least 30–40 feature films a year (*The Sowetan*, April 2009) although this might be overly optimistic, as this would represent a tenfold increase in current major feature film production expenditure in South Africa.

It is also envisaged that the project will employ, temporarily, about 8000 people to work on construction. Although there will be permanent employment, the number of such positions is not yet clear.

The government has supported the project from inception and is investing a great deal of resources in helping to create the enabling infrastructure, such as bulk services and roads.

The Cape Town Partnership and the Creative Cape Town Cluster

The Cape Town Partnership, an umbrella body under which the Creative Cape Town Clusters operate, is a collaborative effort between the public and private sectors working together to develop, promote and manage Cape Town Central City.

The stated key aim is to facilitate 'dynamic partnerships' in the central city, in line with the goals of the central city development strategy, which seeks to transform the central city into 'a leading centre for knowledge, innovation, creativity and culture in Africa and the South' (Cape Town Partnership website, 2010).

This network body brings together stakeholders who are part of Cape Town's creative economy, in what can be broadly be described as a 'virtual cluster'. The initiative started in 2008 and since then the organizers have facilitated at least four meetings, which are referred to as 'Cluster meetings'. According to Zayd Minty, Creative Cape Town executive, 'We create a space for people across disciplines to meet informally to network and hear good talks about "Creative Clusters"' (Minty, 2010).

The organizers see their role as 'facilitating communication' and providing a 'translation service' between civil society and local government.

Creative Cape Town sees itself as an information cluster aimed at increasing interaction amongst like-minded, creative businesses in the city (Minty, 2010). This includes design, architecture, economics, performance art, craft, music, media and cultural tourists, filmmakers and entrepreneurs. The organization helps participants in mega events such as Cape Town's 'Design Indaba' and the annual Cape Town International Jazz Festival.

The Bandwidth Barn

The Cape Town-based Bandwidth Barn (BWB) is situated in the central city in Lower Long Street. BWB has been in operation since 2000 and is today regarded as one of the leading ICT business incubators. The

Bandwidth Barn is owned by the Cape IT Initiative (CITI), a Section 21 company, and the development and promotions agency for the ICT sector in the Western Cape (Bandwidth Barn, 2010).

Focusing on the ICT Sector in the Western Cape, the BWB stated rationale is to encourage innovation and provide training to small and medium-sized organizations so that they can overcome the barriers to entry in the industry and develop into decent-sized businesses (Bandwidth Barn, 2010).

The Bandwidth Barn's 'incubation model' is aimed at attracting resident businesses through a number of programmes offered by the umbrella Cape Town IT Initiative (CITI). Incubation programmes are largely targeted at previously disadvantaged individuals with start-up businesses in the ICT sector.

The BWB has a two-pronged approach to supporting companies. According to their website, 'the first prong of the approach is that we lower the physical barriers of starting up a new business and mitigate the risks by ensuring companies are not bound to long term leases. The second prong of our approach is a carefully considered and proven business development programmes [sic] to equip the budding entrepreneur with basic skills to ensure sustainability' (Levin, 2010).

The strategy has been more successful than expected. The office space was used by 65 companies in 2010, including web media companies, software development start-ups, IT recruitment agents, call centre outsourcers and gaming companies. BWB founding member Allen Levin also points to a key part of Bandwidth Barn's success: creating nimble networks at short notice to compete for government and private sector work. According to Levin, 'our diversity gives us the strength we need, so we can cooperate and bid on big tenders' (Levin, 2010).

CONCLUSION

These relatively humble initiatives in Cape Town (with the exception of the ambitious Film Studios development) and some of the infrastructure developments in Johannesburg take place in an official planning environment that does not foreground media development at all. While some local government policies have a general ICT focus, i.e. a focus on creating the physical wired infrastructure for content to be conveyed over digital channels, none have a strategy to encourage the content creation as an end in itself. And while some official plans for Cape Town and Johannesburg mention facilitating the creation of feature films and TV commercials in South Africa or encouraging design and 'creative industries', there is hardly ever a mention of 'legacy media', be it TV, radio or print, or even web content development.

There are of course some advantages of growing organically. Those clusters that do develop have less interference from the state, which might be a desirable outcome for, for example, news media. But the benign and active neglect of the smaller media sectors has meant that a lot of opportunities have gone begging. A large number of small production houses linked to the SABC have had to close down in the past decade because of lack of content commissions from the public broadcaster which is the main buyer of local content from local broadcast production houses.

From the examples of Johannesburg and Cape Town outlined above, a number of factors come together to create a less than compelling case for either the state or the private sector investing more intensely in the media industry than has been the case in the past 20 years.

First, for the government, there is a lack of appreciation of media as a potential job-creating industry. There may be some basis for this apprehension, but media and communications can, as other countries have shown, be an efficient job creator. The sheer scale of unemployment in South Africa, possibly the highest in the developing world, with only 46 per cent of working age adults in formal employment, seems to predispose the government to look for 'big bang' solutions. These are often sought in so-called 'sunrise' industries that might have the long-term ability to absorb large numbers of unemployed people. (Even traditional large-scale employers in South Africa such as agriculture and manufacturing have not had the kind of state support that might have been expected given their proven labour-absorbing capacity.)

Media, in short, are just not seen as having the kind of job-creation scale that might excite national or local officials.

A second issue is the brittle relationship that governments in general and the South African government in particular have with media. South Africa's ruling African National Congress (ANC) party is fraught with different approaches to media, with some elements in the government and within the ruling party having little tolerance for dissent. ANC Youth League leader Julius Malema's 2010 ousting of a BBC journalist from a press conference may be only the most visible manifestation of this authoritarian tendency (*The Guardian*, 2010).

Other factions in the ruling party are much more supportive of media freedom and the right to critical points of view, and South Africa's constitution has strong protections for freedom of speech and media.

But there is certainly an argument to be made that past and current governments have never been enthusiastic about the idea of encouraging a proliferation of media that might be critical of their performance.

Maybe as a consequence of current low media density South Africa has, by some reports, the second highest level of 'social protests' in the world – after China – which may not be unsurprising for a country with one of the widest Gini-coefficient gaps in the world (Bond, 2010). With this 'outlier' level of social inequality coupled with high levels of poverty and decades of poor education for the majority of South Africans, pre- and post-apartheid, almost every city has a youth unemployment rate of more than 50 per cent.

While it can be argued that large-scale funding of community media might provide an alternative, more constructive channel for popular frustration – and reduce the need for the organizing of social protests in order to be 'heard' – the government has not shown any commitment to the levels of funding that even current community radio and print operations would need, never mind any expansion of these sectors. The sum of ZAR80 million over a decade for community media via the MDDA, as welcome as that has to be, is by any serious measure, desultory.

A third issue has been the relative failure of state media to catalyse the rest of the media industry, particularly in terms of TV and film production. It is common cause that the SABC is badly managed and has been for the better part of a decade. e.tv, the only free-to-air rival to the SABC's three 'public' TV stations, is profit driven to the extent that it often undercuts even the very low rates paid by the SABC for local production. As a result of this mismanagement and lack of vision at the national broadcaster, and e.tv's reliance on low-cost local production (and its predilection for imported films, TV and wrestling programming), the local TV industry has long been adrift.

In addition to the SABC's marginal role in developing local media, and local black-owned and managed media, the government's 'local content' regulations have been set at easy-to-reach levels after intense incumbent lobbying, including lobbying by its 'own' SABC. Quotas are not widely perceived as having been well enforced – even at the low levels they are set.

The FIFA 2010 World Cup is yet another example of what 'could have been' in terms of South African media development. Billions of rands have been invested in ICT infrastructure and temporary broadcast facilities, but there are likely to be few long-term benefits for media in South Africa. South Africa has failed to plan adequately and to allocate resources to ensure that the World Cup leaves a legacy beyond the legacy projects initiated by FIFA. In retrospect all spheres of government, national, provincial and local, needed to approach the planning of the World Cup more strategically. Looking back, they should have perhaps looked harder at how to better use the infrastructure and resources developed during this World Cup process for the economic benefit of various sectors and industries, including media.

This, perhaps above all, would be the most important lesson from South Africa's recent developmental history, and such lessons would be pertinent to any country hosting a large-scale international sporting or business event in the future and thinking it might encourage media development and the benefits of media clustering. This simply does not happen without careful planning, proper funding and good implementation. Other than fine stadia and some transport and airport upgrades, the longer-term impact on economic and social development is likely to be adjudged, at very least, as less than it could have been.

While such critiques are not likely to appear in print and in academic journals until well after the World Cup (and its attendant surges of patriotism and social solidarity) there is nothing to suggest any long-term benefit, at least in terms of media development, in South Africa.

Johannesburg, in particular, as the host city to the final and the host of the 30,000 m^2 International Broadcast Centre, could perhaps have explored how to seed dozens of small start-up companies, taking advantage of the additional bandwidth laid on to NASREC, where the IBC was temporarily erected, and could, for example, have built space for some kind of technology incubation, such as those currently found in Cape Town. Offering free or cheap high-speed broadband, for example, might have been just the spur the local web and mobile industry needed.

In Cape Town, a number of larger-scale projects do, by contrast, have the potential to create opportunities for media industry growth. It is interesting that the main three Cape Town initiatives are likely to promote three different models of clusters. The Cape Town Film Studios initiative promises to deliver a major set of mass media infrastructure, where smaller film, TV and post-production, a film school and allied industries will come together – or at least, so it is hoped by the developers. The Cape Town Creative Cluster is by contrast more of a 'virtual network' of media companies, along the lines described by Picard (2008). The Bandwidth Barn is, in turn, a more organized model of clustering and more centred on the idea of creating economies of scale.

But from the sources this chapter has explored, in both cities, there is no real sense of what a proliferation of new media companies might bring to the spatial and developmental mix of South Africa's major cities.

Despite this, South Africa is likely to remain the strongest player within South African Development Community (SADC) media, especially when it comes to the development of community media. Community media have, in the face of great challenges, given marginalized communities access to more diverse and plural media in South Africa. The Department of Communication has also discussed the issue of developing hubs for community radio, where stronger community radio stations would be the anchor for other struggling stations in terms of skills and resources. This idea has also not been taken up by the sector in any fullness, which means each station still functions independently and is struggling financially, but there are indications that more resources may be on the way soon.

In the context of its locale and developments in both the region and the rest of Africa, South African media are still growing and despite their shortcomings, organizations like the MDDA are still substantially more effective than their counterparts, where these exist, in other African countries. Overall, the legacy of high degrees of apartheid-era concentration and, post-democracy, rather anaemic efforts at media transformation, poor management of the national broadcaster, some antipathy to critical media, and expensive cellular and broadband costs has left many clear opportunities to develop the media industry in South Africa undeveloped.

Until a case for media development is better made and better accepted by South African governments at all levels, media development will in the future, as in the past, be driven more by the private sector than by any government initiatives. The attendant benefits of planned media industry clustering will, in all likelihood, remain elusive.

NOTES

1. The Independent Group's main South African base is in Johannesburg; its international headquarters are in Ireland. Naspers is a multinational media company, based in Cape Town. Although much of its energy is now focused outside of South Africa, Naspers Cape Town HQ is still the hub of substantial operations in South Africa.
2. For example, there have been efforts by the giant Naspers media group to offer Broad-Based Black Economic Empowerment opportunities for some of their businesses, through, for example, the Welkom Yizani scheme to sell part of their Media 24 Group and the Phuthuma Nathi and Futhi share schemes to dilute white ownership of their MultiChoice/DStv business.
3. Within three years of coming to office, the government also offered eight new commercial radio licences in South Africa's three biggest cities – Johannesburg, Cape Town and Durban. This added to the five existing commercial radio licences. This expanded commercial radio options, although most licences went to existing firms, some in collaboration with black partners. Currently, according to the MDDA (2008), '[t]here are 13 private commercial radio stations which are all regional or provincial stations. According to AMPS 2008, these have 16.5 per cent of the total radio adult audience'.
4. The South African Broadcast Corporation (SABC) is a Public Broadcast Service, which owns three free-to-air television stations and 18 radio stations, of which 15 are public broadcasting service (PBS) stations and three are public commercial services (PCS) stations. The SABC accounts for about 41.6 per cent of the total radio audience in the country according to AMPS 2008 (Media Development and Diversity Agency, 2009). e.tv is the only independent free-to-air commercial television licence holder in South Africa. In total, South Africans have access to four free-to-air television stations, with only those with the financial wherewithal gaining access to the DStv bouquet of television offerings.

5. The *Iindaba Ziyafika* project funded by the US-based John S. and James L. Knight Foundation, and located at Rhodes University, is collecting data on all active community newspapers in South Africa.
6. There are four licensed community television stations in South Africa: Soweto Community TV in Johannesburg, Bay Television Station in Durban, Cape Town Community TV and The Trinity Broadcasting Network (TBN) licensed for terrestrial broadcasting in the Eastern Cape and also distributed by satellite on DStv (Media Development and Diversity Agency, 2008).
7. Regional SABC radio stations have studios in different cities, and e.tv, the only free-to-air commercial channel yet licensed in South Africa, has offices in Johannesburg and Cape Town and smaller offices in other cities. With digital migration, both SABC and e.tv will be receiving a large number of digital channels on three multiplexes to be licensed over 2010–2011. Acquiring content for these may lead to some growth in the impendent production industry.
8. The growth rate of the Johannesburg economy has been higher than that of the South African economy over the period 1996 to 2004. Between 2000 and 2004 the Johannesburg economy grew 5.29 per cent on average. The South African economy grew 3.29 per cent per annum on average (City of Johannesburg, 2006).
9. Cape Argus (October, 2008). Films such as 'Lord of War' (2005), 'Blood Diamonds' (2006), '10 000 BC' (2008) and a host of so-called 'Bollywood' movies were shot in Cape Town.
10. Cape Argus (October 2008).

REFERENCES

Acuna, A. (2010), telephone interview with the IBC manager 18 February 2010.

Alfers, D. (2010), telephone interview 27 May 2010.

All Media Product Survey, produced by the South African Advertising Research Foundation, accessible at http://www.saarf.co.za/.

Bandwidth Barn (2010), available at http://www.bandwidthbarn.org/services.html, accessed April 2010.

Barnett, C. (1999). 'The Limits of Media Democratization in South Africa: Politics, Privatization and Regulation', *Media, Culture and Society*, **21**(5), 649–671.

Berger, G. (2006), 'Contested Media Environments in South Africa: Developments in Regard to the Making of Communications Policy since 1994', draft paper for the After Apartheid Conference, 11–12 August 2006, Cape Town, SA.

Berger, G. (2009), 'South Africa's Mediascape Faces the Challenge of Getting More Voices', available at http://www.mdda.org.za/south%20africas_mediascape.htm, accessed 12 April 2010.

Bethlehem, L. (2010), CEO, Johannesburg Development Agency (JDA), telephone interview May 2010.

Blandy, F. (2009), 'Cape Film Studios will be Africa's Largest: Local Industry Certain to Reap Fruits of State-of-the-art Venue, which is Expected to Attract More International Projects', *The Star* (2009).

Bond, P. (2010), 'South Africa's Bubble Meets Boiling Urban Social Protest', *Monthly Review*, **62**(2), available at http://monthlyreview.org/100601bond.php, accessed October 2009.

Boraine, A., O. Crankshaw, C. Engelbrecht, G. Gotz, S. Mbanga, M. Narsoo and S. Parnell (2006), 'The State of South African Cities a Decade after Democracy', *Urban Studies*, **43**(2), 259–284.

Cape Argus (2008), 'South Africa: Lights, Camera and Action at Last', staff reporter.

Cape Town Partnership website (2010), available at http://www.capetownpartnership.co.za/about/, accessed April 2010.

City of Johannesburg (2006), 'Growth and Development Strategy', available at http://www.joburg-archive.co.za/2006/pdfs/gds_book/chapter2.pdf, accessed April 2010.

Creative Cape Town website (2010), available at http://www.creativecapetown.net/creative-cape-town-maps/, accessed 3 March 2010.

Duncan, J. (2009), 'Mobile Network Society? Cellphones and the Overreach of Social Theory', unpublished working paper, Rhodes University.

Guardian, The (2010), 'ANC's Julius Malema Lashes out at "Misbehaving" BBC Journalist', available at http://www.guardian.co.uk/world/2010/apr/08/anc-julius-malema-bbc-journalist, accessed April 2010.

Hadland, A. and K. Thorne (2004), *The People's Voice: The Development and Current State of the South African Small Media Sector*, Cape Town, SA: HSRC Publishers.

Horwitz, R.B. (2001a), *Communication and Democratic Reform in South Africa*, Cambridge, UK: Cambridge University Press.

Horwitz, R.B. (2001b), '"Negotiated Liberalization": Stakeholder Politics and Communication Sector Reform in South Africa', paper presented at the 29th TPRC Conference, in Nancy Morris and Silvio Waisbord (eds), *Media and Globalization: Why the State Matters*, Boulder, CO, USA: Rowman & Littlefield, pp. 34–38.

IOL Technology (2010), 'FISPA Calls for Lower Broadband Price', available at http://www.ioltechnology.co.za/article_page.php?iArticleId=5484642, accessed 25 May 2010.

Johannesburg News Agency (2010a), 'Media', available at http://www.joburg.org.za/content/view/109/58/, accessed 13 April 2010.

Johannesburg News Agency (2010b), 'Jewel City to Sparkle Soon', available at http://www.joburgnews.co.za/2007/may/may9_jewelcity.stm, accessed 12 April 2010.

Levin, A. (2010), telephone interview with Bandwidth Barn founding member, 8 March 2010.

Mayor of Johannesburg (2008), *Executive Mayor's Mid-term Report*, available at http://www.joburg-archive.co.za/2008/pdfs/midterm_Report/chapter3.pdf, p. 88, accessed April 2010.

Media Development and Diversity Agency (2008), *MDDA Annual Report 2007/2008*. The annual reports are numbered 2007/2008, 2008/2009, etc, available at http://www.mdda.org.za/, accessed April 2010.

Media Development and Diversity Agency (2009), *Trends of Ownership and Control of Media in South Africa*, Johannesburg, SA: MDDA.

Minty, Z. (2010), E-mail interview with Creative Cape Town coordinator 4 March 2010, Cape Town, SA [questionnaire in possession of authors].

MyBroadband (2009), 'Internet Access in South Africa', available at http://mybroadband.co.za/news/Internet/7885.html, accessed 5 June 2010.

Picard, R. (2008), *Media Clusters: Local Agglomeration in an Industry Developing Networked Virtual Clusters*, Jonkoping International Business School Working Paper Series No. 2008-3, Jonkoping, SWE: Jonkoping University.

Population Reference Bureau and African Population & Health Research Centre

(2008), *2008 Africa Population Data Sheet*, available at http://www.prb.org/pdf08/africadatasheet2008.pdf, accessed April 2010.

Powell, A. (2008), Film Studios, Digital-media Hub Launched at Faure, *Cape Times* (2008).

Rogerson, C.M. and J.M. Rogerson (1997) 'The Changing Post-apartheid City: Emergent Black-owned Small Enterprises in Johannesburg', *Urban Studies*, **34**(1), 85–103.

Seedat, R. (2010), Head of Strategy, Johannesburg City Metro Council, interview March 2010.

SouthAfrica.info (2010), '2010 broadcast centre "ready to go live"', available at http://www.southafrica.info/2010/wcibc-240510.htm, accessed 5 June 2010.

Sowetan, The (2009), 'South Africa Gets Own Hollywood – Cape Town Film Studios Also Gives Bollywood a Run for its Money', author unknown.

World Wide Worx, Research Notes http://www.worldwideworx.com/2010/05/27/mobile-internet-booms-in-sa/, accessed 17 June 2010.

14. Can Singapore develop into a global media city?

Sören Eriksson

Singapore, one of the very successful examples of Asia's Newly Industrializing Economies, has gone through an impressive economic development since its independence. The progress has been based on various development plans, encompassing a number of industrial policy schemes. The government's vision is to develop Singapore as a global media hub in a general strategy to further transform the economy and move into more modern and value-added tertiary activities. The ambitions to promote the media industry must be seen in the light and context of the nation's overall economic development.

THE FORMATIVE YEARS AND FOUNDING POLICIES

On 3 June 1959 Singapore attained full internal self-government after nearly 140 years of British colonial rule, although Britain retained control of foreign affairs and defence. The first elections held under the new Constitution resulted in a strong mandate for the People's Action Party (PAP), whose platform included total independence for Singapore and a merger with Malaya. The PAP wanted to become part of a larger unit not only for the sake of political stability, but also for the economic benefits of a large market for the island's developing industries. Singapore joined the Federation of Malaysia at its inception in 1963. After only two years – a period of a variety of disagreements – Singapore decided to withdraw from the union.

Singapore's rapid economic growth and good record in solving major social issues such as public housing, crime, corruption and health issues could be traced back to Singapore's model of development (SMD), which refers to nine major policies introduced by the PAP government since 1959 to ensure good life for all Singaporeans through political stability and economic growth (Quah, 1998). The SMD comprises the following nine policies:

1. Promotion of economic development
2. Satisfaction of the population's needs
3. Minimization of corruption
4. Heavy investment in education
5. Emphasis on meritocracy
6. Maintenance of racial harmony
7. Learning from others
8. Rejection of the welfare state
9. Adoption of a comprehensive approach to curbing crime.

In 1959 the prospects for Singapore were unfavourable for a number of reasons. The entrepot trade was declining due to increased trading by the neighbouring countries – the Federation of Malaya and Indonesia. Unemployment was on the rise, especially due to the high population growth rate. Housing was a serious problem with half of the population living in squatter huts, and Singapore had the classical features of a developing country. It lacked natural resources apart from its strategic location and natural harbour and human potential.

The underlying circumstances implied a strategy of industrialization, and in 1960 the government invited a United Nations mission led by the Dutch economist Albert Winsemius. The mission team recommended a strong emphasis on reducing the unemployment as well as a ten-year programme that included creating an investment climate for industrialization, an export drive and incentives to attract foreign investment (Chia, 1986).

During the discussions Winsemius stressed two preconditions for succeeding with the development process. First, get rid of the communists from the government, the unions and the streets. Secondly, let Raffles (the British statesman who founded Singapore in 1819) stand where he stands today, meaning that you accept the heavy ties with the West as you need them in your *economic development* programme (Drysdale, 1984).

Satisfaction of the population's needs embraced a 'nation-building role', i.e. bringing Singaporeans of different ethnic, linguistic or religious groups together, thereby providing them with increased opportunities for interacting with and understanding one another.

The third point, *minimization of corruption*, has been a crucial factor in building up Singapore's economy after independence. Throughout its modern history, Singapore has taken various measures to fight corruption and has a very sound anti-corruption framework, with a strong emphasis on the investigation and prosecution of corruption cases.

Singapore is the least corrupt country in Asia and is also a top performer in the world (Transparency International; various annual surveys). From a global view, Singapore has been ranked 4 to 5 for many years,

Table 14.1 Corruption Perception Index

Rank	Country	CPI 2008 score
1	Denmark	9.3
1	New Zealand	9.3
1	Sweden	9.3
4	Singapore	9.2
5	Finland	9.0
5	Switzerland	9.0
7	Iceland	8.9
7	Netherlands	8.9
9	Australia	8.7
9	Canada	8.7

Source: Transparency International

which implies that Singapore has a unique position in East and South East Asia where many countries suffer from corruption, in some cases endemic. The policy against corruption has been one of many crucial measures to ensure Singapore's successful economic development.

Heavy investment in education is closely linked to Confucian thinking and the 'belief in the perfectibility and educability of human beings' (Tai, 1989, p. 24). Since independence, Singapore has invested heavily in education. The strength of Singapore's education system lies in its bilingual policy (English with Malay/Mandarin/Tamil) and Singapore's public schools have a distinctive record of high standards in teaching and learning, illustrated by international comparative studies such as the Third International Mathematics and Science Study (TIMSS), which showed the majority of students from Singapore schools outperforming the international average in mathematics and science. Students have also excelled in competitions such as world debating championships (English) and International Olympiads (mathematics, physics, chemistry and biology).

At the tertiary level, in addition to boasting three locally grown universities, Singapore has attracted about ten world-class institutions with strong industry links to set up centres of excellence in education and research.

Meritocracy is a central political concept in Singapore. Michael Young coined the term in his book *The Rise of the Meritocracy* (1958). The meritocracy concept was adopted early by Lee Kuan Yew and his government and should be seen in the light of the city-state's rise to independence. One of the reasons behind Singapore's withdrawal from the union with Malaysia in 1965 was the unwillingness of the majority of its population, mostly ethnic Chinese, to accept a 'special position' for the self-proclaimed

Bumiputra, the Malays. The federal Malaysian government had argued for a system that would give special privileges to the Malays as part of their 'birthright' as an 'indigenous' people.

Political leaders in Singapore vehemently protested against this system, arguing instead for the equality of all citizens of Malaysia, with places in universities, government contracts, political appointments, etc going to the most deserving candidates rather than to those chosen on the basis of connections or ethnic background. To this day, Singapore continues to hold up meritocracy as one of its official guiding principles for domestic public policy formulation.

There is criticism that this system has some negative disadvantages, that the Singaporean society is being created from just a narrow segment of the population. Although most Singaporeans still agree that the city-state's tremendous economic success has been due in part to its strong emphasis on developing and promoting talented leaders, there are some who believe that Singapore is becoming an elitist society. A criticism heard, although not officially expressed, is that Singapore's authoritarian political system with censorship and alleged gerrymandering creates people who think increasingly alike.

Maintenance of racial harmony is an important concept in the Singaporean society. Singapore is a multiracial, multilingual and multireligious society. Its population of 4.84 million (2008), of whom 3.64 million are Singaporean citizens and permanent residents, consists of various Chinese linguistic groups (75.2 per cent), Malays (13.6 per cent) and Indians (8.8 per cent), while Eurasians and other groups represent 2.4 per cent (Statistics Singapore). There are four official languages (English, Malay, Mandarin and Tamil) plus several non-official Chinese dialects and Indian languages spoken.

The concept of racial harmony should be seen in the light of the serious riots in Singapore during the 1960s. Racial/religious harmony is looked upon as a very important policy to maintain a stable society and thus stimulate future prosperous development. A number of various measures have been implemented to ensure that both public and private organizations are fair in their treatment of their clientele, regardless of their ethnicity, language or religion.

Culture is a very crucial variable in this multiethnic society. Media issues in Singapore must be viewed as a kind of multilevel chess game with economic considerations constituting only the most apparent variables and political and cultural factors playing themselves out on underlying levels (Edge, 2004).

Singapore's media are strongly censored also from various language perspectives. In TV and in the Singapore cable network only one Chinese dialect is allowed, Mandarin. The other Chinese dialects are filtered through government censorship. It is still (in 2010) prohibited to own a private satellite receiving box, steering the general population towards the content-controllable cable television.

Learning from others instead of reinventing the wheel, has been a long-term solution for policy issues and problems in Singapore. This is closely related to the expression 'let Raffles stand' meaning that you accept the heavy ties with the West, as you need them in your economic development programme. Many of the policies implemented have been modified to suit Singapore's local context. Singapore has been very successful in implementing a number of various policies, and due to the political structure the government has been able to do so very rapidly.

Rejection of the welfare state is a policy that contradicts many people's perception of Singapore as a Southeast Asian welfare state. It implies that the government 'has never committed significant government funds to social security for the unemployed, disabled, aged, or indigent' (Lim, 1989), thus implying more of mandatory savings for each citizen.

The approach to curbing crime has been a fundamental policy in shaping the stability of modern Singapore. During the colonial period, the Singapore Police Force (SPF) had three major problems: the Chinese secret societies, police corruption, and rioting and internal security (Mak, 1981; Phang, 1990). Chinese secret societies were curbed with the help of the Criminal Law Act (CLTPA) of 1958. Police corruption was greatly reduced by various measures and the problem of riots and internal security is no longer there today, although it is still considered the most serious latent threat in the case of a dramatic economic downturn or other external or internal circumstances that can put Singapore's development and stability into jeopardy.

Singapore is well known for its tough law enforcement regarding crime. The crime rate is considerably lower than for most other cities of similar size. Singapore has one of the world's highest rates of executions relative to its population. Curbing crime has been a deliberate choice to secure stable economic development.

ECONOMIC GROWTH

Lee Kuan Yew's government launched Singapore's industrial revolution in the 1960s by attracting foreign investors and multinationals with tax concessions, cheap and reliable labour, efficient public services and political stability. In the first development plan 1961–1964, industrial sites and factories were constructed at Jurong, although it was only from 1967 that foreign companies started to arrive in significant numbers (Huff, 1994, p. 309). This phase of development had a strong emphasis on labour-intensive manufacturing such as electronics equipment, light industrial hardware, wood products and textiles.

In the mid-1960s, the government also prepared Singapore for its future key position in the financial world when it broke up the cartel of British and local banks that had maintained a stranglehold on finance. Two Swiss-style concessions, tax exemption for depositors and strict secrecy, also helped make Singapore the 'Zürich of the East'. In 1967 the Economic Expansion Act superseded the earlier incentives, taxing the profits of export industries at 4 per cent, instead of the usual 40 per cent, for 10–15 years. In addition, the government reinforced the liberal investment regime, renewing Singapore's free port status and limited controls on foreign investment, ownership and profit repatriation (Perry, Kong and Yeoh, 1997).

The 1970s and the 1980s

The second phase of development (1974–1984) was characterized by slower overall growth, mainly associated with two international oil shocks. Even so, economic growth remained high and new taxation incentives were implemented as well as expansion of technical training and efforts to upgrade local industry.

In 1975 a list of priority industries was published, while domestic market and low-value, labour-intensive industries such as food and beverages, textile and wood products declined in relative importance. Chemical products, fabricated metal products, electrical and electronic products and components as well as machinery and precision industries developed strongly. The petroleum industry expanded rapidly and Singapore became the petroleum-refining centre of the Asia-Pacific region and received the epithet 'Houston of Asia' (Doshi, 1989).

In the late 1970s, when Singapore's average annual growth rate of 9.4 per cent was one of the highest in the world, the second international oil crisis resulted in developed countries introducing protectionist measures. The government responded by launching the so-called 'second industrial revolution'. Compared with other Asian NIEs (Hong Kong, South Korea and Taiwan), the Singapore economy seemed to be slow in intensifying the use of capital and skill (Tan, 1995).

The prospects of being squeezed between these apparently more productive economies and lower cost locations opening up in the region (Indonesia, Malaysia and Thailand) also contributed to implementing the new industrial strategy. The government defined new priority sectors, all linked to high technology and more advanced services. At the same time, the National Wages Council moved towards a substantial increase in pay, designed to delocalize industries that were the most labour-intensive and weakest in value-added (Regnier, 1992, p.56). Increase in research and development (R&D) and technical skills was given special focus. The government dramatically increased expenditure on education and special emphasis was placed on engineering studies (Rodan, 1989).

In 1985, for the first time since independence, the Singaporean economy suddenly contracted from a growth rate that had stood at 8.2 per cent in 1984 to one of minus 1.8 per cent in 1985. Trade, transport, communications and financial services were still growing, but construction and manufacturing had tumbled; oil refining and electronics were worst hit. One explanation of the recession was the wage correction policy, but there were also a number of other explanations. Part of the problem was that rises in earnings were beginning to outstrip productivity gains, implying that Singapore was ceasing to be a cheap-labour economy.

The 1986 report of the Economic Committee (*The Singapore Economy: New Directions*, 1986) marked a watershed in the Singaporean leaders' vision of the future, from a strong industrial base to a much more diversified, mostly tertiary economy, concentrating on advanced services (Margolin, 1993, p. 93). Still, several parts of the manufacturing sector were identified as playing an important future role, but there was a need of a general upgrading. Another new opportunity was identified to attract the regional operational headquarters (OHQs) of multinational companies, which was hoped would stimulate demand for business services. An OHQ incentive scheme was introduced designed to make Singapore's taxation environment suitable to regional head offices and competitive with Hong Kong, while other services eligible for the investment incentives were reserved for manufacturers only.

> Singapore aims to become an important strategic node of global companies for the Asia-Pacific region. [. . .] On the one hand, they should integrate backwards into activities such as production engineering, product design, research and development; on the other hand, they should integrate forwards into marketing, technical support, after sales services and ultimately regional management (Economic Development Board, 1988, p.12).

The immediate post-recession recovery was driven primarily by strong manufacturing growth, partly due to increased demand of electronic products and components from the United States as well as increased demand from other Asian Economies (Rodan, 1993). Another very important reason for Singapore's recovery was the large increase of Japanese foreign direct investment into Singapore and the neighbouring economies, which gave further stimulus to Singapore through its emerging role as the regional coordination centre for Japanese MNCs (Aoki and Tachiki, 1992).

The 1990s

In 1991, the Strategic Economic Plan – Towards a Developed Nation – was presented. It was partly a restatement of established goals, but also spoke about Singapore as a global city, by making it a 'total business hub' for the Asia-Pacific offering business location on par with other leading global cities. The National Science and Technology Board (NSTB) was established in 1991, and development of technological abilities has since then been orchestrated through national science and technology plans (NSTP), also accompanied by increasing investments in R&D and technological infrastructure (Blomqvist, 2005). The NSTB identified 13 various industrial clusters (WTEC, 1997) targeted for development.

Industry 21 was launched in 1999 to develop Singapore as a vibrant global hub of knowledge industries in manufacturing and traded services. Strategies for services were grouped under International Business Hub 2000, which aimed at developing the city-state as a global city and a hub for business and finance, logistics and distribution, and communication and information (Chia and Lim, 2003).

Tied to recommendations to develop Singapore's industrial sector is Hutton's (2004) account of an explicit strategy that fosters developmental synergies between technology (mainly ICT), culture in the form of creative and design service industries and 'place' as expressed in the innovative milieu of the inner city. Singapore's tourism sector has become increasingly important and can be considered a key component of the economy. The effort to develop the city-state into a major tourist destination has been successful.

Much of the effort has essentially involved the continuous reinvention of Singapore, as the Singapore Tourism Board has sought to develop attractions in the city-state for tourists (Ooi and Shaw, 2004). Various advertisements, such as 'Instant Asia' and 'Surprising Singapore' have been designed for this purpose promoting the country as a shopping centre (Savage, 1997). In recent years 'Uniquely Singapore' has been used. Singapore's government has actively worked to promote the nation and to attract and host various international events placing it in the global media limelight. One such event is the FIA Formula 1 night race, which took place in 2008 and 2009. Singapore has developed into one of Asia's main tourism spots with over 10 million visitors in 2008.

In early 2010 the 'Resort World Sentosa' was inaugurated, consisting of new hotels, a large casino, the world's largest oceanarium and a large-scale theme park. The latter, The Universal Studios Theme Park, is a part of Singapore's strategic efforts to build up the media industry, due to its heavy use of digital media.

Since the late 1990s Singapore has promoted itself as a regional medical hub. The authorities hope to serve 1 million foreign patients annually by 2012 and generate US$3 billion in revenue. Singapore is known to have world-class medical treatment and a state-of-the-art infrastructure.

The 1985/86 Economic Committee led by Minister of State BG Lee Hsien Loong identified education as one of several other service sectors to be nurtured and promoted (*The Singapore Economy: New Directions*, 1986). Education was recognized for its revenue growth potential and net worth to the economy as well as its export-earning potential. To develop the postgraduate segment of the industry, the EDB in 1998 embarked on a plan to attract at least ten world-class universities to establish a significant presence in Singapore.

Singapore Education is a multi-government agency initiative launched by the Singapore government in 2003 to establish and promote Singapore as a premier education hub and help international students in Singapore. This initiative is led by the Singaporean Economic Development Board and supported by the Singapore Tourism Board, SPRING Singapore, International Enterprise Singapore and the Ministry of Education.

Owing to the Asian financial crisis (1997–1998) and the slowdown of global economic activity in connection with the IT/telecommunication crisis starting in 2001, Singapore's subsequent growth rates have been more volatile. In 2002 Singapore faced its worst economic performance year since 1965. Then a period of strong economic performance followed, but the global economic recession starting in 2008 has had a strong negative impact on the nation.

Singapore has gone through an extensive structural transformation process since the 1960s. From being dependent on a few economic pillars, mainly entrepot trade and the British military base, at the time of independence, it has now established itself as a nation with a number of different very competitive industrial and service sectors.

In 1965, when Singapore became a fully independent nation, the per capita GNP was typical of that of a developing country at US$512 per annum. In 2007, the per capita GNP went up nearly 64 times to US$32,624 per annum (nominal US dollar).

Some of the sectors in Figure 14.1 have only domestic importance, while others have regional or even global influence.

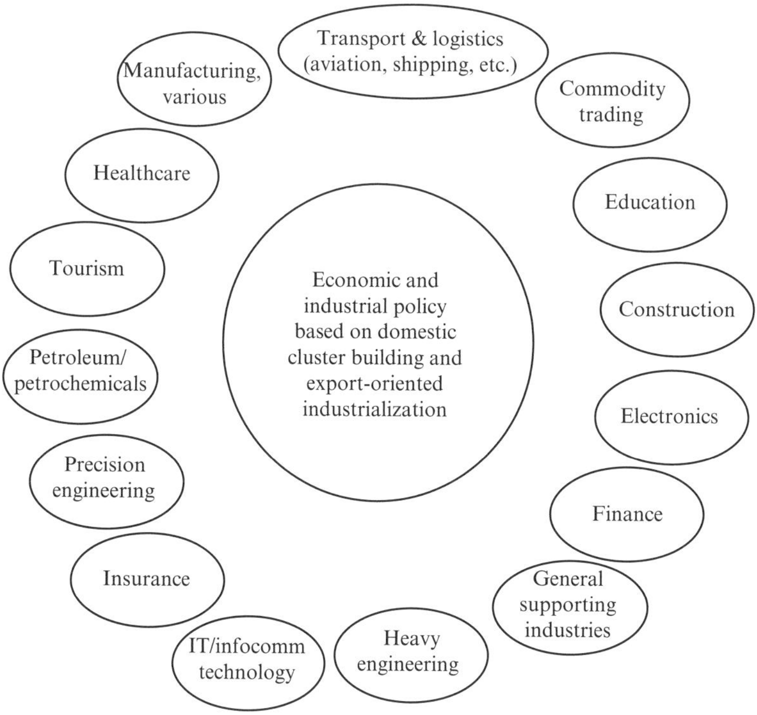

Source: Own adaption.

Figure 14.1 Singapore's main economic and industrial clusters in the early 21st century

MEDIA CLUSTER DEVELOPMENT

Being More Creative

Although Singapore has had 45 years of successful economic development, the government is trying to steer the economy away from traditional manufacturing and trading sectors towards more modern and value-added service and trading sectors. This has also taken place along with a long-term debate in Singapore about the need to be more creative and innovative.

An early step was taken after the release of the 1989 Report of the Advisory Council on Culture and the Arts (Ooi, 2008). When The National Arts Council was formed in 1991, with more support given to arts groups, schools started offering arts programmes and the government started to pay more attention to arts and culture (Chang and Lee, 2003). The next step, based on the 1989 recommendations, was taken when in 1995 the Singapore Tourist Promotion Board (STPB) and the Ministry of Information, Communication and the Arts (MICA) took the initiative to develop Singapore into a 'Global City for the Arts' (Chang, 2000).

In 2000, MICA decided to push the 1995 policy a step further by envisaging Singapore as a 'Renaissance City' (MITA, 2000). This report was the basis for the Economic Review Committee's (2002) 'Creative Industries Development Strategy: Propelling Singapore's Creative Economy' – the most ambitious blueprint on the creative economy – which also includes plans to develop the media and design sectors. Singapore focuses on three creative sectors (Economic Review Committee, 2002, p. iii):

- Arts and Culture: performing arts, visual arts, literary arts, photography, crafts, libraries, museums, galleries, heritage sites, performing arts sites, festivals and arts, etc.
- Design: advertising, architecture, web and software, graphics industrial products, fashion, interior and environmental issues, etc.
- Media: broadcasting (including radio, television and cable), digital media (including software and computer services), film and video, recorded music and publishing.

The main role to spearhead initiatives to promote industry growth in film, television, radio, publishing, music, games, animation and interactive digital media has been given to the Media Development Authority. It was formed in January 2003 from the merger of the Singapore Broadcasting Authority, the Films and Publications Department and the Singapore Film Commission. MDA was created to develop Singapore into a global media city and to foster a creative economy. MDA also has a regulatory role to foster a good business environment for industry players.

Together with the Economic Development Board (EDB) and the Infocomm Development Authority of Singapore (IDA), MDA will be responsible for developing Singapore as the region's media hub. EDB is the leading government agency responsible for planning and executing economic strategies to enhance Singapore's position as a global hub for business and investments. IDA was formed in 1999 when the government merged the National Computer Board (NCB) and the Telecommunication Authority of Singapore (TAS), through the passing of the Info-Communications Development Authority of Singapore Act as a result of a growing convergence of information technology and telephony.

According to Ooi (2006), the authorities use a three-pronged approach to make Singapore into a creative hub:

1. Market Singapore as a creative hub and thus generate the appropriate public image.
2. Formulate and implement business-friendly policies.
3. Use social engineering by building consensus towards the advent of the creative economy, cultivating a creative consumer base, training a workforce suitable for the creative economy and eventually hoping for a place that oozes creativity.

Critics have pointed out that the cultural capital injected into the Singapore cultural economy is basically 'hardware' or the tangible pieces encompassing cultural facilities, programmes and festivals, while there is a lack of nurturing the 'software' or intangible aspects of cultural capital (Wong, Millar and Choi, 2006). Without nurturing the 'soft sides' of culture and divergent expressions and views within film, art and theatre, the basis for Singapore to become a global media city is very slim.

The Media 21 Blueprint

In July 2003 the Media Development Authority (MDA) launched Media 21, a blueprint that is the guiding document concerning measures and strategy to become the regional media hub envisaged as a Global Media City. MDA refers to three key drivers of Singapore's growth as well as that of the global media industry:

- an increased demand for knowledge, information and entertainment spurred by the knowledge economy;
- a growth of broadband networks and usage, which has created large highways on which attractions (or media content) can be developed and marketed;
- technology advancements, particularly digitization, which have transformed the whole value chain of the media industry.

Singapore's method of developing its approach for levelling up with and leapfrogging its competitors is based on six strategic thrusts (MDA and Media 21 Blueprint).

The first step is to establish Singapore as a media exchange centre, positioning Singapore as an Asian media marketplace, including the creation, development and distribution of media content and services. This is also done in partnerships with established international markets. MDA has also developed Media Awards, which are supposed to recognize talent, spur competition and enhance the glamour of the media industry. Other parts are the development of Singapore as a Media Financing Hub and enhancement of knowledge of intellectual property rights (IPR) and digital rights management tools.

The second step is named 'Export Made-by-Singapore Content' aimed at establishing content development schemes for a wider audience, such as the TV Content IDS (Industry Development Scheme). The objectives are to boost the range and quality of local films and TV for export and strengthen niche genres such as digital animation, documentaries, business and education. Some of Singapore's producers are experienced in producing documentaries for international channels like Discovery and National Geographic. There is also a growing demand for educational content, particularly English for the Chinese market. Yet another part is to increase bilateral co-production agreements with targeted countries. MDA and other government agencies are supposed to facilitate co-production agreements and collaborations with overseas governments and industry organizations. This will enable Singapore's media companies to get access to foreign production expertise, financing and foreign distribution networks and markets.

The next step has the overall title 'Deploy Digital Media'. A major trend in the media and entertainment industry is the shift to digital technology across the value chain. This applies all the way from production and user interface to distribution and storage. There is a need to attract high-end digital production companies and to enhance talent and skills in digital production. Content creation is a key to the growth of the digital media industry in Singapore. The Digital Content Development Scheme promotes the development of new ideas and concepts into real content products. It includes episodes for original TV animation, technical demos for game series and interactive media products. This part also includes the development of Singapore into a digital cinema distribution hub for the region.

The fourth step is to internationalize Singapore Media Enterprises. Singapore has a small domestic market and media enterprises need to expand their markets beyond the national borders. MDA's Market Development Scheme assists local media companies in their development of overseas markets. It is seen as crucial for Singapore to nurture its own homegrown media companies if it is to be a global media city. Today Singapore has a few large media companies, which can be an impetus for new emerging companies.

The fifth step is labelled 'Augment Media Talent'. MDA works with various tertiary institutions to increase media education and training at the polytechnic and university levels, such as the National University of Singapore (NUS) and Nanyang Technology University. Feasibility studies of setting up a Media Academy are under way. Such an establishment could take the form of collaboration with renowned international media schools. MDA assists in developing core competencies to support content development. It will mainly focus on enhancing creative writing skills and the art of drawing and illustrating across all media. Another measure is to embed media training into school curricula. MDA works with the Ministry of Education to enhance creative writing and drawing skills at the pre-school, primary and secondary levels. At secondary and tertiary levels, videography and graphic skills training will be implemented.

The last step is to foster a conducive business and regulatory environment. An important part is to promote Fusionopolis@one-north, which is planned as an entire media ecosystem. It aims to be a home for an active community of researchers, content creators, financiers and other industry players from all over the world. This will be a cluster within the greater Singapore cluster creating vertical and horizontal chains in Singapore as well as abroad. MDA plans to make Singapore an attractive place for content development and will work with various agencies to facilitate media production. Sentosa Island has been mentioned as a site for location shoots. MDA has the ambition to ensure that its regulatory policies and business practices are progressive and follow international best practices. Another measure is to increase media literacy and appreciation. MDA works with a series of programmes to foster a culture of appreciation for media products among Singaporeans.

Main Structure and Importance of Singapore's Media Industry

Even if the new emerging media cluster development has its focus on new factors of growth such as digital media, Singapore has had a relatively large media industry based on radio, TV and the publishing sector.

State-owned MediaCorp operates all seven free-to-air terrestrial local television channels licensed to broadcast in Singapore, as well as most of the radio channels except four stations which are operated by SAFRA Radio (a part of Singapore Armed Forces), and the newspaper publisher Singapore Press Holdings Ltd (SPH). Although not directly controlling the SPH by ownership, the government has an indirect control of SPH through a complex web of shareholdings and management influences.

Print media are controlled by the SPH, publisher of the flagship English-language daily *The Straits Times*. The only exception is the daily *Today*, published by MediaCorp.

An interesting media feature regarding *The Straits Times* dates back to the split in 1965 between Malaysia and Singapore. After World War II, *The Straits Times* expanded from its base in Singapore into Malaysia and moved its headquarters to Kuala Lumpur in 1959 after Lee Kuan Yew was elected as Singapore's first prime minister. There had been a tense relationship between Lee and *The Straits Times*, which had opposed much of his policy (Turnbull, 1995).

When the merger between Malaysia and Singapore fell apart in 1965, *The Straits Times* found itself headquartered in a foreign country and the newspaper was forced to move back to Singapore as Malaysia limited foreign ownership of its media. Instead, *The New Straits Times* was established in Malaysia. Since then, owing to political tensions and sensitivities, newspapers from Malaysia cannot be sold in Singapore and vice versa. This is a good example of how old political, racial and social issues still influence the media situation in the region.

The local media industry, covering broadcasting, cinemas, publishing and printing services, music recording, digital and IT-related content services, had an annual turnover of SG$10 billion, contributing 1.56 per cent to Singapore's GDP and employing 38,000 people in 2003 (Media 21). This is planned to increase to 3 per cent of GDP in 2013. The plan also envisages an increase of value-added per worker from SG$66,000 in 2003 to SG$160,000 in 2013 (Media 21, 2003).

According to a report (Deloitte, 2009), the size of Singapore's media industry revenues in 2007 had a total value of SG$19 billion, employing close to 59,000 people (Media Fusion eNewsletter, Issue 28). The core Interactive Digital Media Sector (IDM) revenues grew at a rate of 24.7 per cent from 2007 to 2008 from an estimated SG$1 billion to 1.3 billion. The sector added about 1500 new jobs, growing to an estimated 7400 strong force with around 585 businesses in Singapore conducting an IDM activity.

Overall, exports make up 43 per cent of the revenues, driven by strong business-to-business consumption of IDM services within Singapore, suggesting large domestic investments over the same period. While large companies account for 14 per cent of the number of establishments, the IDM sector is mainly composed of SMEs (67 per cent) and start-ups (19 per cent). Foreign companies account for 21 per cent of the total and domestic firms for 79 per cent (Media Fusion eNewsletter, Issue 28).

Singapore can also be considered a broadcasting hub of Asia, with many of the world's major international satellite and cable networks present and serving the Asia-Pacific Area such as Discovery Channel Asia, Sony Pictures Entertainment Networks, HBO, BBC, CNBC Asia, MTV Asia, ESPN STAR Sports, Walt Disney, etc. Singapore's government has been active in attracting such businesses, also offering various tax incen-

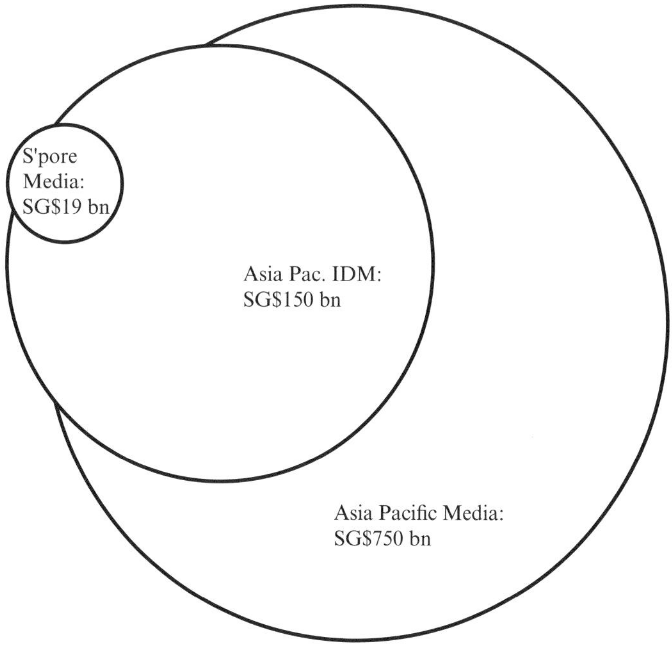

Source: Based on Deloitte (2009).

Figure 14.2 Estimated Media and IDM sector revenues in 2007

tives and financial support. Another basis for attracting foreign companies is the very high quality of Singapore's physical and human infrastructure.

SINGAPORE'S MEDIA CLUSTER – PROSPECTS FOR SUCCESS OR FAILURE

Enabling/Growth Factors

Since the 1980s Singapore has emerged as a major regional industrial hub for information and communication technology (ICT) by leveraging its strategic geographic position, its heavy public investment in telecommunication and transport infrastructure and its public investment in ICT human resource development and by attracting foreign multinational corporations (Wong, 2001).

With the adopted strategy to position Singapore as an ICT hub, Singapore has turned to an overall strategy to develop a more knowledge-based economy. Singapore is well placed for this role due to its rapid and advanced development of ICT and because its other hub activities in commerce and transportation complement the activities of an ICT hub (Chia and Lim, 2003). Thus, for the media industry, Singapore offers a highly developed communication and information technology infrastructure.

Singapore has also positioned itself as a finance, headquarters, logistics and service centre for Southeast Asia. The efforts to build up a media cluster do not evolve from a knowledge vacuum. A very important impetus has been a long-time experience in the manufacturing of electronics goods and subsequent development of supporting service sectors. Singapore's electronics manufacturing started in the early 1970s with labour-intensive assembly of consumer electronics goods. Then it moved into electronics components assembly, and in the early 1980s manufacturing of computer and peripheral products (particularly hard disk drives) became the mainstay of output.

During the last decade there has been considerable downsizing of such production, due to relocation to lower-cost countries in Asia. For instance Seagate, which started disk drive operations in Singapore in 1982, will close manufacturing in 2010 and lay off 2000 workers (*Wall Street Journal*, 5 August 2009). Since the mid-1990s, the focus has shifted more strongly onto electronic components again, mainly in the form of wafer fabrication as well as a growing range of component manufacturing activities for key modules (Wong, 2008).

The electronics goods industry is still an important industrial sector and Singapore is also a trading node in the region for electronics products, parts and components, and supporting services. Singapore's IT software industry is much younger than its hardware counterpart. It is increasingly difficult to distinguish ICT services from traditional non-ICT services as ICT penetrates into all economic sectors.

To develop the media sector, the Singapore government offers various incentives. The Economic and Development Board has allocated SG$500 million to develop the digital media industry for the period between 2006 and 2010. Another SG$500 million will be available for the subsequent five years. Foreign companies are offered tax incentives, resources to set up shops, schemes aimed at education of the workforce and permission to hire foreign specialists (MVD).

A central pillar in Singapore's economic and industrial development has been the strategy of attracting foreign firms, which will also be a key component in the process of developing the nation's media cluster. The ICT sector in general has received key new investments by major overseas firms since the early 21st century. In the digital media industry, players such as

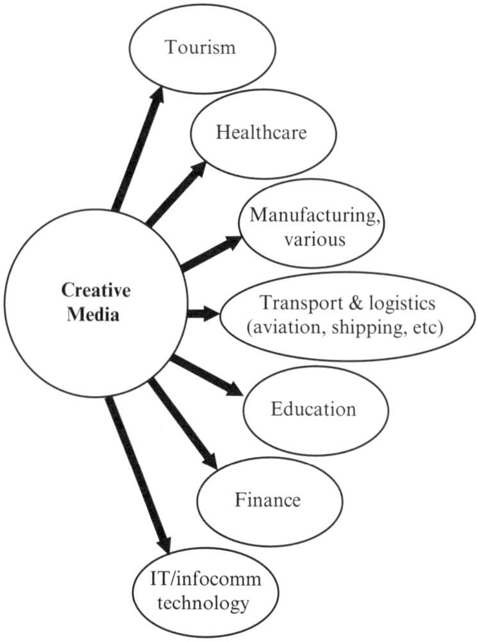

Source: MDA, Media 21 and interviews.

Figure 14.3 Expected spillover from the creative media into other clusters/sectors

Electronic Arts (USA), Genki (Japan), Koei (Japan) and Lucasfilm (USA) have established activities in Singapore. To this should be added numerous other companies in the electronics, IT and telecommunication sectors with direct or indirect applications and technologies that can be used in the IDM sector: Hewlett-Packard (USA), IBM (USA), Motorola (USA), Rohde & Schwarz (Germany), Seagate (USA) and many more.

The Singapore government and the authorities involved in the making of the media cluster hope that the investments in this sector along with production, services, trade and technology flows will spill over into various other industries and sectors, which can lead to the emergence of interrelated clusters.

Impediments to Growth

A problematic view when seeing Singapore as a global media centre is that Singapore is not a nation with free media; it is strongly controlled by the government and this poses dilemmas for a nation with aspiring ambitions of becoming a global communication and media hub. Singapore is seen by many of its larger neighbours in Asia as an economic and political role model, which also has various implications as other authoritarian regimes in Asia are heavily influenced by Singapore's media regulations.

Censorship in Singapore mainly targets political, racial, religious and sexual issues as defined by 'out-of-bounds markers'. These markers, usually abbreviated OB markers, define what topics are allowed for public discussion. However, these markers are not clearly defined; the government can change the markers depending on the political climate and how sensitive issues are. The government argues that censorship of violence and sexual themes is necessary as Singapore's population is deeply conservative. Censorship of political, racial and religious content is seen by authorities as a necessity for maintaining cohesivenesss in a multiracial society. People critical of the censorship argue that it is often used to suppress issues that are sensitive to the government.

Several foreign newspapers/journals have had their circulation capped or otherwise restricted by the government of Singapore, after publishing critical views of the government or being considered slanderous. Examples include *The Economist*, *TIME*, the *Far Eastern Economic Review* and *Asiaweek* (*Asiaweek* ceased publication in 2001), among others. Others have been subject to defamation suits. The *International Herald Tribune* was sued twice after critical articles in 1994, touching sensitive issues about PAP nepotism.

In spite of the strong censorship, major and reputable book publishers such as John Wiley, McGraw-Hill, Addison-Wesley, Simon & Schuster, Reed Elsevier and the Thomson and Times Mirror group have adopted Singapore as their regional base. Evidently, combinations of infrastructure, production and distribution factors, advertising revenue and other considerations have outweighed apprehensions about political control and censorship (Rodan, 2001, p. 72). These types of publishers tend to run into fewer difficulties with authorities than newspapers and news magazines because the content is generally less politically sensitive.

From the very beginning, Singapore's established media outlets were designed to support and justify Singapore's efforts towards nation building. However, Singapore has come a long way in terms of economic and social achievements, and younger generations of Singaporeans will probably demand greater openness.

Freedom of expression is a fundamental condition necessary for creativity, and in recent years there have been signs of more social and political freedom. After following the media debate in Singapore during two decades (author's observations), it seems there are nowadays more open discussions of some political issues and the government seems to be aware that constraining freedom has a negative impact on creativity and innovation. The government is well aware of the importance of innovative capability for the future. Already in the 1990s, issues concerning the Singapore society and creativity/innovation were discussed in a few TV programmes and newspapers (author's observation), although they were not presented as being critical of the government.

Singapore has always been considered a very strict and highly regulated social environment, prone to social engineering, and it seems that some ties have loosened in recent years – this is a concession to the young population and tourists who demand more entertainment and supply of various attractions. Singapore is still rather socially regulated compared with most other countries in the world.

There are still limitations to what one can say about sectors such as art and culture, and criticism of the government is still highly restricted. In 2002 the authorities banned the play *Talaq* by P. Elangovan, as it discusses sensitive issues within an Indian Muslim marriage. Three years later, Martyn See had his film *Singapore Rebel* banned as it was considered political. Producers of films that are considered political can be fined SG$100,000 or be jailed. See was put under police investigation by the Singapore government and forced to surrender all his camera equipment, taped footage and all other materials related to production.

The year after, See made a new film, *Zahari's 17 years*, dealing with Said Zahari's 17 years of incarceration as a political prisoner in Singapore. This film was also banned by the government. Such actions will certainly be counterproductive in the government's effort to build up an internationally competitive media cluster.

Another impedimental factor is the global competition aimed at building media clusters. Singapore is not alone in striving for media industries. Many countries and cities around the world share the same ambitions and search for growth and investments. The situation of the densely populated city-state with very limited space with its very high rental and property costs can be a drawback. Still the emerging Singapore media cluster is very much dependent on foreign specialists and technologies to grow.

CONCLUSIONS AND DISCUSSION

Singapore's ambitions to promote the media industry and the ongoing efforts to develop a competitive media cluster must be seen in the broad light and context of the nation's economic and industrial development. It is not possible to analyse and discuss Singapore's media industry promotion without understanding the complex historical, economic, social and political context.

Singapore is one of the very successful examples of Asia's Newly Industrializing Economies, also labelled economic tigers. This small state has gone through an impressive economic and social development since its independence, and the progress has been based on very deliberate policies such as the SMD and various development plans encompassing a number of industrial policy schemes. Singapore has undergone a huge structural transformation in industry and trade.

Singapore's government has been very ambitious and successful in implementing and executing various economic and industrial policies and adapting to changing global economic conditions. From being dependent on a few economic pillars at the time of independence, it has now established itself as a nation with a number of very different competitive industrial and service sectors.

From the very beginning the economic and industrial polices have been based on export-oriented industrialization. Since the 1990s this has been supplemented by clear statements by the government to develop various economic and industrial clusters. Singapore is striving to become a knowledge-based economy, as it can no longer compete in traditional activities, moving into a much more diversified, mostly tertiary economy.

The most important part of this strategy has been the emergence of Singapore as a very important transportation and logistics hub, an international finance centre and one of Southeast Asia's main tourism spots. This has been accompanied by efforts to establish the country as an educational centre and in recent years as a regional medical service centre.

From early on, the economic policies have been based on a policy to attract foreign investors and multinationals by offering various incentives. This can be traced back to one of the fundamental SMD policies that focuses on *learning from others*.

Singapore's main competitive advantages are a stable legal and political situation, albeit with limited political freedom and freedom of speech, a safe and stable social environment and efficient public service. Other advantages are access to financing due to Singapore's position as a main financial centre and world-class infrastructure including transportation and logistics, IT and telecommunication networks.

A well-educated and loyal workforce and a high-performing educational system also speak in favour of Singapore. As a global top performer in curbing corruption, Singapore is unique in an Asian context where many countries suffer from corruption.

The government's vision since the beginning of the 21st century to develop Singapore as a global media hub is part of the general economic and industrial strategy to further transform the economy and move the nation into more modern and value-added tertiary activities.

As usual when Singapore's government tries to implement new economic or social policies, ambitions and planning take priority. The measures taken influence most parts of society. These influences have been very obvious throughout the last decade as authorities and the state-controlled media have increased and steered the debate more towards the arts and culture, design and media sectors.

The highly increased focus on these creative sectors can be looked upon as a method of making the population more aware of them and their importance. It is like a learning or educational process implemented from above laying the foundation for a more commercialized development of the media sector outlined in the Media 21 blueprint and other documents. It can be considered a way of sending a message, or branding, to the outside world that Singapore is a creative place to be.

What constitutes the basis for the planned development of Singapore's global media cluster? Already before the introduction of the new policy, Singapore had a rather large media sector, mainly structured around domestic newspapers, domestic and international book publishers, radio and TV. The new media cluster will focus on Singapore as a hub where media services and projects are created, developed, traded and distributed to the international market, mainly focusing on the large Asian market.

Due to the limited size of Singapore's media market there is a need to enter export markets, but these are highly competitive and different markets have different characteristics. For instance the large Asian market varies considerably between different countries, due to great variations in development, culture, language, etc. Due to Singapore's multiethnic society there may be a comparative advantage on several markets. Another factor in favour of Singapore is the strong protection of copyrights compared with most other countries in Asia.

Demand refers to three drivers of the global media industry, namely increased demand for knowledge, information and entertainment, i.e. the knowledge economy, growth of broadband networks and advancements in technology, particularly digitization, which have transformed the value chain.

The main focus is now on developing a media cluster, an effort that is divided into six strategic thrusts that aim to establish Singapore as a media exchange centre, promote the export of made-by-Singapore content, deploy digital media, internationalize Singapore media enterprises, promote media talent and foster a conducive business and regulatory environment.

Furthermore, there are hopes for spillover into other sectors of the economy thus creating additional benefits and cross-cluster dynamics.

This we do not know anything about and such effects are only possible to measure in the future.

What are then the obstacles to a successful development? These include lack of free press, constraints on artistic expression and censorship with regard to culture and ethnic and language issues. There are certainly tensions between the economic and political objectives. Another factor that can limit Singapore's possibilities is the circumstance that many other countries and cities have aspiring ambitions to develop their media sectors, posing an increased competition to attract foreign firms necessary to support such development.

Although Singapore is a highly developed society, it is still very much dependent on foreign human resources and technology. In order to succeed there is a need for knowledge transfer through multinational companies and foreign human capital while continuously building up domestic capability in terms of technology, business knowledge and other human resources. The success of Singapore in the future depends on domestic as well as external factors.

This study shows that the Singapore media cluster should be contextualized within a group of clusters that have been planned and started by authorities to gain economic benefits. As such it is a good example of a very deliberate planning process with a broad impact on many sectors in society, where the government also tries to influence and steer the nation's population to adapt to the overall strategy. The policy initiative has the ambition to include actual interaction rather than being a single-sector cluster.

Although planned and steered by the government and the MDA, the actual business side of the cluster development is taken care of by the private marketplace, mostly foreign companies although with various kinds of government support.

As the nature of innovation makes it difficult to plan clusters, especially in a creative sector such as media, it is questionable if Singapore will succeed with that part of the plan. It is likely that other parts of the media sector have better chances to grow, based on Singapore's competitive advantages, i.e. access to financing, an efficient service sector and world-class infrastructure, factors that are not sensitive to political and social issues. The real lessons learnt from this case can only be understood in course of time.

REFERENCES

Aoki, A. and D. Tachiki (1992),'Overseas Japanese Business Operations: The Emerging Role of Regional Headquarters', *Rim: Pacific Business and Industries*, **24**(1), 28–39.

Blomqvist, H.C. (2005), *Swimming with Sharks: Global and Regional Dimensions of the Singapore Economy*, Singapore, Marshall Cavendish Academic.
Chang, T.C. (2000),'Renaissance Revisited: Singapore as a "Global City for the Arts"', *International Journal of Urban and Regional Research*, **24**(4), 818–831.
Chang, T.C. and W.K. Lee (2003),'Renaissance City Singapore: A Study of Arts Spaces', *Area*, **35**(2), 128–141.
Chia, S.Y. (1986), 'The Economic Development of Singapore: A Selective Review of the Literature', in Basant K. Kapur (ed.), *Singapore Studies: Critical Surveys of the Humanities and Social Sciences*, Singapore, Singapore University Press, pp. 183–242.
Chia, S.Y. and J.J. Lim (2003), 'Singapore: A Regional Hub in ICT', in Seiichi Masuyama and Donna Vandenbrink (eds), *Towards a Knowledge-based Economy: East Asia's Changing Industrial Geography*, Tokyo, Numura Research Institute; Singapore, Institute of Southeast Asian Studies, pp. 259–298.
Deloitte (2009), 'Interactive and Global Media: Creating a Vibrant Ecosystem in Singapore', Deloitte Consulting (received from Singapore's Media Development Authority: report not published).
Doshi, T. (1989), *Houston of Asia: The Singapore Petroleum Industry*, Honolulu, HI, USA: Resource Systems Institute; Singapore, Institute of Southeast Asian Studies.
Drysdale, J. (1984), *Singapore: Struggle for Success*, Singapore, Times Books International.
Economic Development Board (1988), *Gearing Up for an Advanced Role in the Global Economy*, Singapore, EDB.
Economic Review Committee (2002), *Creative Industries Development Strategy: Propelling Singapore's Creative Economy*, Report of the ERC Services Subcommittee Workgroup on Creative Industries (ERC-CI), Singapore, ERC.
Edge, M. (2004), 'Pie Sharing or Food Fight? The Impact of Regulatory Changes on Media Market Competition in Singapore', *International Journal of Media Management*, **6**(3), (4), 184–193.
Huff, W.G. (1994), *The Economic Growth of Singapore: Trade and Development in the Twentieth Century*, Cambridge, UK: Cambridge University Press.
Hutton, T.A. (2004), 'Service Industries, Globalization, and Urban Restructuring within the Asia-Pacific: New Development Trajectories and Planning Responses', *Progress in Planning*, **61**(1), 1–74.
Lim, L.Y.C. (1989),'Social Welfare', in Kernial S. Sandhu and Paul Wheatley (eds), *Management of Success: The Moulding of Modern Singapore*, Singapore, Institute of Southeast Asian Studies, pp. 171–197.
Mak, L.F. (1981), *The Sociology of Secret Societies: A Study of Chinese Secret Societies in Singapore and Peninsular Malaysia*, Kuala Lumpur, Oxford University Press.
Margolin, J.-L. (1993),'Foreign Models in Singapore's Development and the Idea of a Singaporean Model', in Garry Rodan (ed.), *Singapore Changes Guard: Social, Political and Economic Directions in the 1990s*, Melbourne, Longman Cheshire.
Media 21: Transforming Singapore into a Global Media City (2003), Singapore, Media Development Authority of Singapore.
Media Fusion eNewsletter, Issue 28, Singapore, Media Development Authority of Singapore.

Ministry of Information and the Arts (MITA) (2000), *Renaissance City Report: Culture and the Arts in Renaissance Singapore*, Singapore, MITA.
Ooi, C.-S. (2006),'Bounded Creativity and the Push for the Creative Economy in Singapore', paper presented to the 16th Biennial Conference of the Asian Studies Association of Australia, Wollongong, 26–29 June 2006.
Ooi, C.-S. (2008),'Creative Singapore: Image and Reality', Conference Proceedings of Arte-Polis2: Creative Communities and the Making of Place', Bandung, 8–9 August 2008, B68-B77.
Ooi, G.L. and B.J. Shaw (2004), *Beyond the Port City: Development and Identity in 21st Century Singapore*, Singapore, Pearson Prentice Hall.
Perry, M., L. Kong and B.Yeoh (1997), *Singapore – A Developmental City State*, Chichester, UK: John Wiley & Sons.
Phang, A.B.L. (1990), *The Development of Singapore Law: Historical and Socio-Legal Perspectives*, Singapore, Butterworths.
Quah, J.S.T. (1998), 'Singapore's Model of Development: Is It Transferable?', in Henry S. Rowen (ed.), *Behind East Asian Growth: The Political and Social Foundations of Prosperity*, London, Routledge, pp. 105–125.
Regnier, P. (1992), *Singapore: City-State in South-East Asia*, Kuala Lumpur, Majeed.
Rodan, G. (1989), *The Political Economy of Singapore's Industrialisation*, London, Macmillan.
Rodan, G. (1993), 'Reconstructing Divisions of Labour: Singapore's New Regional Emphasis', in Richard Higgott, Richard Leaver and John Ravenhill (eds), *Pacific Economic Relations in the 1990s: Cooperation or Conflict?*, Sydney, Allen & Unwin, pp. 223–249.
Rodan, G. (2001),'The Internet and Political Control in Singapore', *Political Science Quarterly*, **113**(1), 63–89.
Savage, V.R. (1997), 'Singapore's Garden City: Translating Environmental Possibilism', in Giok Ling Ooi and Kenson Kwok (eds),*City and the State: Singapore's Built Environment Revisited*, Singapore, Oxford University Press and Institute of Policy Studies, pp. 187–202.
Statistics Singapore. Various issues.
Tai, H.-c. (1989), 'The Oriental Alternative: An Hypothesis on Culture and Economy', in Hung-chao Tai (ed.), *Confucianism and Economic Development: An Oriental Alternative*, Washington, DC, Washington Institute Press, pp. 6–37.
Tan, C.H. (1995), *Venturing Overseas: Singapore's External Wing*, Singapore, McGraw-Hill.
The Singapore Economy: New Directions (1986), Report of the Economic Committee, Singapore, Ministry of Trade and Industry.
Transparency International. Various annual surveys.
Turnbull, C.M. (1995), *Dateline Singapore: 150 years of the Straits Times*, Singapore, Singapore Press Holdings.
Wall Street Journal, 5 August 2009.
Wong, C.Y.L., C.C.J.M. Millar, and C.J. Choi (2006), 'Singapore in Transition: From Technology to Culture Hub', *Journal of Knowledge Management*, **10**(5), 79–91.
Wong, P.-K. (2001), 'Leveraging Multinational Corporations, Fostering Technopreneurship: The Changing Role of S&T Policy in Singapore', *International Journal of Technology Management*, **22**(5)-(6), 539–567.

Wong, P.-K. (2008), 'Coping with Globalization of Production Networks and Digital Convergence: The Challenge of ICT Cluster Development in Singapore', in ShahidYusuf, Karou Nabeshima and Shoichi Yamashita (eds), *Growing Industrial Clusters in Asia: Serendipity and Science*, Washington, DC, The World Bank, pp. 91–145.

WTEC (1997), *WTEC Panel Report on Electronics Manufacturing in the Pacific Rim*, http://144.126.176.216/em/toc.htm (accessed 22 February 2000).

Young, M. (1958), *The Rise of the Meritocracy 1870–2033: An Essay on Education and Equality*, London, Thames & Hudson.

15. Creating a film production cluster in Sweden's west: the case of 'Trollywood'

Leona Achtenhagen

This chapter discusses the case of 'Trollywood', a regional film production cluster in the west of Sweden, which over the past two decades has developed a complete structure for film production (including pre-production, production, and post-production, as well as some distribution activities). This case is interesting to study as it illustrates a rare example of successfully creating a media cluster from scratch. However, the case study deviates from the version which would probably be most preferred by politicians – namely that the successful cluster development was an act engineered and put into practice by regional politics to revive a highly problematic region characterized by unemployment, xenophobia and loss of regional identity. Instead, it provides a complementary perspective by demonstrating how a few key individuals have put their entrepreneurial vision into practice by encouraging and leveraging the political willingness to foster regional development, navigating between and building on the discourses of cultural and/or economic development.

The chapter is structured as follows. First, the policies for regional development and film production as well as their recent developments are discussed as the contextual background of the filmmaking activities in the west of Sweden. This is important as the story of Trollywood is one of new regionalism gaining foothold in a formerly centralized country, thereby enabling the emergence of a regional film production cluster. Then, the origin and development of the 'Trollywood' activities are presented before assessing the current situation in terms of scope of activities, connectedness and financial performance. The focus will be put on 'Film i Väst' (Film in the West), a regional film production centre which is at the heart of the Trollywood activities. This organization also acts as a regional film fund which invests in film and TV productions in the region of Västra Götaland in West Sweden. Since its foundation in 1997, it has co-produced around 200 feature films (http://www.filmivast.se).

The chapter then continues by describing how the cluster works as well as what the drivers for its activities are. Next, the performance of the cluster is evaluated along different criteria, such as linkages developed, ownership of firms, sustainability of activities and number of employees connected to the cluster. Here it is pointed out how the assessment of the performance of regional development activities is necessarily linked to political orientation and the individual beliefs in how much politics should be involved in fostering regional development in the first place. The chapter concludes by discussing current challenges, pointing out possible routes for future development, as well as distilling some policy implications.

THE CONTEXTUAL BACKGROUND: FILM PRODUCTION AND ITS POLICIES IN SWEDEN

The Assumed Role of Film Production for Regional Development

The recent development of the film production activities in and around the western Swedish city of Trollhättan needs to be seen in the light of the political assumption that culture-based activities can play an important role for societal and economic development. The film industry is a key supplier of content to the audiovisual media, which is seen as a creative industry with large growth potential (Kleveland, 2005, p. 5). The investing of taxpayers' money in co-financing of feature movies is motivated with the aim of contributing to regional economic development (Dahlström, 2005, p. 7). This persuasion, however, has not always been evident in that region. Rather, film (production) used to be included mainly in the arena of cultural politics, rather than in economic politics. The success of the Film i Väst ('Film in the West') case discussed in this chapter is interesting from an economic and cultural as well as from a general political point of view, as it has contributed to shifting the power structures in film production from centre to periphery, namely from the capital city Stockholm to regional and local actors by regionalizing film production (Blomgren, 2007). How is political and policy involvement to support film production assumed to foster regional development? Positive effects of film production on regional development are expected to emerge in three, partly overlapping, ways: developing the economy and increasing employment, increasing the attractiveness of the region as well as improving the regional identity and social capital (cf. Dahlström, Hermelin and Rusten, 2005, pp. 14–16).

The Organization of Film Production

Producing feature films means creating cultural products which have an entertainment value for their audience. At the same time, film production creates employment and generates orders to subcontractors as well as revenues for companies in the industry. Film production is characterized by advanced production technologies coupled with artistic creation, turning over large financial and human resources during the period of making the movie (Stern, Svensson and Toll, 2003, p. 8). Film production is project-based, and typically companies are specialized in some part of the value chain. The industry draws on many freelancers who are engaged under one contract at a time. Staffing new teams for a new project is often based on previous experience and personal contacts (DeFilippi and Arthur, 1998). Informal arenas, such as coffee shops and restaurants, have been found to play an important role in facilitating the development of new ideas and cooperation. As such informal arenas tend to locate in larger cities, most film production could historically be found in urban areas. Scepticism towards the attempt of fostering cultural milieus outside of urban centres has been brought forward by, among others, Florida (2002), who argues that a critical mass of different types of people needs to be present to stimulate creativity, and that such critical mass can hardly be found or developed outside of large city environments.

In recent years, film production has undergone extensive changes. For example, it has become increasingly international. Digitization as well as reduced costs of travel and telephony have rendered location less important, and financial resources and trade flows, but also activities of larger companies are increasingly international. In the cultural industries, the dominance of US products (such as Hollywood-produced movies) has increased the demand for cultural products with a clear local, regional and/or national touch. Within the European Union, countries have not only put in place their own quotas of how many films should be produced nationally, but cooperation also occurs between European countries. In the Nordic countries, the Nordic Film and TV Fund partly finances cooperation productions between different Nordic partners (cf. Lange and Westcott, 2004). On the European level, the joint organization 'European Film Agency Directors' lobbies for the national movie subsidies at the European Commission, as national films are argued to play an important role for European identities. Within the programme Interreg IIIC, in 2004 the EU established Cine Regio as a network of regional film funds. In 2006, the head office of Cine Regio moved to Film i Väst ('Film in the West') in Trollhättan (see below).

Film Production and Politics in Sweden Over Time

The role taken on by *cultural politics* regarding movies is to support films of good quality, which should be accessible to a large number of people as well as foster the national language and culture. The role taken by *economic politics* regarding the movie industry is to support the creation of employment, and initiatives have become increasingly regionalized over the years. Developing the infrastructure and educational offers is one way economic policy is put into practice (cf. Dahlström et al., 2005, p. 24).

Since the 1960s, the Swedish film policies are implemented by the Svenska Filminstitutet (Swedish Film Institute, SFI), the board of which is elected by the government. SFI's task is to strengthen, develop and put into the spotlight movies in cultural and societal life, which underlines that the activities of SFI are closely connected to promoting a cultural-political agenda. Different types of production subsidies exist and are granted by SFI, for example for production costs or ticket subsidies. Typically, Swedish feature films are financed at more than 50 per cent by private actors, mainly through industry-internal risk capital (cf. Andersson-Greek, 2004). Swedish film production companies usually do not have the financial means to conduct their projects independent of subsidies and external financing. SFI works with cultural-political aims, meaning that artistic ambition should be supported, while at the same time a proposed movie should be deemed attractive for the audience, and well as have the potential to recuperate its costs.

Towards the end of the 1980s, SFI initiated a discussion about a regional structure of film culture. Regional distribution chains were created, school cinema projects were supported and regional consultants were put in place. Thus, a more regional focus of activities was also supported by SFI. Support for regional activities related to film and video was provided by SFI, if co-financed regionally and locally with the same amount as that provided by SFI. The focus of attention was to support educational media work with children and youth. Among other things, the development of short and documentary films was also supported in nine participating regions. Nonetheless, until the early 1990s, when the activities described in this chapter were initiated, film production was conducted almost exclusively in Stockholm.

In a report to the Swedish government presented in 1998/99, the combined importance of Swedish film to strengthen the Swedish economy as well as culture is outlined for the first time, and its contribution to technological and especially regional development is stressed (cf. Dahlström, Hermelin and Wengström, 2005, p. 45). In a government proposition about the future of film production in Sweden ('Focus på film – en ny svensk filmpolitik' (Focus on film – a new Swedish film policy); proposition 2005/06:3), the economic argument is put into focus: 'From an economic policy perspective, Swedish film production is of great importance for economic growth in Sweden, especially with respect to regional investments and regional development. Film production functions as a locomotive for the entire audiovisual sector' (Proposition 2005/06:3:58; my translation).

In the year 2000, a new 'agreement on film' was put in place (which secured the financing of SFI and redistributed subsidies to other film-related activities). This agreement included support for the production of feature films within three regional production centres, namely Film i Väst, Filmpool Nord and Film i Skåne. From 2007, subsidies were also given to a fourth regional production centre, Film i Mälardalen. The general trend towards a more regionalized policy has led to drastic changes in the geography of Swedish film production. While at the beginning of the 1990s almost all feature films were produced in the Stockholm region, the situation looks very different today (cf. Dahlström, Hermelin and Wengström, 2005). Film i Väst, which is in focus in this chapter, has managed to attract the production of more than 50 per cent of feature films to the Trollhättan region, and even a few other regions have been reasonably successful, for example Film i Skåne leveraging the popularity of Henning Mankell's books about the detective Kurt Wallander in the city of Ystad, which are now produced as movies. But also Filmpool Nord, based in the northern Swedish city of Luleå, is promoting film production. In the year 2005, 80 new Swedish feature films were aired, and 34 per cent of these were co-produced by Film i Väst, 13 per cent by Filmpool Nord and 6 per cent by Film i Skåne (Dahlström, Hermelin and Wengström, 2005: 40).

The focus on the political willingness to invest tax money in regional film activities is also related to a focus of the EU regional structural funds on film production for regional development. Thus, regions which are identified as eligible for EU structural support can receive additional financing. EU co-financing of feature films is possible, as they are considered as a cultural product. By now, the role of culture for regional economic development has been firmly established on the political map.

THE ORIGIN AND DEVELOPMENT OF 'TROLLYWOOD'

In 1992, the predecessor of Film i Väst, Västernfilm, was initiated in Alingsås as part of a mass media policy programme, financed locally with tax money to promote the use of new media. The early activities were geared towards amateur filmmakers, and mainly aimed at providing young people with the opportunity to experiment with video and media production in 36 workshops. In addition, the airing of feature films was facilitated by supporting cinemas. In addition to the workshops, the best 16 students were offered training to make videos more professionally – a first sign of the emerging idea to establish professional film production in the region. The activities were organized in three units in Alingsås, namely 'Children and youth', 'Production' and 'Distribution'. Tomas Eskilsson, formerly cultural secretary in Alingsås, became the CEO of these activities and managed to attract a budget of 11 million SEK to stimulate the theoretical and practical interest in film. In 1994, together with Gunnar Carlsson (then head of the Gothenburg Film Festival, now head of drama at Swedish Television, SVT, in Gothenburg) and Christer Nilsson (CEO of the film production company Götafilm), he established the Västsvenska Filmfonden (West Swedish Film Fund), aiming to support professional filmmaking. The fund was a not-for-profit association based on local and regional public financing, as well as on support from SVT Gothenburg and the marketing partnership Gothenburg & Co. The fund's capital was limited, and therefore it co-financed only a few feature films and short movies. In consequence, SVT pulled out, and even Gothenburg city reduced its support. In spring 1996, the fund was dissolved (Dahlström, Hermelin and Wengström, 2005, p. 52).

In 1996/1997, things started to happen. Alingsås no longer wanted to continue supporting the film activities. At the same time, Tomas Eskilsson created a production alliance with the Danish company Zentropa (with its CEO Peter Aabeen Jensen and the film director Lars von Trier) as well as the Swedish company Memfis Film (with its CEO Lars Jönsson). Zentropa liked the 'fascinating landscape' in Trollhättan, and claimed that when they 'drew lines between Stockholm, Oslo and Copenhagen they had ended up in Trollhättan'. Together, these three actors founded a post-production company. Zentropa developed plans to build a studio in the old industrial complex in Trollhättan. The activities quickly became dubbed 'Trollywood', and Zentropa's aim was to produce at least one feature film a year. The distributor of the film would be Trust Film.

These entrepreneurial activities were coupled with lobbying and political activities. A person in charge of developing the local economy, Bo Melander (Näringslivssekretariatet[1]), suggested investing 2 million SEK over three years in a centre for film production in the old industry premises in Nohab Industri. Trollywood, as it was also called in the political arena, was intended to function as a know-how centre for movie and media production, with Film i Väst as the main player behind the investment. The official argument was that 'through this establishment the four-city region will receive a complementary industry, which is positive for the local needs and the wish to broaden the economic structure'. In addition, the project Film i Väst received EU funding in order to broaden its focus from short films and documentaries to feature films. This money was to be used to co-finance feature film productions which had been granted support by the Swedish Film Institute.

The origin of applying for external funding, which eventually led to the successful EU funding application, dated back to the early 1990s, when Film i Väst started their activities and planned to produce films, for which financing was needed. Through lobbying with allied politicians, they tried to influence the 'film politics' institutionalized by the Swedish Film Institute to pay more attention to regional, rather than big-city activities only. This strategy, however, did not pay off (Blomgren, 2007). Instead, (planned) activities were marketed in their potential of serving as a regional economic engine with the message that regional film production creates growth and increases employment (cf. Blomgren, 2008). This idea received support, and also opened up for applying for EU funding. In order to be eligible for EU funding, regional and local co-financing had to be secured, which the key actors succeeded with. In this process, Tomas Eskilsson's political experience was key, as he not only had many political contacts but also had a very good understanding of how political processes and decision-making happen, which allowed him to navigate his interests. Applying to the EU for more substantial funding opened up the perspective of developing feature film production activities based on longer-term planning. For that, Eskilsson had identified different critical issues, such as the need to build a proper film studio, to build up capacity for post-production as well as to help feature film producing companies establish in the region. In addition, there was a general lack of competence and skills in feature film production. Therefore, a broad infrastructural investment was needed in order to develop sustainable film production activities. The EU application received funding as of 1997. The EU funding was another important reason for moving from Alingsås to Trollhättan. In the 1990s, the formerly booming industrial town was struggling with high levels of unemployment, as many companies were facing bankruptcy and/or laid off many workers, which made it eligible for the European Union's Aim 2 regional financing. The SAAB car factory alone had dismissed 2000 of its staff. Also, the local government in Trollhättan was in favour of the idea of developing a new industry in the region, as they saw that the regional identity suffered due to the economic problems. Eskilsson managed to persuade them by, among other things, drawing on the successful example of Sheffield, where film, media and other creative industry companies had agglomerated (cf. Dahlström, Hermelin and Wengström, 2005, p. 52). Reviving the empty industrial complexes – which had earlier played an important role in the city's identity – with new activities was an attractive prospect, which suddenly appeared realistic as Zentropa and Memfis had promised to produce feature films on these premises.

Changes happened also on the political arena. In 1998, three administrative counties merged to form the region of Västra Götaland. Forming this region was a sign of the decentralization process which gave the region more autonomy and responsibility, and in relation to that also the chance to promote the region in, for example, the EU and its regional structural programme (cf. Assmo, 2005, p. 458). In the same year, eight feature films were produced in the region, and the success of the movie 'Show me Love' (Swedish title: Fucking Åmål) not only meant a commercial breakthrough, but also legitimacy for establishing the regional activities. At this stage, the communicated political plans were to employ 80 people, as culture was seen as an investment and a future job market. In addition, Lars Jönsson, one of the initiators of Film i Väst, wanted to strengthen the role of film producers in Sweden and initiated educational programmes for increasing competences in this area. Persuading existing film production companies to come to the Trollhättan area was successful based on the sales argument that 'Trollhättan provides creative freedom', namely that directors would be less restricted in developing their films according to their own ideas.

During the same period, the formerly centralized national film policy was being increasingly decentralized, and projects could be co-financed by the Swedish Film Institute. In 1999, 11 movies and two long documentaries were shot, and it was communicated that 800 people had been employed through the film-related activities, generating a turnover of 300 million SEK. Ten new companies had been created; the two studios built with EU funding were fully used and a third one was already in planning. Already by that year, half of all Swedish feature film production had moved to Trollhättan. In the same year, an attempt was being made to expand into the experience industry. Based on a model from Denmark of which Zentropa had experience, in December 1999 a 'Dream Factory' was opened, based on the film setting of 'Dancer in the Dark', where 30 'students' per hour could get the script, write their own lines and work with make-up and costumes. In 2003, a stunt show for tourists was opened. However, these experience-based activities never really took off.

In these initial years, some criticism is being voiced. Rumours are spread, for example, that the requirement that the production companies should spend a substantial amount of money in the region is not sufficiently put into practice, that decisions about films and staffing are made based on nepotism, or that small production companies are outcompeted. This criticism illustrates two sides of the difficulty of establishing regional film production outside of Stockholm – first, the struggle of attracting film activities to the Trollhättan area, and secondly, the disapproval of this fact by some people in the Stockholm-based film production activities.

In 2000, a second production company started its activities in Trollhättan, making TV movies, thereby establishing an expansion mode for further activities. By 2001, 33 feature films had been produced and 12 million SEK had been reinvested, providing an important argument to the taxpayers in the region that their money was not wasted. By now, the impact on the region is evaluated very positively. While new jobs have been created as well, the biggest change is seen to have taken place in local attitude. Between 20 and 70 new companies have been created, but the exact scope of the activities is difficult to establish. Ramstad Johansen and Normann (2003) claim that by 2001 around 70 media-related companies had set up business in the region.

These successes calm part of the criticism brought forward against the use of tax money to finance the regional development of the Trollhättan region in the area of film production. Nonetheless, critical voices continue to argue that despite the fact that a substantial amount of the investment should be spent in the region and local people should be employed, many people continue to live in Stockholm while changing their addresses to some relatives in order to be officially local. Dahlström, Hermlin and Wengström (2005, p. 42) found that in 2002 74 per cent of people related to the film industry were registered in the larger Stockholm area. Many people still commute to the productions in the region while a specific project is ongoing. While there are 14 production companies registered as partner companies of Film i Väst on its webpage, many of these continue to have the bulk of their activities in Stockholm.

The decision is taken to work more with young directors in the following years. By 2002, Film i Väst had co-produced more than 75 feature films. By 2003, Film i Väst had increased its resources to more than 60 million SEK, approximately 74 per cent of which derived from public sources (EU funds, Västra Götaland region, and the city municipalities of Trollhättan, Uddevalla, Vänersborg and Lysekil) (Assmo, 2005, p. 460). According to Film i Väst's estimates, the overall business volume related to feature film production in the region (including their own budget) was approximately 376 million SEK in 2003 (Assmo, 2005, p. 461). In that year, the lack of qualified staff still led to the situation that about 65 per cent of the people employed for a film production project came from outside the region. Since then, further studios have been built, which has led to the establishment of further companies and the development of the infrastructure to facilitate not only production but also post-production.

Most film production companies in Sweden are very small, with one or two employees, and small financial resources. Thus, almost all film productions in Sweden need to receive public financing to become reality. Typically, part of this financing is provided by the Swedish Film Institute, and another part of the financing comes from one or several regional film funds. Sometimes, additional private risk capital can be secured. While the financing provided by the SFI is important, the amount of capital provided by the regional film funds is much larger than the national funding through SFI.

The Impact of Film i Väst

Film i Väst has made an ambitious attempt to quantify its impact on the region. In 2003, film production generated a turnover of 380 million SEK in the region, to which Film i Väst contributed with around 28 million SEK in tax money (equivalent to around 8 per cent). Through the number of jobs created through the film production and the taxes paid for these jobs, they estimate that this investment has paid off for the region.

For the region of Västra Götaland, Andersson-Greek (2004) has calculated that Film i Väst receives 25 SEK per capita in subsidies, of which the region's taxpayers cover 22.40 SEK. Until 2005, Film i Väst managed to attract around 90 million SEK in subsidies from the EU regional structural funds, which played an important role in its development. These subsidies are now more and more replaced by regional investments. In the meantime, most critical voices have become silent, and the emergence of the Trollywood cluster is admired as a highly successful initiative.

In 2006, the EU financing through the regional structural funds finished, and many critics had predicted that the regional film production cluster would sink like a ship. Instead, Film i Väst managed to phase out the EU money by attracting more regional funding.

The Current Situation: Size, Connectedness and Profitability

Film i Väst describes itself as having moved 'from mass-media policy to being one of Europe's most successful film centres' (http://www.filmivast.se; my translation). Since the middle of the 1990s, Film i Väst has co-produced long, short, novel and documentary films, almost 200 feature films, several hundreds of short films and documentaries, and many TV dramas. As a consequence of Film i Väst's activities, Västra Götaland now has a complete structure for film production. Today they can offer facilities for productions with competent film workers from the area (to the education of which they have greatly contributed). In recent years

BOX 15.1 MILESTONES OF DEVELOPMENT

1992
The local municipality of Älvsborg sets up Film i Väst's predecessor named Västernfilm, which is based in Alingsås.
1993
Västernfilm changes its name to Film i Väst and presents a study about starting a West-Swedish film fund.
1994
The West-Swedish film fund is established.
1995
Film i Väst receives the Gold Bug prize (Sweden's most prestigious film prize) for its inspiring work.
1996
Film i Väst prepares its move to Trollhättan and receives EU funding for Aim 2 (regional structural development).
1997
Film i Väst moves to the old industrial premises 'Nohab' in Trollhättan; two feature films are co-produced, 'Hela Härligheten' and 'Sjön'.
1998
'Fucking Åmål' is co-produced and becomes a huge success in Sweden.
1999
This year, 11 feature films are produced in Trollywood, among others Lars von Trier's 'Dancer in the Dark'.
2000
The feature films 'Tillsammans' and 'Jalla Jalla' are among the movies which firmly establish Film i Väst's position in the Swedish film production industry. Lars von Trier's 'Dancer in the Dark' receives the Palme d'Or at the Cannes Film Festival.
2001
Film i Väst co-produces 15 feature films during this year.
2002
Lars von Trier produces 'Dogville'.
2003
'Dogville' competes at the Cannes Film Festival.
2004
Film i Väst opens its new studio, Scandinavia's second largest studio, in Trollhättan.

2005
Lars von Trier competes once again in Cannes, this time with the feature film co-produced by Film i Väst, 'Manderley'.
2006
The decision is taken to produce the knights movie 'Arn' in Västra Götaland, which is a huge film project.
2007
Film i Väst celebrates 10 years in Trollhättan.
2008
Film i Väst inaugurates its animation studio, and Ruben Östlund's 'De ofrivilliga' competes in the category Un Certain Regard at the film festival in Cannes.

Source: http://www.filmivast.se; my translation

approximately 50 per cent of all Swedish feature film productions have been co-produced by Film i Väst. Film i Väst has managed to build stable long-term relationships with interesting production companies and film directors. Famous directors like Lukas Moodysson and Lars von Trier continue to come back to the region. Film i Väst cooperates on a long term basis with other public funds in Northern Europe. The office of Cine Regio, Europe's film regions common association, was located in Västra Götaland until January 2010, and helped establish contacts with other regional film funds for co-productions.

In an attempt to quantify the cluster-building activities in the audio-visual industry around Trollhättan, Jonsson (2003) provides the following numbers (Andersson-Greek, 2004, p. 18; see Table 15.1). Interestingly, the communication of the results in terms of the triple helix concept (cooperation between private and public actors as well as higher education) demonstrates once again how Film i Väst masters the adaptation to the political discourse currently in fashion.

According to the CEO of Film i Väst, Tomas Eskilsson, around 3000 people are now employed in film production and related industries in the region. Around 50 per cent of all Swedish feature film productions are co-produced by Film i Väst. In 2008, the production of 30 feature films was started. The general turnover generated through feature films was around 600 million SEK. Film i Väst generated revenues of 88 million SEK and made a profit of 10.5 million SEK. The contribution by the Regional Development Council was 21 million SEK, while the National Council for Cultural Affairs contributed 41 million SEK of taxpayers' money.

Table 15.1 Quantifying the film cluster-building activities around Trollhättan

Educational actors	Entrepreneurship	Political actors
University College Trollhättan-Uddevalla	153 companies	Region Västra Götaland
Gothenburg University		Four-city district
College of Photography and Film		City of Gothenburg

Source: Jonsson (2003) in Andersson-Greek (2004: 18).

Structural and Organizational Characteristics of Trollywood

Film i Väst (FiV) has been successful in attracting the entire value chain of pre-production, production and post-production to Trollhättan. Distribution continues to be centralized to Stockholm, as well as increasingly to Copenhagen, due to the important role played by Zentropa.

Film i Väst acts as co-producer of movies (mainly feature films, but also short films, documentaries, rookie films and TV productions). The region of Västra Götaland owns 100 per cent of the company in order to pursue its vision of becoming the leading film-producing region in Europe through Film i Väst's activities. Films are seen as a vital form of cultural and artistic expression, which also has positive effects for regional development. Film i Väst aims to invest in film projects of high quality.

Therefore, the aims of co-produced projects are fourfold: (1) to strive for high artistic value in film production in the region; (2) to strive for reaching a large audience with films co-produced by Film i Väst; (3) to contribute to broadening and renewing the form, content and financing of Swedish filmmaking through providing a regional perspective; and (4) to contribute to international co-production and international exchange in the area of film with a focus on Europe.

Co-productions by Film i Väst should aim at distribution through several channels. The investment can be up to 20 per cent of the film's budget (or 10 per cent for TV productions). Public financing can go as far as up to 50 per cent of each film's budget. The CEO of Film i Väst decides which feature films to co-produce and reports the decisions to the board.

In order to become eligible for Film i Väst co-production, a number of rules have to be followed. Part of the production of the movie needs to be located in the region of Västra Götaland. Film i Väst must have accepted the manuscript and project plan.

In 2004, the new Studio Fares was opened as Scandinavia's second-biggest sound stage studio (covering an area of 1100 m^2, including facilities such as production offices, scenography workplaces and storage for costumes and props). Today Film i Väst has four studios in the so-called Nohab area, the old industrial premises in Trollhättan. In addition, Film i Väst has expanded into TV drama, and has therefore opened new premises in Gothenburg.

According to CEO Tomas Eskilsson, the cluster has established itself firmly on the Swedish film production market, where chances for further growth are seen to be limited. Opportunities for further expansion, however, are seen in post-production. Regarding post-production, a sound mixer studio opened in April 2004 in collaboration with the Danish sound studio Mainstream. The facility is 100 per cent digital and considered to be the most modern in Sweden. In Spring 2006, Ljudligan and Chimney Pot together expanded from Stockholm to Trollhättan, where they now run three sound studios and Sweden's newest Foley studio.

In addition, more focus is put on developing international contacts and on co-financing international productions. Also, there is a recent move into animation, which is seen to be another area of growth potential.

Cluster Engines

One aspect of implementing a long-term strategy of film production in the region included the development of different types of training. In 2003, Film i Väst investigated the competence structure in the region. It was found that the requirement to recruit at least 50 per cent of the staff locally was rather easy to fulfil. However, at the same time it became clear that certain competences were lacking, especially regarding film directors and cinematographers. The cinematographer is the person in a film team responsible both for the technical and the artistic side of a film's photographic design, in cooperation with the director (Dahlström, Hermelin and Wengström, 2005, pp. 54–5). Typically, directors cooperate with very few cinematographers. In addition, there was a lack of sound technicians, electricians and some other specialist functions. Film i Väst and the regional public service television branch SVT Väst have therefore decided on collaboration to develop such new competences in the region. The lack of film directors in the region was identified early on as a potential threat to further development, and in cooperation with the University College in Trollhättan/Uddevalla, a three-year film producer training was initiated. More recently this programme has received some criticism, referring to, among other things, the fact that the Swedish market is very small and therefore only a limited number of producers are needed in the country. Film i Väst now pays more attention to cooperating with the University of Gothenburg.

In addition, a training course in 3D animation and artistic design was started jointly with the University College in Trollhättan/Uddevalla as well as with Steneby School in Trollhättan. In Trollhättan, Film i Väst together with the adult training centre Komvux is running vocational training for different types of film workers. For film workers and young, not yet established film directors, Film i Väst has developed a trainee programme in cooperation with the employment agency Arbetsförmedlingen Kultur Västra as well as with established production companies (http://www.filmivast.se; Dahlström, Hermelin and Wengström et al., 2005, p. 55).

What are the specific competences that helped Trollywood to become a successful regional cluster? Film i Väst, and especially its CEO Tomas Eskilsson, have developed an excellent flair for judging and selecting proposed feature films. Making successful films is, of course, an important factor not only for economic success, but also for the legitimacy of the activities in the region. In this respect, the role of 'Fucking Åmål' represented a breakthrough for Trollywood when it was aired in 1998 and grew into one of the most successful Swedish feature films of the 1990s. This movie alone generated revenue of more than 36 million SEK, was seen by more than 500,000 people and it also won four Gold Bugs, a prestigious Swedish film prize (cf. Dahlström, Hermelin and Wengström, 2005: 55).

In addition, Film i Väst has developed excellent skills in co-producing films which use rather small teams and a limited number of shooting days. Also, the film directors and producers have a relatively high degree of artistic freedom when making the film. The CEO Eskilsson also mentions the quality of the studios, the availability of skilled and competent staff (as a direct result of the training programmes promoted by Film i Väst), but also the availability of hotel rooms etc, as further factors benefiting the film production cluster.

Linkages and Spillovers Within and to Other Clusters

Film i Väst claims to be active in about 20 formal networks on a local, regional, national, and international level. In 2002, the Swedish Knowledge Foundation (KK-stiftelsen) provided funding to establish Trollhättan as a 'Meeting Place for Film and Media' activities. The work in this project is not restricted to film and media, but aims also at related areas, such as theatre performance, design and experience-based learning. The idea behind the project is to provide opportunities for competence development through meetings across different areas. The triple helix idea (collaboration between academic actors, public actors and private companies) is a basis for this project. A meeting place should be created which continuously enables boundary-crossing meetings to facilitate the exchange and transfer of knowledge as well as to create competence development. In spring 2006, a public seminar about culture and society was organized. In another project named 'Trollhättan Talks' Film i Väst took part in the trade fair 'Film and Tourism' in Gothenburg with a presentation by an Australian researcher.

On an international level, more and more co-productions are made with international partners. While collaboration has taken place on a continuous basis with German and British companies, recently the first feature film co-produced with a Russian company was launched. The importance of developing ties with some key people internationally is stressed, as this facilitates conducting joint projects.

Cine Regio, an interest group for regional film funds in Europe, was founded in 2005 and had its secretariat in Trollhättan 2006-2009. As 25 per cent of the financing of European films comes from regional funds and thereby the relevance of regional activities in film production is increasing, joint lobbying activities towards EU institutions were perceived as necessary. The network today represents 32 regional film funds from 15 countries. The driving force is the belief that regional film support is vital to foster and safeguard the development of the European audiovisual sector and promote local cultural identity, cultural diversity and democratic empowerment. According to its brochure, Cine Regio has three main objectives, knowledge sharing, film policy and co-productions:

(1) *Knowledge sharing*: to exchange views, perspectives, good practices and information for the benefit of the European film industry, including integrating new film funds.
(2) *Film policy*: to raise awareness, represent and promote regional audiovisual interests across Europe, including members' interests towards European institutions and other organizations which play a role in determining the set of rules and conditions for regional film funds.
(3) *Co-productions*: to strengthen the co-development and co-production of audiovisual products, fusing talents and resources in different regions for a wider market – including stimulating artistic, technical and creative exchange and know-how throughout Europe.

International co-production provides additional challenges, as a case study provided by Cine Regio of the shooting of 'Capitaine Achab' by Philippe Ramos reveals. For example, when the French film crew went to Trollhättan to shoot the movie, they were not served dessert after lunch, which they found insulting. As people in Trollhättan were quick to learn, catering is of great importance to French film teams. While the pre-production of that film had been supported by one regional fund only,

Centre Images, another French regional film fund joined the production phase, namely Rhône-Alpes Cinema. The French producer had contacts with another French producer living in Sweden who persuaded him that the surrounding of Trollhättan would fit the film perfectly, and whose contacts led to Film i Väst agreeing on co-producing, thus providing a good example of the relevance of personal ties to cluster activity development. One of the major reasons for Cine Regio to be founded was the different policies and rules of different regional film funds, for example specifying the number of shooting days in the region. All three partner funds in the example above were members of Cine Regio, and eventually managed to agree on a deal, leading to the first Swedish-French co-production in 20 years. Three different crews ended up shooting two weeks in Rhône-Alpes, two weeks in Centre and three weeks in the Trollhättan area. As the director of the Rhône-Alpes regional funds concludes: 'Everything in film is a problem. Why not add an abroad experience to it?' The production ended up winning two prizes at the Locarno Film Festival 2007. Since then, another feature film, 'Les Grandes Personnes', has been co-produced with French companies. Another feature film, 'Kisses', was co-produced with companies from Ireland and 'The Investigator' with companies from Hungary.

Presently, Film i Väst is working towards establishing a Nordic centre for animated film productions, and this project is also sponsored by EU grants. In 2005, Film i Väst and the region evaluated the cluster activities developed to that date, and decided on a strategic direction for the future. This vision included doubling the number of employees in the audiovisual sector in the region within the next ten years, without reducing the quality or weakening the established profile. One of the key areas for growth identified was animated film. A new project was established aimed at developing the sector in the region by providing animation facilities and creating the prerequisites for the production of animated film. As animation is typically a male-dominated sector, additional measures were decided to be taken to increase the percentage of women in this area, for example by stimulating start-ups by immigrant entrepreneurs in the sector. Various workshops and seminars will be arranged during the project period. For example, in March 2008, a seminar about the development of the movie 'Metropia' was organized. Another seminar discussed how the cartoon character Rocky was transformed into an animated film. The project aims at following the triple helix idea by integrating collaboration between private companies, public actors and academic actors.

While the spillover effect to other industries is difficult to establish, the formerly ailing regional identity has developed very positively. People from the region proudly tell anecdotes about how they are getting used to seeing film stars such as Nicole Kidman or Catherine Deneuve in the streets. SAAB, currently still one of the region's more important employers, proudly claims in its marketing to be part of the entertainment industry in Trollhättan (Andersson-Greek, 2004).

Age and Size of Companies, Number of Employees, Spin-offs

Film i Väst is clearly the spider in the cluster web. In addition, Swedish Television (SVT) plays an important role, especially for the TV productions. Due to this crucial role played by one actor, different authors have decided not to call Trollywood a cluster (Lindqvist, Malmberg and Sölvell, 2003), but rather 'an embryo to what could develop into an innovative creative film industry cluster' (Assmo, 2005, p. 465). The arguments for not defining Trollywood as a cluster are first its dependence on Film i Väst and secondly that 'the film production centre is located in an area that largely lacks tradition and skills related to this kind of cultural-oriented industry' (Assmo, 2005, p. 469). As such tradition and skills used to be concentrated in Stockholm only, this definition would *a priori* reject any cluster emergence outside of the capital.

A range of production and other companies have co-located with Film i Väst in Trollhättan. Fourteen production companies and 11 other media companies are located there. In order to facilitate this process, the CEO of Film i Väst identified a number of production companies he found interesting and contacted them to ask whether they were interested in establishing an office in Trollhättan. As the CEO of the production company Migma Film, Anita Oxburgh, states: 'It is not all about money – it was an incredible honour and very inspiring when Tomas Eskilsson (the CEO of Film i Väst) contacted me and said: Come here, I want to work with you! There was someone who wanted to pin his faith on my company and me as a person – that gave me a long-term perspective and thereby a better self-esteem' (in Andersson-Greek, 2004, p. 26, my translation).

The CEO of the first post-production company moving to Trollhättan in 1998, CineStar Rental, Thomas Rogers, has a similar story: 'The decision to establish the company in Trollhättan is based on simple mathematics: if at least five feature films are made each year, it is better for me to have an office there. Moreover, Film i Väst wanted so' (in Andersson-Greek, 2004, p. 30, my translation).

A study conducted by Film i Väst and cited by Dahlström, Hermelin and Wengström (2005, p. 73) identifies three core actors in the media cluster, namely production companies, technology companies and freelancers. It is estimated that 250 production companies with 1200 people work in the modern media sector in this region. In addition, 25 technology companies with 125 people employed as well as 350 freelancers, around 50 of which have their own company. For the year 2003, these companies were calculated to have a turnover of around 1500 million SEK, with TV having a share of 40 per cent. Feature films made for the cinema were calculated to have a turnover of 376 million SEK, and industrial films 272 million SEK. Of the 376 million SEK, 289 million are based on private investments, 28 million on international public investments, 24 on national and 35 on regional public investments.

Tomas Eskilsson estimates the total number of jobs created through the cluster activities at around 3000.

SUSTAINABILITY OF THE CLUSTER

As the cluster has managed to attract more than half of the total number of feature films produced in Sweden, the further growth potential in Sweden can be regarded as limited in this sector. There is still potential to expand TV production, but otherwise international contacts are becoming more and more important. From the outset, international links existed to the Danish production company Zentropa with its director Lars von Trier, who has shot movies such as 'Dancer in the Dark' and 'Dogville', the latter starring Nicole Kidman and Lauren Bacall, as well as more recently the movie 'Antichrist'.

Regarding the sustainability of the cluster, it is obvious that activities are highly dependent on public financing. Film producing activities can be expanded largely based on the level of public financing available. While economic success increases the financial means available for further projects, the existence of the cluster remains dependent on the political willingness to have taxpayers' money invested in these activities. However, as the activities have developed very positively and created many of the desired outcomes, the scenario of stopped funding is rather unlikely. Nonetheless the CEO of Film i Väst, Tomas Eskilsson, emphasizes the importance of public-private relationships and financing as highly crucial for future sustainability. According to him, the future development of the cluster will depend to a large degree on how well these relationships are managed, as well as on continuing support from active filmmakers as well as supportive politicians. Further expansion can be expected to take place in post-production as well as through international collaboration.

Somewhat surprisingly, even many interviewees from Stockholm are now largely positive to the regionalization of film production activities in Sweden. A typical statement is, for example, that Swedish film in general has become more interesting and that the industry has been vitalized. However, some critics point out that there is hardly an alternative for producing films in Sweden than to approach at least one of the regional film pools. As there is a requirement for a production company to have a staffed office in the region, this implies an additional cost on these typically small companies. As many film workers continue to live in Stockholm but have to travel to Trollhättan for several weeks in a row when working with a film production, they are separated from their families for that time. As the CEO of Film i Väst, Tomas Eskilsson, points out, this industry is not made for everybody. He explains that many people get tired of the lifestyle the job implies and change careers.

In terms of competition, the other two more established film production regions in Sweden, Film i Skåne and Filmpool Nord have different foci. Therefore, competition can occur for interesting collaboration partners, rather than for specific film projects.

CONCLUSIONS

One major lesson regarding media cluster development to be learned from this case is the importance of building and leveraging public-private partnerships. The initiator of Film i Väst, Tomas Eskilsson, was able to benefit from his understanding of the political arena which he gained in his former career as cultural affairs secretary. With that background, he also quickly understood that it was much easier to get support for building film production activities when packaging them as economic rather than as cultural activities – drawing on the emerging discourse of clusters as engines of economic development. Thus, rather than to persuade the institutional actors to change their politics to include regional activities, Eskilsson found a way around the existing institutions to turn his ideas into reality. However, with the regionalization of the Swedish Film Institute, he later also managed to get the cultural politicians on board, and activities are now financed by both cultural and economic public development funds.

This case provides a fascinating example of how entrepreneurial vision and drive do not necessarily contradict political intentions, but that these can in fact be leveraged to reach the entrepreneurial aims. Interestingly, many people in Sweden would probably answer the question of who 'owned' the idea of developing Trollywood by saying that this is a political initiative to foster regional development. Thus, Eskilsson needs to be credited with creating strong political commitment to his ideas, which today enjoy a high level of legitimacy, both in the region and on a national and international level.

Was the creation of Trollywood a good idea? To answer this question, the effects of the cluster building need to be assessed comprehensively.

Economic effects mainly relate to spillover effects to other companies and industries, as well as to the number of jobs created. Here, input-output analyses of regional financial flows have been commonly applied to examine the results (cf. Throsby, 2004). The results are typically expressed as multipliers, namely as the relation between the money invested into the film industry and the financial flow in a region which this investment has generated. If the multiplier is larger than 1, the investment has generated more flows than the amount of the investment. The more sourcing and employment has taken place locally, the larger the multiplier. Direct effects refer to regional sourcing within the movie budget, indirect effects refer to regional subcontracting, and inducing effects refer to money spent by the staff of companies which are related to the producing of a movie (cf. Sterngold, 2004a). However, this type of assessment has been criticized for not taking into consideration the increase in quality of life through the access to cultural goods, the strengthening of the cultural heritage and the contribution to a region's social capital (Cohen, 2004). Input-output analyses do not grasp these important effects, which can probably be captured more adequately with qualitative studies as well as longitudinally, as effects might become apparent with a time lag (cf. Sterngold, 2004b). For the film industry, the effect on job creation is difficult to establish, as film production is project-based and many people work as freelancers. Somewhat easier is the calculation of regional economic effects in terms of increase in hotel nights booked and revenues of restaurants or public transport. Also, the development of the housing market could be an indicator for an increasing attractiveness of the region, if more houses are built and/or sold. The number of new start-up companies in the region can also be used as an indicator for evaluating the regional effect. Attempts to integrate the film production activities into the local society might help create positive effects if an identity can be created around those activities, which clearly appears to be the case in Trollhättan. Finally, one point stressed by Film i Väst is that regions can offer new industrial spaces (Dahlström, Hermelin and Wengström, 2005, p. 33), meaning that they provide the opportunity for young and new actors to produce feature films who would not have had this chance in more established, traditional centres of film production. Thus, despite the difficulties in assessing the exact outcome of the cluster, its overall effects clearly seem to be positive.

POLICY IMPLICATION

This case has pointed out the importance of key individuals with a high level of entrepreneurial spirit, a clear vision and sense of achievement, who at the same time have intimate knowledge of how the local, regional and national (as well as EU) political arenas work when attempting to provide political support to regional development. The entrepreneurial drive ensures that an initiative does not fade away when difficulties are met, and the political knowledge facilitates the framing of ideas in a language understood by politicians and policymakers. In this case such framing took place when adapting the discourse flexibly between cultural and economic politics, but it also facilitated getting funding from the EU regional structural funds. Developing competencies to further fuel the activities in the region also appears to play a major role; in this case new degree programmes were initiated to ensure the availability of new film-producing activities in Sweden.

NOTE

1. Näringslivssekretariatet is the trade and industry department at the municipality level.

REFERENCES

Andersson-Greek, U. (2004), *Varför görs det så lite film i Stockholm-Mälardalen? – Rapport om regionaliseringen av svensk film och förutsättningarna för en storregional filmfond i Stockholm-Mälardalen*, Rapport, Länsstyrelsen Stockholms Län.

Assmo, P. (2005), 'Creative Clusters – Ideas and Realities for Cluster Growth: The Example of Film i Väst in the Region of Västra Götaland, Sweden', in Charlie Karlsson, Börje Johansson and Roger R. Stough (eds), *Industrial Clusters and Inter-Firm Networks. New Horizons in Regional Science*, Cheltenham, UK: Edward Elgar Publishing.

Blomgren, R. (2007), 'Att styra eller styras: Från Kulturpolitiska Visioner till Konstpolitisk vardag', *Nordisk Kulturpolitisk Tidsskrift*, **10**(2), 40–59.

Blomgren, R. (2008), *Cultural Industry from Threat to Salvation: Film Production from Art Policy to Regional Development*, Report, Högskolan Väst.

Cohen, R. (2004), 'Commentary: Arthur H. Sterngold's "Do Economic Impact Studies Misrepresent the Benefits of Arts and Cultural Organizations?"', *Journal of Arts Management, Law, and Society*, **34**(3), 235–238.

Dahlström, M. (2005), 'Film och regional utveckling i Norden', in Margareta Dahlström et al. (eds), *Film och Regional Utveckling i Norden*, Stockholm: Svenska Filminstitutet and Nordregio, pp. 7–12.

Dahlström, M., B. Hermelin and G. Rusten (2005), 'Att Analysera Kopplingarna mellan Filmproduktion och Regional Utveckling', in Margareta Dahlström et al. (eds), *Film och regional utveckling i Norden*, Stockholm: Svenska Filminstitutet and Nordregio, pp. 13–38.

Dahlström, M., B. Hermelin and E. Wengström (2005), 'Regionaliserad Filmpolitik i Sverige', in Margareta Dahlströmm et al. (eds), *Film och Regional*

Utveckling i Norden, Stockholm: Svenska Filminstitutet and Nordregio, pp. 39–82.

DeFillippi, R.J. and M.B. Arthur (1998), 'Paradox in Project-based Enterprise: The Case of Film-making', *California Management Review*, **40**(2), 125–139.

Florida, R. (2002): *The Rise of the Creative Class: And How it's Transforming Work, Leisure, Community and Everyday Life*, New York et al.: Basic Books.

Jonsson, S. (2003), *Utveckling av den Audiovisuella Industrin*, Film i Väst/Filmpool Nord.

Kleveland, Å. (2005), 'Förord', in Margareta Dahlström et al. (eds), *Film och Regional Utveckling i Norden*, Stockholm: Svenska Filminstitutet and Nordregio, pp. 5–6.

Lange, A. and T. Westcott (2004), *Public Funding for Film and Audiovisual Works in Europe – A Comparative Approach*, Strasbourg: The European Audiovisual Observatory.

Lindqvist, G., A. Malmberg and Ö. Sölvell (2003), *Svenksa Klusterkartor – En Statistisk Inventering av Kluster i Sverige 2002*, Uppsala: Uppsala University, Centre for Research on Innovation and Industrial Dynamics.

Ramstad Johansen, F. and S. Normann (2003), *Multimediesatsingen i Fredrikstad – Potensiale og Ringvirkninger*, Fredrikstad: Stiftelsen Østfoldsforskning, OR.16.03.

Stern, P., M. Svensson and B. Toll (2003), *Film, TV och Moderna Medier i Västra Götaland*, Göteborg: Film i Väst.

Sterngold, A.H. (2004a), 'Do Economic Impact Studies Misrepresent the Benefits of Arts and Cultural Organizations?', *Journal of Arts Management, Law, and Society*, **34**(3), 166–187.

Sterngold, A.H. (2004b), 'Response to Randy Cohen's Commentary', *Journal of Arts Management, Law, and Society*, **34**(3), 238–240.

Throsby, D. (2004), Assessing the Impacts of a Cultural Industry', *Journal of Arts Management, Law, and Society*, **34**(3), 188–204.

PART III

Conclusion

16. The challenges of media clusters

Charlie Karlsson and Robert G. Picard

The research presented in this book has shown there is great diversity among media clusters and that their structures, operations and scale vary widely. Most media clusters are not directly comparable because of different purposes, histories, structures and sectors emphasized.

The emergence or creation and operation of media clusters is complex because the concept of media itself is complicated by the wide diversity of media in terms of characteristics and methods of production. This is particularly true where some firms' work is characterized as project-based and other firms are engaged in continuous operations. Nevertheless, it is clear that beneficial locations, skilled labour forces and supportive cultural and/or industrial policies are all needed for media clusters to achieve success. The cases in the book reveal that clusters cannot be insular but must reach out to media operations elsewhere and benefit from connections to adjacent cultural industries, such as performance and theatre and appropriate educational institutions.

Some clusters, such as Hilversum, are struggling with legacy characteristics that have narrowed their activities and opportunities and now pose significant challenges for their future. In the case of Munich, the cluster is shifting from film to audiovisual production for TV and advertising, but the changes are altering its economics and market dynamics and making it more vulnerable to changes in the television and advertising industries.

In other cases, such as London and Sydney, there is not a distinct centralized cluster but rather multiple micro-agglomerations of subclusters spread throughout the cities serving advertising, new media, television and film. This would seem to indicate that there are more direct subsector benefits for agglomeration than broader media industry benefits.

In policy terms, the Manchester/Liverpool case shows that national as well as regional policy can play a significant role in development of clusters, particularly where television production by quasi-governmental broadcasters is involved. The Sydney cases reveal that governmental planning can influence and change clusters that have developed on their own, especially by promoting relocation as part of urban renewal projects. The

Vancouver case shows the need for policy initiatives to increase already existing advantages.

The Dubai and Singapore cases show that clusters can be created strategically to serve economic and general developmental goals rather than specific cultural or media objectives. However, the Toronto case reveals how tensions between cultural and economic objectives can affect performance and sustainability of clusters.

The South African case reveals policymakers' difficulties in perceiving and capitalizing on emerging clustering opportunities whereas the Singapore case shows a high appreciation of opportunities and much centralized planning to seek benefits. The Trollhättan case, however, shows that key individuals can use existing regulatory and cultural policies and opportunities to create and achieve at least temporary cluster benefits.

The studies show that media firms may not need to be directly in the cluster location to benefit from it; they may be located on its fringes or nearby. This is particularly so in cases of large urban agglomerations, where firms can still benefit if they are in nearby micro-agglomerations.

The studies reveal that some needs are often left out of the creation of clusters. These include financing organizations and commissioning power for productions, which are often located elsewhere, generally in distant cities and countries. These factors, however, may be more important for the success of motion picture and television production clusters than other factors.

All the studies indicated the need for specialized and high-capacity telecommunications infrastructures as well as access to related media and business services and transportation systems for successful cluster development.

CHALLENGES

One problem with the analyses of urban media clusters is that the traditional basic arguments explaining clustering, which go back to the work of Marshall on industrial districts from the turn from the 19th to the 20th century, only provide a very partial explanation. And this holds even if we consider works in this tradition from the late 20th century, such as Porter (1990), Krugman (1991), Enright (1996) and Fischer (1998), who analyse the conditions under which spatially concentrated industrial clusters emerge. Certainly, the conceptualization of clusters and clustering processes differs somewhat between the different approaches but one thing they have in common is a focus on some kind of intra-regional ties. Some authors, for example, launch the hypothesis that if there is close networking among firms and between firms and regional organizations in a certain region, the competitiveness and development of this region will be promoted. Intra-regional networking is assumed to have the following positive effects:

- Networking enables firms to use a common pool of resources (skilled labour, infrastructure, services from input suppliers and supporting organizations, etc).
- Networking helps firms to exchange information and knowledge and to generate innovations through 'knowledge spillovers' (cf. Bramanti and Maggioni, 1997).
- Networking helps firms to be in close contact with clients or users and their special requirements.
- Networking facilitates a division of labour within a cluster so that highly specialized firms can combine and pool knowledge and competencies.

It also seems obvious that intra-regional networking is advantageous under certain specific circumstances, namely:

- In clusters with a large number of small and medium-sized firms, where flexible cooperation with other firms may substitute the advantages of large organizational size, at least partially (Almeida and Kogut, 1997).
- In clusters with a high rate of technological change and innovation, i.e. in knowledge-intensive clusters (Feldman, 1994; Gehrke and Legler, 1998).
- In clusters where customized goods and services are supplied and where contacts between supplier and customer are particularly important (Scott, 1988).

As is shown in a number of the contributions in this book, many of these conditions can to a great extent be found in urban media clusters, which are characterized by a high degree of intra-regional networking even if the focus many times is more on creativity and design than on innovation. This is natural since many media industries are involved in the production, distribution and consumption of symbolic products that are also experience goods, for which imaginative creativity plays a critical and strategic role (Mommaas, 2004). However, precise definitions of networks and networking are hard to find. The appeal of these concepts seems to stem exactly from the fact that they encompass important intra-regional relationships, which are difficult to summarize under precise definitions.

Networking capacity at a very basic level can be seen as the disposition of economic actors within a cluster to communicate and collaborate to achieve mutually beneficial ends. Yet, we know from the cases presented in this book that the networks of urban media clusters to a great extent go far beyond the border of any of the cluster cities studied and in many cases can be characterized as truly global. Obviously, there are limits to the capacity of the traditional view of clusters to increase our understanding analytically and empirically of urban media clusters.

Thus, urban media clusters can never be studied successfully without also considering their inter-regional, national and international or perhaps rather global connections and the general effects of an increasing globalization. One important aspect of globalization is the continuous scaling-up of markets and the increasing growth of transnational financial and economic networks (Sassen, 1994; Waters, 1995). However, the globalization process is characterized also by the fading of national cultural identities, increasing geographical mobility, worldwide migration, ethnic hybridization and apparent cultural homogenization (Zukin, 1995). Some authors now argue that due to the rapidly advancing globalization, economic structures and flows are increasingly becoming disembedded from regional contexts and that regional embeddeness is losing its importance (see, e.g., Thurow, 1996). On the one hand, these authors have got one aspect right. Today an increasing share of the firms act on a global level and the most globalized companies including global media firms are becoming key actors, whose strategies will increasingly determine the possibilities for development in certain regions.

On the other hand, these authors have not fully understood what globalization implies for firms and regions. The increased importance of global links does not imply that the intra-regional links in clusters lose their importance and this is true for the media sector as for most other sectors. What is important for urban media clusters is that they succeed in combining high quantity and high quality intra-regional networking with high quantity and high quality global networking. Certainly, successful urban media clusters need to preserve strategic positions in the organizational structures and networks of global players but this is impossible if the intra-regional networking is not high quantity and high quality. The critical challenge for urban media clusters is to secure enough synergies between the global and the intra-regional networks. Urban media clusters that successfully secure these synergies might be characterized as global media clusters (cf. Sassen, 1994). Successful global media clusters are those whose networks incorporate an adequate supply of quality knowledge, creativity and design resources, along with the ability, willingness and openness of local firms in cooperation with global firms to make use of external global sources of inspiration, information, knowledge and creativity with a clear focus on developing new superior media products.

The networking logic involves three interrelated organizational principles: flexible specialization, networking and competitive collaboration. Here then, we see why clustering is advantageous, generating three primary benefits (Scott, 2000a): (i) a reduction of transaction costs, (ii) an accelerated circulation of capital and information and (iii) reinforcement of transactionally based modes of social solidarity. Thus, the assets of comparative advantage in a global context of increasingly ubiquitous forms of codified and scientific knowledge are the advantages of proximity associated with (i) the exchange of information, goods and services, (ii) face-to-face contacts, (iii) incremental innovation and (iv) the exchange of tacit knowledge (Amin and Graham, 1997). Thus, clusters are a source of dynamic learning that reinforces and is reinforced by the agglomeration of firms in the same sector. Clustering becomes important in this respect because of (i) the presence of 'quasi-mobile' human capital, (ii) the presence of informal contacts between local economic actors that create a certain 'atmosphere' and (iii) synergy effects stemming from shared experiences, which create common representations and beliefs (Hitters and Richards, 2002). However, clustering of media firms becomes vital also for another reason. A substantial share of the output from the media sector is cultural products, whose demand is characterized by high volatility. To balance this and to reduce risks, production is very often spread out over networks of many different firms. Thus, it is vertically and horizontally disintegrated (Scott, 2006), and only large cities have traditionally been able to sustain such networks, although there is a growing dependence of media firms on virtual networks supplemented with regular regional or global physical networking opportunities (Picard, 2008).

Large cities represent a diversity of human activities and interests that continually create streams of public goods that sustain the workings of what Scott (2000a) calls 'the creative milieu'. Socialization dynamics ensure the preservation and development of local knowledge under the exposure of global information and knowledge flows. Infrastructures such as schools, colleges, universities and training centres secure a continuous supply of skilled and specialized labour, and public-private partnerships promote urban renewal and certain technological, creativity and innovation schemes. Large cities also offer 'institutional thickness' (Amin and Thrift, 1995), overlapping webs of supporting organizations, such as financing organizations, chambers of commerce, local and regional authorities, marketing, innovation and business support agencies that 'create synergy, and a collective sense of identity and purpose within a cluster' (Bassett, Griffiths and Smith, 2002). These features, and the fact that media production requires the overlapping skills of a highly differentiated workforce (cf. Pratt, 1999) imply that full-blown media clusters are normally only present in large cities.

Urban media clusters with both strong intra-regional and strong global networks have the potential to become worldwide forerunners. Whereas strong intra-regional networks facilitate competitive and creative production, global networks provide inputs of external knowledge and access to distant markets and reduce the risks of urban media clusters becoming inflexible. Therefore, a combination of strong intra-regional and strong global networks offers the most favourable conditions for an enduring ability and capacity to secure the long-term competitiveness of urban media clusters (cf. Storper and Harrison, 1991; Freeman, 1995; Markusen, 1996; Freeman and Soete, 1997; Ernst, 1999).

The media value chain is continuously changing not least due to organizational and technological changes including an increasing digitalization but also due to changes in transport costs and distribution systems. Already Driver and Gillespie (1993) showed for printed magazines in the UK that the creative tasks of conception, design and editorial services as well as the preliminary production stage of typesetting and reproduction remained firmly tied to London while the printing of magazines was decentralized from London. Seen from a general perspective, this implies that functions within the media sector are not only outsourced but often also relocated from media clusters to other locations nationally and, increasingly, internationally, i.e. offshored. However, many media functions continue to be clustered irrespective of technological changes and reductions of transport costs, and some media functions might over time even become more clustered. To understand the development of media clusters, the potential need for media cluster policies and what type of media cluster policies to implement, it is necessary to understand the underlying forces, which over time

- change the media value chains in terms of insourcing and outsourcing of functions and the functions making up these value chains;
- change the organization of media firms including mergers and acquisitions and multi-nationalization;
- influence the tendency of functions in media value chains to cluster and to relocate.

These changes reduce the importance of physical location for many media production and distribution activities. However, it is in this connection important to stress that the implications of the digital revolution for spatial relationships simply cannot be predicted from the technology itself, as stressed by Castells (1989, p. 21):

> the newly emerging forms of the informational mode of development, including its spatial forms, will not be determined by the structural requirements of the new technologies seeking to fulfil their development potential, but will emerge from the interaction between its technological and organizational components, and the historically determined process of the restructuring of capitalism.

Against this background, we might now ask the critical question: where will clustering in the media economy continue taking place? If we disregard those clusters that have been created through political decisions, Pratt (2000, p. 429) gives the following answer:

> in the field of new media a clustering of producers will occur where new communications technologies are insufficient to capture the full range of human expression [. . .] clustering of producers will [. . .] occur in particular places, namely those that afford a large degree of chance and random encounter with both similar and different producers, and users.

Thus, the digital revolution will not mean the end of geographical clustering, not even of media industries. Instead, it is the type and form of interactions and transactions that matter, and the need for formal and informal face-to-face communication remains essential and critical. New communications technologies and media cannot substitute all aspects of human interaction. This is particularly true 'in the practices of learning, innovating, contracting, employment, as well as socializing, eating, relaxing . . .' (Pratt, 2000, p. 434). However, the new communications and media technologies have enabled the establishment of new kinds of private and public networks (Sheller, 2004). Irrespective of the advances in technologies, geographical proximity still facilitates untraded interdependencies (Storper, 1997), and since the digital technologies have particular advantages in handling routine information and to keep in contact and set up meetings, they might create more room for face-to-face interaction.

POLICY OPTIONS

The globalization process in recent decades has fundamentally changed the conditions for policymakers (Karlsson, Johansson and Stough, 2010). While the policymakers at the national level have lost many of their traditional policy instruments due to deregulation and the emergence of supranational organizations such as the European Union, local and regional autonomy has been revived (Hitters and Richards, 2002). Cities and regions hosting urban media clusters are today facing the concrete consequences of economic and cultural globalization including increasing competition between cities and regions in general and of course between those hosting urban media clusters (Karlsson, Johansson and Stough, 2009). The increased mobility of capital and the diminishing importance of purely physical location factors imply that cities and regions hosting urban media clusters must carefully follow the development of their clusters as well as the global developments in the media sector and when motivated be prepared to take necessary actions to support the development of 'their' media clusters. In doing so, however, the actual cities and regions have to take into account the shift to the new business logic in the global information economy, where firms increasingly work in network relations (Castells, 1996).

Before going more deeply into basic motivations for cluster policies, it might be useful to consider three different approaches to the governance of clusters (cf. Koch and Fuchs, 2000):

- The *market approach* is based on the assumption that market processes are an efficient coordination mechanism that will guide the development of a cluster's industrial structure in the right direction. The actions and decisions of independent economic actors will direct the development of the cluster, and deliberate cluster policies are considered useless, counterproductive or too costly compared with their benefits.
- The *hierarchical approach* emphasizes the need for political intervention or intraorganizational control to guide the development of clusters, which market forces are unable to provide. Political interventions, using regulatory, planning and/or fiscal instruments or vertical integration of different economic actors are the main instruments for coordinating the development of clusters.
- The *network approach* stresses the importance of cooperative relations between autonomous economic actors in the cluster instead of the invisible hand of the market or the visible hand of the public sector. Instead, private economic actors, and private economic actors and public actors are bound together by network links, which are used to coordinate the development of the cluster. According to this approach, there is room for a special type of cluster policy interventions, namely policy actions aiming to stimulate and support cooperation networks.

The chapter by Davis is devoted to cluster policies with a special focus on media clusters. However, he does not fully consider the basic reasons why cluster policies are motivated at all in market economies. There are two basic motivations for cluster policies. The first basic motivation can be found in traditional static economic welfare theory (Karlsson, 2008). Industrial clustering signals the existence of positive externalities, technological and/or pecuniary, which are not fully exploited automatically. Thus, externalities are a form of market failures and are generally taken as a motivation for political interference (often under the naïve assumption of the existence of perfect policy measures without distorting effects). However, political interference is associated with its own costs and these costs must be balanced against the benefits of better exploitation of the positive externalities.

The second basic motivation for cluster policies is dynamic and comes from endogenous regional growth theory, which emphasizes the importance of local and regional factors and actions in creating and sustaining local and regional economic development (Johansson, Karlsson and Stough, 2001). However, in this case it is less obvious what the practical implications are and how cluster policies should be designed and implemented (Karlsson and Stough, 2002).

Besides the general problem of deciding when cluster policies should be implemented we have the second problem discussed by Davis and that is what policies in each of the two basic cases are suitable for media clusters with their very specific characteristics. Generally speaking, one could claim that there is no agreement in the literature and limited systematic evidence that policy interventions towards clusters are possible and that they can generate value by increasing the effectiveness of existing clusters or by speeding up the process of cluster development or by initiating new clusters (Ketels, 2003). Certainly, the literature is rich with cluster policy recommendations. One example is provided by Power and Scott (2004, pp. 9–10), concerning places that want to develop the cultural economy but where there is a strong overlap between the cultural economy and the media economy. These recommendations also apply for the media economy:

> Policy-makers thus need to pay attention to three main ways of promoting collective competitive advantage, which, on the basis of the modern theory of industrial districts can be identified as (a) the building of collaborative inter-firm relations in order to mobilize latent synergies, (b) the organization of efficient, high-skill local labour markets, and (c) the potential of local industrial creativity and innovation.

The current experience is that policy actions to promote clusters have resulted in an exceedingly diverse range of outcomes (Burfitt and MacNeill, 2008). One comprehensive conclusion that might be drawn from the more general literature is that it is not enough to stimulate local networking, localized learning and agglomeration economies. There is certainly also a strong need to support the development of global pipelines (Bathelt, Malmberg and Maskell, 2004). This is probably important in particular, for media clusters, which are dependent on extra-local links to stimulate creativity but also to be able to market the products over many markets. A simple classification of clusters policies could be into on the one hand policies directed to influence the general preconditions of clusters and on the other hand policies involving active cluster management. The first group of policies includes urban and regional planning, investments in material and non-material infrastructures, development of cluster-relevant education, etc.

An active cluster management by local and/or regional authorities on the other hand involves a number of critical steps and demands (Westrick and Rehfeld, 2003):

- A first success to demonstrate the benefits of cluster management for policymakers as well as most of the firms in the cluster.
- Professionalization, routines and institutional change, especially in local and regional development agencies.
- A sustainable institutional setting that demonstrates the benefits to the firms in the cluster as well as potential entrants to the cluster so that the firms in the cluster over time become ready to pay for the cluster management services themselves.
- The ability of the cluster management in the long run to establish a learning capacity in order to manage rearrangement and adoption of new routines to secure sustainability of the cluster.

From the cases in this book, it would appear that a number of demands or conditions would be useful where, specifically, media clusters are involved:

- Requiring public media firms to spend a portion of production budgets in the region of the cluster.
- Requiring that some actual production takes place rather than firms using the cluster merely as a secondary office meeting some minimum national diversification requirements.
- Requiring broadcasters to spend a percentage of their budgets with domestic independent producers.
- Creating terms of trade conditions that allow independent producers to maintain intellectual property rights in their production because merely outsourcing does not provide sufficient capital accumulation in independent firms for further production.

- Ensuring that tax and labour cost incentives are appropriate to attract and maintain firms in clusters.
- Providing facilities subsidies within clusters to create studios and editing spaces that are available to all participants.
- Creating some incentives for exportable content rather than content primarily to meet domestic needs.
- Ensuring that policy goes beyond merely allocation of production resources to emphasize quality or competitiveness *vis-à-vis* other national and international content.

CHALLENGES FOR FUTURE RESEARCH

Even if the research presented in this book substantially increases our understanding of media clusters there still remain many research challenges including the need for a better comprehension of the social and economic processes of development that characterize urban media clusters. In particular, four topics of major interest for researchers as well as policymakers are evident.

1. *Defining the media economy*. Researchers must continuously work with the definitions of the media economy (cf. Gibson and Kong, 2005), since there are many ad hoc definitions around and since ongoing technological and structural changes continuously change the borders of the media economy and its relations to other sectors in the economy and to the consumers. There are at least four different approaches, which to a certain extent need to be applied simultaneously: (i) the sectoral approach,[1] (ii) the labour market and organization of production approach (cf. Scott, 1996, 2001), (iii) the occupational approach (cf. the creative class approach à la Florida, 2002) and (iv) the convergence of formats approach (cf. Gibson and Kong, 2005). Without proper definitions, it is meaningless to discuss and analyse clusters.

2. *Evaluation of the impact of change on cognitive processes characterizing urban media clusters*. The central element of analysis here is the set of cognitive processes that are the basis of the development path for urban media clusters conceived as creative clusters (cf. Landry and Bianchini, 1995). The relevance of tertiary activities at the urban level was identified decades ago (cf. Jacobs, 1969), however without at that time realizing the prospects of new information, multimedia and telecommunications technologies. This renders the urban media clusters potential entities of analytical studies as a possible motor of economic development associated with the category of immaterial assets which present unique creative characteristics, but which are also characterized by a variety of modes of distribution and consumption (cf. Crane, 1992).

3. *Evaluation of the impact of post-industrial society and globalization processes emerging in urban media clusters.* Large cities containing media clusters are today dominated by tertiary activities, and the development processes that have led to this situation are not only characterized by a decline of some factors, a rejuvenation of some factors and a growth of new ones. They are also characterized by a change of the units of economic analysis themselves, which increasingly have concurrent dimensions at the local and the global level. Urban media clusters in some dimensions can be compared with traditional industrial districts. They must be seen as local systems capable of producing global products. Cultural and media economics contents integrate with those of urban economics and find their synthesis in the urban media cluster as a unit of analysis.

4. *Evaluation of the value-creation mechanisms in urban media clusters.* The evaluation here should not be done only from an economic point of view but also from a socio-cultural point of view due to the strong links between media industries and cultural industries. In particular, value creation in urban media clusters is connected closely to the existence in the city of specific resources able to activate individual as well as collective creative processes for the creation of media products but also for the creation of a cluster identity, i.e. of symbolic capital (cf. Peacock, 1992).

As far as urban economists and geographers are concerned, three interesting research perspectives are opened up: (i) the most suitable *organizational structures* supporting the development of urban media clusters, (ii) feasible *formulas of government* for urban media clusters, both as sources and local competencies in the management mechanisms (both cluster and city management!) and as city promotion instruments (city and cluster marketing!) and (iii) the likely *birth of new leading economic actors in the urban media cluster*, in particular in advanced tertiary activities.

To pursue the above research agenda it is important to return to previous contributions in complex economics and the studies of economic and interorganizational networks for the analysis of urban media clusters, because their variety of organizational forms can be seen as constituting a valid example of complexity. The urban media cluster is a network of formal and informal direct and indirect links or perhaps rather a system of networks or a network of systems related to the network of the information city (Castells, 1989).

The individual networks of the individual actors in the urban media cluster can be thought of at the aggregated level as a macro-network organization to which the analytical categories of strategic management can be applied. Thus, it is possible to introduce the concept of 'media cluster management', which implies the potential of the creation of a cluster 'management' able to govern complexity in the macro-network organization. However, this 'management' does not need to be formal or even informal. There are various institutional mechanisms by which economic activities are coordinated in a cluster (cf. Fuchs, 2002), including networking among economic actors without formal or informal centralized coordination (Hage and Alter, 1997). A point of topical interest here is to turn to theoretical configurations, which either deal with the study of the evolution and sustainable development of media clusters applying analogies to eco-biological models or apply the concept of product or industry life cycle to the media cluster from the perspective of strategic management.

Finally, it is important to apply research perspectives on urban media clusters that focus on the one hand on firm growth in the clusters and on the other hand on the role of entrepreneurship for the continuous renewal of such clusters. A focus on growth of incumbents and new firm entry is critical, since rapid firm growth and new firm entry are two critical signals of a successful cluster (Porter, 1998). It is in this connection important to examine also the potential for the emergence of new leading economic actors in the clusters, since the many small economic actors are dependent on the large leading actors as customers for their services (Scott, 1996, 2000b). A complementary focus to that on growth and new entry is a focus on productivity and innovation, since clusters are expected to generate a higher rate of productivity growth (Henderson, 1986) and a higher rate of innovation (Baptista and Swann, 1998). However, firms in urban media clusters are also affected by the negative effects of success in the form of congestion and competition in input and output markets resulting in increasing land prices, rents and wages and salaries. This will over time lead to a shakeout of firms from the cluster, where those firms with the lowest potential to bear the increasing costs will adapt by slimming their operations, going out of business or relocating their operations (or part of them) to the outskirts of the city or even to other locations with lower costs. If the negative effects grow more rapidly than the positive effects of clustering, this might of course lead to a slowdown in firm and productivity growth and in the rate of net entry and innovation.[2] Thus, the negative effects might lead an urban media cluster to stagnate or even to go into a declining phase of its life cycle (Swann, Prevezer and Stout, 1998).

NOTES

1. It should in this connection be observed that there are strong overlaps between some definitions of the media sector and some definitions of the cultural sector, see for example the following definition of the cultural sector by Pratt (1997): '. . . performance,

fine art, and literature; their reproduction: books, journal magazines, newspapers, film, radio, television, recordings on disc or tape; and activities that link together art forms, such as advertising. Also considered are the production, distribution and display processes of printing and broadcasting, as well as museums, libraries, theatres, nightclubs, and galleries'.

2. Pandit, Cook and Swann (2002) find evidence that clusters can become congested to the extent that they deter entry.

REFERENCES

Almeida, P. and B. Kogut (1997), 'The Exploration of Technological Diversity and the Geographic Localization in Innovation: Start-Up Firms in the Semiconductor Industry', *Small Business Economics*, **9**(1), 21–31.

Amin, A. and S. Graham (1997), 'The Ordinary City', *Transactions of the Institute of British Geographers*, **22**(4), 411–429.

Amin, A. and N. Thrift (1995), 'Globalization, Institutional "Thickness" and the Local Economy', in Patsy Healey, Stuart Cameron, Simin Davoudi, Stephen Graham and Ali Madani-Pour (eds), *Managing Cities: The New Urban Context*, Chichester, UK: John Wiley, pp. 91–108.

Baptista, R. and G.M.P. Swann (1998), 'Do Firms in Clusters Innovate More?', *Research Policy*, **27**(5), 527–542.

Bassett, K., R. Griffiths and I. Smith (2002), 'Cultural Industries, Cultural Clusters and the City: The Example of Natural History Film-making in Bristol', *Geoforum*, **33**(2), 165–177.

Bathelt, H., A. Malmberg and P. Maskell (2004), 'Clusters and Knowledge. Local Buzz, Global Pipelines and the Process of Knowledge Creation', *Progress in Human Geography*, **28**(1), 31–56.

Bramanti, A. and M.A. Maggioni (1997), 'The Dynamics of Milieux: The Network Analysis Approach', in Remigio Ratti, Alberto Bramanti and Richard Gordon (1997) (eds), *The Dynamics of Innovative Regions: The GREMI Approach*, Aldershot, UK: Ashgate, pp. 321–341.

Burfitt, A. and S. MacNeill (2008), 'The Challenges of Pursuing Cluster Policy in the Congested State', *International Journal of Urban and Regional Research*, **32**(2), 492–505.

Castells, M. (1989), *The Informational City: Information Technology, Economic Restructuring and the Urban-Regional Process*, Oxford, UK and Malden, MA, USA: Blackwell.

Castells, M. (1996), *The Network Society: The Information Age: Economy, Society and Culture. Volume I: The Rise of the Network Society*, Oxford, UK and Cambridge, MA, USA: Blackwell.

Crane, D. (1992), *The Production of Culture: Media and Urban Arts*, Newbury Park, CA, USA: Sage.

Driver, S. and A. Gillespie (1993), 'Information and Communication Technologies and the Geography of Magazine Print Publishing', *Regional Studies*, **27**(1), 53–64.

Enright, M.J. (1996), 'Regional Clusters and Economic Development: A Research Agenda', in Udo H. Staber, Norbert V. Schaefer and Basu Sharma (eds), *Business Networks: Prospects for Regional Development*, Berlin and New York, NY, USA: De Gruyter, pp. 190–213.

Ernst, D. (1999), 'How Globalization Reshapes the Geography of Innovation Systems: Reflections on Global Production Networks in Information Industries', paper presented at DRUID 1999 Summer Conference on Innovation Systems, Copenhagen.
Feldman, M.P. (1994), *The Geography of Innovation*, Dordrecht: Kluwer.
Fischer, M. (ed) (1998), *Clusters and Regional Specialisation: On Geography, Technology and Networks*, London: Pion.
Florida, R. (2002), *The Rise of the Creative Class: and How it is Transforming Work, Leisure, Community, and Everyday Life*, New York, NY, USA: Basic Books.
Freeman, C. (1995), 'The "National System of Innovation" in Historical Perspective', *Cambridge Journal of Economics*, **19**(1), 5–24.
Freeman, C. and L. Soete (1997), *The Economics of Industrial Innovation*, 3rd edn, London, UK: Pinter.
Fuchs, G. (2002), 'The Multimedia Industry: Networks and Regional Development in a Globalised Economy', *Economic and Industrial Democracy*, **23**(3), 305–333.
Gehrke, B. and H. Legler (1998), 'Regional Concentration of Innovative Potential in Western Germany', *Vierteljahrshefte zur Wirtschaftsforschung*, **67**(2), 99–112.
Gibson, C. and L. Kong (2005), 'Cultural Economy: A Critical Review', *Progress in Human Geography*, **29**(5), 541–561.
Hage, J. and C. Alter (1997), 'A Typology of Interorganizational Relationships and Networks', in J. Rogers Hollingsworth, and Robert Boyer (eds), *Contemporary Capitalism: The Embeddedness of Institutions*, Cambridge, UK and New York, NY, USA: Cambridge University Press, pp. 94–126.
Henderson, J.V. (1986), 'Efficiency of Resource Usage and City Size', *Journal of Urban Economics*, **19**(1), 47–70.
Hitters, E. and G. Richards (2002), 'The Creation and Management of Cultural Clusters', *Creativity and Innovation Management*, **11**(4), 234–247.
Jacobs, J. (1969), *The Economy of Cities*, New York, NY, USA: Vintage Books.
Johansson, B., C. Karlsson and R.R. Stough (2001) (eds), *Theories of Endogenous Regional Growth: Lessons for Regional Policies*, Berlin and New York, NY, USA: Springer.
Karlsson, C. (2008), 'Introduction', in Karlsson (ed), *Handbook of Research on Innovation and Clusters: Cases and Policies*, Cheltenham, UK and Northampton, MA, USA: Edward Elgar, pp. 1–16.
Karlsson, C., B. Johansson and R.R. Stough (2009) (eds), *Innovation, Agglomeration and Regional Competition*, Cheltenham, UK and Northampton, MA, USA: Edward Elgar.
Karlsson, C., B. Johansson and R.R. Stough (2010), 'Introduction', in Charlie Karlsson, Börje Johansson and Roger R. Stough (eds), *Entrepreneurship and Regional Development. Local Processes and Global Patterns*, Cheltenham, UK and Northampton, MA, USA: Edward Elgar, pp. 1–27.
Karlsson, C. and R.R. Stough (2002), 'Introduction: Regional Policy Evaluation in the New Economic Geography', in Börje Johansson, Charlie Karlsson and Roger R. Stough (eds), *Regional Policies and Comparative Advantage*, Cheltenham, UK and Northampton, MA, USA: Edward Elgar, pp. 1–21.
Ketels, C.H.M. (2003), 'The Development of the Cluster Concept: Present Experiences and Further Developments', paper prepared for NRW conference on clusters, Duisburg, Germany, 5 December 2003.

Koch, A.M. and G. Fuchs (2000), 'Economic Globalization and Regional Penetration: The Failure of Networks in Baden-Württemberg', *European Journal of Political Research*, **37**(1), 57–75.
Krugman, P. (1991), *Geography and Trade*, Cambridge, MA, USA: MIT Press.
Landry, C. and F. Bianchini (1995), *The Creative City*, London, UK: Demos.
Markusen, A. (1996), 'Sticky Places in Slippery Space: A Typology of Industrial Districts', *Economic Geography*, **72**(3), 293–313.
Mommass, H. (2004), 'Cultural Clusters and the Post-Industrial City: Towards the Remapping of Urban Cultural Policy', *Urban Studies*, **41**(3), 507–532.
Pandit, N.R., G.A.S. Cook and G.P. Swann (2002), 'A Comparison of Clustering Dynamics in the British Broadcasting and Financial Services Industries', *International Journal of the Economics of Business*, **9**(2), 195–224.
Peacock, A.T. (1992), 'Economics, Cultural Values and Cultural Policies', in Ruth Towse and Abdul Khakee (eds), *Cultural Economics*, Berlin and Heidelberg: Springer Verlag, pp. 9–20.
Picard, R.G. (2008), *Media Clusters: Local Agglomeration in an Industry Developing Networked Virtual Clusters*, Jönköping: Jönköping International Business School Working Paper Series No. 2008-3.
Porter, M.E. (1990), *The Competitive Advantage of Nations*, New York, NY, USA: Free Press.
Porter, M.E. (1998), 'Clusters and the New Economics of Competition', *Harvard Business Review*, November–December 1998, 77–90.
Power, D. and A.J. Scott (2004), 'A Prelude to Cultural Industries and the Production of Culture', in Dominic Power and Allen J. Scott (eds), *Cultural Industries and the Production of Culture*, Abingdon, UK and New York, NY, USA: Routledge, pp. 3–15.
Pratt, A.C. (1997), 'The Cultural Industries Production System: A Case Study of Employment Change in Britain, 1984–91', *Environment and Planning A*, **29**(11), 1953–1974.
Pratt, A.C. (1999), *Digital Places*, London, UK: London School of Economics.
Pratt, A.C. (2000), 'New Media, the New Economy and New Spaces', *Geoforum*, **31**(4), 425–436.
Sassen, S. (1994), *Cities in a World Economy*, Thousand Oaks, CA, USA: Pine Forge Press.
Scott, A.J. (1988), *Metropolis: From the Division of Labor to Urban Form*, Berkeley, CA, USA: University of California Press.
Scott, A.J. (1996), 'The Craft, Fashion, and Cultural-Products Industries of Los Angeles: Competitive Dynamics and Policy Dilemmas in a Multisectoral Image-Producing Complex', *Annals of the Association of American Geographers*, **86**(2), 306–323.
Scott, A.J. (2000a), *The Cultural Economy of Cities*, London, UK and Thousand Oaks, CA, USA: Sage Publications.
Scott, A.J. (2000b), 'The Cultural Economy of Paris', *International Journal of Urban and Regional Research*, **24**(3), 554–566.
Scott, A.J. (2001), 'Capitalism, Cities, and the Production of Symbolic Forms', *Transactions of the Institute of British Geographers*, **26**(1), 11–23.
Scott, A.J. (2006), 'Entrepreneurship, Innovation and Industrial Development: Geography and the Creative Field', *Small Business Economics*, **26**(1), 1–24.
Sheller, M. (2004), 'Mobile Publics: Beyond the Network Perspective', *Environment and Planning D: Society and Space*, **22**(1), 39–52.

Storper, M. (1997), 'Regional Economies as Relational Assets', in Roger Lee and Jane Willis (eds), *Geographies of Economies*, London, UK and New York, NY, USA: Arnold, pp. 248–258.

Storper, M. and B. Harrison (1991), 'Flexibility, Hierarchy and Regional Development: The Changing Structure of Industrial Production Systems and their Forms of Governance in the 1990s', *Research Policy*, **20**(5), 407–422.

Swann, G.M.P., M. Prevezer and D. Stout (eds) (1998), *The Dynamics of Industrial Clustering: International Comparisons in Computing and Biotechnology*, Oxford, UK: Oxford University Press.

Thurow, L.C. (1996), *The Future of Capitalism: How Today's Economic Forces Shape Tomorrow's World*, New York, NY, USA: William Morrow and Company.

Waters, M. (1995), *Globalization*, London, UK and New York, NY, USA: Routledge.

Westrick, D.G. and D. Rehfeld (2003), 'Clusters and Cluster Policies in Regions of Structural Change – Comparing Three Regions in North Rhine-Westphalia', paper for the International Conference of the Regional Studies Association 12th–15th April 2003 in Pisa, Italy.

Zukin, S. (1995), *The Cultures of Cities*, Oxford, UK and Malden, MA, USA: Blackwell.

Index